METHUEN LIBRARY REPRINTS

SBN/416 12150 O

DOCUMENTS

ILLUSTRATING

THE HISTORY OF CIVILIZATION
IN MEDIEVAL ENGLAND

(1066–1500)

DOCUMENTS
ILLUSTRATING THE
HISTORY OF CIVILIZATION IN
MEDIEVAL ENGLAND
(1066–1500)

R. TREVOR DAVIES, M.A.

TUTOR IN THE HONOUR SCHOOL OF MODERN HISTORY, OXFORD UNIVERSITY
AND VICE-PRINCIPAL OF CULHAM COLLEGE

AUTHOR OF
"A SKETCH OF THE HISTORY OF CIVILIZATION IN MEDIEVAL ENGLAND"

WITH TWO MAPS

BARNES & NOBLE, Inc.
New York
METHUEN & CO. Ltd
London

First Published, 1926

Reprinted, 1969
by
Barnes & Noble, Inc., New York
and
Methuen & Co. Ltd, London

Printed in the United States of America

PREFACE

IT has long been realized that no impartial historian has ever existed or is ever likely to exist. More than half a century ago J. A. Froude wrote : " It often seems to me as if History was like a child's box of letters, with which we can spell any word we please. We have only to pick out such letters as we want, arrange them as we like, and say nothing of those which do not suit our purpose " (*Short Studies*, 3rd ed., 1868, i. 1). Since Froude's time the Teutonic dullness and the pretence of infallible scientific method, that have come to be associated with historical writing, have not blinded many to the fact that twentieth-century textbooks of history suffer from prepossessions—different it may be, but quite as serious in their way as those of other ages. Hence the demand that history shall be studied from contemporary documents, so that the student may have some basis, other than the prejudiced and often obsolete observations of his textbook, upon which to form his opinions.

A sounder reason for the use of original sources is that the application of historical criticism to documents, and the balancing of one document against another, is a process of the highest educational value, and a matchless mental discipline.

The present volume has been compiled with the object of rendering easy of access all the more important documents

b

which are alluded to in the current textbooks of political history, for the period between the Norman Conquest and the Accession of the House of Tudor. All the documents are translated into English for the benefit of those general readers who do not possess a sufficiently accurate knowledge of the medieval Latin and French to deal with the originals. But an attempt has been made to quote the original at the foot of the page in every case in which a particular turn of phrase is of doubtful interpretation or of special importance. Wherever documents are given in thirteenth or fourteenth century English such footnotes are given as, it is hoped, will enable the ordinary reader to understand them without undue difficulty.

Important documents, such as Magna Carta, are given in their entirety ; and only documents of too great bulk for such treatment are given in an abridged form. At the head of each document a few sentences of introduction are intended to give the reader such particulars of date and authorship as will enable him to form an opinion of the historical value of the document or its more important bearings on the history of the period.

The plan and arrangement of the documents follow in the main that of my recent volume, *A Sketch of the History of Civilization in Medieval England* (Macmillan & Co., 1924). That is to say, it turns upon the supposition that the political history of the Middle Ages is best understood in the light of social, economic, and intellectual evolution.

In the choice of sources it has been assumed that letters and State papers, etc., are of higher historical value than extracts from Chroniclers, who so often wrote history with a purpose, and distorted facts accordingly. Hence the very considerable amount of the *Paston Letters* included in this volume. A careful index and a system of cross-references are included in the hope that they will enable students to work out historical problems set by their teacher. This volume is intended for those who have read something of the ordinary textbooks of political history and wish to know a little of the data upon which their conclusions are based. It exactly covers the Board of Education's new Syllabus for the Certificate Examination in Advanced History (Scheme 3 (*a*)) for 1927 ; and it has been formed in the course of lecturing during the past five years to students reading for that examination.

R. TREVOR DAVIES

Oxford, *August 1926*

CONTENTS

ix

DOCUMENTS

ILLUSTRATING

THE HISTORY OF CIVILIZATION
IN MEDIEVAL ENGLAND
(1066-1500)

DOCUMENTS ILLUSTRATING THE HISTORY OF CIVILIZATION IN MEDIEVAL ENGLAND
(1066-1500)

CHAPTER I

THE NORMAN CONQUEST

I. *DOMESDAY BOOK*

[The Survey resulting in *Domesday Book* was discussed at the Christmas sitting of the King's Council in 1085, and completed in 1086. The Survey was carried out by a group of royal

I

officers (*legati*) who held an inquiry, probably in the Shire Courts. The unit of inquiry was the Hundred, and the return for each hundred was sworn by twelve local jurors, half of them English and half Normans. The results of the Survey were afterwards collected and rearranged on a feudal basis, *i.e.* they were classified according to fiefs rather than hundreds and townships.

The original MS. of *Domesday Book* consists of two volumes : the first deals with the greater part of England ; and the second, which is much smaller, is devoted to the three Eastern Counties, Norfolk, Suffolk, and Essex. It is much fuller than the first in certain details, such as the enumeration of live stock. A considerable portion of England was not surveyed. This consisted of Cumberland, which then went with Scotland, Northumberland, Durham, most of Westmoreland, and part of Lancashire. A small portion of North Lancashire, together with a small neighbouring district of Cumberland and Westmoreland, is entered under Yorkshire. The southern part of Lancashire is regarded as an outlying district belonging to Cheshire. There is no survey of Wales or Monmouthshire or of certain large towns, *e.g.* London and Winchester.

The name *Domesday Book* first occurs in the " Dialogus de Scaccario," a treatise compiled by Richard Fitz-Nigel, about 1176. It is there stated that the English called the book of the survey " Domesdei," or " Day of Judgment," because the inquiry was one which none could escape, and because the verdict of this register as to the holding of land was final and without appeal. The book was originally preserved in the royal treasury at Winchester. When the treasury was removed —probably under Henry II.—to Westminster, *Domesday Book* went with it. From 1696 till the middle of the nineteenth century, it was preserved in the Chapter House. It is now in the Public Record Office.

For statistics from *Domesday Book*, see H. Ellis, *General Introduction to Domesday Book* (two vols., 1833).

The Victoria County Histories contain a translation of the Domesday Text, an explanatory introduction, and a map for each county. See also F. W. Maitland's *Domesday Book and Beyond.*]

A. Motives for the Formation of the Domesday Survey

[From the *Anglo-Saxon Chronicle, sub anno* 1085. This part of the Chronicle was probably compiled at Peterborough, *circa* 1120.]

THE year 1085. This year a rumour arose, and it was seriously reported, that Canute, King of Denmark, son of King Sweyn, was proceeding hitherward, with a view to conquering this land with the help of Robert, Count of Flanders, forasmuch as he had married the daughter of Robert.   When William, King of England, who was then in Normandy (for he then held both England and Normandy) was informed of this, he set out for England with a force of cavalry and infantry, raised from France and Brittany, greater than had ever before sought these shores ; so that men began to wonder how the land could support all that army.   But the King scattered his army throughout the whole land amongst his subjects, who contributed to the support of the army each in proportion to his land.   The inhabitants underwent many misfortunes this year ; and the King had the coastlands laid waste, so that, if his enemies were to land, they would find no provisions within easy reach.   But when the King was informed that his enemies had been hindered from coming, and could not make their attack, he sent away a part of the army to their own country, and kept a part in this land over the winter.   For Christmas, the King was at Gloucester with his nobles and held his court there for five days ; afterwards the Archbishop and Clergy held a synod for three days.   Present were Maurice, Bishop-elect of London, William of Norfolk, and Robert of Chester ; all these were the King's clerks.   Afterwards the King held his Great Council, and had deep speech with his nobles about this land, as to how and by what manner of men it was inhabited.   He sent, therefore, into every County throughout the whole of England ministers of his with orders to investigate how many hundred hides there were in each County, and how much land and cattle the King himself had in that County ; and how much in annual revenue he ought to enjoy from that County.   He ordered also to be entered the quantity of land held by his Archbishops, Diocesan Bishops, Abbots, and Earls ; and, to be brief, what and how much each person, who had lands in the English nation, possessed, whether in lands or in cattle, and how much it was worth in money.   So diligently did he have the land surveyed, that not a single hide or virgate of land, and not even (though it is a shame to say what he thought it no shame to do) a single ox or cow or pig was omitted and not returned in the reckoning, and all these writings were afterwards brought to him.[1]

[1] Post haec tenuit Rex Magnum Concilium, et graves sermones habuit cum suis proceribus de hac terra, quo modo incoleretur, et a

B. Extracts from Domesday Book

1. Wallingford, Berkshire (*Domesday Book*, Printed Edition, 1783, pp. 56 sqq.)

In the borough of Walingeford King Edward had eight virgates [1] of land, and in these were 276 closes [2] yielding eleven pounds [3] from rent, and they who dwelt in them used to do service for the king with horses or by water as far as Bildbery,[4] Reddinges,[5] Sudtown,[6] or Bensentone,[7] and to those who did this service the reeve [8] gave hire or payment not from the dues of the king but from his own. There are all the customary dues [9] in this Borough now as there used to be ; but of the closes [2] thirteen are gone ; eight were destroyed to make the castle, and a monyer has one, quit of service so long as he does coining.[10]   Saulf of Öxeneford [11] has one ; the son of Alsi of Ferendone one, which he states that the king gave him ; Humfrey Visdelew has one, for which he claims the king's warranty. Nigel claims one of Henry through inheritance from Soarding, but the burgesses give evidence that he never had it. From these thirteen the king receives no dues ; and besides these William de Warene has one close, from which the king receives no dues. In addition to these are there twenty-

quibus hominibus.   Mittebat idcirco per totam Anglorum terram in singulos Comitatus suos servos, quibus permisit scrutari quot hydarum centenae essent in Comitatu, quidque Rex ipse haberet terrarum et pecorum in eo Comitatu ; et quantum Census annui deberet percipere ex eo Comitatu.   Permisit etiam describi quantum terrarum ejus Archiepiscopi haberent, et Diocesani Episcopi, ac ejus Abbates, ejusque Comites ; et, ne longior in hoc sim, quid aut quantum unusquisque haberet, qui terras possideret in Anglorum gente sive terrarum sive pecoris, quantumque illud pecunia valeret.   Tam diligenter lustrari terram permisit, ut ne unica esset hyda, aut virgata terrae, ne quidem (quod dictu turpe, verum is factu turpe non existimavit), bos aut vacca, aut porcus praeter mittebatur, quod non is retulerat in censum ; omniaque postaea scripta ad eum afferebantur.

[1] A virgate was equivalent to about thirty acres.   [2] Hagae.
[3] The pound usually consisted of 240 silver pennies.
[4] Blewbury, a village on the Berkshire Downs.
[5] Reading.
[6] Possibly Sutton Courtenay, near Abingdon.
[7] Possibly Bensington, in Oxfordshire.
[8] Cf. pp. 291 sqq.   [9] Consuetudines.
[10] Cf. p. 9, for a moneyer in Oxford.   [11] Oxford.

two mansions,[16] held by Frenchmen which pay six shillings[1] and five pence.[2]

King Edward had fifteen acres on which housecarles were settled ; these Miles Crispin[3] holds, by what right is not known ; one of them belongs to Whiteham,[4] a manor of Walter Gifard.

Bishop Walchelin[5] has twenty-seven closes worth twenty-five shillings, and they are appraised in his manor of Brictewalle.[6] The Abbot of Abingdon has two acres on which are seven mansions[7] worth four shillings, and they appertain to Oxeneford.[8]

Miles has twenty mansions worth twelve shillings and ten pence and they belong to Neweham ;[9] and also one acre on which are six closes worth eighteen pence ; in Haselie[10] he has six mansions paying forty-four pence ; in Estoche[11] one mansion worth twelve pence ; in Celgrave[12] one mansion worth four pence ; in Sultone[13] one acre on which are six mansions worth twelve pence ; in Braio[14] one acre and there are eleven mansions worth three shillings. The whole of this land belongs to Oxenefordscire,[15] and yet it is in Walengeforde.

Rainald has one acre on which are eleven mansions[16] worth twenty-six pence, and they appertain to Eldeberie,[17] which is in Oxeneford.[18]

The Archbishop[19] has six mansions worth twenty-six pence ; Walter Gifard has one acre and ten mansions worth six shillings and three halfpence. Robert de Olgi four mansions worth twenty pence ; Gilbert de Gand one mansion worth two pence halfpenny ; Hugh the Tall one mansion worth four pence ; Ralf son of Seifrid two closes worth twelve pence ; Hugh de Molbec one close worth four pence ;

---

[1] The shilling was not a coin but a subdivision of account, equivalent to twelve pence here, though the Saxon shilling was divided into five pennies.

[2] The penny was a silver coin—the only coin in use at this time.

[3] The Lord of Wallingford.

[4] Long Wittenham, a Berkshire village near Abingdon.

[5] The Bishop of Winchester.

[6] Brightwell, a village in Berkshire.

[7] Masurae.   [8] Oxford.

[9] Newnham Murren.   [10] Great Hazeley.

[11] Stoke Bassett.   [12] Chalgrove.   [13] Sutton Courtenay.

[14] Bray.   [15] Oxfordshire.   [16] Masurae.

[17] Albury.   [18] Oxfordshire.   [19] Archbishop of Canterbury.

Ranulf Pevrel one worth four pence; Walter son of Otter six closes worth four pence less one halfpenny; William Lovet one plot of land worth four pence; in Eldeslei three mansions worth three pence. The Abbot of Battle Abbey has five mansions in Berchesire worth twenty pence, and one close which belonged to Bishop Peter, worth four pence. The king has three closes worth six pence; Henry de Ferraris six closes which T.R.E.[1] and also T.R.W.[2] paid sixty-two pence customarily in the King's ferm[3] and now pay nothing.

Bishop Remigius has one close worth four pence; Earl Hugh one close worth sixteen pence; Godric one close worth two pence; Doda one close worth two pence; Algar one close worth two pence; Smiths[4] have five closes worth ten pence.

2. CUMNOR (a Berkshire village four miles west of Oxford; from Printed Edition of *Domesday Book*, 1783, vol. i. p. 59, col. 1)

The Abbey of Abbendone holds Cominore.[5] It has belonged to the Abbey T.R.E., and always it was assessed at fifty hides; now at thirty hides.[6] There is land for fifty ploughs. On the demesne are nine ploughs; and there are sixty villeins and sixty-nine bordars with twenty-six ploughs. There are four serfs and two mills worth fifty shillings; and from the fisheries is yielded forty shillings; and there are two hundred acres of meadow. There is a church. T.R.E. it was worth thirty pounds; and afterwards, as now, fifty pounds.

Of these fifty hides Anschil holds five. Norman held them T.R.E.[6] as one manor. It is called Seuacoorde, and he could not go to what lord he wished. It paid geld for five hides with the others above mentioned. There is land

---

[1] Tempore Regis Edwardi, in the time of King Edward.
[2] Tempore Regis Willelmi, in the time of King William.
[3] In firma regis.   [4] Latin, " fabri."   [5] Cumnor.
[6] The hide consisted of four virgates, or one hundred and twenty acres; but it is not to be taken as an exact measure of area. It was smaller on fertile and larger on less productive ground. Originally it may have been the amount of land which one homestead could till with one plough.

for seven ploughs. On the demesne are two ploughs ; and twelve villeins and fifteen bordars with five ploughs. T.R.E. it was worth a hundred shillings ; and afterwards seventy shillings ; now eight pounds.

3. CUSTOMS OF BERKSHIRE (Stubbs, *Select Charters*, p. 91 ; Printed Edition, *Domesday*, i. 56)

When geld was rendered T.R.E. throughout Bercheschira [1] each hide rendered three pence and a halfpenny before Christmas and as much at Whitsun.

If the king sent the army anywhere, one knight only went from each five hides, and from each hide there was given him for food and pay four shillings for two months. These pennies [2] were not sent to the king but given to the knights. If anyone on being called up for military service did not go, he forfeited all his land to the king. But if anyone having to stay away promised to send a substitute, and the substitute stayed away, his lord was appeased for fifty shillings.

A thegn or knight of the royal demesne dying sent to the king, as a relief, all his arms and one horse with saddle, and one without saddle. Also should he possess dogs or hawks they were offered to the king, that he might accept them, if he would.

If anyone killed a man enjoying the king's peace he forfeited both his body and all his possessions to the king.

Whoever broke out of the city by night [3] made reparation in a hundred shillings to the king, not to the sheriff.

Whoever on being summoned to make ready a hunting lodge [4] did not go, made reparation in fifty shillings to the king.

4. THE CITY OF OXFORD (Stubbs, *Select Charters*, p. 90)

Oxford T.R.E. paid to the King for toll and gable and all other customs yearly twenty pounds, and six sextaries [5] of honey ; but to Earl Algar ten pounds in addition to the mill which he had within the city. When the King went on

---

[1] Berkshire.

[2] Hos vero denarios . . . non mittebantur; lit. "Them pennies . . . were not sent "—an instance of bad grammar in *Domesday Book*.

[3] Qui per noctem effringebat civitatem.

[4] Ad stabilitionem venationis.

[5] The sextaria was a liquid measure of uncertain amount.

expedition twenty burgesses went with him for all the others, or they gave twenty pounds to the King that all might be free.

Now Oxford pays by tale of twenty [pence] in the ora, sixty pounds. In the town as well within the wall as without are two hundred and forty-three houses paying geld, and beside these there are five hundred houses save twenty-two, so waste and destroyed that they cannot pay geld.

The King has twenty mural mansions paying fourteen shillings save twopence which were Earl Algar's T.R.E. then and now, and he has one mansion paying sixpence belonging to Shipton and another paying fourpence belonging to Bloxham and a third belonging to Risborough paying two shillings and sixpence and two others belonging to Tuiford,[1] Buckinghamshire, paying fourpence. One of these is waste. Wherefore they are called mural mansions, because, if there shall be need, and the King command it, they shall repair the walls.

To the lands which Earl Alberic held belong one church and three mansions ; of these two mansions paying two shillings and fourpence lie to the Church of St. Mary, and one mansion paying five shillings lies to Bureford.

To the lands which Earl William held belong nine mansions paying seven shillings. Three of these are waste. The Archbishop of Canterbury has seven mansions paying three shillings and twopence. Four of these are waste. The Bishop of Winchester has nine mansions paying five shillings and twopence. Three are waste. The Bishop of Bayeux has eighteen mansions paying thirteen shillings and fourpence. Four of these are waste. The Bishop of Lincoln has thirty mansions paying eighteen shillings and sixpence. Sixteen of these are waste.

The Bishop of Coutances has two mansions paying one shilling and twopence. The Bishop of Hereford has three mansions paying thirteen pence. One of these is waste. The Abbey of Abingdon has fourteen mansions paying seven shillings and threepence. Eight are waste. The Abbey of Eglesham has thirteen mansions paying nine shillings (seven of these are waste) and one church. The Earl of Mortaine [2] has ten mansions paying three shillings. Nine of these are

[1] Twyford, near Reading.
[2] Cf. pp. 15 and 16.

waste. Earl Hugh has seven mansions paying five shillings and eightpence. Four of these are waste. The Earl of Evreux has one waste mansion paying nothing. Henry of Ferieres has two mansions paying five shillings. William Peverel has four mansions paying seventeen pence. Two of these are waste. Edward the Sheriff has two mansions paying five shillings. Ernulf of Hesding has three mansions paying eighteen pence. One of these is waste. Beringar of Todeni has one mansion paying sixpence. Miles Crispin has two mansions paying twelve pence. Richard de Curci has two mansions paying nineteen pence. Robert d'Oilgi has twelve mansions paying sixty-four pence. Ranulf Flammard has one mansion paying nothing. Wido of Reinbodcurth has two mansions paying twenty pence. Walter Giffard has seventeen mansions paying twenty-two shillings. Seven of these are waste.

The predecessor of Walter has one of these, of the gift of King Edward, of eight virgates which paid customary dues T.R.E.

Jernio holds one mansion paying sixpence belonging to Hamtone.

The son of Manasses holds one mansion paying fourpence belonging to Blecesdone.

All these afore-written hold the afore-named mansions free because they repair the wall. All the mansions which are called mural were T.R.E. free from all customary payment except for expedition and repairing the wall.

The Priests of St. Michael's hold two mansions paying fifty-two pence.

The Canons of St. Frideswide hold fifteen mansions paying eleven shillings. Eight of these are waste.

. . . .

Wluui the Fisherman holds one mansion paying thirty-two pence.

. . . . . .

Suetman the Moneyer holds one house free paying forty pence.

. . . . . .

Alwin holds one house free, for repairing the wall. From this he has thirty-two pence per annum ; and if when there is need the wall is not repaired by him who ought to do it, he shall either forfeit forty shillings to the King or lose his house.

All Burgesses of Oxford have common of pasture,[1] without the wall, which pays six shillings and eightpence.

[In the survey of the County under the heading, " No. XXVIII., the land of Robert di Oigli," is the following entry:]

The same Robert has in Oxford, forty-two houses let to tenants,[2] as well within as without the wall. Of these sixteen pay geld and gable, the rest pay neither, for their poverty they cannot ; and he has eight mansions waste and thirty acres of meadow near the wall, and a mill of ten shillings. The whole is worth three pounds. And for one manor he holds with the benefice of St. Peter[3] . . .

The Church of St. Peter in Oxeneford holds of Robert two hydes in Holywell. Land one carucate. There is one plough and a half there, and twenty-three men having gardens.[4] There are forty acres meadow there. It was worth twenty shillings ; it is now worth forty shillings. This land has not paid tax or rendered any dues.

5. THE CITY OF YORK (EBORAC) (from Printed Edition, *Domesday Book*, 1783, vol. i. p. 298)

In the City of York T.R.E. besides the shire of the Archbishop, there were six shires. Of these one is wasted for the castles.[5] In five shires were 1,418 inhabited houses.[6] Of one of these shires the Archbishop has yet a third part. In these no one else had custom, except Merlesnain in a house which is within the castle, and except the Canons wherever they dwelt ; and except four judges, to whom the King gave the gift by his writ and for so long as they lived.[7] But the Archbishop has full custom of his shire. Of all the above-mentioned mansions there are now inhabited in the hands of the King rendering custom 400, less 9, great and small, and 400 mansions not inhabited which render, the better ones, one penny, and the others less, and 540 mansions so empty that they render nothing at all ; and Frenchmen

[1] The Portmeadow north-west of Oxford.
[2] domos hospitatas.
[3] The sentence is incomplete, a blank space being left in the MS. to be filled in ; which was never done.
[4] Hortulos.
[5] Vastata in castellis.   [6] Mansiones hospitatae.
[7] " et quamdiu vivebant."

hold 145 mansions. St. Cuthbert has one house, which he always had, as many say, quit of all custom ; but the burgesses say that it was not quit T.R.E. unless as belonging to the burgesses, save only that on account of it he had his own toll and that of the Canons. Besides this the Bishop of Durham has of the gift of the King the Church of All Saints and whatsoever pertains to it and the whole land of Uctred and the land of Ernuin, which Hugh the Sheriff has delivered to Bishop Walcher [1] by the King's writ ; and the burgesses who dwell in it say that they hold it under the King.

The Count of Mortaine [2] has there fourteen mansions and two stalls in the shambles, [3] and the Church of St. Crux. These Osbern son of Boson has received and whatsoever pertains to them.

. . . .

T.R.E. the city was worth to the King 53 pounds ; now 100 pounds by weight.

In the shire of the Archbishop there were T.R.E. 200 inhabited mansions, less 11 ; now there are 100 inhabited (mansions) great and small, besides the court of the Archbishop and the houses of the Canons. In this shire the Archbishop has as much custom as the King has in his shires.

. . . .

The King has three ways by land and a fourth by water. In these every forfeiture is the King's and the Earl's wherever the ways lead, be it through the land of the King, or of the Archbishop, or of the Earl.

If peace, given by the hand of the King or his seal, be broken, amend is made to the King alone, by twelve hundreds ; [4] each hundred 8 pounds.

Peace given by the Earl, and broken by anyone, is amended to the Earl himself by six hundreds ; each hundred 8 pounds.

If anyone be exiled according to law, none but the King shall give him peace. But if the Earl or the Sheriff have

---

[1] Bishop of Durham, 1071, till he was assassinated in 1080.
[2] Cf. pp. 8, 15 and 16.   [3] Duo bancos in macello.
[4] This and the following regulations illustrate the system, which prevailed in the Danelagh, of dividing lands into small hundreds of 12 carucates for fiscal and judicial purposes. Similar regulations are found in the Survey of the Counties of Lincoln, Derby, and Nottingham (vide J. H. Round's article in *Victoria County History of Yorkshire*).

sent anyone out of the kingdom, they themselves can recall him, and give him peace, if they will.

Those thegns who had more than six manors, give relief to their lands to the King only. The relief is 8 pounds. But if he had only six manors or less he gives to the sheriff for relief 3 marks of silver.

The Burgesses of the City of York do not give relief.

C. Statistics from " Domesday Book "

1. Recorded Population of each County surveyed

	Total.	Villani.	Bordarii.
Kent . . .	12,205	6,597	3,118, also 1,148 servi.
Sussex . . .	10,410	5,898	2,497, also 420 servi.
Surrey . . .	4,383	2,363	968, also 478 servi.
Hampshire[1] .	9,032	3,416	3,466, also 1,458 servi.
Isle of Wight .	1,124	360	441.
Berkshire . .	6,324	2,623	1,827, also 792 servi.
Wiltshire . .	10,150	3,049	2,754, also 1,539 servi and 1,418 coscez.
Dorsetshire . .	7,807	2,613	2,941, also 1,231 servi.
Somersetshire .	13,764	5,298	4,770, also 2,110 servi.
Devonshire . .	17,434	8,070	4,847, also 3,294 servi and 294 porcarii.
Cornwall . .	5,438	1,730	2,355, also 1,160 servi.
Middlesex . .	2,302	1,141	343, also 112 servi, and 464 cotarii.
Hertfordshire .	4,927	1,830½	1,107, also 550 servi and 837 cotarii.[2]
Buckinghamshire.	5,420	2,893	1,326, also 833 servi.
Oxfordshire . .	6,775	3,545	1,889, also 963 servi.
Gloucestershire .	8,366	3,627	1,792, also 2,044 servi and 30 half villans.
Worcestershire .	4,625	1,520	1,728, also 677 servi and 101 ancillae.
Herefordshire .	5,368	2,124	1,407, also 691 servi, and 99 ancillae, and 104 bovarii.
Cambridgeshire .	5,024	1,902	1,428, also 548 servi.
Huntingdonshire .	2,914	1,933	490.
Bedfordshire .	3,875	1,829	1,132, also 474 servi and 107 sochemanni.

[1] Excluding the New Forest with 217 recorded inhabitants.
[2] Cf. The Consuetudinary of Winchester, p. 131.

	Total.	Villani.	Bordarii.
Northamptonshire	8,441	3,952	2,056, also 1,062 soche-manni and 59 ancillae.[1]
Leicestershire .	6,772	2,665	1,345, also 1,914 soche-manni and 23 ancillae.[2]
Warwickshire .	6,574	3,500	1,775, also 845 servi.
Staffordshire. .	3,178	1,728	912, also 212 servi and 1 ancilla.
Shropshire . .	5,080	1,788	1,157, also 871 servi, 384 bovarii, and 52 ancillae.
Cheshire . .	2,349	797	635, also 193 servi and 172 bovarii.
Derbyshire . .	3,041	1,840	719, also 20 servi and 128 sochemanni.
Nottinghamshire .	5,686	2,603	1,101, also 1,516 soche-manni.
Rutlandshire .	862	730	109, also 5 sochemanni.
Yorkshire . .	8,055	5,079	1,819, also 447 sochemanni.
Lincolnshire . .	25,305	7,723	4,024, also 11,503½ soche-manni.
Essex . . .	16,060	4,087	8,002, also 1,768 servi.
Norfolk . . .	27,087	4,656	9,537, also 4,571 soche-manni, 4,277 liberi homines, and 17 half sochemanni.
Suffolk . . .	20,491	2,812	6,205, also 909 servi, 998 sochemanni, 11 half bordarii, and 5,344 liberi homines.

2. The Boroughs and Cities of " Domesday Book "

On the following page is a list of those about which *Domesday Book* contains incidental notices of the Services, Charges, and Customs.

[1] Northamptonshire had also 807 servi.
[2] Leicestershire had also 400 servi.

	Number of Burgesses Recorded.	Number of Houses Recorded.
Dover (burnt and, therefore, no enumeration possible).		
Canterbury . .	262	
Romney . . .	156	
Pevensey . . .	110	
Lewes. . .	53	
Wallingford . .	491	
Dorchester. . .	1 (only, mentioned)	88 (T.R.E. 172).
Bridport . . .	..	100 (T.R.E. 120).
Wareham . . .	..	70 (T.R.E. 143).
Shaftesbury . .	151	177 (T.R.E. 257).
Taunton . .	64	
Hertford . . .	18 (T.R.E. 146)	37.
Buckingham . .	26	
Oxford . . .	..	721 (478 of these wasted).
Worcester . . .	8 (only, mentioned)	129.
Pershore . . .	28	
Hereford . . .	10	
Cambridge. . .	29	373.
Huntingdon . .	296	
Northampton . .	..	287+.
Leicester . . .	65	318 (+4 wasted).
Warwick . . .	22	225.
Stafford . . .	36	
Shrewsbury . .	334 (43 of them " foreign " burgesses)	252 (+50 wasted and 51 destroyed to make room for the Castle).
Chester . . .	7 monyers and 12 judices, etc.	282 (T.R.E. 487).
The Wiches (i.e. the brine-yielding areas of Worcestershire and Cheshire)		
Nottingham . .	..	
Derby. . . .	140 (T.R.E. 243)	Wasted houses 143, 10 mills (T.R.E. 14).
York	..	1597 (in addition to this, houses had been destroyed to make room for the Castle).
Lincoln . . .	..	1150.

	Number of Burgesses Recorded.	Number of Houses Recorded.
Stamford . . .	..	136 (T.R.E. 143).
Torksey . . .	102 (T.R.E. 213)	
Grantham . . .	..	
Louth	..	
Maldon	180	
Colchester . . .	401	180 (+18 waste houses).
Norwich . . .	1320	
Yarmouth . . .	..	
Thetford . . .	725 (T.R.E. 943)	
Ipswich . . .	210 (T.R.E. about 1000)	Wasted houses, 328.
Dunwich . . .	316	

3. THE WALLED TOWNS (10)

The following are recorded in *Domesday Book* as having walls : Canterbury, Nottingham, York, Oxford, Hereford, Leicester, Stafford, Chester, Lincoln, and Colchester. ,

4. THE CHIEF PROPRIETORS OF LAND IN "DOMESDAY BOOK"

Name.	Total Number of Manors held.
The Monasteries . . . about	1700
The King	1422
The Earl of Mortaine . . .	793
Alan, Earl of Bretagne . . .	442
Odo, Bishop of Bayeux[1] . . .	439
Gosfrid, Bishop of Coutances . .	280
William de Warren, Earl of Surrey, about	228
Roger de Busli	174
Ilbert de Laici	164
William Peverel	162
Roger de Montgomery, Earl of Arundel and Shrewsbury . . .	157
Robert de Stadford . . .	150
Hugh de Abrincis, Earl of Chester .	124
Roger de Laici	116
Walter Giffard, Earl of Buckingham .	107
Hugh de Montford . more than	100

[1] Cf. p. 25.

5. The Manors held by Robert, Earl of Mortaine

County.	Number of Manors.
Sussex	54
Devonshire	75
Yorkshire	196
Wiltshire	5
Dorsetshire	49
Suffolk	10
Hampshire	1
Middlesex	5
Oxfordshire	1
Cambridgeshire	5
Cornwall	248
Nottinghamshire	6
Northamptonshire	99
Gloucestershire	1
Buckinghamshire	29
Hertfordshire	13

6. The Total of Recorded Population in "Domesday Book"

Tenants in Chief, including Ecclesiastical Corporation (approximately)	1,400
Mesne-tenants	7,871
Aloarii (free men, who were tenants in fee simple)	5
Ancillae (female slaves)	467
Angli or Anglici (probably English under-tenants)	26
Bedelli (under-bailiffs of manors)	22
Berquarii (shepherds)	10
Bordarii (bordars)	82,119
Bordarii paupers (poor bordars)	490
Dimidii Bordarii (half-bordars)	15
Bovarii (ox-herds)	749
Burgenses (burgesses)	7,968
Buri, Burs (geburs)	62
Canonici (canons)	59
Carpentarius (carpenter)	1
Censarii (those villeins who paid " censum," a kind of relief)	159

Clerici (Clerks or Clergy)	10
Coliberti (probably tenants who were free but owed certain services to the Lord of the Manor) .	858
Coscets, Coscez (holders of cottages and very small pieces of land)	1,749
Cotarii (unfree holders of small quantities of land)	5,054
Coteri (unfree holders of small quantities of land) .	16
Custodes Apium (bee-keepers) . . .	2
Drenghs (Military tenants found between the Ribble and the Mersey)	6
Fabri (blacksmiths, also carpenters) . .	64
Feminae Cotariae	9
Ferrarii (shoers of horses)	10
Figuli (potters)	5
Flandrenses	9
Forestarii (forest officials of a superior grade) .	3
Franci	50
Francigenae	296
Francigenae servientes (French serjeants) . .	5
Francones homines	3
Homines (Military tenants)	1,287
Homines arantes	3
Homines commendati	33
Homines consuetudinarii	8
Homines de Mercato de Tutberie . . .	42
Homines dimidii	11
Hospites	17
Joculator Regis (a minstrel of the King) . .	1
Joculatrix (a female minstrel) . . .	1
Lagemen (Lawmen of the Danelaw) . .	21
Liberae feminae	31
Liberae feminae commendatae . . .	7
Liberi homines	10,097
Liberi homines commendati . . .	2,041
Liberi homines faldae	21
Dimidii liberi homines	224
Manentes	16
Manentes apud Abbatiam S. Edmund . .	207
Mellitarii (honey and wax manufacturers) . .	9
Mercatores (merchants)	24
Milites (soldiers or knights)	137
Milites Anglici	2

2

Milites Francigenae 3
Molinarii (millers) 5
Monachi (monks) 13
Moniales (nuns) 4
Pauperes Homines 178
Piscatores (fishermen) 111
Porcarii (swineherds) 427
Prepositi Villarum (provosts, reeves, bailiffs or
stewards of Manors) 85
Presbyteri (priests) 994
Radchenistri (a class of freemen) . . . 196
Radmanni, Radmans (a class of freemen) . . 369
Rustici (agricultural labourers) . . . 4
Rustici Porcarii 2
Salinarii (those employed in salt works) . . 108
Servi (the least free of all the unfree classes) . 25,156
Servientes (serjeants) 12
Servientes Francigenae 2
Servientes Regis 9
Sochemanni (inferior landowners whose freedom
was slightly limited) 23,072
Sochemanni dimidii 18
Teini (thegns, the nobility of pre-Conquest times) . 11
Vaccarii (cowmen) 2
Vavassores (Mesne-tenants superior in rank to
knights) 3
Venator (huntsman) 1
Villani (unfree farmers, whose standard holding
was one virgate each) 108,407
Dimidii Villani 49
Waleis, Walenses (Welsh) 111

Total of Recorded Population 283,242

II. WILLIAM OF MALMESBURY'S ACCOUNT OF THE NORMAN CONQUEST

[William of Malmesbury was born between 1090 and 1096, and educated at Malmesbury Abbey, where he afterwards acted as librarian. He is thought to have resided for some time at Glastonbury, as later editions of his *History of the Kings of England* contain notices derived from the history and charters of Glastonbury. He probably died in 1143. The *History of the Kings of England* (*Gesta Regum Anglorum*) was finished in 1125, but a sequel, the *Historiae Novellae*, subsequently brought the history up to the year 1142.

These dates show that William of Malmesbury was not able to narrate the events of the Norman Conquest with the authority of a contemporary. He is, however, the only chronicler of the period who deserves the title of historian. He alone made any serious attempt to investigate cause and effect, and he alone takes up an attitude approaching impartiality to Norman and English in places where the other chroniclers are entirely one-sided in their pro-Norman or pro-English prejudices. It will be noticed, however, in the following extract that even William of Malmesbury does Harold scant justice.]

WILLIAM OF MALMESBURY, *Chronicle of the Kings of England*

[Book III., vide Giles' Translation, pp. 274 seq. (H. G. Bohn, London, 1847.]

IN the meantime Harold returned from the battle with the Norwegians. . . . When the news of the Norman's arrival reached him, reeking as he was from battle, he proceeded to Hastings, though accompanied by very few forces. No doubt the fates urged him on, as he neither summoned his troops, nor, had he been willing to do so, would he have found many ready to obey his call ; so hostile were all to him, as I have before observed, from his having appropriated the northern spoils entirely to himself. He sent out some persons, however, to reconnoitre the number and strength of the enemy ; these being taken within the camp, William ordered them to be led amongst the tents and, after feasting them plentifully, to be sent back uninjured to their lord. On their return, Harold inquired what news they brought. Then, after relating at full the noble confidence of the general, they gravely added, that almost all his army had the appearance of priests, as they had the whole face with both lips shaven. For the English leave the upper lip unshorn, suffering the hair continually to increase ; which Julius Cæsar, in his treatise on the Gallic War,[1] affirms to have been a national custom with the ancient inhabitants of Britain. The king smiled at the simplicity of the relators, observing, with a pleasant laugh, that they were not priests, but soldiers strong in arms, and invincible in spirit. His brother, Girth, a youth, on the verge of manhood, and of knowledge and valour surpassing his years, caught up his words : " Since," said he, " you extol so much the valour of the Norman, I think it ill-advised of you, who are his inferior in strength and desert, to contend with him. Nor can you deny being bound to him, by oath,[2] either willingly or by compulsion. Wherefore, you will act wisely, if, yourself withdrawing from this pressing emergency, you allow us to try the issue of a battle. We, who are free from all obligation, shall justly draw the sword in defence of our country. It is to be apprehended, if you engage, that you will be either subjected to flight or death : whereas, if we only fight, your cause will be safe at all events ; for you will be able both to rally the fugitives, and to avenge the dead."

His unbridled rashness yielded no placid ear to the words of his adviser, thinking it base and a reproach to his past life, to turn his back on danger of any kind ; and, with similar impudence, or to speak more favourably, imprudence, he drove away a monk, the messenger of William, not deigning him even a complacent look ; imprecating only, that God would decide between him and the earl. He was the bearer of three propositions : either that Harold should relinquish the kingdom, according to his agreement ; or hold it of William ; or decide the matter by single combat in the sight of either army. For William claimed the kingdom, on the ground that King Edward,[3] by the advice of

---

[1] *De Bello Gallico*, Book V. ch. xiv.
[2] An allusion to the story that Harold had sworn on certain holy relics to support William's claim to the throne. Cf. the Bayeux Tapestry.
[3] William of Malmesbury derives this statement from William Pictaviensis. Chronology is fatal to it, for Godwin died 1053; Siward in 1055. Moreover, we find Edward the Confessor sending for his nephew from Hungary in 1054, to make him successor to his kingdom.

Stigand, the Archbishop, and of the Earls Godwin and
Siward, had granted it to him, and had sent the son and
nephew of Godwin to Normandy, as sureties of the grant.
If Harold should deny this, he would abide by the judgment
of the Pope, or by battle ; on all which propositions, the
messenger being frustrated by the single answer I have
related, returned, and communicated to his party fresh spirit
for the conflict.

The courageous leaders each prepared for battle, each
according to his national custom. The English, as we have
heard, passed the night without sleep, in drinking and singing, and, in the morning, proceeded without delay towards
the enemy ; all were on foot, armed with battle-axes ; and
covering themselves in front by the junction of their shields,
they formed an impenetrable body, which would have secured
their safety that day, had not the Normans by a feigned
flight induced them to open their ranks, which, till that time,
according to their custom, were closely compacted. The
king [*i.e.* Harold] himself on foot, stood, with his brother,
near the standard, in order that, while all shared equal
danger, none might think of retreating. This standard
William sent, after the victory, to the Pope ; and it was
sumptuously embroidered with gold and precious stones, in
the form of a man fighting.

On the other side, the Normans passed the whole night
in confessing their sins, and received the sacrament in the
morning : their infantry, with bows and arrows, formed the
vanguard, while their cavalry, divided into wings, were
thrown back. The earl, with serene countenance, declaring
aloud that God would favour his as being the righteous side,
called for his arms ; and presently, when, through the hurry
of his attendants, he had put on his hauberk the hind part
before, he corrected the mistake with a laugh, saying, "My
dukedom shall be changed into a kingdom." Then beginning
the song of Roland, that the warlike example of that man
might stimulate the soldiers, and calling on God for assistance, the battle commenced on both sides. They fought
with ardour, neither giving ground, for a great part of the
day. Finding this, William gave signal to his party, that
by a feigned flight they should retreat. Through this device
the close body of the English opening for the purpose of
cutting down the straggling enemy, brought upon itself swift

destruction ; for the Normans facing about, attacked them thus disordered, and compelled them to fly. In this manner, deceived by a stratagem, they met an honourable death in avenging their country ; nor indeed were they at all wanting to their own revenge, as by frequently making a stand, they slaughtered their pursuers in heaps : for, getting possession of an eminence, they drove down the Normans—when roused with indignation and anxiously striving to gain the higher ground—into the valley beneath, where, easily hurling their javelins and rolling down stones on them as they stood below, they destroyed them to a man. Besides by a short passage, with which they were unacquainted, avoiding a deep ditch, they trod underfoot such a multitude of their enemies in that place that they made the hollow level with the plain, by the heaps of carcasses. This vicissitude of first one party conquering then the other, prevailed as long as the life of Harold continued ; but when he fell, his brain pierced with an arrow, the flight of the English ceased not until night. The valour of both leaders was here eminently conspicuous.

Harold, not merely content with the duty of a general in exhorting others, diligently entered into every soldier-like office ; often would he strike the enemy when coming to close quarters, so that none could approach him with impunity ; for immediately the same blow levelled both horse and rider. Wherefore as I have related, receiving the fatal arrow from a distance, he yielded to death. One of the soldiers with a sword gashed his thigh as he lay prostrate ; for which shameful and cowardly action, he was branded with ignominy by William, and dismissed the service.

William, too, was equally ready to encourage by his voice and by his presence ; to be the first to rush forward ; to attack the thickest of the foe. Thus everywhere raging, everywhere furious, he lost three choice horses, which were that day pierced under him. The dauntless spirit and vigor of the intrepid general, however, still persisted, though often called back by the kindly remonstrance of his body-guard ; he still persisted, I say, till approaching night crowned him with complete victory. And no doubt the hand of God so protected him, that the enemy should draw no blood from his person.

This was a fatal day to England, a melancholy havoc

of our dear country, through its change of masters. For it had long since adopted the manners of the Angles, which had been very various according to the times ; for in the first years of their arrival, they were barbarians in their look and manners, warlike in their usages, heathens in their rites ; but, after embracing the faith of Christ, by degrees and in process of time, from the peace they enjoyed, regarding arms only in a secondary light, they gave their whole attention to religion. I say nothing of the poor, the meanness of whose fortune often restrains them from overstepping the bounds of justice : I omit men of ecclesiastical rank, whom sometimes respect to their profession, and sometimes the fear of shame, suffer not to deviate from the truth : I speak of princes, who from the greatness of their power might have full liberty to indulge in pleasure ; some of whom, in their own country, and others at Rome, changing their habit, obtained a heavenly kingdom, and a saintly intercourse. Many during their whole lives in outward appearance only embraced the present world, in order that they might exhaust their treasures on the poor, or divide them amongst monasteries. What shall I say of the multitudes of bishops, hermits, and abbots ? Does not the whole island blaze with such numerous relics of its natives, that you can scarcely pass a village of any consequence, but you hear the name of some new saint, besides the numbers of whom all notices have perished through the want of records ? Nevertheless, in process of time, the desire after literature and religion had decayed for many years before the arrival of the Normans. The clergy, contented with a very slight degree of learning, could scarcely stammer out the words of the sacraments ; and a person who understood grammar was an object of wonder and astonishment. The monks mocked the rule of their order by fine vestments and the use of every kind of food. The nobility, given up to luxury and wantonness, went not to church in the morning after the manner of Christians, but merely in a careless manner, heard matins and masses from a hurrying priest in their chambers, amid the blandishments of their wives. The commonalty, left unprotected, became a prey to the most powerful, who amassed fortunes, either by seizing on their property, or by selling their persons into foreign countries ; although it be an innate quality of this people to be more inclined to revelling, than to the accumulation of wealth. There was one custom, repugnant to nature which they adopted, namely to sell their woman servants, when seduced by them, to an evil life or to foreign slavery. Drinking in particular was a universal practice, in which occupation they passed entire nights as well as days. They consumed their whole substance in mean and despicable houses ; unlike the Normans and French, who, in noble and splendid mansions, lived in frugality. The vices attendant on drunkenness, which enervate the human mind, followed ; hence it arose that engaging William, more with rashness and precipitate fury, than military skill, they doomed themselves and their country to slavery, by one—and that an easy—victory. . . . The English at that time wore short garments reaching to the mid-knee ; they had their hair cropped ; their beards shaven, their arms laiden with golden bracelets ; their skin adorned with punctured designs. They were accustomed to eat till they became surfeited, and to drink till they were sick. These latter qualities they imparted to their conquerors ; as to the rest, they adopted their manners. I would not, however, have these bad propensities universally ascribed to the English. I know that many of the laity, of all ranks and conditions, in this nation, were well-pleasing to God. Be injustice far from this account, the accusation does not involve the whole indiscriminately. . . .

Moreover, the Normans, that I may speak of them also, were at that time, and are even now, proudly apparelled, delicate in their food, but not excessive. They are a race inured to war, and can hardly live without it ; fierce in rushing against the enemy ; and where strength fails of success, ready to use stratagem, or to corrupt by bribery. As I have related, they live in large edifices with economy ; envy their equals ; wish to excel their superiors ; and plunder their subjects, though they defend them from others ; they are faithful to their lords, though a slight offence renders them perfidious. They weigh treachery by its chance of success, and change their sentiments with money. They are, however, the kindest of nations, and they esteem strangers of equal honour with themselves. They also inter-marry with their vassals. They revived by their arrival the observances of religion, which were everywhere grown life-less in England. You might see churches rise in every

village, and monasteries in the towns and cities, built after
a style unknown before ; you might behold the country
flourishing with renovated rites ; so that each wealthy man
accounted that day lost to him, which he had neglected to
signalize with some magnificent action. '

III. AN ESTIMATE OF WILLIAM THE CONQUEROR FROM THE *ANGLO-SAXON CHRONICLE*

[From the *Anglo-Saxon Chronicle, sub anno* 1087. Vide translation
by James Ingram in Dent's Everyman Library (624), pp. 165
sqq. ; also the Rev. J. Stevenson's translation, *The Church
Historians of England*, vol. ii. pt. i. pp. 133 sqq.]

IF any person wishes to know what kind of man he was,
or what honour he had, or of how many lands he was lord,
then will we write about him, just as we found him ; we,
who often looked upon him, and lived sometime in his
court.   This King William, then, that we speak of was a very
wise man, and very rich ; more splendid and powerful than
any of his ancestors were.   He was mild to the good men
that loved God, and beyond all measure severe to the men
that gainsaid his will.   On that same spot where God granted
him that he should gain England, he reared a mighty minster,
and set monks therein, and well endowed it.   In his days
was the great Monastery in Canterbury built, and also very
many others over all England.   This land was, moreover,
well filled with monks, who modelled their lives after the
rule of St. Benedict.   But such was the state of Christianity
in his time, that each man followed what belonged to his
profession as he would.   He was also very dignified.   Thrice
he bare his crown each year, as oft as he was in England.
At Easter he bare it in Winchester, at Pentecost in Westminster, at Midwinter in Gloucester.   And then were with
him all the rich men over all England ; archbishops and
diocesan bishops, abbots and earls, thanes and knights.
So very stern was he also and hot, that no man durst do any
thing against his will.   He had earls in his custody, who
acted against his will.   Bishops he hurled from their
bishoprics, and abbots from their abbacies, and thanes he put
in prison.'   At length he spared not his own brother Odo,[1]
who was a very rich bishop in Normandy.   At Baieux was

---

[1] Cf. p. 15.

his episcopal stall ; and he was the foremost man of all to aggrandize the king. He had an earldom in England ; and when the king was in Normandy, then was he the mightiest man in this land. Him he confined in prison. But amongst other things is not to be forgotten that good peace that he made in this land ; so that a man of any account might go over his kingdom unhurt with his bosom full of gold. No man durst slay another had he never so much evil done to the other ; and if any churl lay with a woman against her will, he soon lost the limb that he played with. He truly reigned over England and by his capacity so thoroughly surveyed it, that there was not a hide of land in England that he wist not who had it, or what it was worth, and afterward set it down in his book. ıſ The land of the Britons was in his power ; and he wrought castles therein ; and ruled Anglesey withal. So also he subdued Scotland by his great strength. As to Normandy, that was his native land ; but he ruled also over the earldom called Maine, and if he might have yet lived two years more, he would have won Ireland by his valour, and without any weapons. Assuredly in his time had men much distress and very many sorrows. Castles he let men build, and miserably oppressed the poor. The king himself was so very rigid, and extorted from his subjects many marks of gold, and many hundred pounds of silver ; which he took of his people, for little need, by right and by unright. He was fallen into covetousness, and greediness he loved withal. ́He made many deer-parks, and he established laws therewith ; so that whosoever slew a hart, or a hind, should be deprived of his eyesight. As he forbad men to kill the harts, so also the boars ; and he loved the tall deer as if he were their father. Likewise he decreed respecting the hares that they should go free. His rich men bemoaned it, and the poor men shuddered at it. But he was so stern that he recked not the hatred of them all ; for they must follow withal the king's will, if they would live or have land, or possessions, or even his peace. ́'Alas ! that any man should presume so to puff himself up, and boast over all men. May Almighty God show mercy to his soul, and grant him forgiveness of his sins ! These things have we written concerning him, both good and evil ; that men may choose the good after their goodness, and flee from the evil withal, and go in the way that leadeth us to the Kingdom of Heaven.

CHAPTER II

THE CONSTITUTIONAL STRUGGLE BETWEEN THE BARONS AND THE MONARCHY

I. CHARTER OF LIBERTIES OF HENRY I.

[For the original, see Stubbs, *Select Charters*, p. 100.]

IN the year of the incarnation of the Lord, 1101, Henry, son of King William, after the death of his brother William, by the grace of God, king of the English, to all faithful, greeting :

1. Know that by the mercy of God, and by the common counsel of the barons [1] of the whole kingdom of England,

---
[1] Cf. pp. 30 and 56.

I have been crowned king of the same kingdom ; and, because the kingdom has been oppressed by unjust exactions, I, from regard to God, and from the love which I have towards you, in the first place, make the holy Church of God free,[1] so that I will neither sell nor place at rent, nor, when archbishop, or bishop, or abbot is dead, will I take anything from the domain of the Church, or from its men, until a successor is installed into it. And all the evil customs by which the realm of England was unjustly oppressed will I take away, which evil customs I partly set down here.

2. If any of my barons, or earls, or others who hold from me shall have died, his heir shall not redeem his land as he did in the time of my brother, but shall relieve it with a just and legitimate relief.[2] Similarly the men [3] of my barons shall relieve their lands from their lords by a just and legitimate relief.

3. And if any one of the barons or other men of mine wishes to give his daughter in marriage, or his sister or niece or relative, he must speak with me about it ; but I will neither take anything from him for this permission, nor forbid him to give her in marriage, unless he should wish to join her to my enemy. And if, when a baron or other man of mine is dead, a daughter remains as his heir, I will give her in marriage according to the judgement of my barons, along with her land. And if when a man is dead his wife remains, and is without children, she will have her dowry and right of marriage, and I will not give her to a husband except according to her will.[4]

4. And if a wife has survived with children, she will have her dowry and marriage portion, so long as she shall have kept her body legitimately, and I will not give her in marriage except according to her will.[5] And the guardian of the land and children shall be either the wife, or another one of the relatives, as shall be the more just. And I require

---

[1] sanctam Dei ecclesiam in primis liberam facio. Cf. p. 40.

[2] haeres suus non redimet terram suam sicut faciebat tempore fratris mei, sed justa et legitima relevatione relevabit eam.

[3] homines.

[4] For this and the following clauses, cf. Magna Carta, *passim*, pp. 41 sqq.

[5] Si vero uxor cum liberis remanserit, dotem quidem et maritationem habebit dum corpus suum legitime servaverit, et eam non dabo nisi secundum velle suum.

that my barons should deal similarly with the sons and daughters or wives of their men.

5. The common tax on money which used to be taken through the cities and counties, which was not taken in the time of King Edward, I now forbid altogether henceforth to be taken. If anyone shall have been seized, whether a monyer or any other, with false money, strict justice shall be done for it.

6. All fines and all debts which were owed my brother, I remit, except my rightful rents, and except those payments which had been agreed upon for the inheritances of others, or for those things which more justly affected others. And if anyone for his own inheritance has stipulated anything, this I remit, and all reliefs which had been agreed upon for rightful inheritances.

7. And if any of my barons or men shall become inferm, however he himself shall give or arrange to give his money, I grant that it shall be so given. Moreover, if he himself, prevented by arms, or by infirmity, shall not have bestowed his money, or arranged to bestow it, his wife or his children or parents, and his lawful men shall divide it for his soul as to them shall seem best.

8. If any of my barons or men shall have committed an offence, he shall not give security to the extent of the forfeiture of his money, as he did in the time of my father, or of my brother, but according to the measure of the offence, so shall he pay, as he would have paid from the time of my father backward, in the time of my other predecessors ; so that if he shall have been convicted of treachery or crime, he shall pay as is just.

9. All murders, moreover, before the day in which I was crowned king, I pardon ; and those which shall be done henceforward shall be punished justly according to the law of King Edward.

10. The forests, by the common agreement of my barons, I have retained in my own hand as my father held them.

11. To those knights who hold their land by the coat of mail, I yield of my own gifts the lands of their demesne ploughs free from all payments and from all labour, so that as they have been favoured by such a great alleviation, so they may readily provide themselves with horses and arms for my service and for the defence of my kingdom.

12. A firm peace in my whole kingdom I establish and require to be kept from henceforth.

13. The law of King Edward, I give to you again with those changes with which my father changed it by the counsel of his barons.

14. If anyone has taken anything from my possessions since the death of King William, my brother, or from the possessions of anyone, let the whole be immediately returned without reparation, and if anyone shall have retained anything hence, he upon whom it is found shall make reparation heavily to me.

Witnesses, Maurice, bishop of London, and Gundulf, bishop, and William, bishop-elect, and Henry, earl, and Simon, earl, and Walter Giffard and Robert de Montfort, and Roger Bigod, and Henry de Port, at London, when I was crowned.

II. THE ASSIZE OF CLARENDON, 1166

[Stubbs, *Select Charters*, p. 143.]

HERE begins the Assize of Clarendon, made by King Henry II., with the assent of the archbishops, bishops, abbots, earls, and barons of all England.

1. In the first place, the aforesaid King Henry, with the consent of all his barons, for the preservation of the peace and the keeping of justice, has enacted that inquiry should be made through the several shires and through the several hundreds, by twelve of the most legal men of the hundred, and by four of the most legal men of each vill, upon their oath that they will tell the truth,[1] whether there is in their hundred or in their vill, any man who has been accused or publicly suspected of being a robber, or murderer, or thief, or of being a receiver of robbers, or murderers, or thieves, since the lord king has been king. And let the justices make this inquiry before themselves, and the sheriffs before themselves.

[1] Inprimis statuit praedictus rex Henricus de consilio omnium baronum suorum, pro pace servanda et justitia tenenda, quod per singulos comitatus inquiratur, et per singulos hundredos, per xii legaliores homines de hundredo, et per iv. legatiores homines de qualibet villata, per sacramentum quod illi verum dicent.

2. And let anyone who has been found by oath of the aforesaid, to have been accused, or publicly suspected of having been a robber, or murderer, or thief, or a receiver of them, since the lord king has been king, be arrested and go to the ordeal of water,[1] and let him swear that he has not been a robber, or murderer, or thief, or receiver of them, since the lord king has been king, to the value of five shillings, so far as he knows.

3. And if the lord of the man who has been arrested or his steward or his men shall have claimed him, with a pledge, within the third day after he has been arrested, let him be given up and his chattels until he himself makes his "law."[2]

4. And when a robber, or murderer, or thief, or receiver of them shall have been seized through the above-mentioned oath, if the justices are not to come very soon into that county where they have been arrested, let the sheriffs send word to the nearest justice by some intelligent man that they have arrested such men, and the justices will send back word to the sheriffs where they wish that these shall be brought before them ; and the sheriffs shall bring them before the justices ; and along with these they shall bring from the hundred and the vill where they have been arrested, two legal men to bring the record of the shire and of the hundred as to why they were arrested, and there before the justice let them make their law.[3]

5. And in the case of those who have been arrested through the aforesaid oath of this Assize, no one shall have court or judgement, or chattels, except the lord king in his court before his justices, and the lord king shall have all their chattels. In the case of those, however, who have been arrested, otherwise than through this oath, let it be as it has been accustomed and ought to be.

6. And the sheriffs who have arrested them shall bring such before the justice without any other summons than they have received from him. And when robbers, or murderers or thieves, or receivers of them, who have been arrested through the oath or otherwise, are handed over to the sheriffs, they also must receive them immediately without delay.

7. And in the several shires where there are no jails, let such be made in a borough or in some castle of the king,

[1] ad juisam aquae. [2] donec ipse faciat legem suam.
[3] et ibi ante Justitiam facient legem suam.

from the money of the king and from his wood, if one shall be near, or from some other neighbouring wood, on the view of the servants of the king ; in order that in them the sheriffs may be able to detain those who have been arrested by the officials who are accustomed to do this or by their servants.

8. And the lord king moreover wills that all should come to the county courts to make the oath, so that no one shall remain behind because of any franchise which he has, or court or jurisdiction which he had, but that they should come to the making of this oath.

9. And there is to be no one within a castle or without a castle, or even in the honour of Wallingford, who may forbid the sheriffs to enter into his court or his land for seeing to the frankpledges and that all are under pledges ; and let them be sent before the sheriffs under a free pledge.

10. And in cities and boroughs, let no one have men or receive them in his house or in his land or his soc, whom he does not take in hand that he will produce before the justice if they shall be required, or else let them be under a frank-pledge.

11. And let there be none in a city or in a borough or in a castle or without or even in the honour of Wallingford who shall forbid the sheriffs to enter into his land or his jurisdiction to arrest those who have been charged or publicly suspected of being robbers or murderers or receivers of them, or outlaws, or persons charged concerning the forest ; but he requires that they should aid them to capture these.

12. And if anyone is captured who has in his possession the fruits of robbery or theft, if he is of bad reputation, and has an evil testimony from the public, and has not a warrant, let him not have "law." [1]   And if he shall not have been publicly suspected, on account of the possession which he has, let him go to [the ordeal of] water. [2]

13. And if anyone shall have acknowledged robbery or murder or theft or the reception of them in the presence of legal men or of the hundreds, and afterwards shall wish to deny it, he shall not have "law." [1]

14. The lord king wills moreover that those who make their law and shall be absolved by the law, if they are of very bad testimony, and publicly and disgracefully spoken ill of

---

[1] non habeat legem ; *i.e.* the ordeal.
[2] eat ad aquam.

by the testimony of many and legal men, shall abjure the lands of the king, so that within eight days they shall go over the sea, unless the wind shall have detained them ; and with the first wind which they shall have afterward they shall go over the sea, and they shall not afterward return into England, except through the mercy of the lord king ; and then let them be outlawed if they return, and if they return they shall be arrested as outlaws.

15. And the lord king forbids any vagabond, that is a wandering and unknown man,[1] to be sheltered anywhere except in a borough, and even there he shall be sheltered only one night, unless he shall be sick there, or his horse, so that he is able to show an evident excuse.

16. And if he shall have been there more than one night, let him be arrested and held until his lord shall come and give securities for him, or until he himself shall have secured pledges ; and let him likewise be arrested who has sheltered him.

17. And if any sheriff shall have sent word to any other sheriff that men have fled from his shire into another shire, on account of robbery or murder or theft, or the reception of them, or for outlawry or for a charge concerning the forest of the king, let him arrest them. And even if he knows of himself or through others that such men have fled into his shire, let him arrest them and hold them until he shall have secured pledges for them.

18. And let all sheriffs cause a list to be made of all fugitives who have fled from their shires ; and let them do this in the presence of their shire courts, and they will carry the written names of these before the justices when they come first before them, so that they may be sought through all England, and their chattels may be taken for the use of the king.

19. And the lord king wills that, from the time when the sheriffs have received the summons of the itinerant justices to appear before them with their shire courts, they shall gather together their shire courts and make inquiry for all those who have recently come into their shire since this assize ; and they should send them away with pledges that they will be before the justices, or else keep them in custody until the justices come to them, and then they shall have them before the justices.

[1] ne aliquis vaivus, id est vagus vel ignotus.

3

20. The lord king moreover prohibits monks and canons and all religious houses from receiving anyone of the lesser people as a monk or canon or brother, until it is known of what reputation he is, unless he shall be sick unto death.

21. The lord king moreover forbids anyone in all England to receive in his land or jurisdiction or in a house under him anyone of the sect of those renegades who have been excommunicated and branded at Oxford.[1] And if anyone shall have received them, he will be at the mercy of the lord king, and the house in which they have been shall be carried outside the village and burned. And each sheriff will take his oath that he will hold this, and will make all his servants swear this, and the stewards of the barons, and all knights and free tenants of the shires.

22. And the lord king wills that this assize shall be held in his kingdom so long as it shall please him.

III. THE ASSIZE OF ARMS, 1181

[Hoveden, ii. 261, and Stubbs, *Select Charters*, p. 154 ; cf. pp. 59–60]

ASSIZE concerning the bearing of arms in England.

1. Let whoever holds one knight's fee have a coat of mail and a helmet, a shield, and a lance ; and let every knight have as many coats of mail, and helmets and shields, and lances as he has knights' fees in his demesne.

2. Also, let every free layman who is worth sixteen marks in chattels or in revenue have a coat of mail and a helmet and a shield and a lance ; also, let every freeman who is worth ten marks in chattels or revenue have a hauberk and a headpiece of iron and a lance.

3. Item let all burghers and the whole body of freemen have a quilted doublet [2] and a headpiece of iron and a lance.

4. Moreover let each one of them swear that before the feast of St. Hilary he will have these arms, and that he will bear faith to our lord King Henry, namely the son of the Empress Matilda, and that he will bear these arms in his

---

[1] Prohibet etiam dominus rex quod nullus in tota Anglia receptet in terra sua vel soca sua vel domo sub se, aliquem de secta illorum renegatorum qui excommunicati et signati fuerunt apud Oxeneforde.

[2] Wambais : said by Stubbs to mean " a doublet or purpoint of mail " (*Select Charters*, 7th ed. p. 551).

service according to his order and for the protection [1] of the lord king and his realm. And let no one who has these arms sell them or pledge them or give them away, or in any other manner alienate them, neither let a lord in any manner take them away from a man, either by forfeiture, or by gift as a pledge, or in any other manner.

5. If anyone having these arms shall die, let his arms remain to his heir. But, if the heir should be of such age that he could not use the arms if there should be need, let the one who has him in custody likewise have custody of his arms and let him find a man who can use arms in the service of the lord king until the heir is of such age that he can bear arms, and then let him have them.

6. Let every burgher who has more arms than he need have according to this assize sell them or give them away or otherwise alienate them to such a man as will keep them in the service of the lord king of England. And let none of them keep more arms than he is required to keep according to this assize.

7. Item let no Jew keep a coat of mail or a hauberk [2] in his possession, but let him sell it or give it away or otherwise dispose of it so that it shall remain in the service of the king.

8. Item let no one carry arms out of England except by the order of the lord king ; neither let anyone sell arms to anyone who will carry them out of England.

9. Item let the justices cause oaths to be taken by lawful knights or other free and lawful men of the hundred or borough as many as they shall see fit, who shall have the value of chattels which make it necessary for him to have a coat of mail, a helmet, a lance, and a shield, according as has been said ; to wit, that one by one they will name to them all from their hundreds and neighbourhoods and boroughs who have sixteen marks either in chattels or in revenue, and likewise those who have ten marks. And afterwards let the justices cause all those jurors and others to be registered ; who have such an amount of chattels and revenues, and afterwards in their presence, in the hearing of all those persons, let them cause this assize concerning the having of arms be read, and that they swear that they will have these arms according to the aforesaid value of chattels or revenue,

---

[1] ad fidem. [2] loricam vel aubergellum.

and that they will hold them at the service of the lord king according to this said assize at the command and for the protection of the lord King Henry and of his realm.[1] If indeed it should happen that any of those who ought to have these arms are not in the shire at the time when the justices shall be in that shire, the justices shall fix for him a time in another shire, in their presence. And if he shall not have come to them in any shire through which they shall go and he has not been in this land, a time shall be appointed for him at Westminster in the octaves of Saint Michael, that he shall be there to make his oath, as he loves his life and all that he has. But let it be commanded him that before the feast of the said Saint Hilary, he shall have arms according as is required of him.

10. Item let the justices cause to be proclaimed throughout all the counties through which they shall go, that whoever has not these arms according as is aforesaid, the lord king shall have recourse to their persons [2] and not at all to their lands or chattels.

11. Item let no man swear concerning lawful and free men, who has not sixteen marks or ten marks in chattels.

12. Item let the justices order throughout all the shires that no one, as he loves his life and property, shall buy or sell any ship to be taken away from England, and that no one shall export or cause to be exported from England, timber. And the king commands that no one shall be received for the oath of arms except a freeman.

IV. TRIALS BEFORE A MANORIAL COURT

[These are taken from *Le Court Baron*, by the kind permission of the Selden Society. It is a book of instructions for the steward who holds the court. In its earliest form it belongs to the thirteenth century. The MS. is written in Norman French.]

(a) A Charge of Battery or Trespass done to
    Strangers (from *Le Court Baron*, pp. 27–8)

Charge.—Sir Steward, Henry of Combe, who is here, complaineth of Stephen Carpenter, who is there, that as he

---

[1] et ea tenebunt in servicio domini regis secundum hanc praedictam assisam in praecepto et fide domini regis Henrici et regni sui.
[2] ad eorum membra.

was going his right way in the peace of God and in the peace
of the Lord through this vill, which is within the surety of
our franchise, at such an hour on such a day in the last year,
there came this Stephen Carpenter and encountered him in
such a place (*naming it*), and assailed him with villain words
which were undeserved, in so much that he called him thief
and lawless man and whatever other names seemed good to
him except only his right name, and told him that he was
spying from house to house the secrets of the good folk of the
vill in order that he might come another time by night with
his fellows to break their houses and carry off their goods
larcenously as a larcener and feloniously as a felon ; whereupon this Henry answered him civilly and said that he was
good and lawful in all things and that he (Stephen) was talking at random ; whereupon the said Stephen was enraged at
this and snatched his staff of holly out of his hand and gave
it him about his head and across his shoulders and his loins
and elsewhere all over his body as he thought fit, and then
went off. This trespass did the said Stephen wrongfully
and against reason and against the peace of the Lord and of
thee, who art charged to guard and maintain the peace, to
his damage 20 shillings and shame half a mark, etc.

Defence.—Tort and force and all that is against the
peace of God and the peace of the Lord and of thee, who art
charged to guard and maintain the peace, and his (Henry's)
damages of 20 shillings and shame of half a mark and every
penny of it, defendeth Stephen who is here, and all manner
of felonies and all manner of villain words against Henry of
Combe, who is there, and against his suit and all that he
surmiseth against him, that never he called him thief nor
gave him villain word, nor surmised villain slander against
him, nor with staff of holly nor other staff beat him across the
head or shoulders or loins or any part of his body as he surmiseth ; and that this is true, he is ready to acquit himself in
all such wise as this court shall award that acquit himself he
ought.

STEWARD : Fair friend, Stephen, this court awardeth
that thou be at law six-handed at the next court to acquit
thyself.

STEPHEN : Willingly, sir.

(*b*) A Case of Horse Stealing (from *Le Court Baron*, pp. 62–64)

STEWARD : Bailiff !

BAILIFF : Sir !

STEWARD : For what cause was this man taken ?

BAILIFF : Sir, for a mare which he took in the field of C. otherwise than he ought.

STEWARD : What is thy name ?

DEFENDANT : Sir, my name is William.

STEWARD : William, thou art taken and attached in this court for a mare, which is here present, which thou art said to have taken larcenously from the field of C. How wilt thou acquit thyself of this larceny and of all others ?

DEFENDANT : Sir, if any man will sue against me for larceny or any other thing that is against the peace of the king and his crown, I am ready to defend myself by my body that I am good and lawful.

STEWARD : William, now answer me by what device thou camest by this mare ; for at least thou canst not deny that she was found with thee, and that thou didst avow her for thine own.

DEFENDANT : Sir, I disavow this mare and never saw I her until now.

STEWARD : Then, William, thou canst right boldly put thyself upon the good folk of this vill that never thou didst steal her.

DEFENDANT : Nay, sir, for these men have their hearts big against me and hate me much because of this ill report which is surmised against me.

STEWARD : Thinkest thou, William, that there would be any who would commend his body and soul to the devils for thee or for love or for hatred of thee ? Nay, verily, they are good folk and lawful, and thou canst oust [1] from among them all those whom thou suspectest of desiring thy condemnation. But do thou what is right and have God before thine eyes and confess the truth of this thing and the other things that thou hast done, and give not thyself wholly to the enticement of the devil, but confess the truth and thou shalt find us the more merciful.

DEFENDANT : Sir, in God's name have pity on me and

[1] *i.e.* You can challenge your jurors.

I will confess to thee the truth, and I will put me wholly upon thy loyalty.[1]

STEWARD : William, by my loyalty thou shalt have nought but justice ! Say, therefore, what thou wilt and conceal nought.

DEFENDANT : Sir, my great poverty and my great neediness and the enticement of the devil made me take this mare larcenously, and often have they made me do other things that I ought not to have done.

STEWARD : God pardon thee ! William, at least thou hast confessed in this court that larcenously thou tookedst this mare and hast done many other ill deeds ; now name some of thy fellows, for it cannot be but that thou hadst fellowship in thy evil deeds.

DEFENDANT : Of a truth, sir, never had I companion in my evil deeds save only the fiend.

STEWARD : William, will thou say or confess aught else ?

DEFENDANT : Nay, sir.

STEWARD : Bailiff !

BAILIFF : Sir !

STEWARD : Take him away, and let him have a priest.[2]

V. MAGNA CARTA, 1215

(Statutes of the Realm, 1810, vol. i. pp. 5 sqq.)

JOHN, by the grace of God, king of England, lord of Ireland, duke of Normandy and Aquitaine, and count of Anjou, to the archbishops, bishops, abbots, earls, barons, justiciars, foresters, sheriffs, stewards, servants, and to all his bailiffs and loyal persons, greeting. Know that, having regard to God and for the salvation of our souls, and those of all our predecessors and heirs, and unto the honour of God and the advancement of Holy Church, and for the reform of our realm, by the counsel of our venerable fathers, Stephen, archbishop of Canterbury, primate of all England and cardinal of the Holy Roman Church, Henry, archbishop of Dublin, William of London, Peter of Winchester, Jocelyn of Bath and Glastonbury, Hugh of Lincoln, Walter of Worcester, William of Coventry, Benedict of Rochester, bishops ;

[1] e me mettrai tut en vostre liaute.

[2] Fet le retrere, si fetes lui aver le prestre. This is the euphemistic phrase in which judgment is given that the defendant shall be hanged.

of master Pandulf, subdeacon and member of the household of our lord the Pope, of brother Aymeric, master of the knights of the Temple in England, and of the illustrious men ; [1] William Marshal, Earl of Pembroke, William, Earl of Salisbury, William, Earl Warenne, William, Earl of Arundel, Alan of Galloway (Constable of Scotland), Waren Fitz Gerald, Peter Fitz Herbert, Hubert de Burgh (Seneshal of Poitou), Hugh de Neville, Matthew Fitz Herbert, Thomas Basset, Alan Basset, Philip D'Aubigny, Robert of Roppesley, John Marshal, John Fitz Hugh, and others our liegemen, we have granted :

I. In the first place we have granted to God, and by this our present charter confirmed for us and our heirs for ever that the English Church shall be free,[2] and shall have her rights entire and her liberties inviolate ; [3] and we will that it be thus observed ; which is apparent from this, that the freedom of elections, which is reckoned most important and very essential to the English Church, we, of pure and un-constrained will, did grant, and did by our charter confirm and did obtain the ratification of the same from our Lord, Pope Innocent III., before the quarrel arose between us and our barons : and this we will observe, and our will is that it be observed in good faith by our heirs for ever. We have also granted to all freemen of our kingdom, for us and our heirs for ever, all the underwritten liberties, to be had and held by them and their heirs, of us and our heirs for ever.[4]

II. If any of our earls or barons, or others holding of us in chief by military service shall have died, and at the time of his death his heir shall be of full age and owe " relief," he shall have his inheritance on payment of the ancient relief, namely the heir or heirs of an earl £100 for a whole earl's barony ; the heir or heirs of a baron £100 for a whole barony ; the heir or heirs of a knight, 100 shillings at most for a whole knight's fee ; and whoever owes less let him give less, according to the ancient custom of fiefs.

III. If, however, the heir of any one of the aforesaid has

[1] Nobiles viri.   [2] Cf. p. 28.
[3] quod Anglicana ecclesia libera sit, et habeat jura sua integra, et libertates suas illesas.
[4] Concessimus etiam omnibus liberis hominibus regni nostri, pro nobis et heredibus nostris in perpetuum, omnes libertates subscriptas, habendas et tenendas, eis et heredibus suis, de nobis et heredibus nostris.

been under age and in wardship, let him have his inheritance without relief and without fine when he comes of age.

IV. The guardian of the land of an heir who is thus under age, shall take from the land of the heir nothing but reasonable produce, reasonable customs, and reasonable services, and that without destruction or waste of men or goods ;[1] and if we have committed the wardship of the lands of any such minor to the sheriff, or to any other who is responsible to us for its issues, and he has made destruction or waste of what he holds in wardship, we will take of him amends, and the land shall be committed to two lawful and discreet men of that fief, who shall be responsible for the issues to us or to him to whom we shall assign them ; and if anyone have given or sold the wardship of any such land to anyone and he has therein made destruction or waste, he shall lose that wardship, and it shall be transferred to two lawful and discreet men of that fief, who shall be responsible to us in like manner as is aforesaid.

V. The guardian, moreover, so long as he has the wardship of the land, shall keep up the houses, parks, fishponds, stanks,[2] mills, and other things pertaining to the land, out of the issues of the same land ; and he shall restore to the heir, when he has come to full age, all his land, stocked with ploughs and "waynage,"[3] according as the season of husbandry shall require, and the issues of the land can reasonably bear.

VI. Heirs shall be married without disparagement, yet so that before the marriage takes place the nearest in blood to that heir shall have notice.

VII. A widow, after the death of her husband, shall forthwith and without difficulty have her marriage portion and inheritance ; nor shall she give anything for her dower, or for her marriage portion, or for the inheritance which her husband and she held on the day of the death of that husband ; and she may remain in the house of her husband for forty days after his death, within which time her dower shall be assigned to her.

[1] et hoc sine destructione et vasto hominum vel rerum.
[2] Stagna : ponds.
[3] Waynagiis, cf. Cap. XX. Coke thought that the term was derived from wain or waggon. More probably it is a Latinized form of the French " gagnage," meaning gain, tillage, crops or grain.

VIII. No widow shall be compelled to marry, so long as she prefers to live without a husband ; provided, however, that she gives security not to marry without our consent if she holds of us, or without the consent of the lord of whom she holds, if she holds of another.

IX. Neither we nor our bailiffs shall seize any land or rent for any debt, so long as the chattels of the debtor are sufficient to repay the debt, nor shall the sureties of a debtor be distrained so long as the principal debtor is able to satisfy the debt ; and if the principal debtor shall fail to pay the debt, having nothing wherewith to pay it, then the sureties shall answer for the debt ; and let them have the lands and rents of the debtor, if they desire them, until they are indemnified for the debt which they have paid for him, unless the principal debtor can show proof that he is discharged thereof as against the said sureties.

X. If one who has borrowed from the Jews any sum, great or small, die before that loan be repaid, the debt shall not bear interest while the heir is under age, of whomsoever he may hold ; and if the debt fall into our hands, we will not take anything except the principal sum contained in the bond.[1]

XI. And if anyone die indebted to the Jews,[2] his wife shall have her dower and pay nothing of that debt ; and if any children of the deceased are left under age, necessaries shall be provided for them in keeping with the holding of the deceased ; and out of the residue the debt shall be paid, reserving, however, service due to feudal lords ; in like manner let it be done touching debts due to others than Jews.

XII. No scutage or aid shall be imposed on our kingdom, unless by common counsel of our kingdom, except for ransoming our person, for making our eldest son a knight, and for marrying our eldest daughter once ; and for them there shall not be levied more than a reasonable aid. In like manner it shall be done concerning aids from the city of London.

XIII. And the city of London shall have all its ancient liberties and free customs,[3] as well by land as by water ; furthermore we decree and grant that all other cities, boroughs, and towns, and ports shall have all their liberties and free customs.

[1] nisi catallum contentum in carta.
[2] Cf. pp. 75 sqq.   [3] Cf. pp. 107 and 123 sqq.

XIV. And for obtaining the common counsel of the kingdom about the assessing of an aid (except in the three cases aforesaid) or of a scutage, we will cause to be summoned the archbishops, bishops, abbots, earls, and greater barons, individually by our letters ; and we will moreover cause to be summoned generally through our sheriffs and bailiffs, all others who hold of us in chief,[1] for a definite date, namely after the expiry of at least forty days, and at a definite place ; and in all letters of such summons we will specify the reason of the summons. And when the summons has thus been made, the business shall proceed on the day appointed, according to the counsel of such as are present, although not all who are summoned have come.

XV. We will not for the future grant to anyone license to take an aid from his own free tenants, except to ransom his body, to make his eldest son a knight, and once to marry his eldest daughter ; and on each of these occasions there shall be levied only a reasonable aid.

XVI. No one shall be distrained for performance of greater service for a knight's fee, or for any other fee tenement than is due therefrom.

XVII. Common pleas shall not follow our court, but shall be held in some definite place.

XVIII. Inquests of novel disseisin, of mort d'ancestor, and of darrein presentment, shall not be held elsewhere than in their own county courts, and in that manner following— we, or if we should be out of the kingdom, our chief justiciar, will send two justiciars through every county four times a year, who shall, along with four knights of the county, chosen by the county, hold the said assizes in the county court, on the day in and the place of meeting of that court.

XIX. And if any of the said assizes cannot be taken on the day of the county court, let there remain of the knights and freeholders, who were present at the county court on that day, as many as may be required for the making of judgements, according as the business be more or less.

[1] Et ad habendum commune consilium regni, de auxilio assidendo aliter quam in tribus casibus praedictis, vel de scutagio assidendo, summoneri faciemus archiepiscopos, episcopos, abbates, comites, et majores barones, sigillatim per litteras nostras ; et praeterea faciemus summoneri in generali, per vicecomites et ballivos nostros, omnes illos qui de nobis tenent in capite. . . .

XX. A freeman [1] shall not be amerced for a slight offence, except in accordance with the degree of the offence ; and for a grave offence he shall be amerced in accordance with the gravity of the offence, yet saving his " contenement " ; [2] and a merchant saving his " merchandise " ; and a villein shall be amerced in the same way, saving his " wainage " [3]— if they have fallen into our mercy ; [4] and none of the aforesaid amercements shall be imposed except by the oath of honest men of the neighbourhood.

XXI. Earls and barons shall not be amerced except through their peers, and only in accordance with the degree of the offence.

XXII. A clerk shall not be amerced in respect of his lay-holding except after the manner of the others aforesaid ; and not in accordance with the amount of his ecclesiastical benefice.

XXIII. No village or individual [5] shall be compelled to make bridges at river banks, except those who were from old times rightfully compelled to do so.

XXIV. No sheriff, constable, coroners, or others of our bailiffs, shall hold pleas of our crown.

XXV. All counties, hundreds, wapentakes, and trithings shall remain at the old " firms " without any additional payment—except the manors on our demesne.

XXVI. If any one holding of us by a lay fief shall die, and our sheriff or bailiff shall show our letters patent of summons for a debt which the deceased owed to us, it shall be lawful for our sheriff or bailiff to seize and catalogue chattels of the deceased, found upon the lay fief, to the value of that debt, under the supervision of law-worthy men, provided always that nothing whatever be thence removed until the debt which is evident be fully paid to us ; and the rest shall be left to the executors to fulfil the will of the

[1] Cf. Cap. I. p. 40.

[2] " Contenementum," derived from French *contenir*, probably means that sufficient to maintain himself and those dependent upon him in the standard of comfort due to his social standing.

[3] For " waynagium " see footnote to Cap V. of the Charter.

[4] Cap. XX. Liber homo non amercietur pro parvo delicto, nisi secundum modum delicti ; et pro magno delicto amercietur secundum magnitudinem delicti, salvo contenemento suo ; et mercator eodem modo amercietur salvo waynagio suo, si inciderint in misericordiam nostram. . . .

[5] Nec villa nec homo. . . .

deceased ; and if there be nothing due from him to us, all the chattels shall go to the deceased, saving to his wife and children their reasonable shares.

XXVII. If any freeman shall die intestate, his chattels shall be distributed by the hands of his nearest kinsfolk and friends, under supervision of the church, saving to everyone the debts which the deceased owed to him.

XXVIII. No constable or other bailiff of ours shall take corn or other provisions from anyone without immediately tendering money in exchange, unless by permission of the seller he is allowed to postpone payment.

XXIX. No constable shall compel any knight to give money in stead of castle guard, when he is willing to perform it in his own person, or (if he himself cannot do it from any reasonable cause) then by another reliable man ; and if we have led him or sent him upon military service, he shall be quit of guard, in proportion to the time during which he has been on service because of us.

XXX. No sheriff or bailiff of ours, or other person, shall take the horses or carts of any freeman [1] for transport duty, against the will of the said freeman.

XXXI. Neither we nor our bailiffs shall take for our castles or for any other work of ours, timber which is not ours, against the will of the owner of that timber.

XXXII. We will not retain beyond one year and one day, the lands of those who have been convicted of felony, and the lands shall thereafter be handed over to the lords of the fiefs.

XXXIII. Henceforth all fish-weirs [2] shall be removed altogether from the Thames and Medway, and throughout all England, except upon the seashore.

XXXIV. The writ which is called " praecipe " [3] shall not for the future be issued to anyone, regarding any tenement whereby a freeman may lose his court. [4]

XXXV. Let there be one measure of wine throughout our whole kingdom, and one measure of ale ; and one measure

---

[1] alicujus liberi hominis.　　　　　　　　　[2] Omnes kydelli.

[3] Praecipe was a writ which ignored private jurisdiction and bade the sheriff command the occupier of a piece of land restore it to the claimant ; or else appear before the royal court to explain his reasons for disobedience.

[4] Breve quod vocatur *precipe* de cetero non fiat alicui de aliquo tenemento unde liber homo amittere possit curiam suam.

of corn, to wit, "the London quarter"; and one width of cloth, whether dyed or russet or "halberget," to wit, two ells within the lists; of weights also let it be as of measures.

XXXVI. Nothing in future shall be given or taken for a writ of inquisition of life or limbs,[1] but freely shall it be granted and never denied.

XXXVII. If anyone holds of us by feefarm, by socage, or by burgage, and holds also land of another lord by knight's service, we will not—by reason of that feefarm, socage, or burgage—have the wardship of the heir, or of such land of his as is of the fief of that other; nor shall we have wardship of that feefarm, socage, or burgage, unless such feefarm owes knight's service. We will not have wardship of the heir or of the land which he holds of another lord by knight service, by reason of any petty serjeantry which anyone may hold of us by the service of rendering to us knives, arrows, or the like.

XXXVIII. No bailiff for the future shall, upon his own unsupported complaint, put anyone to his "law"[2] without reputable witnesses brought for this purpose.

XXXIX. No freeman shall be taken or imprisoned or disseised or exiled or in anyway destroyed, nor will we go upon him nor send upon him, except by the lawful judgement of his peers[3] or by the law of the land.

XL. To no one will we sell, to no one will we refuse right or justice.

XLI. All merchants shall have safe and secure exit from England, and entry to England, with right to tarry there and to move about as well by land as by water, for buying and selling by the ancient and right customs, quit from all evil tolls, except, in time of war, such merchants as are of the land at war with us. And if such are found in our land at the beginning of the war, they shall be detained, without injury to their bodies or goods, until information be received by us or by our chief justiciar how the merchants of our land

---

[1] Better known as the writ "de odio et atia." It was intended to protect from the duellum men unjustly appealed of homicide, etc., by enabling the accused to have a preliminary trial before twelve men of his neighbourhood. If the appeal was found to be groundless, further proceedings were quashed.

[2] The ordeal. Cf. Assize of Clarendon, Cap. 3, p. 31, and Cap. 13, p. 32.

[3] Nisi per legale judicium parium suorum.

found in the land at war with us are treated ; and in our men are safe there the others shall be safe in our land.

XLII. It shall be lawful in future for anyone to leave our kingdom and to return safe and secure by land and water, except for a short period in time of war on grounds of public policy—reserving always the allegiance due to us —excepting always those imprisoned or outlawed in accordance with the law of the kingdom, and natives of any country at war with us, and merchants, who shall be treated as is above provided.

XLIII. If anyone holds of some escheat—such as the honour of Wallingford, Nottingham, Boulogne, Lancaster, or of other escheats which are in our hands and are baronies— and shall die, his heir shall give no other relief, and perform no other service to us than he would have done to the baron, if that barony had been in the baron's hand ; and we shall hold it in the same manner as the baron held it.

XLIV. Men who dwell in the forest need not henceforth come before our justiciars of the forest upon a general summons, except those who are impleaded, or who have become sureties for any person or persons seized for forest offences.

XLV. We will appoint as justices, constables, sheriffs, or bailiffs only such as know the law of the kingdom and mean to observe it well.

XLVI. All barons who have founded abbeys, concerning which they hold charters from the kings of England, or of which they have long continued possession, shall have the wardship of them when vacant, as they ought to have.

XLVII. All forests that have been made such in our time shall forthwith be disafforested ; and a similar course shall be followed with regard to river banks that have been placed " in defence " [1] by us in our time.

XLVIII. All evil customs connected with forests and warrens, foresters and warreners, sheriffs and their officers, river banks and their wardens, shall be immediately inquired into in each county by twelve sworn knights of the same county, and shall, within forty days of the said inquest, be utterly abolished, so as never to be restored, provided always

[1] quae per nos tempore nostro positae sunt in defenso. This was a means of protecting the king's rights of fowling. When put " in defence," a river bank was preserved like a forest for a certain period.

that we previously have intimation thereof, or our justiciar, if we should not be in England.

XLIX. We will immediately restore all hostages and charters delivered to us by Englishmen, as sureties of the peace or of loyal service.

L. We will entirely remove from their bailiwicks, the relations of Gerard of Athee,[1] so that in future they shall have no bailiwick in England ; viz. Engchard of Cigogne, Peter, Guy, and Andrew of Chanceaux, Guy of Cigogne, Geoffrey of Martigny with his brothers, Philip Mark with his brothers and his nephew Geoffrey, and the whole brood [2] of the same.

LI. As soon as peace is restored, we will banish from the kingdom all foreign-born knights, crossbowmen,[3] serjeants, and mercenary soldiers,[4] who have come with horses and arms to the kingdom's hurt.

LII. If anyone has been dispossessed or removed by us, without the legal judgement of his peers,[5] from his lands, castles, franchises, or from his right, we will immediately restore them to him ; and if a dispute arise over this, then let it be decided by the five-and-twenty barons, of whom mention is made below in the clause for securing the peace. Moreover, for all those possessions, from which anyone has, without the lawful judgement of his peers been disseised or removed, by our father, King Henry, or by our brother, King Richard, and which we retain in our hand—or which are possessed by others, to whom we are bound to warrant them—we shall have respite until the usual term of crusaders ; [6] excepting those things about which a plea has been raised, or an inquest made by our order, before our taking of the cross ; but as soon as we return from our pilgrimage—or if by chance we desist from our pilgrimage—we will immediately grant full justice therein.

[1] Gerard of Athee and the rest had followed John to England from his lost dominions in Touraine. They were soldiers of experience and, therefore, greatly feared by the barons.

[2] sequelam : a contemptuous term used of the young of an animal or of the family of a serf.

[3] balistarios.

[4] stipendarios.

[5] Sine legali judicio parium suorum. Cf. Cap. XXXIX.

[6] John, thinking to propitiate the Pope, a few months previously had taken his vow to go on a crusade. This vow entitled one to a three years' respite from all legal proceedings.

LIII. We shall have, moreover, the same respite and in the same manner in rendering justice concerning the de-afforestation or retention of those forests which Henry our father and Richard our brother afforested, and concerning the wardship of lands which are of the fief of another—viz. such wardships as we have hitherto had by reason of a fief which anyone held of us by knight's service—and concerning abbeys founded on fiefs other than our own, in which the lord of the fief claims to have right ; and when we have returned, or if we desist from our pilgrimage, we will immediately grant full justice to all who complain of such things.

LIV. No one shall be arrested or imprisoned upon the appeal of a woman, for the death of any other than her husband.[1]

LV. All fines made by us unjustly and against the law of the land, shall be entirely remitted, or else it shall be done concerning them according to the decision of the five-and-twenty barons of whom mention is made below in (the clause for) securing the peace, or according to the judgement of the majority of the same, along with the aforesaid Stephen, archbishop of Canterbury, if he can be present, and such others as he may wish to bring with him for this purpose ; and if he cannot be present the business shall nevertheless proceed without him, provided always that if any one or more of the aforesaid five-and-twenty barons are in a similar suit, they shall be removed as far as shall concern this particular judgement, others being substituted in their places after having been selected by the rest of the five-and-twenty for this purpose only, and after having been sworn.

LVI. If we have disseised or removed Welshmen from lands or liberties, or other things, without the legal judgement of their peers in England or in Wales, they shall be immediately restored to them ; and if a dispute arise over this, then let it be decided in the marches by the judgement of their peers ; for tenements in England according to the

---

[1] In criminal cases the duellum had to be fought between the appellant in person and the accused. But in certain cases the rule was relaxed and the appellant might fight by proxy. These privileged cases included women, men over sixty, those who had lost a limb, etc. Thus a woman might appeal a man of homicide without incurring any danger. For trial by battle, cf. Jocelyn de Brakelonde's *Chronicle*, p. 92 ; and extracts from Charters to Bristol and Dunwich, p. 112.

4

law of England, for tenements in Wales according to the law of Wales, and for tenements in the marches according to the law of the marches.   Welshmen shall do the same to us and ours.

LVII. But for all those possessions from which any Welshman has, without lawful judgement of his peers,[1] been disseised or removed by King Henry our father, or King Richard our brother, and which we retain in our hand (or which are possessed by others, to whom we are bound to warrant them), we shall have respite until the usual term of crusaders ; excepting those things about which a plea has been raised or an inquest made by our order before we took the cross ; but as soon as we return (or if perchance we desist from our pilgrimage) we will immediately grant full justice in accordance with the laws of the Welsh and in relation to the foresaid regions.

LVIII. We will immediately give up the son of Llywelyn and all the hostages of Wales, and the charters delivered to us as security for the peace.

LIX. We will do towards Alexander, King of Scots, concerning the return of his sisters and his hostages, and concerning his franchises and his right, in the same manner as we shall do towards our other barons of England, unless it ought to be done otherwise according to the charters which we hold of William his father, formerly King of Scots ; and this shall be according to the judgement of his peers in our court.

LX. Moreover, all these aforesaid customs and liberties, the observance of which we have granted in our kingdom as far as pertains to us towards our men, shall be observed by all of our kingdom, as well clergy as laymen, as far as pertains to them towards their men.

LXI. Since, moreover, for God and the amendment of our kingdom and for the better allaying of our quarrel that has arisen between us and our barons, we have granted all these concessions, desirous that they should enjoy them in complete and firm stability for ever, we give and grant to them the underwritten security, namely, that the barons choose five-and-twenty barons of the kingdom, whomsoever they will, who shall be obliged, to observe and hold, and cause to be observed, with all their might, the peace and

---

[1] Sine legali judicio parium suorum.

liberties which we have granted and confirmed to them by
this our present Charter, so that if we, or our justiciar, or
our bailiffs or any one of our officers, shall in anything be at
fault towards anyone, or shall have broken any one of the
articles of the peace or of this security, and the offence be
notified to four barons of the aforesaid five-and-twenty, the
said four barons shall come to us (or to our justiciar, if we
are out of the realm) and, laying the transgression before
us, petition to have that transgression redressed without
delay. And if we shall not have corrected the transgression
(or, in event of our being out of the kingdom, if our justiciar
shall not have corrected it) within forty days, reckoning
from the time it has been notified to us (or to our justiciar,
if we should be out of the kingdom), the four barons aforesaid
shall refer the matter to the rest of the five-and-twenty
barons, and those five-and-twenty barons shall, together
with the community of the whole land, distrain and distress
us in all possible ways, namely, by seizing our castles, lands,
possessions, and in any other way they can, until redress
has been obtained as they deem fit, saving our own person
and the persons of our queen and children ; and when redress
has been obtained, they shall resume their former relations
towards us. And let whoever in the country desires it, swear
to obey the orders of the said five-and-twenty barons for the
execution of all the aforesaid matters, and along with them
to distress us to the utmost of his power ; and we publicly
and freely grant leave to everyone, who wishes, to swear ;
and we shall never forbid anyone to swear. All those, moreover, in the land, who of themselves and their own accord
are unwilling to swear to the twenty-five to help them in
distraining and distressing us, we shall by our command
compel the same to swear to the effect aforesaid. And if
any one of the five-and-twenty barons shall have died or
departed from the land, or be incapacited in any other manner,
which would prevent the aforesaid provisions being carried
out, those of the said twenty-five barons who are left shall
choose another in his place according to their own judgement,
and he shall be sworn in the same way as the others. Further,
in all matters, the execution of which is entrusted to these
twenty-five barons, if perchance these twenty-five are present
and disagree about anything, or if some of them after being
summoned, are unwilling or unable to be present, that

which the majority of those present ordain and command shall be held as fixed and established, exactly as if the whole twenty-five had concurred in this ; and the said twenty-five shall swear that they will faithfully observe all that is aforesaid, and cause it to be observed with all their power. And we shall procure nothing from anyone, directly or indirectly, whereby any part of these concessions and liberties might be revoked or diminished ; and if any such thing has been procured, let it be void and null, and we shall never use it ourselves or by another.

EXTRACT FROM MATTHEW PARIS

The following are the XXV. barons chosen :

The Earl of Clare.
The Earl of Albemarle.
The Earl of Gloucester.
The Earl of Winchester.
The Earl of Hereford.
Earl Roger (Bigot).
Earl Robert (de Vere).
William Marshall, Junior.
Robert, son of Walter, Senior.
Gilbert de Clare.
Eustace de Vesci.
Hugh Bigod.
William de Munbrai.
The Mayor of London.
William de Lanvalay.
Robert de Ros.
The Constable of Chester.
Richard de Perci.
John, son of Robert.
William Malet.
Geoffrey de Say.
Roger de Mumbezon.
William de Huntingfield.
Richard de Muntfichet.
William de Albineio.

VI. WRIT OF SUMMONS

[May 1213. Stubbs, *Select Charters*, p. 276. From Matthew Paris (ed. Wats.), p. 240. The authenticity of this passage has been much disputed. There is no evidence to show that the assembly indicated ever met at St. Albans or elsewhere. *Vide* Medley, *Constitutional History*, 8th ed., ch. iv.]

THE next day the king sent letters to all the sheriffs of the kingdom of England, ordering them to send four legal men from each town in their demesnes, together with the warden, to St. Albans on the fourth of August, that through them and his other servants he might make inquiries about the losses of each of the bishops and abbots, and how much was due to each.

VII. WRIT OF SUMMONS TO A GREAT COUNCIL

[November 1213. Stubbs, *Select Charters*, p. 287.]

THE king to the Sheriff of Oxfordshire, greeting. We direct you to cause all the knights of your bailiwick, who have been summoned to appear before me at Oxford on All Saints' Day, to come in fifteen days with their arms ; but all the barons [1] to come in like manner unarmed : and that you cause four discreet men of your county to meet us there at the same time to consult with us about the business of our realm.

Witness myself at Witney, the seventh day of November.

[Similar writs were directed to all the sheriffs.]

VIII. WRIT OF SUMMONS FOR TWO KNIGHTS OF THE SHIRE TO GRANT AN AID

[February 1254. Stubbs, *Select Charters*, p. 376.]

FORM DIRECTED TO ALL THE MAGNATES AND SHERIFFS OF
ENGLAND

THE king to the Sheriff of Bedfordshire and Buckinghamshire, greeting. Since the earls and barons and other

---

[1] corpora vero baronum.

magnates of our realm have faithfully promised us that they will be in London in three weeks from next Easter, prepared with horses and arms and well equipped to go without delay to Portsmouth, to come over to Gascony to us, to aid us against the king of Castile who intends to invade our territory of Gascony with a strong force, next summer, we have ordered you to constrain to this all those in your bailiwick who hold lands worth twenty pounds a year from us in chief, or from others who are under age and in our wardship ; we straitly command you, that besides all those aforesaid, you cause to come before our council at Westminster on the fifteenth day after Easter next, four lawful and discreet knights from the said shires whom the said shires shall have chosen for this purpose, in place of all and singular of the said shires,[1] that is, two from one shire and two from the other, who together with the knights from the other shires whom we have summoned for the same day, shall arrange what aid they are willing to pay us in our need. And you yourself carefully set forth to the knights and others of the said shires, our need and how urgent is our business, and effectually persuade them to pay us an aid sufficient for the time being ; so that the aforesaid four knights at the aforesaid time shall be able to give definite answer concerning the said aid to the aforesaid council, for each of the said counties. We also give you an absolute command that all dues to us in your bailiwick which are in arrears, and ought to be paid to our exchequer before Easter, you shall have at the aforesaid exchequer on the fifteenth day after the aforesaid Easter, and you are to know that unless you have the aforesaid debts then and there, we shall not only cause you to be placed under arrest, but we shall also cause those dues to be collected from your lands and tenements to your no small loss.

Witness Eleanor the queen and Richard earl of Cornwall, at Windsor, the eleventh day of February.

[1] quos iidem comitatus ad hoc elegerint, vice omnium et singulorum eorundem comitatuum, . . .

IX. WRITS OF SUMMONS TO " THE MODEL PARLIAMENT "

[Sept. 30–Oct. 3, 1295. Stubbs, *Select Charters*, p. 484.]

(*a*) To Clergy

[Sent in the same form to the two archbishops and eighteen bishops ; also, omitting the last clause "citing before hand . . .," to seventy abbots.]

THE king to the venerable father in Christ, Robert, by the same grace archbishop of Canterbury, primate of all England, greeting. As a most just law, established by the careful providence of sacred princes, exhorts and decrees that what affects all, by all should be approved, so also, very evidently, should common danger be met by means provided in common.[1] You know sufficiently well, and it is now, as we believe, divulged through all regions of the world, how the king of France fraudulently and craftily deprives us of our land of Gascony, by withholding it unjustly from us. Now, however, not satisfied, with the aforesaid fraud and injustice, having gathered together for the conquest of our kingdom a very great fleet, and a vast multitude of warriors, with which he has made a hostile attack on our kingdom and the inhabitants of the same kingdom, he now proposes to destroy the English language altogether from the earth, if his power should correspond to the detestable proposition of the contemplated injustice, which God forbid. Because, therefore, darts seen beforehand do less injury, and your interest especially, as that of the rest of the citizens of the same realm, is concerned in this affair, we command you, strictly enjoining you in the fidelity and love in which you are bound to us, that on the Lord's day next after the feast of St. Martin, in the approaching winter, you be present in person at Westminster ; citing beforehand[2] the dean and chapter of your church, the archdeacons and all the clergy of your diocese, causing the same dean and archdeacons in

---

[1] Sicut lex justissima, provida circumspectione sacrorum principum stabilita, hortatur et statuit ut quod omnes tangit ab omnibus approbetur, sic et nimis evidenter ut communibus periculis per remedia provisa communiter obvietur. Cf. pp. 27 and 56.

[2] Praemunientes.

their own persons, and the said chapter by one suitable proctor, and the said clergy by two, to be present along with you, having full and sufficient power from the said chapter and clergy, to consider, ordain, and provide, along with us and the rest of the prelates and nobles and other inhabitants of our kingdom, how the dangers and threatened evils of this kind are to be met.

Witness the king at Wangham, the thirtieth day of September.

(b) TO BARONS

[Summons in this form was sent to seven earls and forty-one barons.]

THE king to his beloved and loyal relative, Edmund, Earl of Cornwall, greeting. Because we wish to have a consultation and meeting with you and with the rest of the nobles of our kingdom, as to provision for remedies against the dangers which in these days are threatening our whole kingdom ; we command you, strictly enjoining you on the fidelity and love in which you are bound to us, that on the Sunday next after the feast of St. Martin, in the approaching winter, you be present in person at Westminster, for considering, ordaining, and doing along with us and with the prelates, and the rest of the nobles and other inhabitants of our kingdom, as may be necessary for meeting dangers of this kind.

Witness the king at Canterbury, the first of October.

(c) TO SHIRE AND BOROUGH REPRESENTATIVES

THE king to the Sheriff of Northamptonshire. Since we intend to have a consultation and meeting with the earls, barons, and other nobles of our kingdom with regard to providing remedies against the dangers which are in these days threatening the same kingdom ; and on that account have commanded them to be with us on the Sunday next after the Feast of St. Martin in the approaching winter, at Westminster, to consider, ordain, and do as may be necessary for the avoidance of these dangers ; we strictly require you to cause two knights from the aforesaid shire, two citizens from each city in the same shire, and two burgesses from each borough, of those who are especially discreet and capable of labouring, to be elected without delay, and to cause them to come to us at the time and place aforesaid.

Moreover, the said knights are to have full and sufficient power for themselves and for the community of the aforesaid shire, and the said citizens and burgesses for themselves, and the communities of the aforesaid cities and boroughs separately, then and there for doing what shall then be ordained according to the common counsel in the premises ; so that the aforesaid business shall not remain unfinished in any way for defect of this power. And you shall have there the names of the knights, citizens, and burgesses, and this writ.

Witness the king at Canterbury, on the third day of October.

X. STATUTE OF WINCHESTER, 1285

[Translation and original in *Statutes of the Realm*, vol. i. pp. 96 sqq., and in Stubbs, *Select Charters*, pp. 472 sqq.]

I. FORASMUCH as from day to day, robberies, murders, burnings, and thefts be more often used than they have been heretofore, and felons cannot be attainted by the oath of jurors which had rather suffer felonies done to strangers to pass without pain, than to indite the offenders of whom great part be people of the same country, or at least if the offenders be of another country the receivers be of places near ; and they do the same because an oath is not put unto jurors, nor upon the country where such felonies were done as to the restitution of damages, hitherto no pain hath been limited for their concealment and laches ; our lord the king, for to abate the power of felons, hath established a pain in this case, so that from henceforth, for fear of the pain more than from fear of any oath, they shall not spare any nor conceal any felonies ; and doth command that cries shall be solemnly made in all counties, hundreds, markets, fairs, and all other places where great resort of people is, so that none shall excuse himself by ignorance, that from henceforth every country be so well kept that immediately upon such robberies and felonies committed fresh suits shall be made from town to town and from country to country.

II. Likewise when need requires, inquests shall be made in towns by him that is lord of the town, and after in the

hundred and in the franchise and in the county, and sometimes in two, three, or four counties, in case when felonies
shall be committed in the marches of shires, so that the
offenders may be attainted. And if the country will not
answer for the bodies of such manner of offenders, the pain
shall be such, that every country, that is to wit, the people
dwelling in the country, shall be answerable for the robberies
done and also the damages ; so that the whole hundred
where the robbery shall be done, with the franchises being
within the precinct of the same hundred, shall be answerable for the robberies done. And if the robbery be done in
the division of two hundreds, both the hundreds and the
franchises within them shall be answerable ; and after that
the felony or robbery is done, the country shall have no
longer space than forty days, within which forty days it
shall behove them to agree for the robbery or offence, or else
that they will answer for the bodies of the offenders.

III. And forasmuch as the king will not that his people
should be suddenly impoverished by reason of this penalty,
that seemeth very hard to many, the king granteth that it
shall not be incurred immediately, but it shall be respited
until Easter next following, within which time the king
may see how the country will order themselves, and whether
such felonies and robberies do cease. After which term let
them all be assured that the foresaid penalty shall run generally ; that is to say, every country, that is to wit, the people
in the country, shall be answerable for felonies and robberies
done among them.

IV. And for the more surety of the country, the king
hath commanded that in great towns being walled, the gates
shall be closed from the sun-setting until the sun-rising ;
and that no man do lodge in suburbs, nor in any place out
of the town, from nine of the clock until day, unless his
host will answer for him ; and the bailiffs of towns every
week, or at the least every fifteenth day, shall make inquiry
of all persons being lodged in the suburbs or in foreign places
of the towns ; and if they do find any that have lodged or
received any strangers or suspicious person against the
peace, the bailiffs shall do right therein. And the king
commandeth, that from henceforth, all watches be made as
it hath been used in times past, that is to wit, from the day
of the Ascension until the day of S. Michael, in every city

by six men at every gate ; in every borough, twelve men ; every town, six or four, according to the number of the inhabitants of the town, and they shall watch the town continually all night from the sun-setting unto the sun-rising. And if any stranger do pass by them he shall be arrested until morning ; and if no suspicion be found he shall go quit ; and if they find cause of suspicion, they shall forthwith deliver him to the sheriff, and the sheriff may receive him without damage, and shall keep him safely, until he be acquitted in due manner. And if they will not obey the arrest, they shall levy hue and cry upon them, and such as keep the watch shall follow with hue and cry with all the town and the towns near, and so hue and cry shall be made from town to town, until that they be taken and delivered to the sheriff as before is said ; and for the arrestments of such strangers none shall be punished.

V. And further it is commanded that highways leading from one market town to another shall be enlarged, whereas bushes, woods, or dykes be, so that there be neither dyke, tree, nor bush whereby a man may lurk to do hurt within two hundred foot of the one side and two hundred foot on the other side of the way ; so that this statute shall not extend unto oaks, nor unto great trees, so as it be clear underneath. And if by default of the lord that will not abate the dyke, underwood, or bushes, in the manner aforesaid, any robberies be done therein, the lord shall be answerable for the felony ; and if murder be done the lord shall make a fine at the king's pleasure. And if the lord be not able to fell the underwoods, the country shall aid him therein. And the king willeth that in his demesne lands and woods, within his forest and without, the ways shall be enlarged, as before is said. And if percase a park be near to the highway, it is requisite that the lord shall minish his park the space of two hundred foot from the highways, as before is said, or that he make such a wall, dyke, or hedge that offenders may not pass, nor return to evil.

VI. And further it is commanded that every man have in his house harness for to keep the peace after the ancient assize [1] ; that is to say, every man between fifteen years of age and sixty years, shall be assessed and sworn to armour according to the quantity of their lands and goods ; that is

[1] Cf. pp. 34 sqq.

to wit, from fifteen pounds lands, and goods forty marks, an hauberke, an helme of iron, a sword, a knife, and a horse ; and from ten pounds of lands, and twenty marks goods, an hauberke, an helme of iron, a sword, and a knife ; and from five-pound lands, a doublet, an helme of iron, a sword, and a knife ; and from forty shillings of land, a sword, a bow and arrows, and a knife ; and he that hath less than forty shillings yearly shall be sworn to keep gisarmes, knives, and other less weapons ; and he that hath less than twenty marks in goods, shall have swords, knives, and other less weapons ; and all other that may shall have bows and arrows out of the forest, and in the forest bows and boults. And that view of armour be made every year two times. And in every hundred and franchise two constables shall be chosen to make the view of armour ; and the constables aforesaid shall present before justices assigned such defaults as they do see in the country about armour, and of the suits, and of watches, and of highways ; and also shall present all such as do lodge strangers in uplandish towns, for whom they will not answer. And the justices assigned shall present at every parliament unto the king such defaults as they shall find, and the king shall provide remedy therein. And from henceforth let sheriffs take good heed, and bailiffs within their franchises and without, be they higher or lower, that have any bailiwick or forestry in fee or otherwise, that they shall follow the cry with the country, and after, as they are bounden, to keep horses and armour, so to do ; and if there be any that do not, the defaults shall be presented by the constables to the justices assigned, and after by them to the king ; and the king will provide remedy as afore is said. And the king commandeth and forbiddeth that from henceforth neither fairs nor markets be kept in churchyards, for the honour of the church. Given at Winchester, the eighth of October, in the thirteenth year of the reign of the king.

XI. CONFIRMATION OF CHARTERS, 1297

[Translation and original in *Statutes of the Realm,* vol. i. pp. 123 sqq., also in Stubbs, *Select Charters,* pp. 496 sqq.]

I. EDWARD, by the grace of God, King of England, Lord of Ireland, and Duke of Guyan, to all those that these present

letters shall hear or see, greeting. Know ye that we to the
honour of God and of holy Church, and to the profit of our
realm, have granted for us and our heirs, that the Charter
of Liberties and the Charter of the Forest, which were made
by common assent of all the realm, in the time of King Henry
our father, shall be kept in every point without breach. And
we will that the same charters shall be sent under our seal
as well to our justices of the forest as to others, and to all
sheriffs of shires, and to all our other officers, and to all our
cities throughout the realm, together with our writs in the
which it shall be contained, that they cause the aforesaid
charters to be published, and to declare to the people that
we have confirmed them in all points, and that our justices,
sheriffs, mayors, and other ministers which under us have
the laws of our land to guide, shall allow the said charters
in pleas before them and in judgments in all their points ;
that is to wit, the Great Charter as the common law and the
Charter of the Forest according to the Assize of the Forest,
for the wealth of our realm.

II. And we will that if any judgment be given from
henceforth, contrary to the points of the charters aforesaid,
by the justices or by any other our ministers that hold plea
before them against the points of the charters, it shall be
undone and holden for nought.

III. And we will that the same charters shall be sent
under our seal to cathedral churches throughout our realm,
there to remain, and shall be read before the people two
times by the year.

IV. And that all archbishops and bishops shall pronounce
the sentence of great excommunication against all those
that by word, deed, or counsel do contrary to the foresaid
charters, or that in any point break or undo them. And
that the said curses be twice a year denounced and published
by the prelates aforesaid. And if the same prelates or any
of them be remiss in the denunciation of the said sentences,
the Archbishops of Canterbury and York for the time being,
as is fitting, shall compel and distrein them to make that
denunciation in form aforesaid.

V. And for so much as divers people of our realm are
in fear that the aids and tasks which they have given to us
beforetime towards our wars and other business, of their
own grant and goodwill, howsoever they were made, might

turn to a bondage to them and their heirs, because they might be at another time found in the rolls, and so likewise the prises taken throughout the realm by our ministers : we have granted for us and our heirs, that we shall not draw such aids, tasks, nor prises into a custom for anything that hath been done heretofore or that may be found by roll or in any other manner.

VI. Moreover, we have granted for us and our heirs, as well to archbishops, bishops, abbots, priors, and other folk of holy Church, as also to earls, barons, and to all the commonalty of the land, that for no business from henceforth will we take such manner of aids, tasks, nor prises, but by the common assent of the realm, and for the common profit thereof, saving the ancient aids and prises due and accustomed.

VII. And for so much as the more part of the commonalty of the realm find themselves sore grieved with the maletote of wools, that is to wit, a toll of forty shillings for every sack of wool, and have made petition to us to release the same ; we, at their requests, have clearly released it, and have granted for us and our heirs that we shall not take such thing nor any other without their common assent and goodwill ; saving to us and our heirs the custom of wools, skins, and leather granted before by the commonalty aforesaid. In witness of which things we have caused these our letters to be made patents. Witness Edward our son at London, the 10th day of October, the five and twentieth year of our reign.

And be it remembered that this same charter in the same terms, word for word, was sealed in Flanders under the king's great seal, that is to say at Ghent, the 5th day of November in the 25th year of the reign of our aforesaid lord the king, and sent into England.

CHAPTER III

THE CATHOLIC CHURCH

I. CANONS OF THE COUNCIL OF LONDON UNDER LANFRANC, A.D. 1075

[Original in Wilkins' *Concilia*, vol. i. pp. 363 sqq.]

1. BECAUSE Councils had fallen out of fashion in England for many years past, some things were renewed which are known to have been defined by ancient canons too. So it was ordained according to the fourth Council of Toledo, and those of Milevis and Braga, that bishops should sit according to the time of their ordination, save those who by old custom, or by privileges of their Churches, have seats by precedence. The old men were asked about this, what they had seen themselves or had

received truly and probably from their elders, and for this answer delay was requested and granted till next day. So on the next day they stated unanimously that the Archbishop of York ought to sit at the right hand of Canterbury, the Bishop of London at the left, Winchester next York; but if York be away, London on the right, Winchester on the left.

2. That monks should hold their proper order by the rule of St. Benedict in the Dialogue of Gregory, and the ancient custom of places under rule, chiefly that children and youths should have guardianship in all places under fit masters assigned them, that all in general should carry lights by night unless they have no property allowed by the authorities. But if anyone be discovered at death to hold any property without the licence aforesaid, and shall not restore it before death, confessing his sin with penitence and grief, let not the bells be tolled for him, nor the saving sacrifice be offered for his absolution, nor let him be buried in the cemetery.

3. By the decrees of Popes Damasus and Leo, and by the Councils of Sardica and Laodicea, whereby it is forbidden that bishops' sees should be in vills,[1] it was granted by royal favour and the Council's authority to the aforesaid three bishops to migrate from vills to cities—Hermann from Sherborne to Salisbury, Stigand from Selsey to Chichester, Peter from Lichfield to Chester. The case of some who were yet in vills or hamlets was postponed for the king's hearing, then at war in parts beyond the sea.

4. By many decrees of the Roman pontiffs and different authorities of the sacred canons, that no one should keep or ordain any clerk or monk without letters dimissory.

5. To restrain the arrogance of some unwise men it was enjoined by general decree that no one speak in the Council, save bishops and abbots, without leave from the metropolitan.

6. By the decrees of Gregory the Great and the Less that none take a wife from his own kin or that of his deceased wife, or any he has as relation, within the seventh degree on either side.

7. That no one buy or sell sacred orders or church office which appertains to cure of souls ; for this crime was originally condemned by the apostle Peter in the case of Simon Magus, afterwards forbidden under excommunication by the holy fathers.

---

[1] villis.

8. That the bones of dead animals be not hung up anywhere as though to avoid diseases of animals, and that sorcery, soothsaying, divination,[1] or any such works of the Devil be practised by no one ; for all such things the sacred canons have forbidden, and those who practised them they have excommunicated by sentence given.

9. That by the Councils of Elvira and Toledo (XI.) no bishop or abbot or any of the clergy should judge concerning a man to be put to death or to mutilation, nor favour with his authority those who so judge.

II. LETTER OF WILLIAM THE CONQUEROR TO POPE GREGORY VII., *circa* A.D. 1076 (?)

[Translated in Giles' *Lanfranc*, Letter x. (Patres Ecclesiae Anglicanae).]

To Gregory, the most noble Shepherd of the Holy Church, William, by the grace of God, renowned king of the English, and duke of the Normans, greeting with amity; Hubert, your legate, Holy Father, coming to me in your behalf, bade me to do fealty to you and your successors, and to think better in the matter of the money which my predecessors were wont to send to the Roman Church : the one point I agreed to, the other I did not agree to. I refused to do fealty, nor will I, because neither have I promised it, nor do I find that my predecessors did it to your predecessors. The money for nearly three years, whilst I was in Gaul, has been carelessly collected ; but now that I am come back to my kingdom, by God's mercy, what has been collected is sent by the aforesaid legate, and what remains shall be dispatched, when opportunity serves, by the legate of Lanfranc our faithful archbishop. Pray for us, and for the good estate of our realm, for we have loved your predecessors and desire to love you sincerely, and to hear you obediently before all.[2]

III. THE CONQUEROR'S MANDATE FOR DIVIDING THE CIVIL AND ECCLESIASTICAL COURTS

[Stubbs, *Select Charters*, p. 85.]

WILLIAM, by the grace of God, king of the English, to R. Bainard, and G. de Magneville, and Peter de Valoines, and all

[1] For divination, etc., cf. *Confessio Amantis*, p. 261.
[2] prae omnibus.

my faithful subjects of Essex, Hertfordshire, and Middlesex, greeting. Know ye and all my faithful subjects resident in England, that I have by my common council, and by the advice of the archbishops, bishops, abbots, and chief men of my realm, determined that the episcopal laws be mended as not having been kept properly nor according to the decrees of the sacred canons throughout the realm of England, even to my own times. Accordingly I command and charge you by royal authority that no bishop nor archdeacon do hereafter hold pleas of episcopal laws in the Hundred, nor bring a cause to the judgment of secular men which concerns the rule of souls.[1] But whoever shall be impleaded by the episcopal laws for any cause or crime, let him come to the place which the bishop shall choose and name for this purpose, and there answer for his cause or crime, and not according to the Hundred, but according to the canons and episcopal laws, and let him do right to God and his bishop. But if anyone, being lifted up with pride, refuse to come to the bishop's court, let him be summoned once, twice and thrice, and if by this means, even, he come not to obedience, let the authority and justice of the king or sheriff be exerted ; and he who refuses to come to the bishop's judgment shall make good the bishop's law [2] for every summons. This, too, I absolutely forbid that any sheriff, reeve, or king's minister, or any other layman, do in any wise concern himself with the laws which belong to the bishop, or bring another man to judgment save in the bishop's court. And let judgment be nowhere undergone but in the bishop's see or in that place which the bishop appoints for this purpose.

IV. THE COMPROMISE OF INVESTITURES, 1107

[Original in *Eadmer* (Rolls Series), p. 186]

ON the first of August an assembly of bishops, abbots, and nobles of the realm was held at London in the king's palace. And for three successive days, in Anselm's absence, the matter was thoroughly discussed between king and bishops concerning investitures, some arguing for this that the king

[1] Propteraea mando et regia auctoritate praecipio, ut nullus episcopus vel archidiaconus de legibus episcopalibus amplius in hundret placita teneant nec causam quae ad regimen animarum pertinet ad judicium secularium hominum adducant ; . . .

[2] emendavit legem episcopalem.

should perform them after the manner of his father and brother, not according to the injunction and obedience of the pope. For the pope in the sentence which had been then published, standing firm, had conceded homage, which Pope Urban had forbidden, as well as investiture, and in this way had won over the king about investiture, as may be gathered from the letter we have quoted above. Afterwards, in the presence of Anselm and a large concourse, the king agreed and ordained that henceforward no one should be invested with bishopric or abbacy in England by the giving of a pastoral staff or the ring, by the king or any lay hand ; Anselm also agreeing that no one elected to a prelacy should be deprived of consecration to the office undertaken on the ground of homage, which he should make to the king. After this decision, by the advice of Anselm and the nobles of the realm, fathers were instituted by the king, without any investiture of pastoral staff or ring, to nearly all the churches of England which had been so long bereaved of their shepherds.

V. CANONS OF ST. ANSELM AT LONDON, 1108

[Eadmer (Rolls Series), pp. 194 sqq.]

IT was ordained that priests, deacons, and subdeacons live in chastity, and have no women in their houses, save those very closely related to them, as the holy Nicene Council defined.

Those priests, deacons, and subdeacons, who after the prohibition of the London Council have retained their women, or have married others, if they wish to celebrate mass after this, shall put them away from themselves entirely so that neither these enter their houses, nor they theirs, nor yet knowingly meet in any house ; nor are such women to live on any church territory.

If they must needs speak with them for any honest reason, let them speak with them outside the house with two lawful witnesses.

And if any of them have been accused of breaking this statute, by two or three lawful witnesses, or public report of the parishioners, he shall purge himself with six witnesses if a priest, four if a deacon, two if a subdeacon. And if this purgation fail he shall be adjudged a breaker of the sacred decree.

Let those priests who, despising God's altar and their holy orders, prefer to live with women, be deprived of office and benefice and put out of the choir, after being pronounced infamous.

And if in rebellion and contempt any leave not the woman and presume to celebrate mass, let him be excommunicated on the eighth day unless he refuse not satisfaction when demanded.

This same sentence comprehends all archdeacons and canons as to leaving their women, and avoiding contact with them, and the censure incurred if they shall transgress the statutes.

All archdeacons shall swear that they will not take money to connive at the breach of this statute, nor will they suffer priests, whom they know to have women, to sing mass, or to have vicars. Deans shall act in like manner, and the archdeacon or dean refusing to swear this shall lose his archdeaconry or deanery.

But priests who choose to leave their women and serve God and His holy altars, vacating their office for forty days, shall in the meantime have vicars, penance being enjoined them according to the bishop's discretion.

All movables belonging to priests, deacons, subdeacons, or canons who fall henceforth, shall be forfeited to the bishops, as well as the concubines, with their effects, as adulteresses.

VI. THE CONSTITUTIONS OF CLARENDON, 1164

[Stubbs' *Select Charters*, p. 137.]

IN the year 1164 from our Lord's Incarnation, the fourth of the pontificate of Alexander, the tenth of Henry II. most illustrious king of the English, in the presence of the same king, was made this memorial or acknowledgment of a certain part of the customs, liberties, and dignities of his ancestors, that is of King Henry his grandfather, and of others, which ought to be observed and held in the realm. And owing to strifes and dissensions which had taken place between the clergy and justices of the lord the king and the barons of the realm, in respect of customs and dignities of the realm, this recognition was made before the archbishops and bishops and clergy, and the earls and barons and nobles of the realm. And these same customs, recognized by the archbishops and bishops, and earls and barons, and by those of high rank and age in the realm, Thomas Archbishop of Canterbury, and Roger Archbishop of York, and Gilbert Bishop of London, and Henry Bishop of Winchester, and Nigel Bishop of Ely, and William Bishop of Norwich, and Robert Bishop of Lincoln, and Hilary Bishop of Chichester, and Jocelyn Bishop of Salisbury, and Richard Bishop of Chester, and Bartholomew Bishop of Exeter, and Robert Bishop of Hereford, and David Bishop of St. David's, and Roger Bishop-elect of Worcester, conceded, and by word of mouth steadfastly promised on the word of truth, to the lord the king and his heirs, should be kept and observed in good faith and without evil intent, these being present : Robert Earl of Leicester, Reginald Earl of Cornwall, Conan Earl of Brittany, John Earl of Eu, Roger Earl of Clare, Earl Geoffrey de Mandeville, Hugh Earl of Chester, William Earl of Arundel, Earl Patrick, William Earl of Ferrers, Richard de Luci, Reginald de St. Valery, Roger Bigot, Reginald de Warenne, Richer de Aquila, William de Braose, Richard de Camville, Nigel de Mowbray, Simon de Beauchamp, Humphry de Bohun, Matthew de Hereford, Walter de Mayenne, Manser Biset the steward, William Malet, William de Courcy, Robert de Dunstanville, Jocelin de Balliol, William de Lanvallei, William de Caisnet, Geoffrey de Vere, William de Hastings, Hugh de Moreville, Alan de Neville, Simon son of Peter, William Maudit the chamberlain, John Maudit, John Marshall, Peter de Mara, and many other magnates and nobles of the realm, as well clerical as lay.

Now of the acknowledged customs and dignities of the realm a certain part is contained in the present document, of which part these are the chapters :

1. If controversy shall arise between laymen, or clergy and laymen, or clergy, regarding advowson and presentation to churches, let it be tried or concluded in the court of the lord the king.

2. Churches belonging to the fief of the lord the king cannot be granted in perpetuity without his own assent and grant.

3. Clerks cited and accused of any matter shall, when summoned by the king's justices, come into his own court

to answer there concerning what it shall seem to the king's court should be answered there, and in the church court for what it shall seem should be answered there ; yet so that the king's justice shall send into the court of holy Church to see in what way the matter is there tried. And if the clerk be convicted, or shall confess, the Church must not any longer protect him.[1]

4. Archbishops, bishops, and beneficed clergy of the realm are not allowed to leave the kingdom without licence of the lord the king ; and if they do leave, they shall, if the king so please, give security that neither in going nor in staying, nor in returning, will they seek the ill or damage of the lord the king or realm.

5. Excommunicate persons are not to give pledge for the future, nor to take oath, but only to give security and pledge of abiding by the Church's judgment that they may be absolved.

6. Laymen are not to be accused save by proper and legal accusers and witnesses in the presence of the bishop, so that the archdeacon do not lose his right nor anything due to him thence. And if the accused be such that no one wills or dares to accuse them, the sheriff, when requested by the bishop, shall cause twelve lawful men from the neighbourhood [2] of the town to swear before the bishop that they will show the truth in the matter according to their conscience.

7. No one who holds of the king in chief, and none of his demesne officers are to be excommunicated, nor the lands of any one of them to be put under an interdict unless first the lord the king, if he be in the country, or his justiciar if he be outside the kingdom, be applied to, in order that he may do right for him ; and so that what shall appertain to the royal court be concluded there, and that what shall belong to the church court be sent to the same to be treated there.

8. In regard to appeals, if they shall occur, they must proceed from the archdeacon to the bishop, and from the

---

[1] Cap. 3. Clerici rectati et accusati de quacunque re, summoniti a Justitia regis venient in curiam ipsius, responsuri ibidem de hoc unde videbitur curiae regis quod ibidem sit respondendum ; et in curia ecclesiastica, unde videbitur quod ibidem sit respondendum ; ita quod Justitia regis mittet in curiam sanctae ecclesiae ad videndum qua ratione res ibi tractabitur. Et si clericus convictus vel confessus fuerit, non debet de cetero eum ecclesia tueri.

[2] de vicineto.

bishop to the archbishop. And if the archbishop fail in showing justice, they must come at last to the lord the king, that by his command the dispute be concluded in the archbishop's court, so that it must not go further without the assent of the lord the king.

9. If a dispute shall arise between a clerk and a layman, or between a layman and a clerk, in respect of any tenement which the clerk wishes to bring to frank-almoign, but the layman to a lay fief, it shall be concluded by the consideration of the king's chief justice on the inquest of twelve lawful men, before the king's justiciar himself. And if the award be that it belongs to frank-almoign, it shall be pleaded in the church court, but if to a lay fief, unless both claim under the same bishop or baron, it shall be pleaded in the king's court. But if both appeal concerning this fief to the same bishop or baron, it shall be pleaded in his own court, so that for making the inquest he who was first seised, lose not his seisin until the matter be settled by the plea.

10. If any one of a city, or castle, or borough, or a demesne manor of the lord the king, be cited by archdeacon or bishop for any offence for which he ought to answer them, and refuse to give satisfaction at their citations, it is well lawful to place him under interdict ; but he must not be excommunicated before the lord the king's chief officer of that town be applied to, in order that he may adjudge him to come for satisfaction. And if the king's officer fail in this, he shall be at the king's mercy, and thereafter the bishop shall be able to constrain the accused by ecclesiastical justice.

11. Archbishops, bishops, and all persons of the realm who hold of the king in chief, have their possessions from the lord the king as barony, and are answerable for them to the king's justices and ministers, and follow and do all royal rights and customs, and like all other barons, have to be present at the trials of the court of the lord the king with the barons until it comes to a judgment of loss of limb, or death.

12. When an archbishopric or bishopric is vacant, or any abbey or priory of the king's demesne, it must be in his own hand, and from it he shall receive all revenues and rents as demesne. And when they come to provide for the church, the lord the king must cite the chief beneficed clergy

of the church, and the election must take place in the chapel of the lord the king himself, with the assent of the lord the king, and the advice of the beneficed clergy of the realm whom he shall have summoned to do this. And the person elected shall there do homage and fealty to the lord the king as to his liege lord for his life and limbs and earthly honour, saving his order, before he be consecrated.

13. If any of the nobles of the realm forcibly prevent the archbishop or archdeacon from doing justice in regard of himself or his people, the lord the king must bring them to justice. And if perchance any one should deforce the lord the king, the archbishops and bishops and archdeacons must judge him, so that he gives satisfaction to the lord the king.

14. The goods of those who are under forfeit of the king, no church or cemetery is to detain contrary to the king's justice, because they belong to the king himself, whether they be found inside churches or outside.

15. Pleas of debts due under pledge of faith or without pledge of faith are to be in the king's justice.

16. Sons of villeins ought not to be ordained without the assent of the lord on whose land they are known to have been born.[1]

Now the record of the aforesaid royal customs and dignities was made by the said archbishops and bishops, and earls and barons, and the nobles and elders of the realm, at Clarendon, on the fourth day before the Purification of the Blessed Mary, ever Virgin, the lord Henry the king's son, with his father the lord king being present there. There are moreover many other great customs and dignities of holy Mother Church and the lord the king and the barons of the realm, which are not contained in this writing. And let them be safe for holy Church and the lord the king and his heirs and the barons of the realm, and be inviolably observed.

VII. MONASTIC LIFE : EXTRACTS FROM THE *CHRONICLE* OF JOCELYN DE BRAKELONDE

[Jocelyn de Brakelonde, from whose *Chronicle* the following extracts are made, was born about the year 1155, and became a novice in the great Abbey of St. Edmundsbury in 1173. Very

---

[1] Cap 16. Filii rusticorum non debent ordinari absque assensu domini de cujus terra nati dignoscuntur.

DIAGRAM
to show the
CHIEF HOUSES OF THE
UNREFORMED BENEDICTINE
ORDER IN MEDIEVAL ENGLAND

little is known of him apart from a few surmises based on his *Chronicle*. He passed under the care of Samson of Tottington, who was the Master of the novices. On the death of Abbot Hugh, as the result of an accident, in 1180, Samson was elected Abbot by his brethren under circumstances which Jocelyn vividly describes. Jocelyn was soon afterwards appointed Chaplain to Sampson. The date of his death, like that of his birth, is uncertain. His *Chronicle* is of the greatest value as a picture of the life of a great medieval monastery as seen through the eyes of an ordinary man of no unusual gifts or ability. It tells of the difficulties, dissensions, and excitements that enlivened the everyday life of the medieval monk. It is also a picture of one great and strong man, Abbot Samson, drawn by one whose knowledge of him was intimate and whose admiration for him was unbounded ; so much so that Carlyle compared Jocelyn to Boswell, the biographer of the great Dr. Johnson. This *Chronicle* covers the period from 1173 to 1190, and, as Jocelyn says at the outset, " he took care to write only what he saw and heard."

The *Chronicle* was printed for the first time by the Camden Society in 1840 under the editorship of G. Rokewood. This was followed in 1843 by Carlyle's famous essay, *Past and Present*, which served to make Jocelyn's *Chronicle* one of the most widely known pieces of medieval literature. The *Chronicle* was translated into English in 1844 by T. E. Tomlins. A new translation was made by L. C. Jane and published together with a valuable introduction by Cardinal Gasquet in the Medieval Library (Chatto & Windus, 1922). The *Chronicle* was edited in the Rolls Series by Thomas Arnold in 1890. *Memorials of St. Edmund's Abbey*, vol. i. pp. 209 sqq.]

ABBOT HUGH was a good and kindly man, a god-fearing and devout monk, but in worldly matters he was inexperienced and improvident.[1] He placed too much confidence in those near him and believed in them too readily, rather trusting to a stranger's advice than using his own judgment. Certainly discipline and the service of God, and all that pertained to the rule, flourished greatly within the cloister, but outside all things were mismanaged. For every man, seeing that he served a simple and ageing lord, did not that which was right, but that which pleased him. The townships and all the hundreds of the abbot were given to farm ; the woods were wasted, and the houses on the manors were almost in ruins ; from day to day all things grew worse. The abbot's sole resource and means of relief was in borrowing money, that so

---

[1] homo pius et benignus, monarchus religiosus et bonus, sed nec bonus nec providus in saecularibus exercitiis : . . .

it might at least be possible to maintain the honour of his house. For eight years before his death, there was never an Easter or Michaelmas in which at least one or two hundred pounds were not added to the debt. The bonds were constantly renewed, and the growing interest was converted into principal.

This disease spread from the head to the members, from the ruler to his subjects. So it came to pass that if any official had a seal of his own, he also bound himself in debt as he listed, both to Jews [1] and Christians. Silken caps, and golden vessels, and the other ornaments of the church, were often placed in pawn without the consent of the monastery. I have seen a bond made to William FitzIsabel for £1040, but know not the why nor the wherefore. And I have seen another bond to Isaac, son of Rabbi Joce, for £400, but know not wherefore it was made. I have also seen a third bond to Benedict, the Jew of Norwich, for £880, and this was the origin and cause of that debt.

Our buttery was destroyed, and the sacristan William received it to restore whether he would or no. He secretly borrowed forty marks [2] at interest from Benedict the Jew, and made him a bond, sealed with a certain seal which usually hung at the shrine of St. Edmund, with which the gilds and brotherhoods used to be sealed ; afterwards, but in no great haste, it was destroyed by order of the monastery. Now when that debt increased to £100, the Jew came, bearing letters of the lord king concerning the sacristan's debt, and then at last that which had been concealed from the abbot and the monks appeared. So the abbot in anger would have deposed the sacristan, alleging a privilege of the lord pope that enabled him to remove William his sacristan when he would. But someone went to the abbot, and pleaded for the sacristan, and so won over the abbot that he suffered a bond to be made to Benedict the Jew for £400, payable at the end of four years, that is, a bond for the £100 to which the interest had increased, and for another £100 which the same Jew had lent to the sacristan for the use of the abbot. And in full chapter the sacristan obtained that all this debt should be paid, and a bond was made and sealed with the seal of the monastery. For the abbot pretended that the

[1] For debts to Jews, cf. Magna Carta, Cap. XI. p. 42.
[2] *i.e.* £26. 13s. 4d.

debt was no concern of his, and he did not affix his seal.
However, at the end of the four years there was nothing
wherewith the debt might be discharged, and a new bond
was made for £880, which was to be repaid at stated times—
£80 every year.

And the same Jew had many other bonds for smaller
debts, and one bond which was for fourteen years, so that
the sum of the debt owing to that Jew was £1200, over and
above the amount by which usury had increased it.

Then came R. the almoner of the lord king and told the
lord abbot that many rumours concerning these great debts
had come to the king. And when counsel had been taken
with the prior and a few others, the almoner was brought
into the chapter. Then, when we were seated and were silent,
the abbot said : " Behold the almoner of the king, our lord
and friend and yours, who, moved by love of God and Saint
Edmund, has shown to us that the lord king has heard some
evil report of us and you, and that the affairs of the church
are ill-managed within and without the walls. And therefore I will, and command you upon your vow of obedience,
that you say and make known openly how our affairs stand."
So the prior arose, and speaking as it were one for all, said
that the church was in good order, and that the rule was well
and strictly kept within, and matters outside the walls carefully and discreetly managed ; and that though we, like
others round us, were slightly involved in debt, there was no
debt which might give us cause for anxiety. When he heard
this, the almoner said that he rejoiced greatly to hear this
witness of the monastery, by which he meant these words
of the prior.

Now I was then a novice, and on a convenient occasion
talked of these things to my master, who was instructing
me in the Rule, and in whose care I was placed : he was
Master Samson, who was afterwards abbot. " What is this,"
I said, " that I hear ? And why do you keep silence when
you see and hear such things—you, who are a cloistered
monk, and desire not offices, and fear God rather than man ? "
But he answered and said, " My son, the newly burnt child
feareth the fire, and so it is with me and with many another.
Prior Hugh has been lately deposed and sent into exile ;
Denis, and Hugo, and Roger de Hingham have but lately

returned to the house from exile. I was in like manner imprisoned, and afterwards was sent to Acre,[1] for that we spoke to the common good of our church against the will of the abbot. This is the hour of darkness ; this is the hour in which flatterers triumph and are believed ; their might is increased, nor can we prevail against them. These things must be endured for a while ; the Lord see and judge ! "

Now in those days the cellarer, like the rest of the officers of the monastery, borrowed money from Jurnet the Jew, without the knowledge of the monastery, on a bond sealed with the seal mentioned above. But when the debt had grown to £60, the monastery was called upon to discharge the debt of the cellarer. He was deposed, though he defended himself by saying that for three years he, by command of the abbot, had received all guests in the guest-house, whether the abbot were at home or no, whom the abbot ought to have received according to the constitution of the abbey.

In his stead Master Denis was appointed, and by his economy and care reduced that debt of £60 to £30. Towards the extinction of that debt we paid the thirty marks [2] which Benedict de Blakeham gave to the monastery for the manors of Newton and Whepstead. But the Jew's bond remains with the Jew to this day, and in it twenty-six pounds are written down as principal and for the debt of the cellarer.

On the third day after Master Dennis was made cellarer, three knights with their squires were brought into the guest-house to be entertained there, the abbot being at home and sitting in his chamber. Now when that great-hearted Achilles heard this, not wishing to fail in his office as did the others, he arose and took the keys of the cellar, and bearing the knights with him to the hall of the abbot, came himself into the abbot's presence. And he said to him, " Lord, you know well that the custom of the abbey is that knights and laymen be received in your hall, if the abbot be at home. I neither wish, nor am I able, to receive guests whose entertainment is your care. But if it be otherwise, take the keys of your cellar, and appoint another cellarer at your pleasure." When the abbot heard this, he received those knights, and ever after-

[1] Castle Acre in Norfolk. [2] *i.e.* £20.

wards knights and laymen in accordance with ancient custom. And they are still so received when the abbot is at home.

.   .   .   .

The abbacy being vacant, we often, as was right, made supplications unto the Lord and to the holy martyr Edmund that they would give us and our church a fit pastor. Three times in each week, after leaving the chapter, did we prostrate ourselves in the choir and sing the seven penitential psalms. And there were some who would not have been so devout in their prayers if they had known who was to become abbot. As to the choice of an abbot, if the king should grant us free election, there was much difference of opinion, some of it openly expressed, some of it privately ; and every man had his own idea.

One said of a certain brother, " He, that brother, is a good monk, a likely person. He knows much of the rule and of the customs of the church. It is true that he is not so perfect a philosopher as are some others, but he is quite capable of being abbot. Abbot Ording was unlettered, and yet he was a good abbot and ruled this house wisely ; and one reads in the fable that the frogs did better to elect a log in which they had confidence to be their king than a serpent, who hissed venomously, and when he had hissed, devoured his subjects." Another answered, " How could this thing be ? How could one who does not know letters preach in the chapter, or to the people on feast days ? How could one without knowledge of the Scriptures have the knowledge of binding and loosing ? For the rule of souls is the art of arts, the highest form of knowledge. God forbid that a dumb idol be set up in the church of Saint Edmund, where many men are to be found who are learned and industrious."

Again, one said of another, " That brother is a literate man, eloquent and prudent, and strict in his observance of the rule. He loves the monastery greatly, and has suffered many ills for the good of the church. He is worthy to be made abbot." Another answered, " From good clerks deliver us, O Lord ! That it may please Thee to preserve us from the rogues of Norfolk ; we beseech Thee to hear us ! "

And again, one said of one, " That brother is a good manager ; this is proved by the state of his office, and from the posts in which he has served well, and from the buildings and improvements which he has brought about. He is well able to work and to defend the house, and he is something of a scholar, though too much learning has not made him mad. He is worthy of the abbacy." Another answered, " God forbid that a man who can neither read nor sing, nor celebrate the holy office, a man who is dishonest and unjust, and a grinder of the poor, should be made abbot."

Again, one said of another, " That brother is a kindly man, friendly and amiable, peaceful and calm, generous and liberal, a learned and eloquent man, and proper enough in presence and deportment. He is beloved of many within and without the walls, and such an one might become abbot to the great honour of the church, if God wills." Another answered, " It is no credit, but rather a disgrace, in a man to be too particular as to what he eats and drinks, to think it a virtue to sleep much, to know well how to spend and to know little how to gain, to snore while others keep vigil, to wish ever to have abundance, and not to trouble when debts daily increase, or whence money spent may bring return ; to be one who hates anxiety and toil, caring nothing while one day passes and another dawns ; to be one who loves and cherishes flatterers and liars ; to be one man in word and another in deed. From such a prelate the Lord defend us ! "

And again, one said of his friend, " That man is almost wiser than all of us, and that both in affairs secular and ecclesiastical. He is a man skilled in counsel, strict in the rule, learned and eloquent, and of noble stature ; such a prelate would become our church well." Another answered, " That would be true, if he were a man of reputation good and approved. But his reputation has been brought in question, whether falsely or truly. And though the man is wise, humble in the chapter, devoted to the singing of psalms, strict in his conduct in the cloister while he is a cloistered monk, this is only from force of habit. For if he have authority in any office, he is too proud, holding monks of no account, and being on familiar terms with secular men, and if he be angry, he will scarce say a word willingly to any brother, even in answer to a question."

I heard in truth another brother abused by some because he had an impediment in his speech, and it was said of him that he had pastry or dregs of malt in his mouth when he should have spoken. And I myself, as I was then young, understood as a child, spake as a child ; and I said that I would not consent that any one should be made abbot unless he knew something of dialectic, and knew how to distinguish the true from the false. One, moreover, who was wise in his own eyes, said, " May Almighty God give us a foolish and stupid pastor, that he may be driven to use our help." And I heard, forsooth, that one man who was industrious, learned, and pre-eminent for his high birth, was abused by some of the older men because he was a novice. The novices said of their elders that they were sickly old men, and little capable of ruling an abbey. And so many men said many things, and every man was fully persuaded in his own mind.

So the prior and the twelve with him, after many labours stood at last in the presence of the king [1] at Waltham, a manor of the bishop of Winchester, on the second Sunday in Lent. And the lord king received them graciously, and declared that he wished to act according to the Will of God and the honour of our church. Then he gave command to the brothers through his proctors, Richard bishop of Winchester and Geoffrey, the chancellor, who was afterwards archbishop of York, that they should nominate three members of our monastery.

Then the prior and the brothers withdrew themselves, as if to discuss this matter, and drew forth the seal and broke it, and found these names written down in this order— Samson, the sub-sacristan, Roger the cellarer, and Hugh the third prior. And at this the brothers who were of greater dignity blushed. Moreover all marvelled that the same Hugh should be both an elector and one of the elected. But because they could not alter the thing they unanimously changed the order of the names, naming Hugh, because he was third prior, first, and Roger the cellarer next, and Samson third. Thus, as far as words went, they made the last first, and the first last.

But the king, having first asked whether they were born in his land, and in whose lordship, said that he did not know them, and commanded that they should name three other members of the monastery with them.

And when this had been granted, William the sacristan said, " Our prior ought to be nominated, for he is our head," and this was readily agreed. Then the prior said, " William

[1] 21st February 1182.

the sacristan is a good man." The same was said of Denis, and was agreed. And when these were named in the presence of the king without any delay, the king marvelled, saying, " These men act quickly. God is with them."

And then the king commanded that for the honour of the kingdom, they should nominate three persons from other houses. When they heard this the brothers were afraid, for they suspected fraud. Yet they agreed to nominate three, but under conditions, viz., that they would receive no one save with the assent of the members of the monastery who were at home. And they named three, master Nicholas de Waringford, who was afterwards sometime abbot of Malmesbury, and Bertrand, prior of St. Faith's, who was afterwards Abbot of Chertsey, and lord H. de St. Neots, a Monk of Bec, a most pious man, and in both secular and spiritual matters very prudent.

When this had been done, the king sent them thanks and commanded that three of the nine should be removed, that is, the prior of St. Faith's, who was afterwards abbot of Chertsey, and Nicholas, the monk of St. Alban's, who was afterwards abbot of Malmesbury, and the prior of St. Neot's.

William the sacristan of his accord withdrew, two of the five were removed by the order of the king, and finally one of the last three, so that there remained then two, namely, the prior and Samson.

Then at last the afore-mentioned proctors of the lord king were summoned to the council of the brothers. And Denis, speaking as one for all, began to commend the persons of the prior and Samson. He said that they were both learned men, both good, both praiseworthy in their lives and of unblemished reputation. But even at the climax of his speech he put forward Samson, multiplying words in his praise, saying that he was a man strict in his conduct, severe in correcting faults, apt for labour, prudent in temporal matters, and proved in divers offices.

Then the bishop of Winchester answered, " We know well what you would say, from your words we gather that your prior has appeared to you to be somewhat remiss, and that you wish to have him who is called Samson." Dennis answered, " Both of them are good men, but we desire to have the better, if God wills." Thereupon the bishop said, " Of two good things, the greater good should be selected.

6

Say openly, do you desire to have Samson ? " And many, and they a majority, answered plainly, " We wish to have Samson," and none spoke against him. Some, however, were silent from caution, wishing to offend neither candidate.

Then Samson was nominated in the presence of the lord king, and when the king had consulted with his men for a while, all were summoned. And the king said, " You have presented to me Samson. I know him not. If you had presented your prior to me, I would have accepted him, for I have seen and known him. Yet I will do only what you will. Beware, by the true eyes of God, if you do ill, I will be avenged upon you."

Then he asked the prior if he assented to the choice and wished it, and the prior answered that he did will it, and that Samson was worthy of much greater honour. He was therefore elected, and fell at the king's feet and embraced them. Then he arose quickly and hastened to the altar, with his head erect and without changing his expression, chanting the " Miserere mei, Deus " with the brothers.

And when the king saw this, he said to those that stood by, " By the eyes of God, this elect thinks himself worthy to rule the abbey."

When king Henry had taken the cross and was come less than a month later [1] that he might pray among us, the abbot secretly made for himself a cross of linen cloth. Then, holding in one hand the cross and a needle and thread, he sought leave from the king that he might take the cross. But leave was refused him, for John, bishop of Norwich, opposed it, and said that it was not well for the land, nor safe for the counties of Norfolk and Suffolk, that the bishop of Norwich and the abbot of St. Edmund's should go away at the same time.

When news had reached London of the capture of king Richard, and of his imprisonment in Germany,[2] and the barons had met to take counsel on the matter, the abbot stood forth in their presence, and said that he was ready to seek his lord the king. He said that he would search for him in disguise or in any other way, until he found him and had certain knowledge of him. And from this speech he gained great praise for himself.

[1] 21st January 1188.   [2] 1193.

The abbot sent many messengers to Rome, and not in vain. The first whom he sent, immediately after his benediction,[1] obtained in detail all the liberties and rights which had been granted to his predecessors, even in the days of schism. Afterwards he, first of the abbots of England, obtained [2] that he might give episcopal benediction wherever he might be. This privilege he gained for himself and for his successors. At a later date [3] he acquired complete exemption for himself and for his successors from all the archbishops of Canterbury, a privilege which abbot Hugh had secured for himself alone. In these confirmations of privileges abbot Samson caused the inclusion of many new liberties, to the great freedom and safety of our church.

Then a certain clerk came to the abbot, bearing letters asking for the grant of some ecclesiastical benefice. And the abbot drew from his desk seven apostolic letters, with leaden seals hanging to them, and answered as follows : " See the apostolic letters, whereby different popes seek that ecclesiastical benefices may be given to this or that clerk. When then I have satisfied those who come first I will give you a benefice, since he who first comes to the mill ought to grind first."

. . . .

On the death of abbot Hugh,[4] the wardens of the abbacy desired to depose the bailiffs of the town of St. Edmund's, and to appoint new bailiffs by their authority, alleging that this right belonged to the king, in whose hand the abbey was. But when we made complaint on this matter and sent our messengers to the lord Ranulf Glanvill,[5] who was then justiciar, he answered that he knew well that forty pounds ought to be rendered from the town to our sacristan annually, and especially for the lights of the church. And he added that abbot Hugh, according to his pleasure and in his chamber, without the assent of the monastery, had given the office of bailiff as often as, and to whomsoever, he would, saving the forty pounds of revenue for the altar. It was, therefore, not out of order for the officials of the king to exact this right on the king's behalf. Then in rough tones, he called all us monks fools in that we had allowed our abbot to do such things, not thinking that the chief duty of monks

[1] 31st March 1182.   [2] 21st January 1187.   [3] 1188.
[4] 1182.   [5] Cf. Giraldus Cambrensis, p. 153.

is to keep silence, and to shut their eyes to all the faults of their prelates, nor thinking of the fact that we are called rogues if, whether rightly or wrongly, we raise opposition in any matter ; and that sometimes we are accused of treason, and sometimes condemned to imprisonment and exile. For these reasons, it seems the wiser to me and those in my position, to die rather as confessors than as martyrs.

When our messenger returned to us and told what he had heard and seen, we took counsel, unwillingly as it seemed and under compulsion, to the effect that, by the common action of the monastery and of the wardens of the abbey, the old bailiffs of the town should be deposed. This was as far as possible to be a joint act, though Samson, who was our subsacristan, was opposed to the proposal.

At a later date, when he had been made abbot, Samson was not unmindful of the injury which had been done to the abbey, and on the morrow of the Easter next after his election, he caused the knights and clerks and many burgesses to be gathered together in our chapter, and in the presence of them all said that this town belonged to the monastery and to the altar, particularly in the matter of finding lights for the church. And he said that he wished to renew the old custom, that all that had to do with the bailiwick of the town and such like matters pertaining to the monastery, should be decided in the presence of the monastery and by common assent.

And at the same time two burghers, Godfrey and Nicholas, were named bailiffs, and there was a dispute as to the question from whose hand they should receive the horn, which is called moot-horn. At last they received it from the hand of the prior, who after the abbot is the chief man in the affairs of the monastery. Then those two bailiffs peacefully exercised their jurisdiction for many years, until they were said to be slack in the administration of the king's justice. Then at the suggestion of the abbot himself, that greater security might be given to the monastery in this matter, they were removed, and the sacristan Hugh received it into his hand. He appointed new officials, who were responsible to him for the bailiwick. In course of time, however—for what reason I know not—new bailiffs were again appointed elsewhere than in our chapter, and without the assent of the monastery, on which account there was apprehension of as much or more danger after the death of abbot Samson than there had been after the death of abbot Hugh.

And one of our brothers, who was fully confident of the love and friendship of the abbot, took an opportunity to address the abbot, with due modesty, on this subject ; and he declared that because of this the monastery murmured. When the abbot heard this he was long silent, as if he were somewhat troubled about it, and at last, so it is said, answered as follows : " Am not I, even I, the abbot ? Is it not my affair to dispose of the goods of the church committed to my care, provided that I act wisely and according to God ? If there be a default in the administration of the king's justice in this town, I shall be called in question about it, I shall be summoned to the court, on me will fall the labour of the journey and the expense, and the defence of the town and of that which pertains thereto. It will be I who am regarded as a fool and not the prior or the sacristan or the monastery. No, it will be I, who am and ought to be their head. By my means and by my counsel, with God's help, the town shall be kept unharmed as far as in me lies, and the £40 of annual rent to the altar shall be preserved. Let the brethren murmur ; let them blame me ; let them say what they will among themselves. I am their father and abbot, and while I live, I will not give mine honour to another."

When he had so spoken the monk left him and told his answers. But I marvelled at such words, and thought the thing over in secret and with care. At last I was forced to doubt still, since the rule of law says and teaches us that all things are in the disposition of the abbot.

The merchants of London wished to be quit from toll [1] at the fair of St. Edmund's. Many, however, though unwillingly and under compulsion, paid it, and on this account, many tumults and a great disturbance occurred between the citizens of London in their hustings. Wherefore, having held a meeting about the matter, they sent word to abbot Samson that they ought to be quit of toll throughout all England, under the authority of the charter which they held from king Henry the Second.

To this the abbot answered that, were it needful, he could easily bring the king to guarantee him that he had never made them a charter in prejudice of our church, or to the

[1] Cf. Henry I.'s Charter to London, p. 108.

injury of the liberties of St. Edmund, to whom the holy
Edward had granted and confirmed toll and theam and all
regalian rights before the conquest of England.   And he
added that King Henry had given to the Londoners quittance
from toll throughout his own demesnes, where he had the
right to give it ; for in the city of St. Edmunds he could not
give it, for it was not his to give.

When the Londoners heard this, they decreed with
common assent that none of them should come to the fair
of St. Edmund's, and for two years they did absent themselves, whence our fair suffered great loss, and the offerings of
our sacristry were greatly diminished.   Eventually, when
the bishop of London and many others had mediated, an
agreement was reached between them and us whereby they
should come to the fair, and some of them should pay
toll, but this should be at once returned to them, that
by such a device the privilege of both parties might be
maintained.

But in the course of time, when the abbot had come to an
agreement with his knights, and as it were rested in peace,
lo ! again " The Philistines be upon thee, Samson ! "   For
the Londoners, with one voice, threatened to level with the
earth the stone houses, which the abbot had built in the
same year, or to take distress an hundredfold from the men
of St. Edmund, if the abbot did not at once make reparation
to them for the wrong which they had suffered from the
bailiffs of the town of St. Edmunds.   For they had taken
fifteen pence from the carts of the citizens of London, which
were coming from Yarmouth and carrying herrings, and
which passed through our town.   And the citizens of London
said that they had been quit of toll of every market, and
always and everywhere, throughout all England, from the
time of the first foundation of the city of Rome, at which
time also the city of London was founded.   They said that
they ought to have this privilege throughout all England,
both because their city was a privileged city, which had been
the metropolis and capital of the kingdom, and because of
the antiquity of the city.

The abbot, however, asked for a truce on this dispute for
a reasonable time, until the return of the king to England,
that he might consult with him on this matter ; and taking
the advice of men skilled in the law, he handed back to the

complainants those fifteen pence as a pledge, without pre-judice to the question of the right of either party.

In the tenth year of the abbacy of abbot Samson,[1] by common council of our charter we made complaint to the abbot in his court and said that the, receipts from all the goods of the towns and boroughs of England were increased, and had grown to the advantage of the possessors and the greater profits of their lords, save in the case of this town, which had been accustomed to pay £40 and had never had its dues increased. And we said that the burghers of the city were responsible for it, since they held so many and such large stands in the market-place, shops and sheds and stalls without the assent of the monastery, and at the gift merely of the bailiffs of the town, who were annual holders of their offices, and servants, as it were, of the sacristan, being removable at his good pleasure.

But when the burghers were summoned, they answered that they were subject to the jurisdiction of the king, and that they were under no obligation to make reply, contrary to the liberty of the town and of their charters, concerning that which they and their fathers had held well and in peace for one year and a day without dispute. And they said that it was the old custom that the bailiffs should, without con-sulting the monastery, give to them places for shops and sheds in the market-place, in return for some annual payment to the bailiwick. But we disputed this, and wished the abbot to dispossess them of such things as they held without having any warrant for them.

Then the abbot came to our council, as if he had been one of ourselves, and informed us privately that he wished, so far as he could, to act rightly by us ; but that he had to proceed in a judicial manner, and that he could not, without the judgment of the court, dispossess his free men of their lands and revenues, which they had held, whether rightly or wrongly, for many years. He added that if he were to do this, he would be liable to punishment at the discretion of the king through the assize of the kingdom.

The burghers, therefore, took council and offered the monastery a revenue of a hundred shillings for the sake of peace, and that they might hold that which they held as they had been accustomed. But we would not grant this,

[1] 1192.

preferring to postpone the matter, and perchance hoping that in the time of another abbot, either we might recover all, or change the place of the fair; and so the matter rested for many years.

But when the abbot had returned from Germany,[1] the burghers offered him sixty marks,[2] and sought his confirmation of the liberties of the town, under the same form of words as that in which his predecessors Anselm and Ording and Hugh had confirmed them to them. And this also the abbot graciously conceded. But while we murmured and grumbled, a charter was made for them, as he had promised to them; and as it would have been a source of shame and confusion to him if he had been unable to do that which he had promised, we would not oppose him, or provoke him to anger. But the burghers, from the time when they had the charter of Abbot Samson and the monastery, were full of confidence that they would never lose their holdings and liberties in the time of abbot Samson; and therefore, never afterwards would they give or offer, as previously, the said revenue of a hundred shillings.

The abbot, however, at length turned his attention to this, and gathering the burghers together about the matter, said that if they would not make their peace with the monastery, he would forbid their sheds to be put up at the fair of St. Edmund's. Then they answered that they would give every year a silken cope, or some other ornament to the value of a hundred shillings, as they had before promised. But they offered this on condition that they should be quit for ever from the tenths of their money which the sacristan sternly exacted from them.

The abbot and the sacristan opposed this offer, and so the dispute was again left unsettled. But we have lost those hundred shillings from that day to this, according as is said in the proverb, " He that will not when he may, shall have nay when he will."

King Richard sent orders [3] to all the bishops and abbots of England that every nine knights should furnish a tenth, and that these should come to him in Normandy without delay, with horses and arms, to help him against the king of France. It was necessary, therefore, for the abbot to be

[1] 1194.   [2] i.e. £40.   [3] 1198.

responsible for the sending of four knights. And when he had caused all his knights to be summoned, and had gathered them together on this matter, they answered that their fiefs, which they held of St. Edmund, were not liable to this, and that neither they, nor their fathers, had ever gone out of England, though they had sometimes paid scutage by command of the king.

Then the abbot was in a difficult position, as on the one hand he saw that the liberty of his knights was endangered, and on the other feared lest he might lose seisin of his barony for default of service to the king, as had happened to the bishop of London and many barons of England. And he at once crossed the sea, and having wearied himself with many labours and expenses and with the many presents which he gave to the king, he was unable at first to come to terms with the king by means of a money payment. And so, when the king said that he needed neither gold nor silver, but instantly demanded the four knights, the abbot offered him four mercenary knights. And the king received these and sent them to the castle of Eu. And the abbot gave them thirty-six marks [1] at once for their expenses for forty days.

But next day there came certain friends of the king, and counselled the abbot that he should act circumspectly, saying that the war might last for a full year or more, and the cost of the knights increase and multiply to the continual loss of him and of his church. They therefore advised that before he left the court, he should come to terms with the king, so that he might be quit of the said knights after forty days. Then the abbot, taking sound advice, gave £100 to the king for this quittance, and so returned to England in high favour with his lord. And he bore with him the king's writ that distraint should be levied on the fees of his knights to repay him for the service which he had made to the king on their behalf.

.   .   .   .

At that time, though the abbot incurred great expenses over sea, he did not return empty-handed to his church, but brought with him a golden cross and a precious copy of the Scriptures, which was worth twenty-four marks.[2] And on another occasion, when he had returned from across the sea, sitting in his chapter he said that had he been cellarer

[1] *i.e.* £24.   [2] *i.e.* £16.

or chamberlain he would have sought for something which would be helpful in the administration of his office. And he added that as he was abbot he ought to acquire something which was fitting for an abbot, and saying this he offered the monastery a costly chasuble and a mitre inlaid with gold, and sandals with silken buskins, and the head of a pastoral staff, made of silver and well worked. In the same way, as often as he returned from beyond the sea, he brought some ornament with him.

. . . . . .

After these things an agreement was made between abbot Samson and Robert de Scales as to the half of the advowson of a church of Wetherden,[1] and the same Robert acknowledged the right of St. Edmund and of the abbot. The abbot, when no agreement had yet been made, and no promise given, gave the half of that church which belonged to him to master Roger de Scales, brother of the same knight, on condition that he would render an annual pension of three marks[2] by the hand of our sacristan to the master of the schools, who should read in the town of St. Edmunds.

The abbot was led to do this by motives of memorable generosity, and since he had already bought stone houses for the purposes of the school that the poor clerks might be quit from house rent, so henceforth they were free from all exaction of money, which the master of the schools had, according to custom, gathered for their education. Then by the will of God and in the lifetime of the abbot, the whole half of that church, which was worth, so it is said, a hundred shillings, was turned to such uses.

. . . .

Many marvelled at the changes in the customary dues which took place with the orders or consent of the lord abbot Samson. From the time when the town of St. Edmunds received the name and liberty of a borough, the men of every house had been accustomed to give to the cellarer one penny at the beginning of August for the reaping of our corn, which tax was called "rep-selver." And before the town was free all were accustomed to reap as serfs, and only the houses of the knights and the chaplains and servants of the court were free from this tax. But as time passed, the

[1] 1198.   [2] *i.e. £2.*

cellarer spared some of the richer men of the town and gathered nothing from them.

When the other burghers saw this, they said publicly that no one who had a messuage of his own ought to pay that penny, but only those who rented the houses of others. Afterwards, all in common sought this freedom, coming to the lord abbot about it, and offering an annual payment in place of this exaction. Then the abbot learnt that the cellarer had gone through the town to collect " rep-selver " in a wrongful manner, and that he had caused sureties to be taken from the houses of the poor men, taking sometimes tripods, and at others doors, and other goods, and how the old women appeared with their distaffs, threatening and cursing the cellarer and his men. And he decreed that twenty shillings should be given to the cellarer every year at the next portman-moot, by the hand of the bailiff, before August, by the burghers liable to pay this money.

And this was done, and confirmed by our charter. And they were given quittance from a certain customary due which is called " sorpenny," in return for four shillings to be paid at the same time. For the cellarer had been wont to receive one penny a year for each cow, belonging to the men of the city, which went out to pasture, unless the cows were those of the chaplains or servants of the court, and these cows he used to impound, and about this he used to have much trouble.

But later on, when the abbot spoke of this in the chapter, the monastery was indignant and angry, and so Benedict, the sub-prior, made answer for all in the chapter, and said, " He, abbot Ording, who lies there, would not have done such a thing for five hundred marks of silver." But the abbot was angry at this, and postponed the matter for a time.

Also a dispute arose between Roger the cellarer and Hugh the sacristan concerning the profits of their offices, so that the sacristan would not lend to the cellarer the prison in the town for the imprisonment of robbers, who were taken in the fee of the cellarer. Wherefore the cellarer was often vexed, and when the robbers escaped, was blamed for the default of justice.

But it happened that a certain free tenant of the cellarer who remained without the gate, a man called Ketel, being accused of robbery and defeated in a trial by battle,[1] was hanged. And the monastery was grieved at the abusive words of the burghers, who said that if the man had lived within the gate, the matter would not have come to trial by battle, but that he would have been acquitted by the oaths of his neighbours, as was the privilege of those who dwelt within the borough.

And when the abbot and the more reasonable section of the monastery saw this, and observed that the men, both without and within the borough are our men, and that all should enjoy the same liberty within the jurisdiction of the abbey, except the land-sets at Hardwick and their like, provided with care that this should be so.

Then the abbot in his anxiety clearly to define the offices of the cellarer and of the sacristan, and to calm disputes as though he favoured the side of the sacristan, gave orders that the servants of the bailiff of the town and the servants of the cellarer should enter together the fee of the cellarer to take robbers and malefactors. And he ordered that the bailiff should have half the pay due for the imprisonment and guarding of the men and for the labour required, and that the court of the cellarer should go to the portman-moot, and that there cases which had to be adjudged should be adjudged by common assent. And it was also resolved that the men of the cellarer should go to the roll-house with the rest, and there renew their sureties, and that they should be inscribed in the roll of the bailiffs, and pay a penny to the bailiff there, which payment is called " borth-selver," and that the cellarer should have half of it. Now, however, the cellarer receives nothing on this account.

All this was done that all might enjoy equal liberty. But the burghers still say that those who dwell without the town ought not to be free from market toll, unless they are members of the guild merchant.[2] And the bailiff, with the assent of the abbot, claims the pleas and forfeitures of the fee of the cellarer to this day.

---

[1] For trial by battle, cf. Magna Carta, Cap. LV., p. 49, and extracts from Charters of Bristol and Dunwich, p. 112.

[2] For merchant guilds, cf. Chapter IV. *passim*, particularly pp. 109 and 123.

VIII. ANSWER OF INNOCENT III. CONCERNING THE INTERDICT, 1208

[Wilkins, *Consilia*, vol. i. p. 526.]

INNOCENT the bishop, etc., to the Bishops of London, Ely, and Worcester, greeting and apostolic blessing. We reply to your inquiries, that whereas by reason of the interdict new chrism cannot be consecrated on Maundy Thursday, old must be used in the baptism of infants, and, if necessity demand, oil must be mixed by hand of the bishop or else priest, with the chrism, that it fail not. And although the viaticum seem to be meet on the repentance of the dying, yet, if it cannot be had, we who read it believe that the principle holds good in this case, " believe and thou hast eaten," when actual need, and not contempt of religion, excludes sacrament, and the actual need is expected soon to cease. Let neither gospel nor church hours be observed in the accustomed place, nor any other, though the people assemble in the same. Let religious men, whose monasteries people have been wont to visit for the sake of prayer, admit pilgrims inside the church for prayer, not by the greater door, but by a more private place. Let church doors remain shut save at the chief festival of the church, when the parishioners and others may be admitted for prayer into the church with open doors. Let baptism be celebrated in the usual manner with old chrism and oil inside the church with shut doors, no lay person being admitted save the god-parents, and if need demand, new oil must be mixed. Penance is to be inflicted as well on the whole as the sick ; for in the midst of life we are in death. Those who have confessed in a suit, or have been convicted of some crime, are to be sent to the bishop or his penitentiary, and, if need be, are to be forced to this by church censure. Priests may say their own prayers in private. Priests may on Sunday bless water in the churchyard and sprinkle it ; and can make and distribute bread when blessed, and announce feasts and fasts and preach a sermon to the people. A woman after childbirth may come to church, and perform her purification outside the church walls. Priests shall visit the sick, and hear confessions, and let them perform the commendation of souls in the accustomed manner, but they shall not follow the corpses of the dead, because they will not have church burial. Priests shall, on the day of the Passion, place the cross outside the church, without ceremony, so that the parishioners may adore it with the customary devotion.

IX. JOHN'S SURRENDER OF THE KINGDOM TO THE POPE, 1213

[Stubbs, *Select Charters*, pp. 284 sqq.]

JOHN, by the grace of God king of England, lord of Ireland, duke of Normandy and Aquitaine, count of Anjou, to all the faithful in Christ who shall inspect this present charter, greeting. We will it to be known by all of you by this our charter, confirmed by our seal, that we, having offended God and our mother the holy Church in many things, and being on that account known to need the Divine mercy, and unable to make any worthy offering for the performance of due satisfaction to God and the Church, unless we humble ourselves and our realms—we, willing to humble ourselves for Him who humbled Himself for us even to death, by the inspiration of the Holy Spirit's grace, under no compulsion of force or of fear, but of our good and free will, and by the common consent of our barons, offer and freely grant to God and His holy apostles Peter and Paul, and the holy Roman Church, our mother, and to our lord the Pope Innocent and his catholic successors, the whole realm of England and the whole realm of Ireland with all their rights and appurtenances, for the remission of our sins and those of all our race, as well quick as dead ; and from now receiving back and holding these, as a feudal dependant, from God and the Roman Church, in the presence of the prudent man Pandulf, subdeacon and familiar of the lord the pope, do and swear fealty for them to the aforesaid our lord the Pope Innocent and his catholic successors and the Roman Church, according to the form written below, and will do liege homage to the same lord the Pope in his presence if we shall be able to be present before him ; binding our successors and heirs by our wife, for ever, that in like manner to the supreme pontiff for the time being, and to the Roman Church, they should pay fealty and acknowledge homage without contradiction. Moreover, in proof of this our perpetual obligation and grant, we will and establish that from the proper and special revenues of our realms aforesaid, for all service and custom that we should render for ourselves, saving in all respects the penny of blessing Peter, the Roman Church receive 1000 marks sterling each year, to wit at the feast of St. Michael, 500 marks, and at Easter 500 marks ; 700 to wit for the realm of England, and 300 for the realm of Ireland ; saving to us and our heirs our rights, liberties and royalties. All which, as aforesaid, we willing them to be perpetually ratified and confirmed, bind ourselves and our successors not to contravene. And if we or any of our successors shall presume to attempt this, whoever he be, unless he come to amendment after due admonition, let him forfeit right to the kingdom, and let this charter of obligation and grant on our part remain in force for ever.

The Oath of Fealty

I, John, by the grace of God king of England and lord of Ireland, from this hour forward will be faithful to God and the blessed Peter and the Roman Church, and my lord the Pope Innocent and his successors following in catholic manner : I will not be party in deed, word, consent, or counsel, to their losing life or limb or being unjustly imprisoned. Their damage, if I am aware of it, I will prevent, and will have removed if I can ; or else, as soon as I can, I will signify it, or will tell such persons as I shall believe will tell them certainly. Any counsel they entrust to me, immediately or by their messengers or their letter, I will keep secret, and will consciously disclose to no one to their damage. The patrimony of blessed Peter, and specially the realm of England and the realm of Ireland, I will aid to hold and defend against all men to my ability. So help me God and these holy gospels. Witness myself at the house of the Knights of the Temple near Dover, in the presence of the lord H. Archbishop of Dublin ; the lord J. Bishop of Norwich ; G. Fitz-Peter, Earl of Essex, our justiciar ; W. Earl of Salisbury, our brother ; W. Marshall, Earl of Pembroke ; R. Count of Boulogne ; E. Earl of Warenne ; S. Earl of Winchester ; W. Earl of Arundel ; W. Earl of Ferrers ; W. Brewer ; Peter, son of Herbert ; Warren, son of Gerald. The 15th day of May in the 14th year of our reign.

X. THE FRIARS

(a) Extract from " The Rule of St. Francis "

[Vide Henderson, *Historical Documents of the Middle Ages*, pp. 344
   sqq.   The rule was confirmed by Pope Honorius in 1223.]

THOSE brothers to whom God has given the ability to labour,
shall labour faithfully and devoutly ; in such way that idleness, the enemy of the soul, being excluded, they may not
extinguish the spirit of holy prayer and devotion ; to which
other temporal things should be subservient.   As a reward,
moreover, for their labour, they may receive for themselves
and their brothers the necessaries of life, but not coin or
money ; and this humbly as becomes servants of God and
the followers of most holy poverty.   The brothers shall
appropriate nothing to themselves, neither a house nor a
place nor anything ; but as pilgrims and strangers in this
world, in poverty and humility serving God, they shall go
confidently seeking for alms.   Nor need they be ashamed,
for the Lord made Himself poor for us in this world.

(b) Extract from Thomas of Eccleston's " Chronicle." The Coming of the Franciscan Friars to England, 1224

[Thomas of Eccleston was an English friar of the Order of
St. Francis.   He wrote his *De Adventu Minorum* about 1258.   It
is edited in the Rolls Series by J. S. Brewer, *Monumenta Fran-
ciscana*, pt. i. 1858.]

THESE nine [1] having then been charitably conveyed across
to England, and cordially provided for in their necessities
by the nuns of Fécamp, on arriving at Canterbury sojourned
for two days at the priory of the Holy Trinity.   Then four
of them at once set off for London. . . .   The other five went
to the Priest's Hospice, where they remained until they found
for themselves a dwelling.   But very shortly after their
arrival they were given a small chamber at the back of a
schoolhouse, where from day to day they remained almost
continuously shut up.   But when the schoolboys had gone
home in the evening, the brethren went into the schoolhouse,

[1] *i.e.* Agnellus of Pisa and his eight brethren.

and there made a fire and sat by it. And sometimes at the
evening conference they would put on the fire a small pot in
which were the dregs of beer, and they would dip a cup into
the pot and drink in turn. . . . One who merited to be a
companion and participator in this unblemished simplicity
and holy poverty has testified that at times the beer was so
thick that when the pot was to be put on the fire they had
to put in it water, and so they drank rejoicing.[1]

XI. THE MORTMAIN ACT OF 1279

[Translated in *Statutes of the Realm*, vol. i. p. 51.]

WHEREOF late it was provided, that religious men should not
enter into the fees of any without the licence and will of the
chief lords, of whom those fees be holden immediately ; and
notwithstanding, religious men have entered as well into their
own fees, as into the fees of other men, appropriating and
buying them, and sometimes receiving them of the gift of
others, whereby the services that are due from such fees,
and which at the beginning were provided for defence of the
realm, are wrongfully withdrawn, and the chief lords lose
their escheats of the same :

We therefore, to the profit of our realm, intending to
provide convenient remedy by the advice of our prelates,
earls, barons, and other our subjects, being of our council,
have provided, established, and ordained, that no person,
religious or other, whatsoever he be, presume to buy or sell
any lands or tenements, or to receive them under the colour
of gift or lease, or any other title, whatsoever it be, or by any
other craft or device appropriate them to himself, under
pain of forfeiture of the same, whereby such lands or tenements may in any wise come into mortmain.

We have provided also, that if any person, religious or
other, do presume either by craft or trickery to offend against
this statute, it shall be lawful to us and other chief lords of
the fee immediate, to enter into the land so alienated, within
a year from the time of the alienation, and to hold it in fee
and inheritance.

And if the chief lord immediate be negligent, and will
not enter into such fee within the year, then it shall be lawful

---

[1] For Friars, cf. Chaucer's " Prologue," pp. 283 sqq., and the
Vision of Piers Plowman, p. 301 ; also the *Paston Letters*, p. 334.

7

to the next chief lord immediate of the same fee to enter into the same land within half a year next following, and to hold it as is aforesaid ; so every lord immediate may enter into such land, if the next lord be negligent in entering into the same fee, as is aforesaid.

Witness myself at Westminster the Fifteenth day of November, the seventh year of our reign.

XII. THE " CLERICIS LAICOS " BULL OF 1296

[Vide Rymer's *Foedera*, vol. ii. p. 706.]

BONIFACE BISHOP, servant of the servants of God, for the perpetual memory of the matter. That laymen have been very hostile to clerks antiquity relates, which too the experiences of the present times manifestly declare, whilst not content with their own bounds they strive for those forbidden and loose the reins for things unlawful. Nor do they prudently consider how power over clerks or ecclesiastical persons or goods is forbidden them : they impose heavy burdens on the prelates of the churches and ecclesiastical persons regular and secular, and tax them, and impose collections : they exact and demand from the same the half-tithe, or twentieth, or any other portion or proportion of their revenues or goods ; and in many ways they essay to bring them under slavery, and subject them to their authority. And (as we sadly relate), some prelates of the churches and ecclesiastical persons, alarmed where there should be no alarm, seeking transient peace, fearing more to offend the temporal majesty than the eternal, acquiesce in such abuses, not so much rashly as improvidently, permission or licence of the Apostolic See not having been obtained.

We therefore, desirous of preventing such wicked actions, do, with apostolic authority, decree with the advice of our brethren, that whatsoever prelates and ecclesiastical persons, religious or secular, of whatsoever orders, condition or standing, shall pay or promise or agree to pay to lay persons collections or taxes for the tithe, twentieth, or hundredth of their own rents, or goods, or those of the churches, or any other portion, proportion, or quantity of the same rents, or goods, at their own estimate or value, under the name of aid, loan, relief, subsidy, or gift, or by any other title, manner, or pretext demanded, without the authority of the same see,

And also whatsoever emperors, kings, or princes, dukes, earls, or barons, powers, captains, or officials, or rectors, by whatsoever names they are reputed, of cities, castles or any places whatsoever, wheresoever situate, and all others of whatsoever rank, pre-eminence or state, who shall impose, exact, or receive the things aforesaid, or arrest, seize, or presume to occupy the things anywhere deposited in holy buildings, or to command them to be arrested, seized, or occupied, or receive them when occupied, seized, or arrested, and also all who knowingly give aid, counsel, or favour, openly or secretly, in the things aforesaid, by this same should incur sentence of excommunication.   Universities, too, which may have been to blame in these matters, we subject to ecclesiastical interdict.

The prelates and ecclesiastical persons above mentioned we strictly command, in virtue of their obedience, and under pain of deposition, that they in no wise acquiesce in such things without express licence of the said see, and that they pay nothing under pretext of any obligation, promise, and acknowledgment whatsoever, made so far, or in progress heretofore, and before such constitution, prohibition, or order come to their notice, and that the seculars aforesaid do not in any wise receive it, and if they do pay, or the aforesaid receive, let them fall under sentence of excommunication by the very deed.

Moreover, let no one be absolved from the aforesaid sentences of excommunications and interdict, save at the moment of death, without authority and special licence of the Apostolic See, inasmuch as it is part of our intention that such a terrible abuse of secular powers should not in anywise pass under dissimulation, any privileges whatsoever notwithstanding, in whatsoever tenors, forms or modes, or arrangement of words, conceded to emperors, kings and the others aforesaid ; against which premises aforesaid we will that aid be given by no one, and by no persons in any respect.

Let it then be lawful to none at all to infringe this page of our constitution, prohibition, or order, or to gainsay it by any rash attempt ; and if any one presume to attempt this, let him know that he will incur the indignation of Almighty God, and of his blessed apostles Peter and Paul.

Given at Rome in St. Peter's on the 24th of February in the second year of our Pontificate.   (1296.)

XIII. THE ARTICULI CLERI OF 1316

[Translated in *Statutes of the Realm*, vol. i. p. 171.]

THE king to all to whom, &c., greeting. Know ye, that whereas of late in the times of our progenitors formerly kings of England, in divers their Parliament, and likewise after that we had undertaken the governance of our realm, in our Parliament, many articles containing divers grievances, committed, as was asserted in the same, against the English Church, the prelates, and clergy, were propounded by the prelates and clerks of our realm ; and further, great instance was made that convenient remedy might be provided therein : and of late in our Parliament holden at Lincoln, the ninth year of our reign, we caused the articles underwritten, with certain answers made to some of them heretofore, to be rehearsed before our council, and caused certain answers to be corrected ; and to the residue of the articles underwritten, answers were made by us and our council ; of which said articles, with the answers to the same, the tenors here ensue :

First, laymen purchase prohibitions generally upon tithes, obventions, oblations, mortuaries, redemption of penance, violent laying hands on clerk or conversus, and in cases of defamation ; in which cases proceeding is had to enjoin canonical penance. The king answers to this article, that in tithes, oblations, obventions, mortuaries, when they are propounded under these names the king's prohibition has no place, even if for the long withholding of these they come to a pecuniary settlement of the same. But if a clerk or a religious man sells his tithes, being gathered in his barn, or otherwise, to any man for money, if the money be demanded before a spiritual judge, the prohibition shall lie ; for by the sale the spiritual goods are made temporal, and the tithes turned into chattels.

Also if dispute arise upon the right of tithes, having its origin in the right of patronage, and the quantity of the same tithes comes to the fourth part of the goods of the church, the king's prohibition has place, if this cause come before a judge spiritual. Also if a prelate enjoin a pecuniary penance to a man for his offence, and it be demanded, the king's prohibition has place.   But if prelates enjoin penances corporal, and they which be so punished will redeem, upon their accord, such penances by money, if money be demanded before a judge spiritual, the king's prohibition has no place.

Moreover, if any lay violent hands on a clerk, the amends for the peace broken shall be before the king, and for excommunication before the prelate, that penance corporal may be enjoined ; which if the offender will redeem of his own good will, by giving money to the prelate, or to the party grieved, it can be required before the prelate, and the king's prohibition shall not lie.

In defamations, also, prelates shall correct in the manner abovesaid, the king's prohibition notwithstanding first enjoining a penance corporal, which if the offender will redeem, the prelate may freely receive the money, though the king's prohibition be tendered.

.   .   .   .

Also if any cause or matter, the knowledge whereof belongs to a court spiritual, and shall be definitely determined before a spiritual judge, and pass into a judgment, and shall not be suspended by an appeal, and afterwards, if upon the same thing a question is moved before a temporal judge between the same parties, and it be proved by witnesses or instruments, such an exception shall not be admitted in a temporal court.   The answer :   When the same case is debated before judges spiritual or temporal (as above appears upon the case of laying violent hands on a clerk) they say, notwithstanding the spiritual matter, the king's court shall discuss the same matter as the party shall think expedient for himself.

Also the king's letter is directed to ordinaries that have wrapped those that be in subjection to them in the sentence of excommunication, that they should assoil them by a certain day, or else that they should appear, and show wherefore they have excommunicated them.   The answer : The king decrees, that hereafter no such letters shall be suffered to issue, except in case where it is found that the king's liberty is prejudiced by the excommunication.

Also barons of the king's Exchequer, claiming by their privilege that they ought to make answer to no complaint out of the same place, extend the same privilege to clerks abiding there, called to orders or to residence, and inhibit ordinaries that by no means or for any cause, so long as they be in the Exchequer or in the king's service, shall they call them to judgment. The answer : It pleases our lord the king, that such clerks as attend in his service, if they offend, shall be corrected by their ordinaries, like as other ; but so long as they are occupied about the Exchequer, they shall not be bound to keep residence in their churches. Here it is thus added anew by the king's council : The king and his ancestors, time out of mind, have used that clerks, who are employed in his service, during such time as they are in service, shall not be compelled to keep residence at their benefices ; and such things as be thought necessary for the king and the commonwealth, ought not to be said to be prejudicial to the liberty of the Church.

Also the king's officers, as sheriffs and others, enter the fees of the Church to take distresses, and they sometimes take the rector's beasts in the king's highway, where they have nothing but the land belonging to the Church. The answer : The king's pleasure is, that from henceforth such distresses shall neither be taken in the king's highway, nor in the fees wherewith churches in times past have been endowed ; nevertheless he wills that distresses be taken in possessions newly purchased by ecclesiastical persons.

Also where some, flying to the church,[1] abjure the land, according to the custom of the realm, and laymen, or their enemies, do pursue them, and they are taken from the king's highway, are hanged or beheaded, and whilst they be in the church are kept in the churchyard by armed men, and sometimes in the church, so straitly, that they cannot depart from the hallowed ground to relieve nature, and are not suffered to have necessaries brought to them for their living. The answer : They that abjure the land, so long as they be on the common way, are in the king's peace, nor ought they to be disturbed by any man ; and when they be in the church, their keepers ought not to abide in the churchyard, except necessity or peril of escape so require it. And so long as they be in the church, they shall not be compelled to flee away, but they shall have necessaries for their living and may go forth to relieve nature. And the king's pleasure is, that robbers being appellants, whensoever they will, may

[1] For the right of Sanctuary, cf. More's *Richard III*. p. 397.

confess their offences to priests ; but let the confessors beware lest such appellants erroneously inform.

Also it is desired that our lord the king, and the great men of the realm, do not charge religious houses or spiritual persons, for corrodies, pensions, or provisions in religious houses, and other places of the Church, or with taking up horses and carts, whereby such houses are impoverished, and God's service is diminished, and, by reason of such charges, priests and other ministers of the Church, deputed to divine service, are oftentimes compelled to depart from the places aforesaid. The answer : The king's pleasure upon the contents in the petition is that from henceforth they shall not be unduly charged. And if the contrary be done by great men or others, they shall have remedy after the form of the statutes made in the time of King Edward, father to the king that now is. And like remedy shall be made for corrodies and pensions extracted by compulsion, whereof no mention is made in the statutes.

Also if any persons of the king's tenure be called before their ordinaries out of the parish where they continue, and they be excommunicated for their manifest contumacy, and after forty days a writ goes forth to take them, they pretend their privilege that they ought not to be cited out of the town and parish where their dwelling is, and so the king's writ for taking the same is denied. The answer : It was never denied, nor shall be hereafter.

Also it is prayed that spiritual persons, whom our lord the king presents to benefices of the Church, if the bishop will not admit them, either for lack of learning or for other cause reasonable, may not be under the examination of lay persons in the cases aforesaid, as it is at this time, in fact, attempted, contrary to the decrees canonical ; but that they may sue for remedy to the spiritual judge, to whom of right it belongs. The answer : Of the ability of a parson presented to a benefice of the Church, the examination belongs to a spiritual judge ; and so it has been used heretofore, and shall be hereafter.

Also if any dignity be vacant where election is to be made, it is prayed that the electors may freely make their election without fear of any temporal power and that all prayers and oppressions shall in this behalf cease. The answer : They shall be freely made according to the form of statutes and ordinances.

Moreover, though a clerk ought not to be judged before a temporal judge, nor anything done against him that concerns life or member ; nevertheless temporal judges cause clerks fleeing to the Church, and peradventure confessing their offences, to abjure the realm, and for the same cause admit their abjurations, although hereupon they cannot be their judges, and so power is wrongfully given to lay persons to put to death such clerks, if they chance to be found within the realm after their abjuration. The prelates and clergy desire such remedy to be provided herein, that the immunity or privilege of the Church and spiritual persons may be saved and unbroken. The answer : A clerk fleeing to the Church for felony, to obtain the privilege of the Church, if he affirm himself to be a clerk shall not be compelled to abjure the realm ; but yielding himself to the law of the realm, shall enjoy the privilege of the Church, according to the laudable custom of the realm heretofore used.

Also notwithstanding that a confession made before him that is not lawful judge thereof, is not sufficient whereon process may be awarded, or sentence given ; yet some temporal judges with respect to clerks—who in this behalf are not of their jurisdiction—confessing before them their heinous offences, such as thefts, robberies, or murders, do admit their accusation, which they call an appeal, and do not, after the premises, deliver them, so confessing, accusing or making appeal to their prelates, although they the judges be sufficiently required therein ; albeit they cannot be judged or condemned before them by their own confession without breaking the Church's privilege. The answer : The privilege of the Church shall not be denied to one appealing, when summoned in due form, as a clerk, by his ordinary.

We—desiring to provide for the state of the English Church, and for the tranquillity and quiet of the prelates and clergy aforesaid, so far as we may lawfully do, to the honour of God, and emendation of the Church, prelates, and clergy of the same, ratifying, confirming, and approving all and every of the articles aforesaid, with all and every of the answers made and contained in the same—do grant and command them to be kept firmly, and observed for ever ; willing and granting for us and our heirs, that the aforesaid prelates and clergy, and their successors, shall use, execute, and practise for ever the jurisdiction of the Church in the premises after the tenor of the answers aforesaid, without let, molestation, or vexation of us or of our heirs, or of any of our officers whosoever they be. Witness the king at York, the 24th day of November, in the tenth year of the reign of King Edward, the son of King Edward.

CHAPTER IV

TRADE GUILDS AND UNIVERSITIES

I. Trade Guilds—
    A. Charter of William I. to the City of London.
    B. Charter of Henry I. to the Citizens of London.
    C. Charter of Henry III. to Gloucester, 1227.
    D. Extracts from Charters to illustrate the Chief Borough
        Privileges.
        (i) Exemption from Scotale—
            (a) Malmesbury, 1205–1222.
        (ii) Exemption from Trial by Battle—
            (a) Bristol, 1188.
            (b) Dunwich, 1215.
        (iii) Grant of a Market—
            (a) Portsmouth, 1194.
            (b) Wells, 1201.
        (iv) Grant of a Fair—
            (a) Portsmouth, 1194.
            (b) Wells, 1201.
            (c) Ilchester, 1204.
            (d) Pevensey, 1207.
        (v) Grant of a Merchant Guild—
            (a) Leicester, 1103–1118.
            (b) Burford, 1087–1107.
            (c) Wallingford, 1156.
        (vi) Grants of Craft Guilds—
            (a) Oxford Cordwainers (about 1175).
            (b) Abolition of London Weavers' Guild, 1202.
    E. Prelude to FitzStephen's *Life of Becket*.
    F. Extracts from the Ancient Ordinances of the Guild
        Merchant of Southampton.
    G. Abstract of an Ancient Consuetudinary of the City of
        Winchester.
    H. Extracts from the Regulations of the Guild of Berwick-
        on-Tweed, 1283.
    I. Craft Guild Ordinances—
        (i) The Peltyers of Norwich.
        (ii) The Cordwainers of Exeter.
        (iii) The Guild of St. Mary, Lynn.
    J. Indenture of Apprenticeship, 1459.

II. Universities—
A. Extract from a Letter of Theobald of Etampes to
  Faricius, Abbot of Abingdon, about 1115.
B. Lectures of Robert Pullein at Oxford, 1133.
C. The Miraculous Cure of an Oxford Student, about 1180.
D. Giraldus Cambrensis reads his *Topography of Ireland*
  at Oxford, 1186.
E. Nominalism and Realism.
F. A Coroner's Inquest at Oxford, 1297.
G. Licences to Beg given to Scholars. Statute of 1388.
H. The Mythical Origin of Oxford.
I. Statute of 1421 relating to University Discipline.

I. TRADE GUILDS

A. CHARTER OF WILLIAM I. TO THE CITY OF LONDON, 1066

[This was written in Old English. For original and translation,
see Stubbs, *Select Charters*, pp. 82–83.]

WILLIAM, king, greets William, bishop, and Gosfrith,
port reeve, and all the burghers within London, French
and English, friendly ; and I do you to wit that ye
two be worthy of all the laws that ye were worthy of in King
Edward's day. And I will that every child be his father's
heir, after his father's day. And I will not endure that any
man offer any wrong to you.

God keep you.

B. CHARTER OF HENRY I. TO THE CITIZENS OF LONDON

[For the original, see Stubbs, *Select Charters*, p. 108.]

HENRY, by the grace of God, king of England, sends greeting
to the Archbishop of Canterbury, bishops, abbots, earls,
barons, justiciars, and sheriffs, and to all his liege subjects,
French and English, of all England.

Know ye that I have granted my citizens of London that
Middlesex shall be held at farm for three hundred pounds
by account, by themselves and their heirs of me and my
heirs, so that the citizens shall appoint as sheriff whomsoever they will from among themselves, and as justiciar
whomsoever they will from among themselves, to keep the

pleas of my crown and to conduct the same ; and none other shall be justiciar over the men of London.

And citizens shall not be impleaded outside the walls of the City for any plea ; and they shall be quit of Scot and Lot, Danegeld and Murdrum, and none of them shall undergo trial by battle.[1]

And if any of the citizens be impleaded concerning pleas of the crown he shall prove his case by the oath which shall be adjudged him in the City.

And within the walls of the City entertainment shall be given to no one, either of my own family, or of any other, unless hospitality be freely given.

And all the citizens of London shall be quit and free, and all their possessions, both throughout England and throughout the sea ports, of toll and passage and lastage and all other customs.

And both Church and barons and citizens shall have and hold well and in peace their jurisdictions [2] with all their customs, so that guests who are entertained within their jurisdictions shall give their customs to none except to him of whose jurisdiction he is, or to a servant whom he appoints there.

And a man of London shall not be condemned to a discretionary fine of money [3] except to the extent of his " were," [4] viz., One hundred shillings concerning the said plea as regards money.

And further there shall be no " miskenning " [5] in husting nor in folk-moot nor in any other pleas within the city.

And the husting shall sit once a week, to wit on Monday.

And I will cause my citizens to possess their lands and ward moot and dues within the City and without.

And as for lands, about which suit is made to me, I will conduct it for them in accordance with the law of the City.

And if any one shall take toll or custom from citizens of London,[6] the citizens of London shall take from that borough or township where toll or custom was taken, as much as the man of London paid for toll, and in addition he shall receive

[1] et nullus eorum faciat bellum.   [2] Socnas.
[3] Non judicetur in misericordia pecuniae.
[4] The " were " was the pecuniary estimation of a man, by which the value of his oath and the payment for his death were determined.
[5] " Miskenning " was a fine for shifting the ground of an action after it had come into court. It was sometimes levied on very trivial occasions.   [6] Cf. Jocelyn de Brakelonde, p. 85.

compensation for the injury. And all debtors who owe debts to citizens shall pay them or else disprove their liability in London. But if they will not pay nor come to plead their cause, then the citizens to whom they owe their debts shall make seizure of their goods within the City or from the shire in which the debtor resides.

And the citizens shall have their rights of coursing as to the fullest and best extent that their ancestors enjoyed, viz., the Chilterns, Middlesex, and Surrey.[1] Witnesses, the Bishop of Winchester, Robert son of Richer, Hugh Bigot, Alfred de Toteney, William Abini, Hubert the King's Chamberlain, William de Montfichet, Hagulf de Tainus, John Belet, Robert son of Siward. Given at Westminster.

C. Charter to Gloucester, a.d. 1227

[From Charter Roll, 11 Henry III., p. 1, m. 10, No. 88. Brown, Bland and Tawney's *Economic History : Select Documents*, pp. 119–121, by kind permission of Messrs. G. Bell & Sons and G. H. Tawney, Esq.]

HENRY, King of England, etc., greeting. Know ye that we have granted and by this our charter confirmed to our burgesses of Gloucester the whole borough of Gloucester with the appurtenances, to hold of us and our heirs for ever at fee farm rendering yearly £55 sterling, as they were wont to render the same, and £10 by tale of increment of farm, at our Exchequer at the term of Easter and at the term of Michaelmas. We have granted also to our burgesses of Gloucester of the Merchants' Gild that none of them plead without the walls of the borough of Gloucester touching any plea save pleas of foreign tenures, except our moneyers and ministers. We have granted also to them that none of them suffer trial by battle [2] and that touching pleas pertaining to our crown they may deraign [3] according to the ancient custom of the borough. This also we have granted to them that all the burgesses of Gloucester of the merchants' guild [4] be quit of toll and lastage [5] and pontage [6] and stallage [7]

---

[1] Cf. Magna Carta, Cap. XIII. p. 42 ; also FitzStephen, p. 122.
[2] Cf. pp. 49, 92, 112, etc.   [3] plead.
[4] For merchant guilds, cf. Jocelyn de Brakelonde's *Chronicle*, p. 92 ; cf. also pp. 114, 123, etc.
[5] A toll per load of goods exacted at fairs, markets, and ports.
[6] Bridge toll.   [7] Tolls for having a stall or booth at a fair.

within fairs and without and throughout seaports of all our lands on this side of the sea and beyond the sea, saving in all things the liberties of the City of London, and that none be judged touching a money penalty save according to the ancient law of the borough which they had in the time of our ancestors, and that they justly have all their lands and tenements and sureties and debts, whosoever owe them, and that right be done them according to the custom of the borough touching their lands and tenures which are within the borough, and that pleas touching all their debts by loans which have been made at Gloucester, and touching sureties made there, be held at Gloucester. And if any man in the whole of our land take toll or custom from the men of Gloucester of the Merchants' gild, after he have failed to do right, the sheriff of Gloucester or the provost of Gloucester shall take distress thereon at Gloucester, saving in all things the liberties of the City of London. Furthermore for the repair of the borough we have granted to them that they be all quit of " gyeresyeve "[1] and of " scotale ",[2] if our sheriff or any other bailiff exact " scotale." We have granted to them these aforesaid customs and all other liberties and free customs which they had in the times of our ancestors, when they had them well and freely. And if any Customs were unjustly levied in time of war, they shall be annulled. And whosoever shall come to the borough of Gloucester with his wares, of whatsoever place they be, whether strangers or others, shall come, stay and depart in our safe peace, rendering right customs. And let no man disturb them touching this our charter. And we forbid that any man commit wrong or damage or molestation against them thereon on pain of forfeiture of £10 to us. Wherefore we will, etc. that the aforesaid burgesses and their heirs have and hold all these things aforesaid in inheritance of us and our heirs well and in peace, freely, quietly and honourably, as is above written. We will also and grant that the same our burgesses of Gloucester elect by the common council of the borough two of the more lawful and discreet burgesses of Gloucester and present them to our chief justice at Westminster, which two or one of them shall well and faithfully keep the provostship of the borough and shall not be removed so long as they

---

[1] A compulsory gift exacted every year.
[2] Compulsory purchase of a certain quantity of ale ; cf. p. 112.

be of good behaviour in their bailiwick, save by the common council of the borough. We will also that in the same borough of Gloucester by the common counsel of the burgesses be elected four of the more lawful and discreet men of the borough to keep the pleas of the crown and other things which pertain to us and our crown in the same borough, and to see that the provosts of that borough justly and lawfully treat as well poor as rich, as the charter of the lord King John, our father, which they have thereon, reasonably testifies. We have granted also to the same burgesses of Gloucester that none of our sheriffs intermeddle with them in aught touching any plea or plaint or occasion or any other thing pertaining to the aforesaid borough, saving to us and to our heirs for ever pleas of our crown, which ought to be attached by the same our burgesses, until the coming of our justices, as is aforesaid. We have granted also to the same that if any bondman or any man stay in the aforesaid borough and maintain himself therein and be in the merchants' gild and hanse and lot and scot with the same our burgesses for a year and a day without claim, thenceforth he shall not be reclaimed by his lord, but shall abide freely in the same borough. Witnesses : Wm. Archbishop of York, Wm. Bishop of Carlisle, Hubert de Burgo, etc., Wm. Earl Warrenne, Osbert Giffard, Ralph son of Nicholas, Richard de Argentem, our stewards, Henry de Capella, John de Bassing and others. Dated by the hand of the venerable father Ralph, Bishop of Chichester, our Chancellor, at Westminster, on the sixth day of April in the eleventh year of our reign.

D. Extracts from Charters to Illustrate the Chief Borough Privileges

[For a fine collection of extracts from Charters, see A. Ballard, *British Borough Charters*, 2 vols. (Cambridge Univ. Press, 1913). The following extracts are given by the kind permission of the Syndics of Cambridge University Press.]

(i) Exemption from Scotale, etc.

(a) *Extract from a grant of the Abbot of Malmesbury to the Town of Malmesbury*, 1205–1222 (Ballard, p. 86)

To all the faithful in Christ who shall see or hear this present writing, Walter, by the grace of God, Abbot of Malmesbury, and the whole convent of the same place, send greeting in the Lord. Be it known to you all, that we, by the inspiration of divine piety, and for the salvation of our souls, at the devout instance and petition of the burgesses of Malmesbury, have released for ever to them and their successors, as far as we can, the suit of three scotales [1] which they were accustomed to attend every year : that is to say, one at Michaelmas, the second at Christmas, and the third in Lent. To them therefore we release that suit, who are of the Merchant guild in the town of Malmesbury, and to all others outside the merchant guild, who should and ought to pay as much to the said scotales as they of the aforesaid guild. For this release, however, of the said scotales the said burgesses have given us one mark of silver as a fine ; and that we may not incur a loss in our rent, which ought to be paid to us from the said scotales, the said burgesses will give us yearly, as rent of the said scotales, xxx shillings at the three terms, to wit, x shillings on the Sunday next before Michaelmas, and x shillings on the Sunday next before Christmas, and x shillings on the second Sunday in Easter. And these sums shall be collected at the fixed terms, by the hands of the stewards of the said guild, and by the hand of our serjeant.

(ii) Exemption from Trial by Battle

(a) *Extract from Charter to Bristol*, 1188 (Ballard, p. 133)

THAT no burgess fight [2] a duel unless he is appealed of the death of a foreigner who was killed in the town and did not belong to the town.

(b) *Extract from Charter to Dunwich*, 1215 (Ballard, p. 134)

THAT although any of them be appealed he shall not fight a duel either in his borough or outside it, either in a suit for land or for larceny or for felony or for any other plea, except only the death of a foreigner.

---

[1] Cf. Charter to Gloucester, p. 110.
[2] faciat duellum. For trial by battle, cf. Magna Carta, Cap. LIV. p. 49 ; also Jocelyn de Brakelonde's *Chronicle*, p. 92.

(iii) Grant of a Market

(a) Extract from Charter to Portsmouth, 1194 (Ballard, p. 171)

THAT our burgesses in the same borough have every week
in the year on one day in the week, to wit on Thursday, a
market with all the liberties and free customs which our
citizens of Winchester or Oxford or others of our lands have
or ought to have.

(b) Extract from Charter to Wells, 1201 (Ballard, p. 171)

THERE shall be a free market on Sunday as there is now and
is wont to be.

(iv) Grant of a Fair

(a) Extract from Charter to Portsmouth, 1194 (Ballard, p. 172)

KNOW ye that we have retained our borough of Portsmouth
in our own hand with all its appurtenances, and in it have
established and given and granted a fair [1] to continue, once
a year, for fifteen days, at the Feast of St. Peter's Chains.
(Aug. 1.)

(b) Extract from a Charter to Wells, 1201 (Ballard, p. 173)

AND free fairs [2] as there they were wont to be there every
year, in the feast of the blessed Andrew,[3] of the blessed
Calixtus,[4] in the Invention of the Holy Cross,[5] and on the
morrow of the blessed John the Baptist,[6] and moreover,
one fair of our own gift every year, at the Translation of
the Blessed Andrew, to continue for eight days in the streets
of the same borough in the places in which the aforesaid
fair of the blessed Andrew was wont to be held, provided
that it be not a nuisance to the neighbouring fairs.

*(c) Extract from a Charter of King John to Ilchester, 1204
(Ballard, p. 174)*

AND they shall have one fair every year at Ilchester lasting
for one day, to wit on the day of the Beheading of St. John

---

[1] nundinas. [2] et liberae feriae. [3] 30th November.
[4] 14th October. [5] 3rd May. [6] 25th June.

8

the Baptist,[1] with all the liberties and free customs pertaining to fairs of this kind, since they had this fair with all the aforesaid customs by a charter of King Henry our father.

(d) *Extract from a Charter to Pevensey*, 1207 (Ballard, p. 175)

MOREOVER, we have granted to our aforesaid barons of Pevensey that they may have there every year a fair to continue for seven days, to wit, three days next before the Birthday of St. John the Baptist,[2] and the feast day, and the three following days, and a market on every Sunday, provided that the aforesaid fair and market shall not be a nuisance to the neighbouring fairs and markets.

(v) GRANT OF A MERCHANT GUILD

(a) *Extract from a Charter to Leicester*, 1103–18
(Ballard, p. 202)

KNOW ye that I have granted to my merchants of Leicester their guild of merchants with all the customs with which they held it in the time of King William and of King William his son, and now in the time of King Henry.

(b) *Extract from a Charter to Burford*, 1087–1107
(Ballard, p. 203)

. . . guild of merchants.[3]

(c) *Extract from a Charter to Wallingford*, 1156
(Ballard, p. 204)

THAT is to say, they shall have their merchant guild with all its customs and laws freely, so that no reeve or justice of mine shall intermeddle concerning their guild, except their own Alderman and minister.

(vi) GRANTS OF CRAFT GUILDS

(a) *Grant of Henry II. to the Oxford Cordwainers* (*about* 1175)
(Ballard, p. 208)

KNOW ye that I have granted and confirmed to the corvesars of Oxford all the liberties and customs which they had in

---

[1] 29th August.   [2] 24th June.
[3] . . . gilda mercatorum. The preceding words are illegible. This is probably the earliest mention of a merchant guild in an English Charter ; cf. pp. 92, 109, 123, etc.

the time of King Henry my grandfather, and that they have their guild, so that none carry on their trade in the town of Oxford, except he be of that guild.

I grant also that the cordwainers who afterwards may come into the town of Oxford shall be of the same guild and shall have the same liberties and customs which the corvesars had or ought to have.

For this grant and confirmation, however, the corvesars and cordwainers ought to pay me every year an ounce of gold.

(b) *Grant of King John to London abolishing the Weavers' Guild*, 1202 (Ballard, p. 209).

KNOW ye that at the petition of our Mayor and citizens of London we have granted and by this present charter confirmed that the Weavers' Guild shall not exist henceforth in our City of London, nor shall it on any account be revived. But because we have been wont to receive yearly eighteen marks of silver from that Weavers' Guild, the aforesaid citizens shall pay every year to us and our heirs twenty marks of silver at the feast of St. Michael at our Exchequer.

E. THE PRELUDE TO FITZSTEPHEN'S "LIFE OF BECKET"

[FitzStephen was a clerk in the service of Becket, and was present at his martyrdom. He afterwards wrote a *Life* of his great master, and prefaced it with the following description of the City of London. It is edited in the Rolls Series by J. C. Robertson, *Materials for the History of Thomas Becket*, vol. iii. pp. 2 sqq. FitzStephen died about 1190.]

AMONG the noble cities of the world that Fame celebrates, the City of London of the Kingdom of the English is the one seat that pours out its fame more widely, sends to farther lands its wealth and trade, lifts its head higher than the rest. It is happy in the healthiness of its air, in the Christian religion, in the strength of its defences, the nature of its site, the honour of its citizens, the modesty of its matrons; pleasant in sports; fruitful of noble men. Let us look into these things separately.

If the clemency of the skies there softens minds, it is not so that they corrupt in Venus, but that they be not fierce and bestial, rather benign and liberal.

There is in the church there the Episcopal Seat of St. Paul ; once it was Metropolitan, and it is thought will again become so if the citizens return into the island, unless perhaps the archiepiscopal title of Saint Thomas the Martyr, and his bodily presence, preserve to Canterbury, where it now is, a perpetual dignity. But as Saint Thomas has made both cities illustrious, London by his rising, Canterbury by his setting, in regard of that saint, with admitted justice, each can claim advantage of the other. There are also, as regards the cultivation of the Christian faith, in London and the suburbs, thirteen larger conventual churches, besides lesser parish churches one hundred and twenty-six.

It has on the east the Palatine Castle,[1] very great and strong, of which the ground plan and the walls rise from a very deep foundation, fixed with a mortar tempered by the blood of animals. On the west are two towers very strongly fortified, with the high and great wall of the city having seven double gates, and towered to the north at intervals. London was walled and towered in like manner on the south, but the great fish-bearing Thames river which there glides, with ebb and flow from the sea, by course of time has washed against, loosened, and thrown down those walls. Also upwards to the west the royal palace [2] is conspicuous above the same river, an incomparable building with ramparts and bulwarks, two miles from the city, joined to it by a populous suburb.

Everywhere outside the houses of those living in the suburbs are joined to them, planted with trees, the spacious and beautiful gardens of the citizens.

Also there are, on the north side, pastures and a pleasant meadow land, through which flow river streams, where the turning wheels of mills are put in motion with a cheerful sound. Very near lies a great forest, with woodland pastures, coverts of wild animals, stags, fallow deer, boars, and wild bulls. The tilled lands of the city are not of barren gravel but fat plains of Asia, that make crops luxuriant, and fill their tillers' barns with Ceres' sheaves.

There are also about London on the north side, excellent suburban springs, with sweet, wholesome, and clear water

[1] The Tower of London.
[2] Westminster Palace, of which Westminster Hall, built by William Rufus, still remains.

that flows rippling over the bright stones ; among which
Holy Well, Clerken Well, and Saint Clements are held to be
of most note : these are frequented by greater numbers,
and visited more by scholars and youth of the city when they
go out for fresh air on summer evenings.   It is a good city
indeed when it has a good master.

That city is honoured by her men, adorned by her arms,
populous with many inhabitants, so that in the time of
slaughter of war under King Stephen, of those going out to
a muster twenty thousand horsemen and sixty thousand
men on foot were estimated to be fit for war.   Above all
other citizens, everywhere, the citizens of London are regarded as conspicuous and noteworthy for handsomeness of
manners and of dress, at table, and in way of speaking.   The
citizens of other cities are called inhabitants ; of this one they
are called barons.   For them an oath finishes any dispute.

The city matrons are true Sabine women.

In London three principal churches have, by privilege and
ancient dignity, famous schools ; yet very often by support
of some personage, or of some teachers who are considered
notable and famous in philosophy, there are also other
schools by favour and permission.   On feast days the masters
have festival meetings in the churches.   Their scholars
dispute, some by demonstration, others by dialectics ; some
recite enthymemes,[1] others do better in using perfect
syllogisms.   Some are exercised in disputation for display,
as wrestling with opponents ; others for truth, which is the
grace of perfectness.   Sophists who feign are judged happy
in their heap and flood of words.   Others paralogize.   Some
orators, now and then, say in their rhetorical speeches something apt for persuasion, careful to observe rules of their
art, and to omit none of the contingents.   Boys of different
schools strive against one another in verses, and contend
about the principles of grammar and rules of the past and
future tenses.   There are others who employ in epigrams,
rhymes, and verses the old trifling banter, and with
Fescennine [2] license freely pull their comrades to pieces,
without giving their names, fling at them scoffs and sarcasms,

---

[1] *i.e.* syllogisms in which one premiss is suppressed.
[2] This adjective is derived from the town of Fescennium, in Etruria,
whence the Romans are said to have derived certain coarse and
boisterous songs which were bandied about at harvest festivals.

touch the faults of schoolfellows or perhaps of greater people with Socratic salt, or bite harder with theonine tooth. The hearers ready to laugh much

" Ingeminant tremulos naso crispante cachinnos." [1]

Those engaged in the several kinds of business, sellers of several things, contractors for several kinds of work, are distributed every morning into their several localities and shops. Besides, there is in London on the river bank, among the wines in ships and cellars sold by the vintners, a public cook shop ; there eatables are to be found every day, according to the season, dishes of meat, roast, fried and boiled, great and small fish, coarser meats for the poor, more delicate for the rich, of game, fowls, and small birds. If there should come suddenly to any of the citizens friends, weary from a journey and too hungry to like waiting till fresh food is brought and cooked, with water to their hands comes bread,[2] while one runs to river bank, and there is all that can be wanted. However great the multitude of soldiers or travellers entering the city, or preparing to go out of it, at any hour of the day or night—that these may not fast too long and those may not go out supperless—they turn hither, if they please, where every man can refresh himself in his own way ; those who would care for themselves luxuriously, when set before the delicacies there to be found, would not desire sturgeon nor the bird of Africa nor the Ionian godwit. For this is the public kitchen, very convenient to the city, and part of its civilization ; hence we read in the Gorgias of Plato that next to medicine the office of the cooks, as the adulation of imitators, makes the fourth part of civility.[3] Outside one of the gates there, immediately in the suburb, is a certain field, smooth [Smith] field in fact and name. Every Friday, unless it be a higher duty of appointed

---

[1] FitzStephen is quoting Persius, iii. 86–7.
[2] FitzStephen here quotes Virgil's *Aeneid*, i. 702 :
     " Dant famuli manibus lymphas, Cereremque canistris
      Expediunt,"
shortening the last clause to " panesque."
[3] Quotation of Plato by a twelfth-century writer is worth noting. Very little of the Greek classics—even of Aristotle—was known in Western Europe at this time.

solemnity, there is in it a famous show of noble horses for
sale. Earls, barons, knights, and many citizens who are in
town, come to see or to buy. It is pleasant to see the
steppers in quick trot going gently up and down, their feet
on each side alternately rising and falling. On this side are
the horses most fit for esquires, moving with harder pace yet
swiftly, that lift and set down together, as it were, the
opposite fore and hind feet ; on that side colts of fine breed
who not yet well used to the bit :

"Altius incedunt, et mollia crura reponunt." [1]

In that part are the sumpter horses, powerful and
spirited : here costly chargers, elegant of form, noble of
stature, with ears quickly tremulous, necks lifted, haunches
plump. In their stepping, the buyers first try for the
gentler, then the quicker pace, which is by the fore and the
hind feet moving in pairs together. When a race is ready
for such thunderers, and perhaps for others of like kind,
powerful to carry, quick to run, a shout is raised, orders
are given that the common horses stand apart. The boys
who mount the wing-footed by threes or twos according to
the match, prepare themselves for contest ; skilled to rule
horses, they restrain the mouths of the untamed with bitted
bridles. For this chiefly they care, that no one should get
before another in the course. The horses rise too in their
own way to the struggle of the race ; their limbs tremble,
impatient of delay they cannot keep still in their place ; at
the sign given their limbs are stretched, they hurry on their
course, are borne with stubborn speed. The riders contend for the love of praise and hope of victory, plunge spurs
into the loose-reined horses, and urge them none the less
with whips and shouts. You would think with Heraclitus
everything to be in motion, and the opinion to be wholly
false of Zeno,[2] who said there was no motion and no goal to
be reached. In another part of the field stand by themselves
the goods proper to rustics, implements of husbandry, swine

---

[1] Virgil's *Georgics*, iii. 76 :
      " Continuo pecoris generosi pullus in arvis
        Altius ingreditur, et mollia cura reponit."
[2] Zeno of Elea, born about 490 B.C. He was the author of in-
genious arguments to deny the reality of motion.

with long flanks, cows with full udders, oxen of bulk immense, and woolly flocks. There stand the mares fit for plough, dray, and cart, some big with foal, and others with their young colts closely following. To this city from every nation under heaven merchants delight to bring their trade by sea :

" Aurum mittit Arabs ; species et thura Sabæus ;
 Arma Scythes ; oleum palmarum divite sylva
 Pingue solum Babylon ; Nilus lapides preciosos ;
 Norwegi, Russi, varium grisium, sabelinas ;
 Seres, purpureas vestes ; Galli sua vina." [1]

London is, on the faith of the chroniclers, a much older city than Rome, for by the same Trojan forefathers this was founded by Brutus before that by Romulus and Remus. Whence it is that they still have the same laws established in common. This city, like that, is divided into wards, has annual sheriffs for its consuls, has senatorial and lower magistrates, sewers and aqueducts in its streets, its proper places and separate courts for cases of each kind, deliberative, demonstrative, judicial ; has assemblies on appointed days. I do not think there is a city with more commendable customs of church attendance, honour to God's ordinances, keeping sacred festivals, almsgiving, hospitality, confirming betrothals, contracting marriages, celebration of nuptials, preparing feasts, cheering the guests, and also in care for funerals and the interment of the dead. The only pests of London are the immoderate drinking of fools and the frequency of fires.[2] To this may be added that nearly all the bishops, abbots, and magnates of England are, as it were, citizens and freemen of London ; having there their splendid houses, to which they resort, where they spend largely when summoned to great councils by the king or by their metropolitan, or drawn thither by their own private affairs.

Let us now come to the sports and pastimes, seeing it is

[1] The Arabian sends gold ; Sabæan, spice and incense ; Scythian, arms ; from its rich wood fat soil, Babylon sends oil of palms ; Nile, precious stones ; Norwegians, Russians, many furs and sables ; Seres, her purple clothing ; Gaul, her wines. Cf. Virgil, *Georgics*, i. 57 and ii. 117.

[2] solae pestes Londoniae sunt immodica stultorum potatio, et frequens incendium,

fit that a city should not only be commodious and serious,
but also merry and sportful ; whereupon in the seals of the
popes, until the time of Pope Leo, on the one side was
St. Peter fishing, with a key over him, reached as it were by
the hand of God out of heaven, and about it this verse :

" Tu pro me navem liquisti, suscipe clavem."

And on the other side was a city, and this inscription
on it : " *Aurea Roma.*" Likewise to the praise of Augustus
Cæsar and the city in respect of the shows and sports was
written :

" Nocte pluit tota, redeunt spectacula mane," etc.

" All night it raines, and shows at morrow tide returne again,
  And Cæsar with almighty Jove hath matcht an equal raign."

But London, for the shows upon theatres, and comical
pastimes, hath holy plays, representations of miracles, which
holy confessors have wrought, or representations of torments
wherein the constancy of martyrs appeared. Every year
also at Shrove Tuesday, that we may begin with children's
sports, seeing we all have been children, the schoolboys do
bring cocks of the game to their master, and all the forenoon
they delight themselves in cock-fighting : after dinner, all
the youths go into the fields to play at the ball.

The scholars of every school have their ball, or baton, in
their hands ; the ancient and wealthy men of the city come
forth on horseback to see the sport of the young men, and to
take part of the pleasure in beholding their agility. Every
Friday in Lent a fresh company of young men comes into
the field on horseback and the best horseman conducteth
the rest. Then march forth the citizens' sons, and other
young men, with disarmed lances and shields, and there they
practise feats of war. Many courtiers likewise, when the
king lieth near, and attendants of noblemen, do repair to
these exercises ; and while the hope of victory doth inflame
their minds, do show good proof how serviceable they would
be in martial affairs.

In Easter holidays they fight battles on the water ; a
shield is hung upon a pole, fixed in the midst of the stream, a

boat is prepared without oars, to be carried by violence of the water, and in the fore part thereof standeth a young man, ready to give charge upon the shield with his lance; if so be he breaketh his lance against the shield, and doth not fall, he is thought to have performed a worthy deed; if so be, without breaking his lance, he runneth strongly against the shield, down he falleth into the water, for the boat is violently forced with the tide; but on each side of the shield ride two boats, furnished with young men, which recover him that falleth as soon as they may. Upon the bridge, wharfs, and houses, by the river's side, stand great numbers to see and laugh thereat.

In the holidays all the summer the youths are exercised in leaping, dancing, shooting, wrestling, casting the stone, and practising their shields; the maidens trip in their timbrels, and dance as long as they can well see. In winter, every holiday before dinner, the boars prepared for brawn are set to fight, or else bulls and bears are baited.

When the great fen, or moor, which watereth the walls of the city on the north side, is frozen, many young men play upon the ice; some, striding as wide as they may, do slide swiftly; others make themselves seats of ice, as great as millstones; one sits down, many hand in hand to draw him, and one slipping on a sudden, all fall together; some tie bones to their feet and under their heels; and shoving themselves by a little picked staff, do slide as swiftly as a bird flieth in the air, or an arrow out of a cross-bow. Sometime two run together with poles, and hitting one the other, either one or both do fall, not without hurt; some break their arms, some their legs, but youth desirous of glory in this sort exerciseth itself against the time of war. Many of the citizens do delight themselves in hawks and hounds; for they have liberty of hunting [1] in Middlesex, Hertfordshire, all Chiltern, and in Kent to the water of Cray.

---

[1] Cf. Magna Carta, Cap. XIII. p. 42 ; also p. 109.

F. Extracts from the Ancient Ordinances of the Guild Merchant of the Town of Southampton

[The document from which the following extracts, translated from the French, are made is contained in a small parchment book of miscellaneous documents. The handwriting is of various dates, but mainly of the fourteenth century. The whole document was published in the original language by Edward Smirke in the *Archæological Journal* for September 1859, vol. xvi. pp. 284 sqq. ; see the revised translation in *The Oak Book of Southampton*, edited by P. Studer (Publications of the Southampton Record Society, No. 10, vol. i. p. 22 sqq.)]

1. *How the Aldermen, Seneshal, Chaplain and eskevins are wont to be elected in the Guild.*—First that of the Guild Merchant [1] there be elected and established an Alderman, a Seneshal, a Chaplain and four eskevins and an usher. And it is customary that he who shall be Alderman shall have of each one entering the guild fourpence, the Seneshal twopence, the Chaplain twopence and the usher one penny. And the guild should meet twice in the year, that is to say, on the Sunday next after the Feast of St. John the Baptist,[2] and the Sunday next after St. Hilary.[3]

2. *When the Guild meets none shall come with them except by permission of the Alderman.*—And when the guild assembles no member thereof may bring with him any stranger unless he be invited to do so by the Alderman or Seneshal. And the Alderman must have a serjeant to serve before him, and the Seneshal another serjeant and two eskevins a serjeant. And the other two eskevins a serjeant and the Chaplain shall have his clerk.

3. *What the Alderman shall have every night when the Guild meets.*—And when the guild meets the Alderman shall have each night that the guild sits two gallons of wine and two candles, and the seneshal also and the four eskevins and the Chaplain each of them one gallon of wine and one candle, and the usher one gallon of wine.

4. *What the dependents [4] shall have of the Guild whenever it meets.*—And when the guild meets the dependents of the

[1] Cf. pp. 92, 109, 114, etc.   [2] 24th June.   [3] 13th January.
[4] meseaus.

Madeline shall have in alms of the guild brethren two "cestres" of beer. And the sick of the Hospital [1] and of St. Julian shall have two "cestres" of beer. And the Franciscan Friars [2] shall have two "cestres" of beer and one "cestre" of wine. And four "cestres" of beer shall be given to the poor of the place wheresoever the guild shall meet.

5. *None of the Guild brethren shall go out of the town when the Guild meets in the town.*—And when the guild sits no member of the guild shall go outside the town for any purpose without the permission of the Seneshal. If any one does so he shall be "in mercy" for two shillings and shall pay this fine.

6. *How two worthy men shall visit the sick of the Guild brethren and each one shall have a Guild brother alotted to him.*[3]—And when the guild meets and any one of them have gone out of the town without being aware of his obligation he shall have a gallon of wine if his servants come to seek it. And if a guild brother is sick, wine should be sent to him, viz. two loaves and a gallon of wine and a mess from the kitchen, and two worthy men of the guild shall go and visit him and find out how he fares.

7. *When a Guild brother dies all belonging to the Guild who are in the town shall meet at the Service for the Dead.*— And when a guild brother dies, all those who belong to the guild and are in the town must be present at the Service for the Dead and guild brethren must bear his body and conduct the body to the burial. And whosoever shall fail to come shall pay by oath two pence to the poor. And each of the ward where the dead man shall be must find a man to watch by the body throughout the night during which the dead man remains in his own house. And when the Service of the Dead shall take place, that is to say the vigil and the mass, there shall be burnt four tapers of the guild, each taper of two pounds' weight or more, until the body be interred. And these four tapers must remain in charge of the Seneshal of the guild.

11. *If a Guild brother be in prison in any place in England.* —And if any guild brother be imprisoned in England in time of peace the Alderman or the Seneshal or one of the eskevins must go at the cost of the guild to bring about the liberation of him who shall be in prison.

19. *No one shall bring into the town to sell again unless he*

---

[1] la maysun Deu. [2] les freres menors. [3] Text amended.

be a Guild brother.—And no one shall bring anything into the town of Southampton to sell again in the same town unless he be of the Guild Merchant or of the Franchise. And if any one do so and be arrested all that he has so brought is forfeit to the King. . . .

22. *If any fall into poverty and have not the wherewithal to live.*—And if any guild brother fall into poverty and have not the wherewithal to live and cannot work where he would, he shall have one mark from the guild to relieve his condition when the guild shall meet. . . .

23. *And no private person or stranger shall sell merchandise nor buy before a burgess.*—And no private person or stranger shall bargain for or buy any merchandise whatsoever, which comes into the town, before a burgess of the Guild Merchant whenever such guild brother is present and wishes to bargain or to buy, and if any one does so and is arrested, that which he bought is forfeit to the King.

G. Abstract of an Ancient Consuetudinary of the City of Winchester

[An old certificate or exemplification of the customs of the city of Winchester was found among the muniments of Winchester College about 1850. It was published in full in the original French by E. Smirke in the *Archæological Journal* for March 1852 (vol. ix. pp. 70 sqq.). The following is an abstract of the document, which is too lengthy to translate here in full. It probably belongs in the main to the end of the thirteenth century.]

These are the ancient usages of the city of Winchester which have been used in the times of our ancestors. The mayor is chosen annually by twentyfour jurats, and the commonalty to be the chief upholder of the franchise ; which mayor shall be removeable from year to year. He has not, per se, jurisdiction on any plaint or plea touching the provostry of the city.

There ought to be twentyfour jurats chosen from "the wisest and most worthy men of the city," [1] to aid and counsel the mayor in maintaining the franchise. They may be convened by summons, and, in default, are liable to be fined one besant.[2]

---

[1] plus prudeshomes et plus sages.

[2] A coin of gold or of silver, and, therefore, of varying value, which spread over Europe from Constantinople (Byzantium) at the time of the Crusades.

Two sworn bailiffs are annually chosen to keep the provostry and to do justice to the commonalty. The mayor and twentyfour select worthy men [1] at the Michaelmas Burgmote, of whom the commonalty choose two to be the bailiffs. Four city serjeants are sworn verge-bearers to execute the commands of the mayor and bailiffs.

None of the twentyfour are to maintain any party in the city courts, or to act as advocates to the prejudice of the franchise.

Two coroners are sworn in the King's name to execute their office as well in the soke as in the city.

The bailiffs annually return their rolls of pleas and terrage into the public custody of the city.

No citizen shall cause burells [2] or chalons [7] to be made without the walls on pain of forfeiture of the article made or its value.

Every great loom for making burells [2] pays five shillings per annum towards the farm of the city, unless it makes only one cloth.

No one ought to be free who keeps in his house, or elsewhere, more than one to the use of the mayor, one to the use of the hospital [3] and a third to the use of the city clerk.

The telers of burells [2] ought to take eighteen pence for the working of cloth from All Saints [4] to the Annunciation of Our Lady,[5] and thence again to All Saints, two shillings.

None but freemen can make burells, except that each fuller may make one every year, and every teler one towards the king's farm.

Of the small looms for making chalons, each turs loom pays to the city farm twelve pence a year, and each single loom sixpence unless only one cloth be made in the year. And no one can be a freeman who does not at least render this amount.

Cloth must be of the length and breadth required by the old assize of the mystery on pain of forfeiture ; chalons 4 ells long must be 2 yards wide "before the tapener " ;[6] chalons [7] $3\frac{1}{2}$ yards long must be $1\frac{3}{4}$ yards wide. If $3\frac{1}{4}$ yards

---

[1] prudeshomes. [2] A kind of coarse or roughed up cloth.
[3] *i.e.* the Hospital of St. John, Winchester.
[4] 1st November. [5] 25th March.
[6] One who regulates the width of the cloth.
[7] A kind of blanket or bed-cloth.

long they must be an ell and a half and half a quarter wide.
If 3 ells long, they must be an ell and a half wide.

An apprentice put to work at the loom of a tapener [1] to
oil must pay ten shillings to the king, if he be not the son,
or sister's son, of the master.

None of the mystery [2] may engage the servant of another
until after St. Andrew's Day, on pain of half a mark to the
King.

None of the mystery [2] of a tapener may work at night
except from the feast of St. Thomas [3] to Christmas, on pain
of sixpence for every offence.

None of the mystery of buriller may work at night except
from St. Nicholas [4] to Christmas.

Two worthy men are to be chosen from the mystery of
tapeners and sworn to maintain the ancient usages of it,
and to take pledges from defaulters, and present them at
the next court of the bailiffs. They are also to have care
and oversight of the *send*, or shop, where the yarn is sold,
so as to prevent regrating before the hour of tierce.[5] Articles
so sold are forfeited to the city farm.

No regrater is to have there a box or locker by which
such regratings may be concealed ; and if they find an
article wetted, or any fraud practised, it shall be delivered
to the bailiffs for adjudication and punishment.

No butcher or other is to have a stall in the High Street
except upon payment of a consideration to the city.

No one can buy undressed leather or skins if he be not
of the franchise, on pain of forfeiture ; and no one of
the franchise can take them in the same state out of the
liberty.

No fishmonger or poulterer can buy for resale before the
hour of tierce [5] has sounded.

No victuals brought into the city, and once put up for
sale, can be taken out of it without leave of the bailiff.

No regrater is to leave the city for the purpose of buying
victuals on their way to the city, in order to raise their price,
on pain of forty days' imprisonment.

The custom as to fish is, that no one may have a board
except of the king ; and each board is charged towards the

---

[1] One who regulates the width of the cloth.   [2] craft.
[3] 22nd December.   [4] 9th December.
[5] An office said about 9 a.m.

king's rent a farthing for each day on which there is fish on it to sell. No franchise can exempt from this charge.

Every cart bringing fish for sale into the city pays a halfpenny to the king's rent for the board which it stands before. And if the cart be not of the franchise, it pays to the king 2½d. ; and every horse-load of fresh fish not of the franchise pays 1½d., and of salt fish a halfpenny.

A cart, not of the franchise, bringing salmon pays 4d. unless it brings only one salmon ; and a horse-load, 2d., unless there be only one fish ; and if on a man's back, 1d.

For every 100 lampreys there are due 5 lampreys to the bailiffs to their own use and no other custom.

Every seller of herrings in Lent by retail is to pay 6d. to the king, and a pitcher of wine to the bailiffs, of whatever franchise he be.

The usage of butchers is that every butcher not of the franchise, who keeps a stall, is to pay to the king, of custom 25d. per annum.

All persons, not of the franchise, who bring cattle, sheep, or pigs, and sell them alive, are to pay 5d. a year to the king for custom of paddocks, and to the city clerk, 1d., for enrolling their names, provided the number sold exceeds one. And to this duty all dealers in those animals, not being freemen, who frequent the city, are chargeable, if they come more than once. And they are to stand to their beasts in the paddocks without the West-gate from Michaelmas to St. Nicholas from morning till high tierce, and afterwards in Minster Street, where they are to stand all the rest of the year.

Every baker of bread for sale is charged 2d. per annum to the king, and 1d. to the city clerk ; and he must make white bread, well baked, according to the vend of corn and the assise of the king's marshalsea ; that is to say, if the farthing loaf be at all deficient, beyond 2d. he is to be amerced, and so in proportion to every default within 3 shillings. If the deficiency exceeds 3 shillings he is subject to the judgment of the city.

Every woman selling bread [1] in the High Street, not having the freedom, pays to the king 2 shillings a year, and to the city clerk, 1d., if she sells by the year ; if less, then in proportion. If she sells in the *blind streets*, 6d. or 3d., according to

[1] Cf. *Piers Plowman*, " Prologue," p. 307.

her handiwork; and she is not to procure bread except where the baskets shall stand, on pain of amercement of buyer and seller, before the hour of noon; nor shall she procure bread of any baker from whom she cannot have security. If she does, she shall herself be security for him.

Every baker is to have his known seal on the bread, so that he may not gainsay it when found bad.

Every women who brews for sale [1] within the jurisdiction of the city is to make good beer, according to the price of corn and the appointed assize, on pain of amercement to the king on conviction by the bailiffs.

In like manner no man, whatever his trade, not free of the city, can keep a shop, or sell or buy within its jurisdiction, without compounding with the bailiffs.

Every cart sold in the city to a non-freeman pays to the king a halfpenny.

The following are the petty customs of the city, viz.—

A stone of wool brought separately into the city by a non-freeman pays a farthing to the king; two together, a farthing; three, a halfpenny; four or five, the like sum; six or seven, 3 farthings; eight, 1d.; and if one man brings nine stone, either separately or together, at one time, he shall pay 2d. to the king for pesage, of whatever franchise he be. And the like duty is payable for cheese, butter, lard,[2] and suet, as in the case of wool. In these cases as much is due for each separate half weight as for whole weight; and where pesage attaches to articles brought for sale, it is payable by whatever weight it may be weighed, and whatever be the franchise of the owner. If any private person or stranger conceals the pesage due from him beyond a night, he is liable to amercement in proportion to his offence.

When tallage is levied in the city by command of the king, or for the common business of the city, six sworn " prudeshomes " are to be chosen by common assent, three from the twenty-four and three from the commonalty, to assess the taillage and to collect and lawfully expend and account for it. And when the mayor, bailiffs, or other " prudeshomes " are absent for the common profit of the city, and at the common expense, they must account to the

---

[1] Cf. *Piers Plowman*, " Prologue," p. 307, also p. 132.   [2] oinct.

above six without delay on their return ; and if any " prudehome " of the city advances money for the use of the city,
it is to be lent by tally, and repaid by the hands of the
same six.

When provision is made for " drinking the guild merchant," the trades of the city are by common assent to
seek suitable persons of good repute to collect the guild,[1]
each of whom ought to have goods to the value of 4 pounds
or more ; and those who shall be so chosen shall be lotted
into four houses,[2] according to the immemorial usage. And
when the guild merchant has been drunk, the four houses
shall assemble themselves to see what they shall have
levied and can levy ; and if any trespass has been done,
amendment is to be made by common assent ; and if
any house be worth more than another, it is to be
charged according to its value. The money so levied
on the four houses is to be paid to the above-mentioned
six " prudeshomes," who are sworn to account to the
" prudeshomes " of the city twice a year by tally or by
writing.

If any one of the twenty-four finds a foreigner within the
city jurisdiction who owes him a debt, he may himself compel
him by distress to come before the bailiffs. And no freeman
of the city ought to give anything to the bailiffs of the city
for making a distress on his private or foreign debtors,
provided he offers gages and pledges to prosecute his suit
against them.

The following customs are taken by the bailiffs at the
gates of Winchester from persons who are not freeman of
the city :

Every cart not carrying corn for sale pays a halfpenny
every time it comes ; a horse-load pays a farthing.

A cart with iron or steel, 2d. ; a horse-load, 1d.

A cart carrying new cart-gear, 2d. ; a horse-load, 1d.

A cart carrying mill-stones, 4d. ; whet-stones, 2d.

A cart carrying tin or lead for sale, 4d. ; a horse-load, 2d.

A cart carrying korc for dyeing, 2d. ; a horse-load, 1d.

Scythes and sickles in a cart pay 1d. ; a horse-load, ½d.

A cart with tanned leather for sale, 2d. ; a horse-load, 1d.

A cart with wood for sale, 4d. ; a horse-load, 1d.

[1] Or, possibly, " to entertain the guild."

[2] hlotez a quatre meisuns.

Every cottar [1] who brings ashes for wood is to pay 6d. a year to the king, and 1d. to the clerk, for enrolling his name, unless he comes only once in the year.

The usage of the mystery [2] of dyeing is that two " prudes-homes " are to be chosen by common assent, and sworn to assay the wood brought by strange merchants for sale, and to enforce the assise against buyer and seller.

Every tanner who has a board in the High Street is to pay 2 shillings a year for the space occupied by him in the street, and 1d. to the clerk in the name of *Tangable* ; and every woman who buys suet or lard by retail pays 1d. at Easter in the name of *Smergable*. Every shoemaker who makes new shoes of cows-leather pays to the city 2d. in the name of *Scogable*.

These usages are binding on freemen as well as others.

The city has a common and authentic seal, with which charters of feoffment of the city are sealed. Such charters are to be in the custody of the *alderman* who shall have delivered seisin under them for a year and a day, and if after that time the charters are presented by the aldermen, who testify due delivery of seisin and the keeping of them without challenge or objection by anyone, then, after bans or pro-clamation made in the city three days before the sealing, they shall be sealed by the above seal and made good for ever.

For the sealing of this seal there is due 7d. for wax, which shall include everything. The seal itself shall be kept under the keys, of which two are to be kept by two " prudes-homes " of the twenty-four, and one by a prudehome of the commonalty ; and the coffer, containing the seal, shall be put into a large coffer closed with two locks, and the key of one kept by a prudehome of the twenty-four, and the key of the other by one of the commonalty. . . .

[The remainder of the document gives a detailed account of the procedure in the city courts.]

[1] chescun cutere ; cf. *Domesday Book*, p. 12.
[2] craft.

H. Extracts from the Regulations of the Guild of Berwick-on-Tweed, 1283

[This guild was formed by uniting into one all the guilds that had previously existed in the town. See Toulmin Smith, *The English Gilds* (Early English Text Society, No. 40, reprinted 1924), pp. 338 sqq.]

X. If any brother die, leaving a daughter true and worthy and of good repute, but undowered, the Guild shall find her a dower, either on marriage, or on going into a religious house.

XII. If a brother is charged, on a matter of life or limb, outside the borough, two or three guildmen shall help him, at the cost of the Guild, for two days ; afterwards, it must be at the brother's cost. If the brother has been rightly charged, he shall be dealt with as the Alderman and Brethren think well.

XV. No leper shall come within the gates of the borough ; and if one gets in by chance, the serjeant shall put him out at once. If one wilfully forces his way in, his clothes shall be taken off him and burnt, and he shall be turned out naked. For we have already taken care that a proper place for lepers shall be kept up outside the town, and that alms shall be there given to them.

XIX. No one shall grind wheat or other grain in hand-mills, unless there be urgent need. The miller must have his share—the thirteenth part for grain, and the twenty-fourth part for malt.

XX. No one, not being a brother of the Guild, shall buy wool, hides, or skins, to sell again, or shall cut cloths, save stranger merchants in the course of trade. Such a one shall have neither Lot nor Cavil with any brother.

XXIII. If anyone buys goods misled by false top samples, amends must be made.

XXVI. No woman shall sell ale, from Easter to Michaelmas, at dearer than twopence a gallon[1] ; nor from Michaelmas till Easter, at dearer than a penny. And the names of the ale-wives shall be registered.

XXIX. Goods shall not be bought up before they reach the market. Goods so bought up, shall be forfeited to the Guild.

XXXVII. Whoever buys a lot of herrings, shall share

[1] Cf. p. 129.

them, at cost price, with the neighbours present at the buying. Anyone not present and wanting some shall pay to the buyer twelve pence for profit.

I. Craft Guild Ordinances

(i) The Gild of Peltyers,[1] Norwich, 1376

[For many Craft Gild Ordinances, see *The English Gilds*, issued by the Early English Text Society in 1870, and edited by Toulmin Smith.]

Constitutiones.—In the name of the Father and Son and Holy Ghost, three persons one God in Trinity ; and in the worship of Saint Mary his dear mother, and of Saint William the Holy Innocent and worthy martyr, and All Saints. In the year of Our Lord Jesus Christ, one thousand three hundred and seventy-six, Peltyers and other good men began this gild and this brotherhood of Saint William the Holy Innocent and martyr in Norwich. And all these ordinances underwritten, all the brethren and sisters shall hold and keep upon their power.

At the first all the brethren and sisters have thus been commanded ; that they, every year, on the Sunday next after the Feast of St. Peter and St. Paul,[2] in worship of the Trinity and Our Lady and St. William and All Saints, shall offer two flowered[3] candles before St. William's Tomb, in the minster of the Trinity, and every one of them offer a half-penny at the Mass, and hear all the Mass. And whosoever shall be absent, then he shall pay to St. William's light three pounds of wax. And it shall be raised and gathered by the Alderman and his fellows. Also a boy child, innocent, shall carry a candle that day, two pounds in weight, led between two good men, betokening the Holy Martyr.

Also it is ordained, that no man shall be excused for absence from that Mass, except it be for the king's service, or for serious sickness, or for dwelling twenty miles from this city, that he should not pay the penalty of three pounds of wax.

And whosoever shall be excused for any other reason, it shall be at the will of the Alderman and of the Company.

[1] Furriers. [2] 29th June. [3] *i.e.* dressed with flowers.

Also all the brethren and sisters have ordained and granted, for any ordinance that is made or shall be made amongst them, that they shall save the king his rights, and that no injury be done against his law and ordinance.

Also it is ordained, that every brother and sister of this gild, early on the morrow after the gild day, shall hear a requiem mass for the souls of all the brothers and sisters of this gild, and for all Christian souls at St. William's altar in the minster of the Trinity at Norwich and offer a farthing. And whosoever be absent shall pay a pound of wax.

And when the mass is done, by their Alderman's consent they shall go all together to an Inn. And every man that has any property of the gild shall lay it down ; and they shall make ordinances there according to their desires by common assent, and choose officers for the next year. And whosoever fails shall pay two pounds of wax.

And eight men of the Alderman's choosing, on the gild day, shall choose an alderman, and two fellows, and a beadle, for the next year.

Also it is ordained, in the worship of the Trinity and of Our Lady St. Mary, and of St. William and of All Saints, that whatsoever brother or sister, by God's sending, fall into trouble or misease, and have not wherewith to help himself, he shall have alms of every brother and every sister every week, a farthing, as long as his trouble lasts ; of which farthings he shall have fourteen pence and the remainder shall go to the property [of the Guild]. But if the trouble be the outcome of his folly he shall not have of the alms.

Also it is ordained by common consent, that whosoever be chosen in office, and refuse it, he shall pay to St. William's light three pounds of wax,[1] and in accordance with the penalty of his oath.

Also if any brother or sister die, he shall have of the guild four tapers, and four poor men clothed, around his body. And every brother and sister shall make an offering at his mass, and hear the whole of the mass, and wait for his interring, and at mass offer a farthing and a halfpenny given as alms for his soul. And there shall be given towards a mass a penny, which shall be gathered by the alderman and his fellows, the mass to be done for his soul and the souls of all Christians.

[1] Cf. p. 138, etc.

Also if any brother or sister die seven miles from the city, the Alderman and seven other brethren, at his burial services, shall go in company to the body and ordain and do for his soul as is done for one of the brethren.

Also it is ordained, by common assent, that these brethren, in worship of the Holy Trinity and St. William, shall eat together that day at their common cost.

And whosoever be summoned to the assembly or meeting before the alderman and the brethren, and come not, he shall pay a pound of wax to the light.

Also it is ordained, by common assent, that no brother nor sister in this gild shall be received except by the alderman and twelve brethren.

Also it is ordained by common consent that the common bellman shall go through the city on the gild day, after noon, and recommend the souls of all the brethren and sisters by name, and all Christian souls ; and say that a Requiem mass shall be said early on the morrow, at dawn, as a memorial of their souls and the souls of all Christians ; and summoning all the brethren and sisters, that they be at the mass at the altar of St. William at the time of Prime,[1] on pain of three pounds of wax.

(ii) THE GUILD OF CORDWAINERS, EXETER

To all men that shall see or hear these presents, greeting in Our Lord everlasting. Whereas the master of the Craft of Cordwainers, of the fraternity of the Blessed Trinity, in the City of Exeter, hath divers times in humble wise, sued to the honourable mayor and bailiffs, and common council of the said city, concerning the said Craft, under the favour of the said mayor, bailiffs and common council in reforming divers inconveniences that have been down before this time, and hereafter might ensue, and for the conservation of the polite government of the same, to the lawde and honour of the said fraternity of the Blessed Trinity, and the weel of the king, our sovereign lord's people. Wherefore Mayor, bailiffs and common council, considering their desires, will and grant that the Master and Wardens of the said craft shall enjoy and use such ordinances and rules within the jurisdiction of the said city as followeth.

[1] The first office of the day, said about 6 a.m.

First, that the said Master and Wardens, and their successors with three other men of the said craft convenient, shall make due search, at all times, of everything necessary pertaining to the said craft, as by sufferance they have used within the jurisdiction of the said city ; that is to wit, of all white leather and dry boots, thigh boots, galaches,[1] pattens,[2] and all other ware pertaining to the said craft, made and unmade, which is deceitfully wrought, as in tanning, currying, cutting or sowing, or in any otherwise made, whereby the king's liege people should be deceived ; that then such goods so found defective, to be by the said Master and Wardens forfeited and taken ; and to be valued lawfully in the Guild Hall of the said city ;—half of the same to go to the profit of the said city, and the other half to the profit of the said fraternity.

Also whereas they have an election amongst the said craft, of a Master and Wardens for the convenient government of the same ; that he that is so elected by the said fraternity to be a master, if he were to refuse to take the governance upon him, so that an inordinate rule should ensue, that then he so elected, for his refusal should pay twenty shillings ; half whereof to be to the profit of the said city, and the other half to the profit of the said fraternity so often as they so do offend.

Also whereas the said fraternity have, by sufferance, to elect Wardens of the said craft, for the year following, whereof two of them shall be shop-holders, and two other journeymen, within the said city ; that if he so elect for the warden of the shop-holders, refuse to take upon him, to forfeit thirteen shillings and four pence ; half thereof to the profit of the said city, and the other half to the profit of the said fraternity, as oft as it shall so happen to offend. And if any of the journeymen of the said craft be elected Warden, refuse to take the office of Wardenship, that then they forfeit six shillings and eightpence ; the one half to be to the profit of the said city, and the other half to the profit of the said fraternity, as often as it shall happen.

Also, if any person of the said craft, whatsoever degree or condition he be of, be warned in reasonable time, to come

---

[1] pyncouz : a word of doubtful meaning; it probably means "high unsoled shoes of thin leather."

[2] galegez.

before the said Master and Wardens, at their place accustomed, and he so warned absent him, and no reasonable excuse had, that then for every default so done, that they shall pay for the said disobedience three shillings and fourpence ; the said city to have the one half and the said fraternity the other half.

Also that no manner of man, whatsoever condition he be of, of the said craft, hold no open shop within the jurisdiction of the said city, except he be an enfranchised man, according to the old custom contained in the black roll of the said city, upon pain of six shillings and eightpence ; half to the profit of the said city, and the other half to the profit of the said fraternity.

Also, that no manner of man of the said craft, dwelling within the jurisdiction of the said city, as well in the suburbs as in the city, wear the livery of any lord or other gentleman upon pain of six shillings and eightpence ; the half thereof to the profit of the said city, the other half to the profit of the said fraternity.

Also, that if any shop-holder of the said craft within the said city, set any man awork by the space of a month, that the stranger is to pay fourpence to the wax of the said fraternity ; and that he that so setteth him awork shall answer for the said fourpence.

Also, that no man of the said craft in the said city, set any man to work that is retainèd in any man's service, on the time that he be had, in examination before the said master, wardens and fellowship, to understand the departure of him ; if any do the contrary, he to forfeit six shillings and eightpence ; the half thereof to the profit of the said city, the other half to the profit of the said fraternity.

And also, if any man of the said mystery, of whatsoever degree or condition he be, that such sums of money as he or they have been set to pay, for the sustentation of the Priest and of their chapel, after being once warned, refuse to pay his due, he shall loose for every default forty pence ; and that every master answer for his servants to the same, upon the same penalty : the forfeit whereof, the one half to go to the city, the other half to the said fraternity.

Provided alway, that the said Master and Wardens of the said Mystery, shall come every year to the Guild Hall of the said City, the next Monday upon the election of the new Mayor, Bailiffs, and other officers of the said city ; and there by the payment of fourpence, to surrender all their said power on to the said Mayor, Bailiffs and commonalty ; and then and there to take and resume it, by the new Mayor's grant, of the said city, according to the said enrollment under the seal of office, without any fees therefore to be paid ; provided also, that the liberties of the said city, franchises, and old usages, alway be saved, and in no wise interrupted by the said grant.

And that these said ordinances and constitutions with other convenient rules, as accordeth with reason, shall be firm and stable, we the said Mayor, bailiffs and common council have had them enrolled in a roll, bearing the date the Monday next after the Purification of Our Lady [1] in the twenty-first year of the reign of the king and sovereign lord, King Edward the IVth,[2] amongst the records of the said city.

(iii) THE GUILD OF ST. MARY, LYNN

[Toulmin Smith, *English Gilds*, pp. 65 sqq.]

IN the worship of Jesus Christ of Heaven, and of His dear worthy Mother, Saint Mary, and of the Purification, in whose worship this fraternity is begun. By the will of the Brothers and Sisters of the Guild, to have four " morning speeches " by the year. The first " morning speech " shall be on the first general day, after meat ; the second shall be on the Sunday next after St. Dunstan's Day [3] in May ; the third shall be the Sunday next after St. Matthew's Day ; [4] the fourth shall be on the Sunday before St. Thomas' Day [5] before Christmas Day. And also if any brother or sister be summoned to any of these " morning speeches," and he be in town, and he will not come, nor make any attourney for himself, nor ask leave of the alderman, he shall pay, to amendment of the light, half a pound of wax,[6] unless he have grace. And if the dean faileth of his summons, he shall pay, for every brother or sister one penny. And whoever enters into this fraternity, he shall pay the rights of the house ; that is for to say, to the alderman one penny ;

---

[1] 2nd February.   [2] 1481.
[3] 19th May.   [4] 21st September.
[5] 21st December.   [6] Cf. p. 134, etc.

the clerk a halfpenny ; the dean a halfpenny ; and for wax a halfpenny. And if any brother or sister of the Guild be dead, the dean shall bring the candles of the guild to the " dirige," and warn all the brothers and sisters to come after, giving for the dead a farthing, and a farthing for alms ; and he that offers not for the dead, he shall pay to amendment of the light, one penny. And whoso betrays the counsel of this Guild to any strange man or woman, he shall pay to amendment of the light, a pound of wax. And if the alderman be chosen and he forsake his office, he shall pay, to amendment of the light, two pounds of wax ; every " skevyn " half a pound ; the dean half a pound of wax. And if any brother or sister of this Guild be dead, he shall have masses for his soul of the proper chattels of the Guild, that is to wit, xii masses. And whoso enters the chamber where the ale lieth in, and asks not leave of the officers of the Guild, he shall pay, for amendment of the light, one penny, unless he have grace. Also the dean shall have for his work, by the year sixpence ; the clerk eightpence. Also the " skevyns " that have the chattels of the Guild, they shall find sureties for the chattels, to bring [an account of it] before the alderman and the Guild brothers and sisters at general " morning speech." He that does not, he shall pay, to amendment of the light, two pounds of wax, unless he have grace. And that no man remain in the house where the Guild is held longer than the Alderman : he that does, he shall pay, to amendment of light, one penny, unless he have grace. And the Alderman shall have for his allowance, in time of drinking, two gallons of ale ; every " skevyn " a gallon ; the clerk a pottle ; [1] and the Dean a pottle.[1] Also, if any brother or sister be sick, of this Guild, in time of drinking, he shall have a pottle of ale. Also, if any brother or sister of this Guild falleth in poverty, and may not help himself, he shall have, of every brother or sister, at each " morning speech " a penny. And whoso enters into this fraternity, he shall pay for his entry two shillings, and find two sureties for the chattels.

Robert Thornegge, warden of the same [Guild] has in goods five shillings.

[1] *i.e.* half a gallon.

J. Indenture of Apprenticeship, 1459

[Ancient Deeds, A. 10,022.]

THIS indenture made between John Gibbs of Penzance in the County of Cornwall of the one part and John Goffe, Spaniard, of the other part, witnesses that the aforesaid John Goffe has put himself to the aforesaid John Gibbs to learn the craft of fishing, and to stay with him as apprentice and to serve from the feast of Philip and James [1] next to come after the date of these presents until the end of eight years then next ensuing and fully complete ; throughout which term the aforesaid John Goffe shall well and faithfully serve the aforesaid John Gibbs and Agnes his wife as his masters and lords, shall keep their secrets, shall everywhere willingly do their lawful and honourable commands, shall do his masters no injury, nor see injury done to them by others, but prevent the same, as far as he can, shall not waste his master's goods nor lend them to any man without his special command. And the aforesaid John Gibbs and Agnes his wife shall teach, train and inform or cause the aforesaid John Goffe, their apprentice, to be informed in the craft of fishing in the best way they know, chastising him duly, and finding for the same John, their apprentice, food, clothing, linen and woollen, and shoes, sufficiently, as befits such an apprentice to be found, during the term aforesaid. And at the end of the term aforesaid the aforesaid John Goffe shall have of the aforesaid John Gibbs and Agnes his wife twenty shillings sterling without any fraud. In witness whereof the parties aforesaid have interchangeably set their seals to the parts of this indenture. These witnesses : Richard Bascawen, Robert Martyn and Robert Cosyn and many others. Given at Penzance, 1 April in the thirty-seventh year [2] of the reign of King Henry the Sixth after the conquest of England.

II. UNIVERSITIES

A. Extract from a Letter from Theobald of Etampes to Faricius, Abbot of Abingdon, about 1115

[This is one of the earliest mentions of Oxford as a place of learning. Theobald here describes himself as a "Master at

[1] 1st May. [2] 1459.

Oxford "—an expression which some have thought to imply the existence of a university at Oxford as early as this. Faricius was Abbot of Abingdon from 1101 to 1117 : consequently the letter must have been written some time before the latter date. This letter is printed in D'Archery's *Spicilegium*, vol. iii.]

THEOBALD, Master at Oxford, to Faricius, Venerable Prelate of the Church of Abingdon and his undoubted friend. . . .

[Here he repels a charge made by the Abbot of false teaching on the subject of unbaptized infants.]

. . . but if any enemy of truth wishes to raise an outcry against the Catholic statement, I am ready to refute that impious wretch and vile dog, both in speech and in writing. . . .

[He concludes with compliments to the Convent, and especially to his friend, the Prior.]

B. THE LECTURES OF ROBERT PULLEIN AT OXFORD, 1133

Extract from the Oseney Chronicle

[Oseney Abbey was founded in 1129. But this Chronicle begins in the year 1016. It is edited by Luard in the Rolls Series, *Annales Monastici*, vol. iv. p. 19.]

IN the year 1133. Master Robert Pullein began to lecture at Oxford on the Holy Scriptures, which had come to be neglected in England. Afterwards when the Church both in England and in France had profited much from his teaching he was sent for by Pope Lucius II. and made Chancellor of the Holy Roman Church.

C. THE MIRACULOUS CURE OF AN OXFORD STUDENT, *circa* 1180

[From the " Historia Miraculorum Sanctae Frideswidae Virginis, cum prologo per Philippum ejusdem Monasterii Priorem," *Acta Sanctorum*, vol. viii. p. 579. The passage is of interest owing to its early date, *circa* 1180.]

THERE was at that time staying at Oxford for purposes of study a certain clerk named Stephen, a Yorkshireman, in the flower of his youth and of unusually handsome appearance. He was attacked by a quotidian fever, and hastened to avail himself of medical assistance. And by so doing he only impoverished himself for no purpose, for the fever grew worse and worse every day. When, therefore, human help failed he sought as a last resort the help of God, and now extremely emaciated, with his limbs scarce holding together, eyes leaden, and face ghastly pale, he implored the patronage of the glorious Virgin. Then, having drunk a goblet of holy water, the fever died down, his strength in a little while returned and he was completely restored to health.

D. Giraldus Cambrensis reads his Work on the Topography of Ireland at Oxford, 1186

[For a notice of Giraldus Cambrensis, see Chapter V. p. 151. *Extract from De Rebus a se Gesto*, c. xvi. (Rolls Series, ed. Brewer, vol. i. pp. 72–73).]

THE work having been completed and revised in the process of time, desiring not to place his light under a bushel but on a candlestick that it might give light, he resolved to read his work at Oxford, where the clergy in England most did congregate, and excelled in clerkly lore, before that great audience.[1] And since his book was in three divisions and one division a day was read, the readings lasted three days in succession ; and the first day he invited and entertained at his lodgings all the poor of the entire town. Next day he entertained all the doctors of the various faculties and their more distinguished pupils. On the third day he entertained the rest of the Scholars together with the knights [2] of the town and many burgesses. It was a sumptuous and noble function ; for the authentic and ancient times of the poets were thus in some measure renewed ; neither the present day nor the days of old can recall such a great solemnity's ever having taken place in England.

E. Nominalism and Realism

[The following extract from Boethius' translation of the *Isagoge* of Porphyry launched the great debate between the Nominalists and the Realists of medieval Universities.]

THE question concerning genera and species—whether they have a substantial existence or are found only in bare

[1] apud Oxoniam, ubi Clerus in Anglia magis vigebat et clericatu praecellebat, opus suum in tanta audentia recitare disposuit.
[2] milites.

concepts of the mind ; whether supposing them to have a substantial existence, they are corporeal or incorporeal, and whether again they are found a part from things   which the Senses can perceive, or exist in those things and with them and about them, I shall forbear to say. For this kind of question is a very deep one and demands a fuller investigation.[1]

F. A CORONER'S INQUEST IN OXFORD, 1297

[This is translated from *Oxford City Documents, 1268–1665*, edited by Thorold Rogers for the Oxford Historical Society (Clarendon Press, 1891), pp. 150 sqq. It is the record of the inquest on John Metescharp, February 6, 1297, and a good illustration of the lawlessness of medieval students, which led to such strained relations between town and university.]

IT happened on the Monday next after the Feast of the Purification of the Blessed Virgin Mary [2] in the 25th year of the reign of King Edward that John Metescharp of Oxford died in the house of Radulf " le Cyrgien " in the Parish of St. Aldate's Oxford and was viewed the same day by John de Oseney, the Coroner of Our Lord the King, and he had a wound in his left side half a thumb in width and five thumbs in depth in which was a small arrow.[3] And the same day an inquest was held before the aforesaid Coroner by the oaths of Thomas de Morton, Thomas " le Parmenter," John de Staunford, Richard de Bampton, Thomas de Lewes, Walter the Smith and Thomas " le Turnur," Jurors of the parish of St. Aldate's, Nicholas de Lyncoln, Nicholas de Weston, Richard Sutton, John de Themele, William Kynge and John le Furnur, Jurors of the parish of St. Ebbs, Adam de Tylhurst, William de Godestowe, Richard de Eynsham, Alexander de Bloxham, Robert de Quenynton, and Robert de Fulbroke, Jurors of the parish of St. Peter in the Bailey, Thomas de Weston, Thomas de Boleworth, Walter de Eynesham and Gilbert de Couele, Jurors of the Parish of St. Martin.   And all the aforesaid Jurors say upon oath that on

---

[1] " Mox de generibus et speciebus illud quidem sive subsistant sive in solis nudis intellectibus posita sint, sive subsistantia corporalia sint an incorporalia, et utrum separata a sensibilibus an in sensibilibus posita et circa haec consistentia, dicere recusabo ; altissimum enim negotium est hujusmodi et majoris egens inquisitionis."

[2] February 2.   [3] cum quadam sagitta minuta.

Saturday in the Feast of the Purification of the Blessed Virgin Mary in the aforesaid year, one Michael, Manciple of the clerks dwelling in Bolehall in the parish of St. Aldate's and one John de Skurf, a clerk, and one Madoc, a Welsh clerk went through the streets with swords and arrows and bows [1] after the hour of curfew and molested all the passers-by. Wherefore a hue-and-cry was raised, and the aforesaid John Metescharp and others hearing the hue-and-cry came out of their houses to keep the peace of Our Lord the King and as soon as the aforesaid John came into the street, the aforesaid Michael shot him with an arrow and inflicted upon him the above mentioned wound, whereof he died on the day aforesaid, but he had all the ordinances of the Church, and immediately after the aforesaid deed the aforesaid Michael and all the others fled so that they could not be arrested, nor could any of their goods be found.

G. Licences to Beg given to Scholars

Extract from a Statute made at Cambridge, 1388

[From *Enactments in Parliament specially concerning the Universities of Oxford and Cambridge*, edited by L. L. Shadwell, 1912, vol. i. pp. 2 sqq.]

For the common profit and universal wealth of all the Realm of England, our Lord the King at his Parliament holden at Cambridge, the morrow after the nativity of Our Lady, the Twelfth Year of his Reign, by the assent of the Lords and Commons there assembled, hath made certain Statutes and Ordinances in the Form following.

．　　　．　　　．　　　．　　　．

VII. Item, It is accorded and assented, that of every person that goeth begging, and is able to serve or labour, it shall be done of him as of him that departeth out of the Hundred and other Places aforesaid without Letter Testimonial as afore is said, except People of Religion, and Hermits having Letters testimonial of their Ordinaries. And that the Beggars impotent to serve, shall abide in the Cities and Towns where they be dwelling at the Time of the Proclamation of this Statute ; and if the People of Cities or other Towns will not or may not suffice to find them, that

[1] Cf. p. 147.

then the said Beggars shall draw them to other Towns within the Hundreds, Rape, or Wakentake, or to the Towns where they were born, within Forty Days after the Proclamation made, and there shall continually abide during their Lives. And that of all them that go in Pilgrimage as Beggars, and be able to travail, it shall be done as of the said Servants and Labourers, if they have no letters testimonial of their pilgrimage under the said seals. And that the Scholars of the Universities [1] that go so begging, have Letters testimonial of their Chancellor upon the same Pain.

H. The Mythical Origin of Oxford

Extract from the " Historia Regum Angliae " of John Rous

[John Rouse was a chantry priest at Warwick. He lived a large portion of his life at Oxford, and was famous for his work as an antiquary. He wrote the Chronicle from which the following extract is taken towards the close of the fifteenth century. He died, according to Leland, on 24th January 1491.]

ABOUT this time Samuel the Servant of God was judge in Judæa ; and king Magdan had two sons ; that is to say Mempricius and Malun. The younger of the two having been treacherously killed by the elder, he left the kingdom to the fratricide. He (Mempricius) was a man full of envy and cruelty, and according to that passage in the second of Proverbs, " Anger hath no mercy," so had he none, but he was against everyone and everyone against him. This Mempricius entered upon his rule as a monarch badly, and he continued his rule still worse by killing his nobles. At length, in the twentieth year of his reign, he was surrounded by a large pack of very savage wolves, and being torn and devoured by them, ended his existence in a horrible manner. Nothing good is related of him except that he begot an honest son and heir by name Ebrancus, and built one noble city which he called from his own name *Caer-Memre*, but which afterwards in course of time was called *Bellisitum*, then *Caerbossa*, at length *Ridohen*, and last of all *Oxonia*, or by the Saxons *Oxenfordia*, from a certain egress out of a neighbouring ford ; which name it bears to the present day. There arose here in after years an universal and noble seat

[1] Cf. Chaucer's " Clerk of Oxenford," p. 285.

of learning, derived from the renowned University of Grek-laad.[1]

It is situated between the rivers Thames and Cherwell which meet there. This city, just as Jerusalem, has, to all appearance, been changed ; for as Mount Calvary, when Christ was crucified, was just outside the walls of the city, and is now contained within the circuit of the walls ; so also now there is a large level space outside Oxford contiguous to the walls of the town which is called Belmount, and which means beautiful mount ; and this in a certain way agrees with one of the older names of the city before named and recited ; that is to say Bellisitum ; whence many are of opinion that the University from Greklaad was transferred to this very *Bellus mons* or *Bellesitum* before the coming of the Saxons, and while the Britons ruled in the island ; and the Church of St. Giles, which was dedicated under the name of some other saint, was the place for the creation of graduates, as now is the Church of St. Mary which is within the walls. Of this noble University I shall touch more fully when I come to the times of King Alfred.

.   .   .   .

He [King Alfred] amongst the praiseworthy acts of his munificence, in the year 873 at the instigation of St. Nest established public schools for the several arts in Oxford ; to which city on account of his special love for the scholars he granted many privileges, not allowing anyone who was illiterate to be promoted to any dignity. The Masters and Scholars, who had been converted to the faith taught in the Monasteries and in other places set apart according to the manner of the ancient Schools of Greklade, Lecklade, Stamford, Caerleon, Cambridge and Bellisitum, and of such other schools [2] of this kind as were already in the island. . . .

At the first foundation of this University this noble King Alfred established at his own expense within the city of Oxford three Doctors, namely in Grammar, in the Arts, and in Theology, in three different places in the name of the Holy Trinity. In one of these which was situated in High Street [3] towards the East Gate he endowed the hall with all that was necessary for twenty-six grammarians ; and because of its inferiority in knowledge, he ordered it to be called " *Parva Aula Universitatus* " ; and so it was called in my own

---

[1] Cricklade, in Wilts.   [2] studia.   [3] in alto vico.

time. Towards the northern walls of the city in what is now called " *Vicus Scholarum* " he founded another Hall with abundance of means necessary for twenty-six Logicians or Philosophers, and this he ordered to be called " *Aula Minor Universitatis.*" The third Hall, which he founded in High Street, near East gate and close to the first on the west side, he called *Aula Magna* and arranged for twenty-six theologians who should promote the study of Holy Scripture, and for this he provided abundant means to meet their costs.

Besides this there grew up in a short time many other Halls of the different faculties, established by the burgesses of the city and of the neighbourhood and then by those from a distance ; yet not at the King's expense, but through the King's gracious example.

I. A STATUTE OF 1421 RELATING TO UNIVERSITY DISCIPLINE

[From L. L. Shadwell, *Enactments in Parliament*, vol. i. pp. 15 sqq.]

AT the Parliament holden in Westminster, the Second Day of May, the Ninth year of the Reign of King Henry the Fifth after the Conquest, the same our Lord the King, by the Assent of the Lords Spiritual and Temporal, and at the special instance and request of the Commons, assembled in the same Parliament, hath caused to be ordained and stablished certain Statutes and Ordinances in the Form following.

. . . .

VIII. Item, Because that many Clerks and Scholars of the University of Oxford unknown, armed, and arrayed in the Manner of War,[1] have oftentimes disseised and put out divers Persons of their Lands and Tenements in the Counties of Oxford, Berks, and Bucks, and also have hunted with Dogs and Greyhounds in divers Warrens, Parks and Forests in the same Counties, as well by days as by nights, and taken Deer, Hares and Conies, and moreover threatening the Keepers of the same of their Lives ; and also with strong Hand taken Clerks convict of Felony by due Process of the Law, out of the Ward of the Ordinaries, and those Prisoners have brought with them, and let go at large, as the King, by

[1] Cf. p. 144.

open complaint to him made in this Parliament, hath conceived : Our said Sovereign Lord the King, willing upon the same to set Remedy, hath ordained and established, That due Process shall be made against such Scholars wrong doers, for their Offences, as the Law and also the statutes of the Land require, according to the Case, till they come to answer, or else be outlawed. And if any such Scholar be so outlawed, then the Justices before whom such Outlawry shall be returned, shall certify the Chancellor of the said University, for the time being, of the same Outlawry ;[1] and that the same Chancellor upon such Certification had, shall do to be banished maintenant, and without Difficulty, such Outlaws out of the same University, upon Pain that pertaineth. And that this Ordinance endure till the next Parliament to be holden, after the King's Return from beyond the Sea into England.

[1] Et si ascun tiel escoler soit ensi utlagee, adonques les Justices devaunt queux celle Utlagarie soit retournee facent certifier le Chanceller del Universite suisdicte pur le temps esteant de mesme Utlagarie.

CHAPTER V

THE AGE OF THE CRUSADES

I. The First Crusade : Extract from William of Malmesbury's *Chronicle of the Kings of England.*
II. Extracts from the *Itinerarium Kambriae* of Giraldus Cambrensis.
III. Extracts from Joinville's *Chronicle of the Crusade of St. Louis.*
IV. Extracts from the *Voyages and Travels* of Sir John Maundeville—
    A. Introduction.
    B. To Teach you the Way out of England to Constantinople.
    C. How the Earth and Sea are of Round Form, as is proved by the Star called Antarctic, which is Fixed in the South.
    D. Prester John.
V. Extracts from Roger Bacon—
    A. Bacon's Labours and Difficulties.
    B. A Plea for the Study of Books in their Original Languages.
    C. The Importance of Mathematics.
    D. The Necessity of Experiment.
    E. Forecast of Mechanical Inventions.

I. THE FIRST CRUSADE : EXTRACT FROM WILLIAM OF MALMESBURY'S *CHRONICLE OF THE KINGS OF ENGLAND*

[A notice of William of Malmesbury appears at the head of Section II., Chapter I. p. 19.]

IN the month of November [1] in which this Council [of Clermont] was held, each departed to his home : and the report of this good resolution soon becoming general it gently wafted a cheering gale over the minds of Christians :

----

[1] 1095.

which being universally diffused, there was no nation so
remote, no people so retired, as not to contribute its portion.
This ardent love not only inspired the continental provinces,
but even all who had heard the name of Christ, whether
in the most distant islands, or savage countries.   The Welshman left his hunting ; the Scot his fellowship with lice ; the
Dane his drinking party ; the Norwegian his raw fish.   Lands
were deserted of husbandmen ; houses of their inhabitants ;
even whole cities migrated.   There was no regard of relation-
ship ; affection to their country was held in little esteem ;
God alone was placed before their eyes.   Whatever was stored
in granaries, or hoarded in chambers, to answer the hopes
of the avaricious husbandman, or the covetousness of the
miser, all, all was deserted ; they hungered and thirsted after
Jerusalem alone. . . . You might see the husband departing
with his wife, indeed, with all his family ; you would smile
to see the whole household laden on a carriage about to
proceed on their journey. . . . The number surpassed all
human imagination, though the itinerants were estimated
at six millions. . . .

In the fourth year, then, of the expedition to Jerusalem,
and the third after the capture of Nice, and the second after
that of Antioch, the Franks laid siege to Jerusalem—a city
well able to repay the toils of war. . . . As they saw, therefore, that the city was difficult to carry on account of the
steep precipices, the strength of the walls, and the fierceness
of the enemy, they ordered engines to be constructed. . . .
There was one engine which we call the Sow, the ancients
Vinaea ; because the machine, which is constructed of slight
timbers, the roof covered with boards and wickerwork, and
the sides defended with undressed hides, protects those who
are within it, who, after the manner of a sow, proceed to
undermine the foundations of the walls. . . . During the
whole of that day the battle was such that neither party
seemed to think they had been worsted ; on the following
which was the fifteenth of July [1099], the business was
decided. . . . There was no place of refuge for the Turks,
so indiscriminately did the insatiable rage of the victors
sweep away both the suppliant and the resisting.   Ten thousand were slain in the Temple of Solomon ; more were thrown
from the tops of the churches and of the citadel. . . . The
city being thus expiated by the slaughter of the infidels,

they proceeded with hearts contrite and bodies prostrate
to the sepulchre of the Lord, which they had so long earnestly
sought after, and for which they had undergone so many
labours.

II. EXTRACTS FROM THE *ITINERARIUM KAMBRIAE* OF GIRALDUS CAMBRENSIS

[Gerald " the Welshman " (Cambrensis) was born about 1147 at
Marnobier Castle, Pembrokeshire. On his father's side he was
of Norman blood ; but he was descended through his mother
from Rhys ap Tewdwr Mawr, the last independent prince of
South Wales. His grandmother was the beautiful Princess
Nesta, whose romantic love affairs have made her one of the
famous characters of the Middle Ages. In spite of the fact that
his uncles were heroic soldiers, who played no small part in the
Conquest of Ireland, Gerald devoted himself to the life of a
cleric. He studied, and afterwards lectured, at Paris, paid
several visits to Rome, and afterwards became Court Chaplain
to King Henry II. He accompanied Prince John to Ireland—a
visit which resulted in his *Topographia Hibernica*, on which he
afterwards lectured at Oxford. In 1188 he accompanied Archbishop Baldwin on a journey through Wales to preach the Third
Crusade. The following extracts are taken from his record of
this expedition, the *Itinerarium Kambriae*, which he composed
shortly afterwards, and revised in later years. Gerald was
Archdeacon of Brecon ; and set his ambition on becoming
Bishop of St. David's. He was offered other bishoprics by
Richard I. and John, but refused them, caring for none but the
See of St. David's. Twice, at least, in the course of his lifetime
he thought that he had at last gained the coveted See, only to
be bitterly disappointed. For many years he fought hard in
an attempt to make the Welsh Church independent of Canterbury, but without success. He removed in 1216 to a life of
scholarly retirement at Lincoln, where he remained till his
death in 1223. Gerald was one of the most learned men of that
age of intellectual ferment which called the universities into
existence. The range of subjects which interested him, and his
linguistic knowledge, particularly, is quite wonderful. His
works are characterized by a shrewd knowledge of men and
things, and a power of vivid portrayal of incidents and characters. Notice also in these extracts his vanity and credulity.
    Gerald's works were published in the Rolls Series during the
middle of the last century. In addition to the *Itinerarium
Kambriae* and the *Topographia Hibernica*, already mentioned,
they include the *Expugnatio Hibernica, Descripto Kambriae,
Gemma Ecclesiastica, De Rebus a se Gestis, De Instructione Princi-*

pum, etc. A handy volume of the *Itinerarium Kambriae* is issued in Dent's Everyman's Library under the title *The Itinerary through Wales.* See also *The Historical Works of Giraldus Cambrensis*, edited by Thomas Wright (H. G. Bohn, 1863).]

IN the year 1188 of the Incarnation of Our Lord, Urban the Third being the head of the Apostolic See ;[1] Frederick,[2] emperor of Germany and king of the Romans ; Isaac, emperor of Constantinople ; Philip, the son of Louis, reigning in France ; Henry the Second in England ; William in Sicily ; Bela in Hungary ; and Guy in Palestine : in that same year, when Saladin, prince of the Egyptians and Damascenes, by a signal victory possessed himself of the kingdom of Jerusalem ; Baldwin, archbishop of Canterbury, a venerable man, distinguished for his learning and sanctity, journeying from England for the service of the holy cross, entered Wales near the borders of Herefordshire.

The archbishop proceeded to Radnor, on Ash Wednesday,[3] accompanied by Ranulph de Glanville, privy counsellor and justiciar of the whole kingdom, and there met Rhys, son of Gruffyd,[4] prince of South Wales, and many other nobles of those parts ; where a sermon being preached by the archbishop, upon the subject of the Crusades, and explained to the Welsh by an interpreter, the author of this Itinerary, impelled by the urgent importunity and promises of the king, and the persuasions of the archbishop and the justiciar, arose the first, and falling down at the feet of the holy man, devoutly took the sign of the cross. His example was instantly followed by Peter, bishop of St. David's, a monk of the abbey of Cluny, and then by Eineon, son of Eineon Clyd, prince of Elvenia, and many other persons. Eineon rising up, said to Rhys, whose daughter he had married, " My father and lord ! with your permission I hasten to revenge the injury offered to the Great Father of All." Rhys himself was so fully determined upon the holy pilgrimage, as soon as the archbishop should enter his territories on his return, that for nearly fifteen days he was employed with great solicitude in making

---

[1] As a matter of fact Urban III. died in October 1187. Clement III. was Pope at this time.

[2] *i.e.* Frederick Barbarossa.

[3] Caput Jejunii.

[4] He was grandson of Rhys ap Tewdwr. Rhys, son of Gruffyd, was a prince of most brilliant gifts, and made a conspicuous figure in Welsh history. His effigy may be seen in St. David's Cathedral.

the necessary preparations for so distant a journey ; till his wife, and, according to the common vicious licence of the country, his relation in the fourth degree, Gwenllian, daughter of Madoc, prince of Powys, by female artifices diverted him wholly from his noble purpose ; since, as Solomon says, " A man's heart deviseth his way, but the Lord directeth his steps." As Rhys before his departure was conversing with his friends concerning the things he had heard, a distinguished young man of his family, by name Gruffydd, who afterwards took the cross, is said thus to have answered : " What man of spirit can refuse to undertake this journey, since, amongst all imaginable inconveniences, nothing worse can happen to any one than to return." [1]

On the arrival of Rhys in his own territory, certain canons of Saint David's, through a zeal for their church, having previously secured the interest of some of the prince's courtiers, waited on Rhys, and endeavoured by every possible suggestion to induce him not to permit the archbishop to proceed into the interior parts of Wales, and particularly to the metropolitan see of Saint David's (a thing hitherto unheard of), at the same time asserting that if he should continue his intended journey, the church would in future experience great prejudice, and with difficulty would recover its ancient dignity and honour. Although these pleas were most strenuously urged, the natural kindness and civility of the prince would not suffer them to prevail, lest by prohibiting the archbishop's progress, he might appear to wound his feelings.

Early on the following morning, after the celebration of mass, and the return of Ranulph de Glanville [2] to England, we came to Cruker Castle, two miles distant from Radnor, where a strong and valiant youth, named Hector, conversing with the archbishop about taking the cross, said, " If I had the means of getting provisions for one day, and of keeping fast on the next, I would comply with your advice " ; on the following day, however, he took the cross. The same evening, Malgo, son of Cadwallon, prince of Melenia, after a short but efficacious exhortation from the archbishop, and not without

[1] " Quis ' inquam ' animi virilis peregrinationis hujus iter abhorreat, cum inter universa quae excogitari poterunt ejus incommoda, nihil incommodius cuiquam, nihil deterius accidere possit quam redire,"

[2] Cf. Jocelyn de Brakelonde's *Chronicle*, p. 83.

the tears and lamentations of his friends, was marked with the sign of the cross.

But here it is proper to mention what happened during the reign of king Henry the First to the lord of the castle of Radnor, in the adjoining territory of Builth, who had entered the church of Saint Avan (which is called in the British language Llan Avan), and, without sufficient caution or reverence, had passed the night there with his hounds. Arising early in the morning, according to the custom of hunters, he found his hounds mad, and himself struck blind. After a long, dark, and tedious existence, he was conveyed to Jerusalem, happily taking care that his inward sight should not in a similar manner be extinguished ; and there being accoutred, and led to the field of battle on horseback, he made a spirited attack upon the enemies of the faith, and, being mortally wounded, closed his life with honour.

Another circumstance which happened in these our days, in the province of Warthrenion,[1] distant from hence only a few furlongs, is not unworthy of notice. Eineon, lord of that district, and son-in-law to prince Rhys, who was much addicted to the chase, having on a certain day forced the wild beasts from their coverts, one of his attendants killed a hind with an arrow, as she was springing forth from the wood, which, contrary to the nature of her sex, was found to bear horns of twelve years' growth, and was much fatter than a stag, in the haunches as well as in every other part. On account of the singularity of this circumstance, the head and horns of this strange animal were destined as a present to king Henry the Second. This event is the more remarkable, as the man who shot the hind suddenly lost the use of his right eye, and being at the same time seized with a paralytic complaint, remained in a weak and impotent state until the time of his death.

In this same province of Warthrenion, and in the church of Saint Germanus, there is a staff of Saint Cyric, covered on all sides with gold and silver, and resembling in its upper part the form of a cross ; its efficacy has been proved in many cases, but particularly in the removal of glandular and strumous swellings ; insomuch that all persons afflicted with these complaints, on a devout application to the staff, with the offering of one penny, are restored to health. But it

[1] Gwyrthrynion, a district of Radnorshire.

happened in these our days, that a strumous patient on presenting one halfpenny to the staff, the humour subsided only in the middle ; but when the oblation was completed by the other halfpenny, an entire cure was accomplished. Another person also coming to the staff with the promise of a penny, was cured ; but not fulfilling his engagement on the day appointed, he relapsed into his former disorder ; in order, however, to obtain pardon for this offence, he tripled the offering by presenting threepence, and thus obtained a complete cure.

At Elevein, in the church of Glascum, is a portable bell, endowed with great virutes, called Bangu, and said to have belonged to Saint David. A certain woman secretly conveyed this bell to her husband, who was confined in the castle of Raidergwy, near Warthrenion (which Rhys, son of Gruffydd, had lately built), for the purpose of his deliverance. The keepers of the castle not only refused to liberate him for this consideration, but seized and detained the bell ; and in the same night, by divine vengeance, the whole town, except the wall on which the bell hung, was consumed by fire.

The church of Luel, in the neighbourhood of Brecheinoc,[1] was burned, also in our time, by the enemy, and everything destroyed, except one small box, in which the consecrated host was deposited.

It came to pass also in the province of Elvenia, which is separated from Hay by the river Wye, in the night in which king Henry I. died, that two pools of considerable size, the one natural, the other artificial, suddenly burst their bounds ; the latter, by its precipitate course down the hillsides, emptied itself ; but the former, with its fish and contents, obtained a permanent situation in a valley about two miles distant. In Normandy, a few days before the death of Henry II., the fish of a certain pool near Seez, five miles from the castle of Exme, fought during the night so furiously with each other, both in the water and out of it, that the neighbouring people were attracted by the noise to the spot ; and so desperate was the conflict, that scarcely a fish was found alive in the morning ; thus, by a wonderful and unheard-of prognostication, foretelling the death of one by that of many.

But the borders of Wales sufficiently remember and abhor the great and enormous excesses which, from am-

[1] Brechinia.

bitious usurpation of territory, have arisen amongst brothers and relations in the districts of Melenyth, Elvein, and Warthrenion, situated between the Wye and the Severn.

. . . .

The Journey by Coed Grono and Abergevenni

From thence we proceeded through the narrow, woody tract called the evil pass of Coed Grono, leaving the noble monastery of Lanthoni, inclosed by its mountains, on our left. The castle of Abergevenni is so called from its situation at the confluence of the river Gevenni with the Usk.

It happened a short time after the death of king Henry I. that Richard de Clare, a nobleman of high birth, and lord of Cardiganshire, passed this way on his journey from England into Wales, accompanied by Brian de Wallingford, lord of this province, and many men-at-arms. At the passage of Coed Grono, and at the entrance into the wood, he dismissed him and his attendants, though much against their will, and proceeded on his journey unarmed ; from too great a presumption of security, preceded only by a minstrel and a singer, one accompanying the other on the fiddle. The Welsh awaiting his arrival, with Iorwerth, brother of Morgan of Caerleon, at their head, and others of his family, rushed upon him unawares from the thickets, and killed him and many of his followers. Thus it appears how incautious and neglectful of itself is too great presumption ; for fear teaches foresight and caution in prosperity, but audacity is precipitate, and inconsiderate rashness will not await the advice of the leader.

A sermon having been delivered at Abergevenni, and many persons converted to the cross, a certain nobleman of those parts, named Arthenus, came to the archbishop, who was proceeding towards the castle of Usk, and humbly begged pardon for having neglected to meet him sooner. Being questioned whether he would take the cross, he replied, " That ought not to be done without the advice of his friends." The archbishop then asked him, " Are you not going to consult your wife ? " to which he modestly answered, with a downcast look, " When the work of a man is to be undertaken, the counsel of a woman ought not to be asked " ; and instantly received the cross from the archbishop.

We leave to others the relation of those frequent and

cruel excesses which in our times have arisen amongst the inhabitants of these parts, against the governors of castles, and the vindictive retaliations of the governors against the natives. But king Henry II. was the true author, and Ranulf Poer, sheriff of Hereford, the instrument, of the enormous cruelties and slaughter perpetrated here in our days, which I thought better to omit, lest evil men should be induced to follow the example ; for although temporary advantage may seem to arise from a base cause, yet, by the balance of a righteous judge, the punishment of wickedness may be deferred, though not totally avoided, according to the words of the poet :

"Non habet eventus sordida praeda bonos." [1]

For after seven years of peace and tranquillity, the sons and grandsons of the deceased, having attained the age of manhood, took advantage of the absence of the lord of the castle (Abergevenni) and, burning with revenge, concealed themselves, with no inconsiderable force, during the night, within the woody moat of the castle. One of them, name Sitsylt [2] son of Eudaf, on the preceding day said rather jocularly to the constable, "Here will we enter this night," pointing out to him a certain angle in the wall where it seemed the lowest ; but since

"... Ridendo dicere verum
Quis vetat ? " [3]

and

"... fas est et ab hoste doceri," [4]

the constable and his household watched all night under arms, till at length, worn out by fatigue, they all retired to rest on the appearance of daylight, upon which the enemy attacked the walls with scaling-ladders, at the very place that had been pointed out. The constable and his wife were taken prisoners, with many others, a few persons only escaping, who had sheltered themselves in the principal tower. With the exception of this stronghold, the enemy violently seized and burned everything ; and thus, by the righteous judgment of God, the crime was punished in the

[1] " Ill-gotten gains lead to no good."
[2] Sisillus, the modern Cecil.
[3] " Many a true word is spoken in jest."
[4] " It is lawful to pick up information from an enemy."

very place where it had been committed. A short time after the taking of this fortress, when the aforesaid sheriff was building a castle at Landinegat, near Monmouth, with the assistance of the army he had brought from Hereford, he was attacked at break of day, when

"Tythoni croceum linquens Aurora cubile" [1]

was only beginning to divest herself of the shades of night, by the young men from Gwent and the adjacent parts, with the descendants of those who had been slain. Though aware of this premeditated attack, and prepared and drawn up in battle array, they were nevertheless repulsed within their defences, and the sheriff, together with nine of the chief men of Hereford, and many others, were pierced to death with lances. It is remarkable that, although Ranulf, besides many other mortal wounds, had the veins and arteries of his neck and his windpipe separated with a sword, he made signs for a priest, and from the merit of his past life, and the honour and veneration he had shown to those chosen into the sacred order of Christ, he was confessed, and received extreme unction before he died. And, indeed, many events concur to prove that, as those who respect the priesthood, in their latter days enjoy the satisfaction of friendly intercourse, so do their revilers and accusers often die without that consolation. William de Braose, who was not the author of the crime we have preferred to pass over in silence, but the executioner, or, rather, not the preventer of its execution, while the murderous bands were fulfilling the orders they had received, was precipitated into a deep foss, and being taken by the enemy, was drawn forth, and only by a sudden effort of his own troops, and by divine mercy, escaped uninjured. Hence it is evident that he who offends in a less degree, and unwillingly permits a thing to be done, is more mildly punished than he who adds counsel and authority to his act. Thus, in the sufferings of Christ, Judas was punished with hanging, the Jews with destruction and banishment, and Pilate with exile. But the end of the king, who assented to and ordered this treachery, sufficiently manifested in what manner, on account of this and many other enormities he had committed (as in the book, *De Instructione Principis*, by God's guidance, we shall set forth), he began with accumu-

---

[1] "Aurora leaving Tithonus's saffron couch."

lated ignominy, sorrow, and confusion, to suffer punishment
in this world.

It seems worthy of remark, that the people of what is
called Gwent[1] are more accustomed to war, more famous
for valour, and more expert in archery, than those of any
other part of Wales. The following examples prove the
truth of this assertion. In the last capture of the aforesaid
castle, which happened in our days, whilst two soldiers were
passing over a bridge to take refuge in a tower built on a
mound of earth, the Welsh took them in the rear, and penetrated with their arrows the oaken portal of the tower, which
was almost four fingers thick ; in memory of which circumstance, the arrows were preserved in the gate.[2] William
de Braose also testifies that one of his soldiers, in a conflict
with the Welsh, was wounded by an arrow, which passed
through his thigh and the armour with which it was cased
on both sides, and through that part of the saddle which is
called the " alva," and mortally wounded the horse. Another
soldier had his hip, equally sheathed in armour, penetrated
by an arrow, right up to the saddle, and on turning his horse
round, received a similar wound on the opposite hip, which
fixed him to his seat on both sides. What more could be
expected from a ballista ? Yet the bows used by this people
are not made of horn, ivory, or yew, but of wild elm ; un-
polished, rude, and awkward, but stout ; not calculated to
shoot an arrow to a great distance, but to inflict very severe
wounds in close fight.

But let us again return to our Itinerary.

* * * * * * *

Of Haverford and Ros

A sermon having been delivered at Haverford by the
archbishop, and the word of God preached to the people by
the archdeacon, whose name appears on the title-page of this
work, many soldiers and plebeians were induced to take the
cross. It appeared wonderful and miraculous, that, although

[1] Venta.

[2] In praetaxata castri proditione, militibus duobus in turrim, cumu-
lato terrarum aggere sitam, per pontem transfugientibus, Gualenses,
ut ipsos a tergo percuterent, sagittas arcu mittentes, portam turris
iliceam, palmalis fere spissitudinis, transpenetrarunt; ad tantorum
ictuum vehementiae perpetuam memoriam, sagittis in porta ferro
repercusso reservatis.

the archdeacon addressed them both in the Latin and French tongues, those persons who understood neither of those languages were equally affected, and flocked in great numbers to the cross.

An old woman of those parts, who for three preceding years had been blind, having heard of the archbishop's arrival, sent her son to the place where the sermon was to be preached, that he might bring back to her some particle, if only of the fringe of his garment. The young man being prevented by the crowd from approaching the archbishop, waited till the assembly was dispersed, and then carried a piece of the earth on which the preacher had stood. The mother received the gift with great joy, and falling immediately on her knees, applied the turf to her mouth and eyes ; and thus, through the merits of the holy man, and her own faith and devotion, recovered the blessing of sight, which she had entirely lost.

The inhabitants of this province derived their origin from Flanders, and were sent by king Henry I. to inhabit these districts ; a people brave and robust, ever most hostile to the Welsh ; a people, I say, well versed in commerce and woollen manufacture ; a people anxious to seek gain by sea or land, in defiance of fatigue and danger ; a hardy race, equally fitted for the plough or for the sword ; a people brave and happy, if Wales (as it ought to have been) had been dear to its sovereign, and had not so often undergone the vindictive resentment and ill-treatment of its governors.

.   .   .   .

We continued our journey over the Traeth Mawr, and Traeth Bachan, that is, the greater and the smaller arm of the sea, where two stone castles have newly been built ; one called Deudraeth, belonging to the sons of Conan, situated in Evionyth, towards the northern mountains ; the other named Carn Madryn, the property of the sons of Owen, built on the other side of the river towards the sea, on the headland Lleyn. Traeth, in the Welsh language, signifies a tract of sand flooded by the tides, and left bare when the sea ebbs. We had before passed over the noted rivers, the Dissenith, between the Maw and Traeth Mawr, and the Arthro, between the Traeth Mawr and Traeth Bachan. We slept that night at Nevyn, on the eve of Palm Sunday, where the archdeacon, after a long inquiry and research, is said to have found Merlin Sylvestris.

Beyond Lleyn, there is a small island inhabited by very religious monks, called Caelibes, or Colidei.[1] This island, either from the wholesomeness of its climate, owing to its vicinity to Ireland, or rather from some miracle obtained by the merits of the saints, has this wonderful peculiarity, that the oldest people die first, because diseases are uncommon, and scarcely any die except from extreme old age. Its name is Enlli in the Welsh, and Berdesey in the Saxon language ; and very many bodies of saints are said to be buried there, and amongst them that of Daniel, bishop of Bangor.

The archbishop having, by his sermon the next day, induced many persons to take the cross, we proceeded towards Banchor, passing through Caernarvon, that is, the castle of Arvon, it is called Arvon, the province opposite to Mon, because it is so situated with respect to the island of Mona. Our road leading us to a steep valley, with many broken ascents and descents, we dismounted from our horses, and proceeded on foot, rehearsing, as it were, by agreement, some experiments of our intended pilgrimage to Jerusalem. Having traversed the valley, and reached the opposite side with considerable fatigue, the archbishop, to rest himself and recover his breath, sat down on an oak which had been torn up by the violence of the winds ; and relaxing into a pleasantry highly laudable in a person of his approved gravity, thus addressed his attendants : " Who amongst you, in this company, can now delight our wearied ears by whistling ? " which is not easily done by people out of breath. He affirming that he could, if he thought fit, the sweet notes are heard, in an adjoining wood, of a bird, which some said was a wood-pecker, and others, more correctly, an aureolus. The wood-pecker is called in French, spec, and with its strong bill perforates oak trees ; the other bird is called aureolus, from the golden tints of its feathers, and at certain seasons utters a sweet whistling note, instead of a song. Some persons having remarked, that the nightingale was never heard in this country, the archbishop, with a significant smile, replied, " The nightingale followed wise counsel, and never came into Wales ; but we, unwise of counsel, who have penetrated and gone through it." We remained that night at Banchor, the metropolitan see of

[1] *i.e.* Culdees.

North Wales, and were well entertained by the bishop of the diocese. On the next day, mass being celebrated by the archbishop before the high altar, the bishop of that see, at the instance of the archbishop and other persons, more importunate than persuasive, was compelled to take the cross, to the general concern of all his people of both sexes, who expressed their grief on this occasion by loud and lamentable cries.

III. EXTRACTS FROM JOINVILLE'S *CHRONICLE* OF THE CRUSADE OF ST. LOUIS

[Joinville came of a wealthy and noble family of the County of Champagne. His mother was a cousin of the famous Emperor Frederick II. He was born probably in 1224, and embarked with St. Louis on his Crusade in August 1248, returning to France again, after nearly six years of perilous adventure, in July 1254. The *Chronicle*, from which the following extracts are taken, was written in 1309, when Joinville was about eighty-five years of age. It describes the events of more than half a century before with the garrulousness and discursiveness of old age. Therein is its great value. Joinville is never tired of discussing those intimate and trivial details of everyday life, which the ordinary chronicler of the period would omit as beneath the dignity of history, but which bring us very close to the life and mentality of medieval man. The world of the Crusades lives in his pages as nowhere else in the literature of the Middle Ages. It is for this reason that Joinville cannot be omitted from a volume of documents dealing with Medieval England, in spite of the fact that it has no direct connexion with this country. As we read Joinville we are enabled to get some glimpse of the vision that caused millions of men from Western Europe—Englishmen not a few among them—to give up so much that men commonly hold dear, in order to seek peril and hardship and death in far distant lands in striving to win Jerusalem from the Infidel.

A handy volume of Joinville in the original French is that edited by M. Natalis de Wailly (Libraire Hachette, Paris, 1921). Joinville's *Chronicle* was translated into English by Johnes of Hafod—from whose translation of Froissart a selection will be found in Chapter VI.—about 1804. Another translation was made by James Hutton in 1868 (Sampson Low, Marston & Co.), and yet another by Ethel Wedgewood in 1906 (John Murray). The handiest volume of Joinville is the translation by Sir F. Marzials in the Everyman's Library (No. 333) under the title *Chronicles of the Crusades by Villehardouin and Joinville*, first published 1908.]

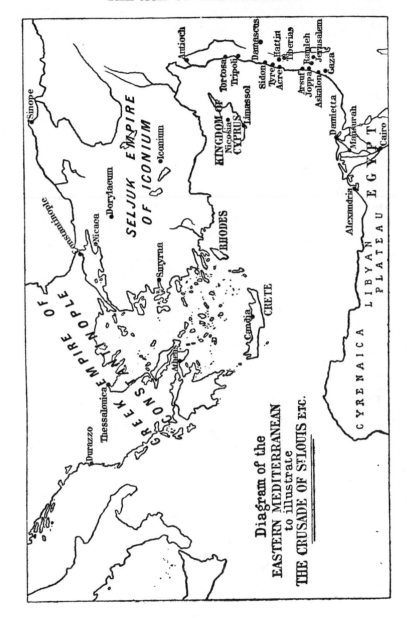

Diagram of the
EASTERN MEDITERRANEAN
to illustrate
THE CRUSADE OF ST. LOUIS ETC.

Beginning of the First Book—Principal Virtues of St. Lewis

IN the name of God the Almighty, I, John, Lord of Join-ville, seneschal of Champagne, dictate the life of our holy King Lewis ; [1] that which I saw and heard during the six years that I was in his company on pilgrimage beyond the sea, and after we returned. And before I tell you of his great deeds, and of his chivalry, I will tell you that I saw and heard of his good teachings and of his holy words, so that these may be found here set in order for the edifying of those who shall hear thereof.

This holy man loved God with all his heart, and followed Him in His acts ; and this appeared in that, as God died for the love He bore His people, so did the king put his body in peril, and that several times, for the love he bore to his people ; and such peril he might well have avoided,[2] as you shall be told hereafter.

The great love that he bore to his people appeared in what he said during a very sore sickness that he had at Fontainebleau, unto my Lord Lewis, his eldest son. " Fair son," he said, " I pray thee to make thyself beloved of the people of thy kingdom ; for truly I would rather that a Scot should come out of Scotland and govern the people of the kingdom well and equitably than that thou shouldest govern it ill in the sight of all men." [3] The holy king so loved truth, that, as you shall hear hereafter, he would never consent to lie to the Saracens as to any covenant that he had made with them.

Of his mouth he was so sober, that on no day of my life did I ever hear him order special meats, as many rich men are wont to do ; but he ate patiently whatever his cooks had made ready, and was set before him. In his words he was temperate ; for on no day of my life did I ever hear him speak evil of any one ; nor did I ever hear him name the Devil—which name is very commonly spoken throughout the kingdom, whereby God, as I believe, is not well pleased.

He put water into his wine by measure, according as he saw that the strength of the wine would suffer it. At

---

[1] Au nom de Dieu le tout puissant je Jean, Sire de Joinville, Sénéchal de Champagne, fais écrire là vie notre saint roi Louis. . . .
[2] s'en fût bien soufers ; . . .
[3] que ce que tu le gouvernasses malapertement.

Cyprus he asked me why I put no water into my wine ; and I said this was by order of the physicians, who told me I had a large head and a cold stomach, so that I could not get drunk. And he answered that they deceived me ; for if I did not learn to put water into my wine in my youth, and wished to do so in my old age, gout and diseases of the stomach would take hold upon me, and I should never be in health ; and if I drank pure wine in my old age, I should get drunk every night, and that it was too foul a thing for a brave man to get drunk.

He asked me if I wished to be honoured in this world, and to go into paradise at my death ? And I said " Yes." And he said : " Keep yourself then from knowingly doing or saying anything which, if the whole world heard thereof, you would be ashamed to acknowledge, saying ' I did this,' or ' I said that.' " He told me to beware not to contradict or impugn anything that was said before me—unless indeed silence would be a sin or to my own hurt—because hard words often move to quarrels, wherein men by the thousand have died.

He said that men ought to clothe and arm their bodies in such wise that men of worth [1] would never say, this man has done too much, nor young men say, this man has done too little. And I repeated this saying to the father [2] of the king that now is, when speaking of the embroidered coats of arms that are made nowadays ; and I told him that never, during our voyage oversea, had I seen embroidered coats, either belonging to the king or to any one else. And the king that now is told me that he had such suits, with arms embroidered, as had cost him eight hundred pounds *parisis*. And I told him he would have employed the money to better purpose if he had given it to God, and had had his suits made of good taffeta (satin) ornamented with his arms, as his father had done.

St. Lewis's Horror of Sin—His Love for the Poor

He called me once to him and said : " Because of the subtle mind that is in you I dare not speak to you of the things relating to God ; so I have summoned these two friars that are here, as I want to ask you a question." Now

[1] les prudhommes.   [2] *i.e.* Philippe le Hardi.

the question was this : " Seneschal," said he, " what manner
of thing is God ? " And I said : " Sire, it is so good a thing
that there cannot be better." " Of a truth," said he, " you
have answered well ; for the answer that you have given is
written in this book that I hold in my hand."

" Now I ask you," said he, " which you would the better
like, either to be a leper,[1] or to have committed a mortal
sin ? " And I, who never lied to him, made answer that
I would rather have committed thirty mortal sins than be a
leper. And when the friars had departed, he called me to
him alone, and made me sit at his feet, and said, " How
came you to say that to me yesterday ? " And I told him
that I said it again. And he answered, " You spoke hastily
and as a fool.[2] For you should know that there is no
leprosy so hideous as the being in mortal sin, inasmuch as
the soul that is in mortal sin is like unto the Devil ; wherefore
no leprosy can be so hideous. And true indeed it is that,
when a man dies, he is healed of the leprosy in his body ;
but when a man who has committed mortal sin dies, he
cannot know of a certainty that he has, during his lifetime,
repented in such sort that God has forgiven him ; wherefore
he must stand in great fear lest that leprosy of sin should
last as long as God is in paradise. So I pray you," said he,
" as strongly as I can, for the love of God, and for the love
of me, so to set your heart that you prefer any evil that can
happen to the body, whether it be leprosy, or any other
sickness, rather than that mortal sin should enter into your
soul."

He asked me if I washed the feet of the poor on Holy
Thursday. " Sire," said I, " it would make me sick ! The
feet of these villains will I not wash." [3] " In truth," said
he, " that was ill said ; for you should never disdain what
God did for our teaching. So I pray you, for the love of
God first, and then for the love of me, that you accustom
yourself to wash the feet of the poor."

Regard of St. Lewis for Worth and Uprightness

He so loved all manner of people who had faith in God
and loved Him, that he gave the constableship of France to

[1] que vous fussiés mesiaus.   [2] Vous dîtes comme hastis musarz.
[3] Les piez de ces vilains ne laverai-je jà.

my Lord Giles Le Brun,[1] who was not of the kingdom of
France, because men held him in so great repute for his faith
and for love to God. And verily I believe that his good repute
was well deserved.

He caused Master Robert of Sorbon [2] to eat at his table,
because of the great repute in which he was held as a man
of uprightness and worth. One day it chanced that Master
Robert was eating at my side, and we were talking to one
another. The king took us up, and said : " Speak out, for
your companions think you are speaking ill of them. If
you talk at table of things that can give us pleasure, speak
out, and, if not, hold your peace."

When the king would be mirthful he would say to me :
" Seneschal, tell me the reasons why a man of uprightness
and worth [3] is better than a devotee ? " [4] Then would begin
a discussion between me and Master Robert. When we had
disputed for a long while, the king would give sentence and
speak thus : " Master Robert, willingly would I bear the
title of upright and worthy [5] provided I were such in reality
—and all the rest you might have. For uprightness and
worth [6] are such great things and such good things that even
to name them fills the mouth pleasantly."

On the contrary he said it was an evil thing to take other
people's goods. " For," said he, " to restore is a thing so
grievous, that even in the speaking the word restore [7] scratches
the throat by reason of the r's that are in it, and these r's
are like so many rakes with which the Devil would draw to
himself those who wish to ' restore ' what they have taken
from others. And very subtly does the Devil do this ; for
he works on great usurers and great robbers in such sort that
they give to God what they ought to ' restore ' to men."

He told me to warn King Thibaut,[8] from him, to beware
of the house of the Preachers of Provins, which he was building, lest he should encumber his soul on account of the great
sums he was spending thereon. " For wise men," said he,
" should, while they live, deal with their possessions as
executors ought to do. Now the first thing a good executor

---

[1] Gilles de Trasignies, called " The Brown," was of Flemish origin.
[2] Robert was the founder of the Sorbonne at Paris.
[3] preudhomme.   [4] beguin.   [5] preudhomme.
[6] preudome.   [7] rendres.
[8] Thibaut II., King of Navarre, married in 1255 to Isabelle, daughter
of St. Lewis.

does is to satisfy all the claims upon the dead, and pay back to others what is due to them, and it is only after having done this that he should spend in alms what remains of the dead man's possessions."

How St. Lewis thought Men ought to Clothe Themselves

The holy king was at Corbeil one Whitsun, and there were there eighty knights. The king came down after dinner into the court below the chapel, and was talking, at the entrance of the door, to the Count of Brittany, the father of the count that now is—whom may God preserve ! [1]—when Master Robert of Sorbon came to fetch me thither, and took me by the skirt of my mantle and led me to the king ; and all the other knights came after us. Then I said to Master Robert, " Master Robert, what do you want with me ? " He said, " I wish to ask you whether, if the king were seated in this court, and you were to seat yourself on this bench, and at a higher place than he, ought you to be greatly blamed ? " And I said, " Yes." And he said, " Then are you to be blamed when you go more nobly apparelled than the king, for you dress yourself in fur and green cloth, and the king does not do so." And I replied : " Master Robert, saving your grace, I do nothing blameworthy when I clothe myself in green cloth and fur, for this garment was left to me by my father and mother. But you are to blame, for you are the son of a common man and a common woman, and you have abandoned the vesture worn by your father and mother, and wear richer woollen cloth [2] than the king himself." Then I took the skirt of his surcoat, and of the surcoat of the king, and said, " See if I am not speaking sooth." Then the king set himself to defend Master Robert with all his power.

After this my lord the king called my Lord Philip, his son, the father of the king that now is, and King Thibaut, and sat himself at the entrance to his oratory, and put his hand to the ground and said : " Sit yourselves down here, quite close to me, so that we be not overheard." " Ah ! sire,"

---

[1] John I., Count of Brittany. His son, John II.—curiously enough —died just about the time when Joinville wrote these words (18th November 1305).

[2] camelin.

they replied, " we should not dare to sit so close to you."
And he said to me, "Seneschal, sit you here." And I did
so—so close that my robe touched his. And he made them
sit after me, and said to them : " You have done very ill,
seeing you are my sons, and have not, at the first word,
done what I commanded you. See, I pray you, that this
does not happen again." And they said it should not so
happen. Then he said to me that he had so called us together
to confess that he had wrongly defended Master Robert
against me. " But," said he, " I saw that he was so discouraged that he had great need of my help. Nevertheless,
you must not attach import to anything I may have said to
defend Master Robert ; for, as the seneschal says, you ought
to clothe yourselves well and suitably, so that your wives
may love you the better, and your people hold you in the
greater honour. For, as the sage tells us, our garments
should be of such fashion as neither to cause the aged and
worthy [1] to say that too much has been spent upon them, nor
the young to say that too little has been spent."

The Warnings of God—How they are to be Turned to Advantage

You shall now hear of one of the lessons he taught me
at sea, when we were returning from the lands oversea. It
chanced that our ship struck before the island of Cyprus,
when a wind was blowing which is called " guerbin " ; and
this wind is not one of the four great winds. And at the
shock that our ship received, the mariners so despaired that
they rent their garments and tore their beards. The king
sprang from his bed, barefoot, for it was night, and clothed
only in his tunic,[2] and went and placed himself cross-wise
before the body of our Lord, as one who expected nothing
but death. The day after this happened, the king called me
to him alone, and said : " Seneschal, God has just showed us
a portion of His great power ; for one of these little winds,
a wind so little that one can scarcely give it a name, came
near to drown the King of France, his children, his wife, and
his men. Now St. Anselm [3] says that such are warnings from
our Lord, as if God meant to say to us, ' See how easily I
could have compassed your death, had it been my will.'

[1] preudome.   [2] une cote.   [3] Sainz Anciaumes.

'Lord God,' says the saint, 'why dost Thou thus threaten us ? For when Thou dost threaten us, it is not for Thine own profit, nor for Thine advantage—seeing that if Thou hadst caused us all to be lost, Thou wouldst have been none the poorer, and if Thou hadst caused us all to be saved, Thou wouldst have been none the richer. Therefore, this Thy warning is not for Thine own advantage, but for ours, if so be that we suffer it do its work.' Let us therefore take the warning that God has given us in such sort that, if we feel that we have, in our hearts or bodies, anything displeasing to God, we shall remove it hastily ; and if there be anything we think will please Him, let us try hastily to do it. If we so act, then our Lord will give us blessings in this world, and in the next blessings greater than we can conceive. And if we do not act thus, He will deal with us as the good lord deals with his wicked servant ; for if the wicked servant will not amend after warning given, the lord punishes him with death, or with other great troubles that are worse than death."

Let the king that now is beware ; for he has escaped from peril as great as that in which we then were, or greater. Therefore let him amend from his evil deeds in such sort that God treat him not grievously, either in himself or in his possessions.

What St. Lewis thought about Faith

The holy king endeavoured with all his power—as you shall here be told—to make me believe firmly in the Christian law, which God has given us. He said that we ought to believe so firmly the articles of faith that neither from fear of death, nor for any mischief that might happen to the body, should we be willing to go against them in word or deed. And he said that the Enemy is so subtle that, when people are dying, he labours all he can to make them die doubting as to some points of the faith.[1] For he knows that he can in no wise deprive a man of the good works he has done ; and he knows also that the man is lost to him if he dies in true faith.

Wherefore we should so guard and defend ourselves from this snare, as to say to the Enemy, when he sends such a

---

[1] Et disoit que li ennemis est si soutilz que, quant les gens se meurent, il se travaille tant comme il puet que il les puisse fair mourir en aucune doutance des poins de la foy.

temptation : " Away ! " Yes, " Away ! " must one say to
the Enemy. " Thou shalt not tempt me so that I cease to
believe firmly all the articles of the faith. Even if thou
didst cause all my members to be cut off, yet would I live and
die in the faith." And whosoever acts thus, overcomes the
Enemy with the very club and sword that the Enemy desired
to murder him withal.

He said that the Christian faith and creed were things
in which we ought to believe firmly, even though we might
not be certain of them except by hearsay. On this point he
asked me what was my father's name ? And I told him his
name was Simon. And he asked how I knew it. And I
said I thought I was certain of it, and believed it firmly,
because my mother had borne witness thereto. Then he
said, " So ought you to believe all the articles of the faith,
to which the Apostles have borne witness, as also you chant
of a Sunday in the Creed."

William, Bishop of Paris, comforts a Certain Theologian

He told me that the bishop, William of Paris,[1] had related
how a great master of divinity had come to him and told
him he desired to speak with him. And the bishop said to
him : " Master, say on." And when the master thought to
speak to the bishop, he began to weep bitterly. And the
bishop said : " Master, say on ; be not discomfited ; no one
can sin so much but that God can forgive him more." " And
yet I tell you," said the master, " that I cannot choose but
weep for I fear me I am a miscreant, inasmuch as I cannot
so command my heart as to believe in the sacrifice of the
altar, like as Holy Church teaches ; and yet I know well
that this is a temptation of the Enemy."

" Master," said the bishop, " pray tell me, when the
Enemy sends you this temptation, does it give you pleasure ? "
And the master said : " Sir, far from it ; it troubles me as
much as anything can trouble me." " Now," said the
bishop, " I will ask you whether, for gold or silver you would
utter anything out of your mouth that was against the
sacrament of the altar, or the other holy sacraments of the
Church ? " " Sir ! " said the master, " be it known to you
that there is nothing in the world that would induce me so

[1] William of Auvergne, Bishop of Paris, 1228–48.

to do ; I would much rather that every limb were torn from my body than that I should say such a thing."

"Now I will say something more," said the bishop. "You know that the King of France is at war with the King of England, and you know too that the castle that lies most exposed in the border-land between the two is the castle of la Rochelle in Poitou. Now I will ask you a question : If the king had set you to guard la Rochelle, which is in the dangerous border-land, and had set me to guard the castle of Montlehéry, which is in the heart of France, where the land is at peace, to whom, think you, would the king owe most at the end of the war—to you who had guarded la Rochelle without loss, or to me, who had guarded the castle of Montlehéry without loss ? " "In God's name, sir," said the master, " to me, who had guarded la Rochelle without loss."

"Master," said the bishop, " my heart is like the castle of Montlehéry ; for I have neither temptation nor doubt as to the sacrament of the altar. For which thing I tell you that for the grace that God owes to me because I hold this firmly, and in peace, He owes to you four-fold, because you have guarded your heart in the war of tribulation, and have such good-will towards Him that for no earthly good, nor for any harm done to the body, would you relinquish that faith. Therefore I tell you, be of good comfort, for in this your state is better pleasing to our Lord than mine." When the master heard this, he knelt before the bishop, and considered himself for well rewarded.[1]

Faith of the Count of Montfort—One must not enter into Controversy with Jews

The holy king told me that several people among the Albigenses came to the Count of Montfort,[2] who was then guarding the land of the Albigenses for the king, and asked him to come and look at the body of our Lord, which had become blood and flesh in the hands of the priest. And the Count of Montfort said, " Go and look at it yourselves, you

[1] Quant li maistres oy ce, il s'agenouilla devant l'evesque, et se tint bien pour paié.

[2] Amaury de Montfort, who died 1241, the father of Simon, Earl of Leicester.

who do not believe it. As for me, I believe it firmly, holding as Holy Church teaches of the sacrament of the altar. And do you know what I shall gain," said the count, " in that during this mortal life I have believed as holy Church teaches ? I shall have a crown in the Heavens, above the angels, for the angels cannot but believe, inasmuch as they see Him in whom they believe."

He told me that there was once a great disputation between clergy and Jews at the monastery of Cluny. And there was at Cluny a poor knight, to whom the abbot gave bread at that place for the love of God ; and this knight asked the abbot to suffer him to speak the first words, and they suffered him, not without doubt. So he rose, and leant upon his crutch, and asked that they should bring to him the greatest clerk and most learned master among the Jews ; and they did so. Then he asked the Jew a question, which was this : " Master," said the knight, " I ask you if you believe that the Virgin Mary, who bore God in her body and in her arms, was a virgin mother, and is the mother of God ? "

And the Jew replied that of all this he believed nothing. Then the knight answered that he had acted like a fool [1] when—neither believing in her, nor loving her—he had yet entered into her monastery and house. "And verily," said the knight, " you shall pay for it ! " Whereupon he lifted his crutch and smote the Jew near the ear, and beat him to the earth.[2] Then the Jews turned to flight, and bore away their master, sore wounded. And so ended the disputation.

The abbot came to the knight and told him he had committed a deed of great folly. But the knight replied that the abbot had committed a deed of greater folly in gathering people together for such a disputation ; for there were a great many good Christians there who, before the disputation came to an end, would have gone away mis-believers through not fully understanding the Jews. " And I tell you," said the king, " that no one, unless he be a very good clerk, should dispute with them ; but a layman, when he hears the Christian law missaid, should not defend the Christian law, unless it be with his sword, and with that

---

[1] Et li chevaliers li respondi que mout avoit fait que fous.

[2] Et lors il hauça sa potence, et feri le Juif lès l'oye, et le porta par terre.

he should pierce the mis-sayer in the midriff, so far as the sword will enter." [1]

The Devotions of St. Lewis—How he did Justice in his Land

The government of his land was so arranged that every day he heard the hours sung, and a *Requiem* mass without song : and then, if it was convenient, the mass of the day, or of the saint, with song. Every day he rested in his bed after having eaten, and when he had slept and rested, he said, privily in his chamber—he and one of his chaplains together —the (office for the) dead ; and afterwards he heard vespers. At night he heard compline.

A gray-friar [2] (Franciscan) came to him at the castle of Hyeres, where we disembarked ; and said in his sermon, for the king's instruction, that he had read the Bible, and the books pertaining to misbelieving [3] princes, and that he had never found, either among believers or misbelievers, [3] that a kingdom had been lost, or had changed lords, save there had first been failure of justice. " Therefore let the king, who is going into France, take good heed," said he, " that he do justice well and speedily among his people, so that our Lord suffer his kingdom to remain in peace all the days of his life." It is said that the right worthy man who thus instructed the king, lies buried at Marseilles, where our Lord, for his sake, performs many a fine miracle. He would never consent to remain with the king, however much the king might urge it, for more than a single day.

The king forgat not the teaching of the friar, but ruled his land very loyally and godly, as you shall hear. He had so arranged that my Lord of Nesle, [4] and the good Count of Soissons, [5] and all of us who were about him, should go, after we had heard our masses, and hear the pleadings at the gate which is now called the Requests.

And when he came back from church, he would send for us and sit at the foot of his bed, and make us all sit round him, and ask if there were any whose cases could not be

---

[1] Ne doit pas desfendre la loi crestienne, ne mais de l'espée, de quoy il doit donner parmi le ventre dedans, tant comme elle y puet entrer.

[2] Uns cordeliers.   [3] mescreans.   [4] Simon, Lord of Nesle.

[5] John II. of Nesle, called the Good, was Count of Soissons from 1237 to 1270. He was a cousin-germain of Joinville.

settled save by himself in person. And we named the
litigants ; and he would then send for such and ask : " Why
do you not accept what our people offer ? " And they
would make reply, " Sire, because they offer us very little."
Then would he say, " You would do well to accept what is
proposed, as our people desire." And the holy man endeavoured thus, with all his power, to bring them into a
straight path and a reasonable.

Ofttimes it happened that he would go, after his mass,
and seat himself in the wood of Vincennes, and lean against
an oak, and make us sit round him. And all those who
had any cause in hand came and spoke to him, without
hindrance of usher, or of any other person. Then he would
ask, out of his own mouth, " Is there any one who has cause
in hand ? " And those who had a cause in hand stood up.
Then would he say, " Keep silence all, and you shall be heard
in turn, one after the other." Then he would call my Lord
Peter of Fontaines and my Lord Geoffry of Villette, and
say to one of them, " Settle me this cause."

And when he saw that there was anything to amend in
the words of those who spoke on his behalf, or in the word
of those who spoke on behalf of any other person, he would
himself, out of his own mouth, amend what they had said.
Sometimes have I seen him, in summer, go to do justice
among his people in the garden of Paris, clothed in a tunic
of camlet, a surcoat of tartan without sleeves, and a mantle
of black taffeta about his neck, his hair well combed, no cap,
and a hat of white peacock's feathers upon his head.[1] And
he would cause a carpet to be laid down, so that we might
sit round him, and all the people who had any cause to bring
before him stood around. And then would he have their
causes settled, as I have told you previously he was wont to
do in the wood of Vincennes.

St. Lewis refuses an Unjust Demand made by the Bishops

I saw him, yet another time, in Paris, when all the prelates
of France had asked to speak with him, and the king went

---

[1] Je le vi aucune foiz, en estei, que pour delivrer sa gent il venoit ou
jardin de Paris, une cote de chamelot vestue, un seurcot de tyreteinne
sanz manches, un mantel de cendal noir entour son col, mout bien
pigniez et sans coife, et un chapel de paon blanc sus sa teste.

to the palace to give them audience. And there was present Guy of Auxerre, the son of my Lord William of Mello, and he spoke to the king on behalf of all the prelates, after this manner : " Sire, the lords who are here present, archbishops and bishops, have directed me to tell you that Christendom, which ought to be guarded and preserved by you, is perishing in your hands." The king crossed himself when he heard that word, and he said, " Tell me how that is."

" Sire," said Guy of Auxerre, " it is because excommunications are at the present day so lightly thought of that people suffer themselves to die before seeking absolution, and will not give satisfaction to the Church. These lords require you therefore, for the sake of God, and because it is your duty, to command your provosts and bailiffs to seek out all such as suffer themselves to remain excommunicated for a year and day, and constrain them, by seizure of their goods, to have themselves absolved.

And the king replied that he would issue such commands willingly whensoever it could be shown to him that the excommunicate persons were in the wrong. The bishops said they would not accept this condition in anywise, as they contested his jurisdiction in their causes.[1] Then the king told them he would not act otherwise ; for it would be against God and reason if he constrained people to seek absolution when the clergy were doing them wrong. " And of this," said the king, " I will give you an example, viz. that of the Count of Brittany, who, for seven years long, being excommunicated, pleaded against the prelates of Brittany, and carried his cause so far that the Apostles [2] condemned them all. Wherefore, if I had constrained the Count of Brittany, at the end of the first year, to get himself absolved, I should have sinned against God and against him." Then the prelates gave in ; nor did I ever hear tell that any further steps were taken in the aforesaid matters.

The Loyalty of St. Lewis

The peace that he made with the King of England was made against the advice of his council, for the council said

---

[1] Et li evesques dist que il ne feroient à nul fuer, que li deveissient la court de lour cause.

[2] *i.e.* the Apostolic See of the West, the Court of Rome.

to him : " Sire, it seems to us that you are giving away the
land that you make over to the King of England ; for he
has no right thereto, seeing that his father lost it justly."
To this the king replied that he knew well that the King of
England had no right to the land, but that there was a reason
why he should give it him, " for," said he, "we have two
sisters [1] to wife, and our children are cousins-german ;
wherefore it is fitting that there should be peace between
us.   Moreover, a very great honour accrues to me through
the peace that I have made with the King of England, seeing
that he is now my liegeman, which he was not aforetime."

The uprightness of the king may be seen in the case of
my lord Renaud of Trie,[2] who brought to the saint a
charter, stating that the king had given to the heirs of the
Countess of Boulogne, lately deceased, the county of Dammartin in Gouelle.   The seal on the charter was broken, so
that nothing remained save half the legs of the image on the
king's seal, and the stool [3] on which the king set his feet.
And the king showed the seal to all those who were of his
council, and asked us to help him to come to a decision.
We all said, without a dissentient, that he was not bound to
give effect to the charter.   Then he told John Sarrasin, his
chamberlain, to give him a charter which he had asked him
to obtain.   When he held this charter in his hands, he said :
" Lords, this is the seal I used before I went overseas, and
you can see clearly from this seal that the impression on the
broken seal is like unto that of the seal that is whole ; wherefore I should not dare, in good conscience, to keep the said
county."   So he called to him my lord Renaud of Trie, and
said, " I give you back the county."

* * * * * * *

St. Lewis falls Ill, and takes the Cross in 1244

[N. de Wailly's Ed., pp. 47 sqq.]

After the things related above, it happened, as God so
willed, that a very grievous sickness came upon the king in

---

[1] Marguerite, wife of St. Louis, and Elanor, wife of Henry III. of
England, were daughters of Béranger IV., Count of Provence.

[2] The name should be Mathieu of Trie.   Renaud is a mistake of
Joinville.

[3] eschamel.

12

Paris, and brought him to such extremity, so it was said, that one of the ladies who were tending him wished to draw the cloth over his face,[1] saying he was dead ; but another lady, who was on the other side of the bed, would not suffer it, and said the soul was still in his body.

And as he listened to the dispute between these two ladies, our Lord wrought within him, and soon sent him health, for before that he had been mute, and could not speak. And as soon as he was in case to speak, he asked that they should give him the cross, and they did so. When the queen, his mother, heard say that speech had come back to him, she made as great joy thereof as ever she could. But when she knew that he had taken the cross—as also he himself told her—she made as great mourning as if she had seen him dead.

After he had taken the cross, so also took the cross, Robert, Count of Artois ; Alfonse, Count of Poitiers ; Charles, Count of Anjou, who afterwards was King of Sicily—all three brothers of the King—and there also took the cross, Hugh, Duke of Burgundy ; William, Count of Flanders, and brother of Count Guy of Flanders, lately deceased ;[2] the good Hugh, Count of St. Paul ; and my Lord Gaucher, his nephew, who did right well oversea, and would have done much good service if he had lived.

With them also took the cross, the Count of la Marche and my Lord Hugh Le Brun, his son, the Count of Sarrebruck, and my Lord Gobert of Apremont, his brother—in whose company I, John, Lord of Joinville, passed over the sea in a ship which we hired, because we were cousins—and we passed over with twenty knights, of whom he was over ten, and I over ten.

Joinville prepares to join the Crusade

At Easter, in the year of grace that stood at 1248, I summoned my men, and all who held fiefs from me, to Joinville ; and on the vigil of the said Easter, when all the people that I had summoned were assembled, was born my son John, Lord of Ancerville, by my first wife,[3] the sister of the Count of Grandpré. All that week we feasted and danced, and my brother, the Lord of Vaucouleurs, and the other rich

---

[1] traire le drap sur le visage.
[2] Guy died 7th March 1305.
[3] Alix, sister of Henry IV., Count of Grandpré.

men who were there, gave feasts on the Monday, the Tuesday, the Wednesday, and the Thursday.

On the Friday I said to them : " Lords, I am going oversea, and I know not whether I shall ever return. Now come forward ; if I have done you any wrong, I will make it good, as I have been used to do, dealing, each in turn, with such as have any claim to make against me, or my people." So I dealt with each, according to the opinions of the men on my lands ; and in order that my presence might not hinder them, I retired from the council, and agreed, without objection, to what they recommended.

Because I did not wish to take away with me any penny wrongfully gotten,[1] I went to Metz, in Lorraine, and placed in pawn the greater part of my land. And you must know that on the day when I left our country to go to the Holy Land, I did not hold more than one thousand livres a year in land, for my lady mother was still alive ; and yet I went, taking with me nine knights, and being the first of three knights-bannerets.[2] And I bring these things to your notice, so that you may understand that if God, who never yet failed me, had not come to my help, I should hardly have maintained myself for so long a space as the six years that I remained in the Holy Land.

As I was preparing to depart, John, Lord of Apremont, and Count of Sarrebruck in his wife's right, sent to tell me he had settled matters to go oversea, taking ten knights, and proposed, if I so willed, that we should hire a ship between him and me ; and I consented. His people and mine hired a ship at Marseilles.

Of a Clerk who killed three of the King's Sergeants

The king summoned all his barons to Paris, and made them take oath that, if anything happened to him while away, they would give faith and loyalty to his children. He asked me to do the same ; but I would not take the oath, because I was not his " man." [3]

---

[1] Pour ce que je n'en vouloie porter nulz deniers à tort. . . .

[2] et moy tiers de bannieres.

[3] Joinville was at this time a vassal of the Count of Champagne. He afterwards became a vassal of St. Louis in 1253, when St. Louis conferred a fief upon him.

While I was on my way to Paris, I found three men dead upon a cart, whom a clerk had killed ; and I was told they were being taken to the king. When I heard this, I sent one of my squires after, to know what befell. And my squire, whom I had sent, told me that the king, when he came out of his chapel, went to the entrance steps to look at the dead, and inquired of the provost of Paris how this thing had happened.

And the provost told him that the dead men were three of his sergeants of the Chatelet, who had gone into unfrequented streets to rob people. " And they found," said he to the king, " this clerk, whom you see here, and robbed him of all his clothes. The clerk, being only in his shirt, went to his lodging, and took his crossbow, and caused a child to bring his falchion. Then when he saw them again, he cried out upon them, and said they should die. So the clerk drew his crossbow, and shot, and pierced one of the men through the heart. The two others made off flying. And the clerk took the falchion which the child handed to him, and followed them in the moonlight, which was fine and clear. The one man thought to pass through a hedge into a garden, and the clerk struck him with his falchion," said the provost, " and cut right through his leg, in such sort that it only holds to the boot,[1] as you may see here. The clerk then followed the other, who thought to go down into a strange house, where the people were still awake ; but the clerk struck him in the middle of the head with his falchion, so that he clove his head to the teeth, as you may see here," said the provost to the king. " Sire," continued he, " the clerk showed what he had done to the neighbours in the street, and then came and made himself your prisoner. And now, sire, I have brought him to you, to do with him what you will. You see him here."

" Sir clerk," said the king, " you have lost your priesthood by your prowess ;[2] and for your prowess I take you into my service, and you shall go with me overseas. And this thing I do for you, because I would have my men to fully understand that I will uphold them in none of their wickednesses."

When the people there assembled heard this, they cried

[1] l'estival.
[2] vous avez perdu à estre prestre par vostre proesce.

out to our Saviour, and prayed God to give the king a good and a long life, and bring him back in joy and health.

Joinville leaves his Castle

After these things I returned to our county, and we agreed, the Count of Sarrebruck and I, that we should send our baggage in carts to Ausonne, thence to be borne on the river Saone, and to Arles by the Saone and the Rhone.

The day that I left Joinville I sent for the Abbot of Cheminon, who was held to be one of the most worthy of the order of the white monks.[1] I heard this testimony regarding him given at Clairvaux on the festival of Our Lady, when the holy king was present, by a monk, who showed the abbot to me, and asked if I knew who he was ; and I inquired why he asked me this, and he answered, " because I think he is the worthiest monk in all the white order.   For listen," said he, " what I heard tell by a worthy man who slept in the same dormitory as the Abbot of Cheminon.   The abbot had bared his breast because of the great heat ; and this did the worthy man see who lay in the same dormitory : he saw the Mother of God go to the abbot's bed, and draw his garment over his breast, so that the wind might do him no hurt."

The Abbot of Cheminon gave me my scarf and staff of pilgrimage ; [2] and then I departed from Joinville on foot, barefoot, in my shirt—not to re-enter the castle till my return ; and thus I went to Blécourt, and Saint-Urbain, and to other places thereabouts where there are holy relics.   And never while I went to Blécourt and Saint-Urbain would I turn my eyes towards Joinville for fear my heart should melt within me at thought of the fair castle I was leaving behind, and my two children.[3]

I and my companions ate that day at Fontaine-l'Archeveque, before Donjeux ; and the Abbot Adam of Saint-Urbain — whom God have in His grace ! — gave a great quantity of fair jewels to myself and the nine knights I had with me.   Thence we went to Auxonne, and thence again,

---

[1] *i.e.* Monks of the Cistercian Order.

[2] m'escharpe et mon bourdon.

[3] je ne voz onques retourner mes yex vers Joinville, pour ce qui li cuers ne me attendrisist dou biau chastel que je lessoie et de mes dous enfans.

with the baggage, which we had placed in boats, from
Auxonne to Lyons down the river Saone ; and along by the
side of the boats were led the great war-horses.[1]

At Lyons we embarked on the Rhone to go to Arles the
White ; and on the Rhone we found a castle called Roche-de-
Glun, which the king had caused to be destroyed, because
Roger, the lord of the castle, was accused of robbing pilgrims
and merchants.

The Crusaders Embark, August 1248

In the month of August we entered into our ship at the
Roche-de-Marseille. On the day that we entered into our
ship, they opened the door of the ship and put therein all the
horses we were to take oversea ; and then they reclosed the
door, and caulked it well, as when a cask is sunk in water,
because, when the ship is on the high seas, all the door is under
water.

When the horses were in the ship, our master mariner
called to his seamen, who stood at the prow, and said : " Are
you ready ? " and they answered, " Aye, sir—let the clerks
and priests come forward ! " As soon as these had come
forward, he called to them, " Sing, in God's name ! " and they
all, with one voice, chanted, " *Veni Creator Spiritus.*"

Then he cried to his seamen, " Unfurl the sails, in God's
name ! " and they did so.

In a short space the wind filled our sails and had borne
us out of sight of land, so that we saw naught save sky and
water, and every day the wind carried us further from the
land where we were born. And these things I tell you, that
you may understand how foolhardy is that man who dares,
having other's chattels in his possession, or being in mortal
sin, to place himself in such peril, seeing that, when you lie
down to sleep at night on shipboard, you lie down not knowing whether, in the morning, you may find yourself at the
bottom of the sea.[2]

At sea a marvellous thing befell us ; for we came across
a mountain quite round, before the coast of Barbary. We
came across it about the hour of vespers, and sailed all night,

---

[1] les grans destriers.
[2] car l'on se dort le soir là où on ne sait se l'on se trouvera ou font
de la mer au matin.

and thought to have gone about fifty leagues ; and, on the morrow, we found ourselves before the same mountain ; and this same thing happened to us some two or three times. When the sailors saw this, they were all amazed, and told us we were in very great peril ; for we were before the land of the Saracens of Barbary.

Then a certain right worthy priest,[1] who was called the Dean of Maurupt, said to us that no mischance had ever occurred in his parish—whether lack of water, or overplus of rain, or any other mischance—but so soon as he had made three processions, on three Saturdays, God and His Mother sent them deliverance. It was then a Saturday. We made the first procession round the two masts of the ship. I had myself carried in men's arms, because I was grievously sick.[2] Never again did we see the mountain ; and on the third Saturday we came to Cyprus.

.   .   .   .

The Departure from Cyprus, 1249

[De Wailly's Ed., pp. 62 sqq.]

As soon as March came in, by the king's command, the king, the barons, and the other pilgrims ordered that the ships should be reladen with wine and provisions, so as to be ready to move when the king directed. And when the king saw that all had been duly ordered the king and queen embarked on their ships on the Friday before Whitsun,[3] and the king told his barons to follow in their ships straight to Egypt. On the Saturday the king set sail and all the others as well, which was a fair thing to look upon, for it seemed as if all the sea, so far as the eye could reach, were covered with the canvas of the ships' sails ; and the number of the ships, great and small, was reckoned at eighteen hundred.

The king anchored at the head of a hillock [4] which is called the Point of Limassol, and all the other vessels anchored round about him. The king landed on Whitsunday. After we had heard mass a fierce and powerful wind, coming from the Egyptian side, arose in such sort that

---

[1] un preudom prestres.

[2] je-meismes m'i fiz porter par les braz, pour ce que je estoie grief malades.

[3] May 21, 1249.   [4] ou bout d'un tertre.

out of two thousand eight hundred knights, whom the king
was taking into Egypt, there remained no more than seven
hundred whom the wind had not separated from the king's
company and carried away to Acre and other strange lands ;
nor did they afterwards return to the king of a long while.
The day after Whitsunday the wind had fallen. The king
and such of us as had, according to God's will, remained with
him, set sail forthwith, and met the Prince of Morea, and the
Duke of Burgundy, who had been sojourning in Morea. On
the Thursday after Whitsunday the king arrived before Damietta, and we found there, arrayed on the seashore, all the
power of the soldan—a host fair to look upon, for the soldan's
arms are of gold, and when the sun struck upon them they
were resplendent. The noise they made with their cymbals
and horns was fearful to listen to.[1]

The king summoned his barons to take counsel what
they should do. Many advised that he should wait till his
people returned, seeing that no more than a third part had
remained with him ; but to this he would by no means
agree. The reason he gave was, that to delay would put
the foe in good heart, and, particularly, he said that there
was no port before Damietta in which he could wait for his
people, and that, therefore, any strong wind arising might
drive the ships to other lands, just as the ships had been
driven on Whitsunday.

Preparation for Disembarkation in Egypt

It was settled that the king should land on the Friday
before Trinity and go to battle with the Saracens, unless
they refused to stand. The king ordered my Lord John of
Beaumont to assign a galley to my Lord Everard of Brienne
and to myself, so as that we might land, we and our knights,
because the great ships could not get close up to the shore.

Also as God willed, when I returned to my ship, I found
a little ship that my Lady of Beyrout, who was cousin-
german to my Lord of Montbéliard and to myself, had given
me, and where there were eight of my horses.

When the Friday came I and my Lord Everard went,
fully armed, to the king and asked for the galley ; where-

---

[1] La noise que il menoient de lour nacaires et de lour cors sarrazi n-
nois, estoit espouentable à escouter.

upon my Lord John of Beaumont told us that we should not have it. When our people saw that they would get no galley, they let themselves drop from the great ship into the ship's boat, pell-mell, and as best they could, so that the boat began to sink. The sailors saw that the boat was sinking, little by little, and they escaped into the big ship and left my knights in the boat. I asked the master how many more people there were in the boat than the boat could hold. He told me twenty men-at-arms ; and I asked him whether he could take our people to land if I relieved him of so many, and he said " Yes." So I relieved him in such sort that in three journeys he took them to the ship that had carried my horses.

While I was conducting these people a knight belonging to my Lord Everard of Brienne, and whose name was Plonquet, thought to go down from the great ship into the boat ; but the boat moved away, and he fell into the sea and was drowned.

When I came back to my ship I put into my little boat a squire whom I made a knight, and whose name was my Lord Hugh of Vaucouleurs, and two very valiant bachelors —of whom the one was named my Lord Villain of Versey, and the other my Lord William of Dammartin—who were at bitter enmity the one against the other. Nor could any one make peace between them, because they had seized each other by the hair in Morea.[1] And I made them forgive their grievances and embrace, for I swore to them on holy relics that we should not land in company of their enmity.

Then we set ourselves to get to land, and came alongside of the barge belonging to the king's great ship, where the king himself was. And his people began to cry out to us, because we were going more quickly than they, that I should land by the ensign of St. Denis, which was being borne in another vessel before the king. But I heeded them not, and caused my people to land in front of a great body of Turks, at a place where there were full six thousand men on horseback.

So soon as these saw us land, they came toward us, hotly spurring. We, when we saw them coming, fixed the points of our shields into the sand and the handles of our

[1] Ne nulz n'en pooit faire la paiz, car il s'estoient entrepris par les cheveus à la Morée.

lances in the sand with the points set towards them.[1] But when they were so near that they saw the lances about to enter into their bellies, they turned about and fled.

The Crusaders disembark in Front of the Saracens

My Lord Baldwin of Rheims, a right good man,[2] who had come to land, requested me, by his squire, to wait for him ; and I let him know I should do so willingly, for that a right good man such as he ought surely to be waited for in like case of need,—whereby I had his favour all the time that he lived. With him came to us a thousand knights ; and be well assured that, when I landed, I had neither squire, nor knight, nor varlet that I had brought with me from my own country, and yet God never left me without such as I needed.

At our left hand landed the Count of Jaffa, who was cousin-german to the Count of Montbéliard, and of the lineage of Joinville.[3] It was he who landed in greatest pride, for his galley came all painted, within and without, with escutcheons of his arms, which arms are or with a cross of gules patée. He had at least three hundred rowers in his galley, and for each rower there was a targe with the count's arms thereon, and to each targe was a pennon attached with his arms wrought in gold.[4]

While he was coming it seemed as if his galley flew, so did the rowers urge it forward with their sweeps ; and it seemed as if the lightning were falling from the skies at the sound that the pennants made, and the cymbals, and the drums, and the Saracenic horns that were in his galley. So soon as the galley had been driven into the sand as far up as they could drive it, both he and his knights leapt from the galley, well armed and well equipped, and came and arrayed themselves beside us.

I had forgotten to tell you that when the Count of Jaffa landed he immediately caused his tents and pavilions to be pitched ; and so soon as the Saracens saw them pitched,

---

[1] nous fichames les pointes de nos escus ou sablon et le fust de nos lances ou sablon et les pointes vers aus.

[2] uns preudom.

[3] He was related through the female line with the Joinville family.

[4] et a chascune targe avoit un pennoncel de ses armes batu à or.

they all came and gathered before us, and then came on
again, spurring hotly, as if to run in upon us. But when
they saw that we should not fly, they shortly turned and
went back again.

On our right hand, at about a long-crossbow-shot's
distance, landed the galley that bore the ensign of St. Denis.
And there was a Saracen who, when they had landed, came
and charged in among them, either because he could not
hold in his horse, or because he thought the other Saracens
would follow him ; but he was hacked to pieces.

.   .   .   .

Greek Fire hurled against the Towers that guarded the Cat-castles

[De Wailly's Ed., pp. 85 sqq.]

One night when we were keeping guard over the towers
that guarded the cat-castles, it happened that the Saracens
brought an engine called a petrary,[1] which they had not
hitherto done, and put Greek fire into the sling of the engine.
When my Lord Walter of Ecurey, the good knight who was
with me, saw it, he spoke thus : " Lords, we are in the
greatest peril that we have ever been in, for if they set fire
to our towers and we remain here we are but lost and burnt
up ; while if we leave these defences which we have set to
guard, we are dishonoured. Wherefore none can defend us
in this peril save God alone. So my advice and counsel is,
that every time they hurl the fire at us, we throw ourselves
on our elbows and knees, and pray to our Saviour to keep
us in this peril."

So soon as they hurled the first cast, we threw ourselves
on our elbows and knees as he had taught us. That first
cast fell between our two towers guarding the covered ways.
It fell on the place in front of us, where the host had been
working at the dam. Our firemen were ready to put out
the fire ; and because the Saracens could not shoot straight
at them, because of two pavilion wings that the king had
caused to be set up, they shot up into the clouds, so that
the darts fell on the firemen's heads.

[1] perriere. This engine, as its name implies, was generally used to
hurl stones. In this instance the Saracens employed it to hurl Greek
fire.

The fashion of the Greek fire was such that it came front-wise as large as a barrel of verjuice, and the tail of fire that issued from it was as large as a large lance.[1] The noise it made in coming was like heaven's thunder. It looked like a dragon flying through the air. It gave so great a light, because of the great quantity of fire making the light, that one saw as clearly throughout the camp as if it had been day. Three times did they hurl Greek fire at us that night, and four times did they discharge it with the swivel crossbow.[2]

Every time that our holy king heard them hurling the Greek fire, he would raise himself in his bed, and lift up his hands to our Saviour, and say, weeping : " Fair Lord God, guard me my people ! " And verily I believe that his prayers did us good service in our need. At night, every time the fire had fallen, he sent one of his chamberlains to ask how we fared, and whether the fire had done us any hurt.

Once when they hurled it at us, the fire fell near the tower which the people of my Lord of Courtenay were guard-ing, and struck the bank of the stream. Then, mark you, a knight, whose name was l'Aubigoiz, came to me, and said, " Lord, if you do not come to our help we shall all be burned ; for the Saracens have shot so many of their shafts that it is as if a great hedge were coming burning against our tower." We sprang up, and went thither, and found that he spoke the truth. We put out the fire, and before we had put it out, the Saracens had struck us all with shafts that they shot across the stream.

The Cat-castles burned by Greek Fire

The king's brothers kept guard over the cat-castles by day, and went to the top of the towers to shoot bolts from the crossbows at the Saracens who were in the Saracens' camp ; for the king had decided that the King of Sicily was to keep guard over the towers by day, while we were to keep guard over them by night ; and now on a day when the King of Sicily was thus keeping guard, and we were to keep guard by night, we were in sore trouble of heart, because the Saracens had well-nigh shattered our towers. And the Saracens brought out their petrary in full daylight, whereas they had

---

[1] aussi grans comme uns grans glaives.   [2] à l'arbalestre à tour.

so far only brought it out by night, and they threw Greek fire
on to our towers.   And they had brought their engines so near
to the causeway which the host were building that no one
dared to go to the towers because of the great stones that the
engines cast, and that fell upon the causeway.   Whence it
happened that the two towers were burned, and the King
of Sicily was so beside himself that he wished to throw himself
where the fire was, in order to put it out ; and if he was
incensed, I and my knights could but praise God, seeing
that if we had been on guard that night, we should all have
been burned.[1]

When the king saw this, he sent for all the barons of the
host, and begged them each to give him wood from their
ships to build a tower to help to dam up the stream ; and
he showed them clearly that there was no wood with which
this could be done, save the wood of the vessels that had
brought our goods up the river.   Each brought according
to his will, and when the tower was made, the wood was
valued at ten thousand livres and more.

The king decided also that the tower should not be pushed
forward on to the causeway until the day came when it was
the turn of the King of Sicily to mount guard, so that he
might thus repair the loss of the other towers that had been
burned while he was on guard.   As it had been decided, so
was it done ; as soon as the King of Sicily came on guard,
he caused the tower to be pushed forward along the causeway,
to the point where the other towers guarding the covered
way had been burned.

When the Saracens saw this, they so arranged that all
their sixteen engines should cast their missiles upon the
causeway, to the place whither the tower had been brought ;
and when they saw that our people feared to go to the tower
because of the stones from the engines that fell on the causeway, they brought up the petrary, and cast Greek fire at the
tower, and burned it utterly.   Great was the courtesy that
God showed to me and my knights in this matter, for if we
had mounted guard that night we should have done so in
as great peril as on the former occasion, of which I have
already spoken to you.

· · · · · · ·

[1] car se nous eussiens guietié le soir, nous eussiens estei tuit ars.

The Christians begin to suffer from Disease and Famine

[De Wailly's Ed., pp. 121 sqq.]

After the two battles aforementioned, the host began to suffer very grievously ; for at the end of nine days the bodies of our people, whom the Saracens had slain, came to the surface of the water ; and this was said to be because the gall had putrified. The bodies came floating to the bridge between our two camps, and could not pass under because the bridge touched the water. There was such great quantity of them that all the river was full of corpses, from the one bank to the other, and, lengthwise, the cast of a small stone.

The king had hired a hundred vagabonds,[1] who took full eight days to clear the river. They cast the bodies of the Saracens, who were circumcised, on the other side of the bridge, and let them go down with the stream ; the Christians they caused to be put in great trenches, one with another. I saw there the chamberlains of the Count of Artois, and many others, seeking for their friends among the dead ; but never did I hear tell that any was found.

We ate no fish in the camp the whole of Lent save eels ;[2] and the eeles ate the dead people, for they are a gluttonous fish. And because of this evil, and for the unhealthiness of the land—where it never rains a drop of water—there came upon us the sickness of the host, which sickness was such that the flesh of our legs dried up, and the skin upon our legs became spotted, black and earth colour, like an old boot ; and with us, who had this sickness, the flesh of our gums putrified ; nor could any one escape from this sickness, but he was certain to die. The sign of death was this, that when there was bleeding of the nose, then death was sure.

A fortnight afterwards the Turks, in order to starve us—which very much astonished our people—took several of their galleys that were above our camp, and caused them to be dragged by land and put into the river, a full league below our camp. And these galleys brought famine upon us ; for no one, because of these galleys, dared to come up the stream from Damietta and bring us provisions. We knew naught of these things till such time as a little ship, belonging to the Count of Flanders, escaped from them by force and told us

[1] ribaus.   [2] bourbetes.

of them, as also that the galleys of the soldan had taken
full eighty of our galleys coming from Damietta, and put to
death the people that were therein.

Thus there arose a great dearth in the camp, so that as
soon as Easter was come an ox was valued at eighty livres,
and a sheep at thirty livres, and a pig at thirty livres, and an
egg twelve deniers, and a measure of wine ten livres.

The Host re-crosses the River—Six of Joinville's Knights punished for their Wickedness

When the king and the barons saw this, they agreed
that the king should shift his camp,[1] which was on the
side towards Babylon, to the camping ground [1] of the
Duke of Burgundy, which was on the river that went to
Damietta. In order to collect his people with greater safety,
the king caused a barbican to be constructed before the
bridge between our two camps, in such wise that one could
enter the barbican from either side on horseback.

So soon as the barbican was ready, all the king's host
got under arms, and the Turks made an attack in force
upon the king's camp. Nevertheless, neither the king nor
his people moved till all the baggage had been carried over,
and then the king passed, and his body of troops after him,
and after them all the other barons, save my Lord Walter of
Chatillon, who had the rearguard. As they were entering
into the barbican, my Lord Everard of Valery delivered my
Lord John, his brother, whom the Turks were carrying away
captive.

When all the host had passed, those who remained in
the barbican were in great peril, for the barbican was not
high, so that the mounted Turks shot full at them, and the
Saracens on foot threw clods of earth right into their faces.
All would have been lost had it not been for the Count of
Anjou—afterwards King of Sicily—who went to their rescue,
and brought them out safe and sound. Of that day did my
Lord Geoffry of Mussambourc bear the prize—the prize of
all who were in the barbican.

On the eve of Shrove Tuesday [2] I beheld a marvel, of
which I will now tell you ; for on that day was buried my Lord
Hugh of Landricourt, who was with me, carrying a banner.

[1] ost.   [2] Le vegile de quaresme-pernant.

There as he lay on a bier in my chapel, six of my knights were leaning on a number of sacks full of barley; [1] and because they were speaking loud in my chapel, and disturbing the priest, I went to them, and told them to be quiet, and said it was a discourteous thing for knights and gentlemen to talk while mass was being sung. And they began to laugh and told me, laughing, that they were re-marrying the dead man's wife. And I spoke sharply to them, and told them that such words were neither good nor seemly, and that they had forgotten their companion over soon. And God took such vengeance upon them, that on the morrow was the great battle of Shrove Tuesday, in which they were all killed or mortally wounded, so that the wives of all six were in case to marry again.

Joinville falls Sick—Death of his Priest

Owing to the wounds I had received on Shrove Tuesday, the sickness of the host took hold upon me, in my mouth and legs, as also a double tertian fever, and so great a cold in my head that the rheum flowed from the head through the nostrils ; and because of the said sicknesses, I took to sickbed at mid-Lent ; and thus it befell that my priest sang mass for me, before my bed, in my pavilion. And he had the same sickness as I. Now it chanced that at the consecration, he turned faint. When I saw that he was about to fall, I, who had on my tunic,[2] leapt from my bed barefoot, and took him in my arms, and told him to do all leisurely, and to proceed fairly with the consecration, for that I should not leave him till he had brought it to an end. He came to himself, and finished the consecration,[3] and sang his mass fully. But never did he sing mass again.

Attempt to treat with the Saracens—Pitiful Condition of the Host

After these things the king's councillors and the councillors of the soldan appointed a set day on which to come to an agreement. The proposed conditions were these : that we should surrender Damietta to the soldan, and the soldan surrender to the king the kingdom of Jerusalem ; and that

[1] sus plusours saz pleins d'orge.　　　　[2] ma cote vestue.
[3] et fist son sacrement.

the soldan should take charge of the sick that were at Damietta, and also of the salted meats—because they did not eat
pork—and of the king's engines of war, until such time as
the king was able to send and fetch all these things.

They asked the king's councillors what security would be
given that the soldan should repossess Damietta. The
king's councillors offered to deliver over one of the king's
brothers, either the Count of Anjou, or the Count of Poitiers,
to be kept until such time as Damietta was placed in the
soldan's hands. The Saracens said they would consent to
nothing unless the person of the king were left with them as
a pledge ; whereupon my Lord Geoffry of Sargines, the good
knight, said he would rather that the Saracens should have
them all dead or captive than bear the reproach of having
left the king in pledge.

The sickness began to increase in the host so much,
and the dead flesh so to grow upon the gums of our people,
that the barbers [1] had to remove the dead flesh in order that
the people might masticate their food and swallow it.   Great
pity it was to hear the cry throughout the camp of the people
whose dead flesh was being cut away ; for they cried like
women labouring with child.

The Host attempts to retreat by Land and Water

When the king saw that he could only remain there to
die, he and his people, he ordered and arranged that they
should strike their camp, late on Tuesday,[2] at night, after
the octave of Easter, to return to Damietta.   He caused the
mariners who had galleys to be told that they should get
together the sick, and take them thither.   He also commanded Josselin of Cornaut, and his brothers, and the other
engineers, to cut the ropes that held the bridge between us
and the Saracens ; but of this they did nothing.

We embarked on the Tuesday, after dinner, in the afternoon, I and two of my knights whom I had remaining, and
the rest of my followers.   When the night began to fall, I
told my mariners to draw up their anchor, and let us go down
the stream ; but they said they dared not, because the

[1] Certain surgical operations, such as bleeding, were formerly
performed by barbers.

[2] 5th April 1250.

13

soldan's galleys, which were between us and Damietta, would surely put us to death. The mariners had made great fires to gather the sick into their galleys, and the sick had dragged themselves to the bank of the river. While I was exhorting the mariners to let us begone, the Saracens entered into the camp, and I saw, by the light of the fires, that they were slaughtering the sick on the bank.

While my mariners were raising their anchor, the mariners appointed to take away the sick cut the ropes of their anchors and of their galleys and came alongside our little ship, and so surrounded us on one side and the other that they well-nigh ran us down. When we had escaped from this peril, and while we were going down with the stream, the king, who had upon him the sickness of the host and a very evil dysentery, could easily have got away on the galleys, if he had been so minded ; but he said that, please God, he would never abandon his people. That night he fainted several times ; and because of the sore dysentery from which he suffered, it was necessary to cut away the lower part of his drawers, so frequent were his necessities.

They cried to us, who were floating on the water, that we should wait for the king ; and when we would not wait, they shot at us with crossbow bolts ;[1] wherefore it behoved us to stop until such time as they gave us leave to proceed.

The King made Prisoner—The Saracens violate the Truce

Now I will leave off speaking of this matter, and tell you how the king was taken, as he himself related it to me. He told me how he had left his own division and placed himself, he and my Lord Geoffry of Sargines, in the division that was under my Lord Gaucher of Chatillon, who commanded the rearguard.

And the king told me that he was mounted on a little courser[2] covered with a housing of silk ; and he told me that of all his knights and sergeants there only remained behind with him my Lord Geoffry of Sargines, who brought the king to a little village, there where the king was taken ; and as the king related to me, my Lord Geoffry of Sargines defended him from the Saracens as a good servitor defends his lord's drinking-cup from flies ;[3] for every time that the

---

[1] quarriaus.   [2] sur un petit roncin.
[3] comme li bons vallez deffent le hanap son signour des mouches.

Saracens approached, he took his spear, which he had placed
between himself and the bow of his saddle, and put it to his
shoulder, and ran upon them, and drove them away from the
king.

And thus he brought the king to the little village ; and
they lifted him into a house, and laid him, almost as one
dead, in the lap of a burgher-woman of Paris, and thought
he would not last till night.   Thither came my Lord Philip
of Montfort, and said to the king that he saw the emir with
whom he had treated of the truce, and if the king so willed,
he would go to him, and renew the negotiation for a truce in
the manner that the Saracens desired.   The king begged
him to go, and said he was right willing.   So my Lord Philip
went to the Saracen ; and the Saracen had taken off his
turban from his head, and took off the ring from his finger
in token that he would faithfully observe the truce.

Meanwhile, a very great mischance happened to our
people ; for a traitor sergeant, whose name was Marcel,
began to cry to our people : " Yield, lord knights, for the
king commands you, and do not cause the king to be slain ! "
All thought that the king had so commanded, and gave up
their swords to the Saracens.   The emir saw that the Saracens
were bringing in our people prisoners, so he said to my Lord
Philip that it was not fitting that he should grant a truce to
our people, for he saw very well that they were already
prisoners.

So it happened to my Lord Philip that whereas all our
people were taken captive, yet was not he so taken, because
he was an envoy.   But there is an evil custom in the land of
paynimry that when the king sends envoys to the soldan, or
the soldan to the king, and the king dies, or the soldan, before
the envoy's return, then the envoys, from whithersoever they
may come, and whether Christians or Saracens, are made
prisoners and slaves.

.   .   .   .

IV. EXTRACTS FROM THE *VOYAGES AND TRAVELS* OF " SIR JOHN MAUNDEVILLE "

[" Sir John Maundeville " was born at St. Albans about 1300. On
Michaelmas Day, 1322, he set out to travel extensively in the
East, and spent thirty years visiting distant lands that were

almost unknown to Western Europe in the fourteenth century. At last he was compelled by a severe attack of rheumatic gout to return home and rest. He wrote the account of his travels, from which the following extracts are made, in French, afterwards issuing a version in Latin. The book is planned as a guide to pilgrims to the Holy Places at Jerusalem, but Maundeville takes his readers much farther afield than this—to India and China and the Malay Archipelago. It became the most popular of all books of travel in the later Middle Ages, as is shown by the large number of MSS. that have survived. It illustrates the way in which the horizon of the medieval Englishman expanded as a result of the Crusades. It is also one of the best surviving expositions of medieval geography. Maundeville died at Liége in 1372. His book is printed in its entirety in *Early Travels in Palestine*, in Bohn's Antiquarian Library (Messrs. George Bell & Son). A handy little volume of Maundeville in modern spelling is published in Cassell's National Library, No. 11 (Messrs. Cassell & Co. Ltd., 1886).]

A. INTRODUCTION

AND forasmuch as it is long time passed that there was no general passage or voyage over the sea, and many men desiring to hear speak of the Holy Land, and have thereof great solace and comfort, I, John Maundeville, knight, albeit I be not worthy, who was born in England, in the town of Saint Albans, passed the sea in the year of our Lord Jesus Christ 1322, on the day of St. Michael ; and hitherto have been a long time over the sea, and have seen and gone through many different lands, and many provinces, and kingdoms, and isles, and have passed through Tartary, Persia, Ermony (Armenia) the Little and the Great ; through Lybia, Chaldea, and a great part of Ethiopia ; through Amazonia, India the Less and the Greater, a great part ; and throughout many other isles that are about India ; where dwell many different folks, and of divers manners and laws, and of divers shapes of men. Of which lands and isles I shall speak more plainly hereafter. And I shall devise you some part of things that are there, when time shall be as it may best come to my mind ; and especially for them that will and are in purpose to visit the holy city of Jerusalem, and the holy places that are thereabout. And I shall tell the way that they shall hold thither ; for I have ofttimes passed and ridden the way, with good company of many lords : God be thanked !

And ye shall understand that I have put this book out of Latin into French, and translated it again out of French into English,[1] that every man of my nation may understand it ; and that lords and knights and other noble and worthy men that know Latin but little, and have been beyond the sea, may know and understand, if I err from defect of memory, and may redress it and amend it. For things passed out of long time from a man's mind or from his sight turn soon into forgetting ; because a man's mind may not be comprehended or withheld, on account of the frailty of mankind.

B. TO TEACH YOU THE WAY OUT OF ENGLAND TO CONSTANTINOPLE

In the name of God, glorious and Almighty. He that will pass over the sea to go to the city of Jerusalem may go many ways, both by sea and land, according to the country that he cometh from : many ways come to one end. But you must not expect that I will tell you all the towns, and cities, and castles, that men shall go by ; for then I should make too long a tale : but only some countries and the principal places that men shall go through to go the right way.

First, if a man come from the west side of the world, as England, Ireland, Wales, Scotland, or Norway, he may, if he will, go through Almaine,[2] and through the kingdom of Hungary, which borders on the land of Polaine,[3] and to the land of Pannonia, and so to Silesia. And the king of Hungary is a great and mighty lord, and possesses great lordships and much land. For he holds the kingdom of Hungary, Sclavonia, and a great part of Comania and Bulgaria, which men call the land of Bougres, and the realm of Russia, a great part, whereof he hath made a duchy, that extendeth unto the land of Nyflan, and borders on Prussia. And we go through the land of this lord, through a city that is called Cypron, and by the castle of Neaseborough, and by the evil town, which is situated towards the end of Hungary.

And there men pass the river Danube, which is a very great river, and it goeth into Almaine,[4] under the hills of Lombardy ; and it receives forty other rivers, and runs

---

[1] As a matter of fact the book was translated into English, long after the author's death, about 1400.

[2] Germany.   [3] Poland.   [4] Germany.

through Hungary, and through Greece, and through Thrace, and entereth into the sea, towards the east, so roughly and so sharply, that the water of the sea is fresh and keeps its sweetness twenty miles from shore.

And after, men go to Belgrave, and enter the land of Bougres ; and there men pass a bridge of stone, which is upon the river Marrok. And men pass through the land of Pyncemartz, and come to Greece to the city of Nye, and to the city of Fynepape, and after to the city of Adrianople, and then to Constantinople, which was formerly called Byzantium, where the Emperor of Greece usually dwells.

And there is the fairest and noblest church in the world, that of St. Sophia. And before the church is the image of the emperor Justinian, covered with gold, and he sits crowned upon a horse ; and he formerly held a round apple of gold in his hand, but it is fallen down ; and they say there, that it is a token that the emperor hath lost a great part of his lands and lordships. For he was emperor of Romania and of Greece, of all Asia the Less, and of the land of Syria, of the land of Judea, in which is Jerusalem, and of the land of Egypt, of Persia, and of Arabia ; but he hath lost all but Greece ; and men would many times restore the apple to the hand of the image, but it will not hold it. The apple betokens the lordship which he had over all the world, which is round ; and the other hand he lifts up towards the east, in token to menace the misdoers. This image stands upon a pillar of marble at Constantinople.

C. How the Earth and the Sea are of Round Form, as is proved by the Star called Antarctic, which is fixed in the South

Neither in that land, nor in many others beyond it, may any man see the polar star, which is called the Star of the Sea, which is immovable, and is towards the north, and which we call the load-star. But they see another star opposite to it, towards the south, which is called Antarctic. And right as shipmen here govern themselves by the load-star, so shipmen beyond these parts are guided by the star of the south, which appears not to us. This star, which is towards the north, that we call the load-star, appears not to them. For which cause, we may clearly perceive that the land and sea are of round shape and form, because the part of the firmament appears in one country which is not seen in another country.

And men may prove by experience and their understanding, that if a man found passages by ships, he might go by ship all round the world, above and beneath ; which I prove thus, after what I have seen. For I have been towards the parts of Brabant, and found by the astrolabe that the polar star is fifty-three degrees high ; and further, in Germany and Bohemia, it has fifty-eight degrees ; and still further, towards the north, it is sixty-two degrees and some minutes ; for I myself have measured it by the astrolabe. Now you shall know that opposite the polar star is the other star, called antarctic, as I have said before. These two stars are fixed ; and about them all the firmament turns as a wheel that turns on its axle-tree ; so that those stars bear the firmament in two equal parts ; so that it has as much above as it has beneath. After this I have gone towards the south, and have found that in Lybia we first see the antarctic star ; and I have gone so far in those countries that I have found that star higher, so that, towards Upper Lybia, it is eighteen degrees and certain minutes. After going by sea and land towards the country of which I spoke last, and to other isles and lands beyond that country, I have found the antarctic star thirty-three degrees in altitude and some minutes. And if I had had company and shipping to go further, I believe certainly that we should have seen all the roundness of the firmament all about.

For, as I have told you before, the half of the firmament is between the two stars, which half I have seen. And the other half I have seen towards the north, under the polar star, sixty-two degrees and ten minutes ; and, towards the south, I have seen under the antarctic thirty-three degrees and sixteen minutes ; and the half of the firmament in all contains but one hundred and eighty degrees, of which I have seen sixty-two on the one part, and thirty-three on the other, which makes ninety-five degrees, and nearly the half of a degree ; so that I have seen all the firmament except eighty-four degrees and the half of a degree ; and that is not the fourth part of the firmament. By which I tell you, certainly, that men may go all round the world, as well under as above, and return to their country, if they had

company, and shipping, and guides ; and always they would
find men, lands, and isles, as well as in our part of the world.
For they who are towards the antarctic are directly feet
opposite feet of them who dwell under the polar star ; as
well as we and they that dwell under us are feet opposite feet.
For all parts of sea and land have their opposites, habitable
or passable.

And know well that, after what I may perceive and
understand, the lands of Prester John, emperor of India, are
under us ; for in going from Scotland or from England,
towards Jerusalem, men go always upwards ; for our land
is in the low part of the earth, towards the west ; and the
land of Prester John is in the low part of the earth, towards
the east ; and they have there the day when we have night ;
and, on the contrary, they have the night when we have the
day ; for the earth and the sea are of a round form, as I
have said before ; and as men go upward to one part, they
go downward to another. Also you have heard me say that
Jerusalem is in the middle of the world ; and that may be
proved and shown there by a spear which is fixed in the
earth at the hour of midday, when it is equinoxial, which
gives no shadow on any side.

They, therefore, that start from the west to go towards
Jerusalem, as many days as they go upward to go thither,
in so many days may they go from Jerusalem to other
confines of the superficialities of the earth beyond. And
when men go beyond that distance, towards India and to
the foreign isles, they are proceeding on the roundness of the
earth and the sea, under our country. And therefore hath
it befallen many times of a thing that I have heard told
when I was young, how a worthy man departed once from
our country to go and discover the world ; and so he passed
India, and the isles beyond India, where are more than five
thousand isles ; and so long he went by sea and land, and
so environed the world by many seasons, that he found an
isle where he heard people speak his own language, calling
an oxen in the plough such words as men speak to beasts in
his own country, whereof he had great wonder, for he knew
not how it might be. But I say that he had gone so long,
by land and sea, that he had gone all round the earth, that
he was come again to his own borders, if he would have
passed forth till he had found his native country. But he

turned again from thence, from whence he was come ; and so he lost much painful labour, as himself said, a great while after, when he was coming home ; for it befell after that he went into Norway, and the tempest of the sea carried him to an isle ; and when he was in that isle he knew well that it was the isle where he had heard his own language spoken before, and the calling of the oxen at the plough.

But it seems to simple and unlearned men that men may not go under the earth, but that they would fall from under towards the heaven. But that may not be any more than we fall towards heaven from the earth where we are ; for from what part of the earth that men dwell, either above or beneath, it seems always to them that they go more right than any other people. And right as it seems to us that they be under us, so it seems to them that we are under them ; for if a man might fall from the earth unto the firmament, by greater reason the earth and the sea, that are so great and so heavy, should fall to the firmament, but that may not be, and therefore saith our Lord God, " He hangeth the earth upon nothing."

And although it be possible so to go all round the world, yet of a thousand persons not one might happen to return to his country ; for, from the greatness of the earth and sea, men may go by a thousand different ways, that no one could be sure of returning exactly to the parts he came from, unless by chance or by the grace of God ; for the earth is very large, and contains in roundness and circuit, above and beneath, 20,425 miles, after the opinion of the old wise astronomers ; and, after my little wit, it seems to me, saving their reverence, that it is more ; for I say thus : let there be imagined a figure that has a great compass ; and, about the point of the great compass, which is called the centre, let there be made another little compass ; then, afterwards, let the great compass be divided by lines in many parts, and all the lines meet at the centre ; so that in as many parts as the great compass shall be divided, in so many shall the little one that is about the centre be divided, although the spaces be less. Let the great compass be represented for the firmament, and the little compass for the earth ; now the firmament is divided by astronomers into twelve signs, and every sign is divided into thirty degrees. Also let the earth be divided into as many parts as the firmament, and let every part answer to a degree of the firmament ; and I know well that, after the authorities in astronomy, seven hundred furlongs of earth answer to a degree of the firmament, that is eighty-seven miles and four furlongs. Now, multiplied by three hundred and sixty times, it makes 31,500 miles, each of eight furlongs, according to miles of our country. So much hath the earth in circuit after my opinion and understanding.

D. Prester John

Many other isles there are in the land of Prester John, and many great marvels, that were too long to tell, both of his riches and of his nobleness, and of the great plenty also of precious stones that he has. I think that you know well now, and have heard say, why this emperor is called Prester John. There was some time an emperor there, who was a worthy and a full noble prince, that had Christian knights in his company, as he has that now is. So it befell that he had great desire to see the service in the church among Christians ; and then Christendom extended beyond the sea, including all Turkey, Syria, Tartary, Jerusalem, Palestine, Arabia, Aleppo, and all the land of Egypt. So it befell that this emperor came, with a Christian knight with him, into a church in Egypt ; and it was the Saturday in Whitsuntide. The bishop was conferring orders ; and he beheld and listened to the service full attentively ; and he asked the Christian knight what men of degree they should be that the prelate had before him ; and the knight answered and said that they were priests. And then the emperor said that he would no longer be called king or emperor, but priest ; and that he would have the name of the first priest that went out of the church ; and his name was John. And so, evermore since, he is called Prester John.

V. EXTRACTS FROM THE WORKS OF ROGER BACON

[According to John Rous the Antiquary, who had been a student in Oxford about 1440, Roger Bacon was born of a " noble family of the inhabitants of the County of Dorset near Ilchester." Ilchester, it may be noted, is actually in Somersetshire, but it is only a few miles from the Dorset border. Other traditions make Bacon's birthplace the Parish of Bisley, in Gloucester-shire, and the town of Witney, in Oxfordshire. The Ilchester tradition, however, is the earliest and the most generally accepted. The date of Bacon's birth is fixed from a passage in the *Opus Tertium* as about the year 1214. He went to Oxford probably when he was about thirteen years of age, and studied there with extraordinary industry and ability. Some time about 1235 he went on to the greater university of Paris to continue his studies. By the year 1250 we find him back in England.

Some time during his student life either at Oxford or at Paris he joined the Franciscan Order. The motives which led this great scholar to join a mendicant order have been the subject of endless conjectures. The rule of St. Francis, with its ideal of utter poverty, made it difficult for a member of his order to possess the mathematical instruments and paraphernalia of science necessary to pursue the researches to which Bacon wished to devote his life. Bacon's advanced views on many subjects, together with his violent denunciations of those with whom he disagreed, soon brought him into trouble with his order. It is commonly stated that he was imprisoned for ten years in Paris from 1257 to 1267 by the order of the General of the Franciscans. This is probably a mistake. A document discovered in the Vatican Library in 1896 makes it more likely that Bacon was not hampered in his researches by imprisonment, but by a serious illness during these ten years. In 1266, Pope Clement IV., who had in his earlier days made the acquaintance of Bacon, asked him to send him an account of his researches, and a treatise on the sciences. In spite of almost overwhelming difficulties Bacon worked with incredible industry, and within eighteen months dispatched to the Pope three long treatises, the *Opus Majus*, the *Opus Minus*, and the *Opus Tertium*. These works are the fullest record that we have of the immense knowledge, the curiously modern outlook, and the wonderful forecasts of modern inventions that have caused many to consider Friar Bacon the greatest man of the Middle Ages. In 1268 Bacon was allowed to return to Oxford. But ten years later his works were condemned by the Franciscan Order, and Bacon seems to have spent some years of his old age in prison, where he wrote a small book on methods of prolonging life, the *De Retardandis Senectutis Accidentibus*. He survived his imprisonment, and in 1292 we find him writing his *Compendium Studii Theologiae*. Soon after this, his long and troubled life of industry and failure must have come to an end. John Rous says in his *Historia Regum Angliae*: " The noble doctor Roger Bacon was buried at the Grey Friars in Oxford A.D. 1292, on the feast of St. Barnabas the Apostle " (June 11). The best book on Bacon's life and works is *Roger Bacon : Commemoration Essays* edited by A. G. Little (Oxford University Press, 1914).

See also Bridges, *The Opus Majus of Roger Bacon*, 2 vols. (Oxford University Press), and Brewer, *Opera Inedita Rogeri Baconis*, London, 1859 (Rolls Series, No. 15). For the legends of Roger Bacon, see *The Famous Historie of Fryer Bacon* (London, 1615).]

A. Bacon's Labours and Difficulties

From the " Opus Tertium," ch. ii.

WHEN your holiness wrote to me, on the last occasion, the writings you demanded were not yet composed, although you supposed they were. For whilst I was in a different state of life [1] I had written nothing on Science ; nor in my present condition had I ever been required to do so by my superiors ; nay, a strict prohibition had been passed to the contrary, under penalty of forfeiture of the book, and many days' fasting on bread and water, if any work written by me, or belonging to my house, should be communicated to strangers. Nor could I get a fair copy [2] made except by employing transcribers unconnected with our Order ; and then they would have copied my works to serve themselves or others, without any regard to my wishes, as authors' works are often pirated by the knavery of transcribers at Paris. And certainly if it had been in my power to have communicated my discoveries freely, I should have composed many things for my brother, the scholar, and for others, my most intimate friends. But as I despaired of the means of communicating my thoughts, I forbore to commit them to writing. When, therefore, I professed to you my readiness, you must understand that it was for writings to be composed, not for such as had been composed already. And, therefore, your chaplain, Raymond of Laon, was altogether mistaken when he made mention of me to your holiness. For although I had at various times put together, in a hasty manner, some few chapters on different subjects, at the request of my friends, there was nothing noteworthy in these writings : nothing of such a nature as I could think of presenting to your wisdom. They were such as I myself hold in no estimation, as being deficient in continuity and perfection.

[1] *i.e.* before entering the Franciscan Order.
[2] littera bona.

From the " Opus Tertium," ch. iii.

I wrote to my brother, a rich man in my country. But
he, belonging as he did to the king's party, was in exile with
my mother, brothers and whole family. Ruined and reduced
to utter poverty, he was unable to help me, and up to the
present day has sent me no reply.

From the " Opus Tertium," ch. xvii.

I sought the friendship of all wise men among the Latins ;
and I caused young men to be trained in languages, in geo-
metrical figures, in numbers, in the construction of tables,
in the use of instruments and in many other necessary things.
During this time I spent more than two thousand pounds in
those things and in the purchase of books and instruments.

From the " Opus Tertium," ch. xx.

I have laboured much in the sciences and in languages,
and it is now forty years since first I learned the alphabet,
and I have always been industrious ; and except for two
years of these forty I have always been studying in a
university.[1]

B. PLEA FOR THE STUDY OF BOOKS IN THEIR ORIGINAL LANGUAGES

From the " Compendium Studii Philosophiae," viii. 465

THE Latins never originated a single text, either in theology
or philosophy. All texts were composed in the first and
second instance in Hebrew, in the third in Greek, and in the
fourth in Arabic. . . .
Waters drawn from the fountains were sweeter than those
taken from turbid rivulets, and wine was purer and more
wholesome when kept in the original cask than when poured
from vessel to vessel. If, therefore, the Latins wish to
drink the pure and wholesome liquor from the fount of wisdom,
they must turn their attention to the Hebrew, Greek and
Arabic languages. It is impossible to recognize the proper

[1] in studio.

form and beauty and wisdom in all their dignity except in
the languages in which they were originally laid down.   Oh,
how delicious is the taste of wisdom to those who draw from
the well of wisdom in its primary fullness and purity !   All
others are like those stricken with paralysis, who could not
judge of the sweetness of food ; like those born deaf who are
unable to enjoy the harmony of sound.

From the " Opus Tertium," ch. xxv.

Jerome says that one language cannot possibly be represented by another.   That which sounds well in one tongue
becomes ridiculous when expressed in another.   Homer
became ridiculous when translated into Latin, and that most
eloquent poet could hardly be said to speak at all.

C. The Importance of Mathematics

From the " Opus Majus," vol. i. p. 97

THE neglect of mathematics for thirty or forty years has
nearly destroyed the entire studies of Latin Christendom.
For he who knows not mathematics cannot know any other
sciences ; what is more, cannot discover his own ignorance
or find its proper remedies.   So it is that the knowledge of
this science prepares the mind, and elevates it to a well-
authenticated knowledge of all things.   For without mathematics neither antecedents nor consequents can be known ;
they perfect and regulate the former, and dispose and prepare
the way for that which succeeds.

From the " Opus Majus," vol. i. p. 108

These reasons are of universal application ; to descend
to particulars would be nothing more than to show how all
parts of philosophy are learned by the application of mathematics ; in other words, that the sciences cannot be known
by logical and sophistical arguments, as is ordinarily the
case, but by mathematical demonstrations descending into
the truths and operations of other sciences, and regulating
them, for without mathematics they cannot be understood
or set forth, taught, or learned.

From the " Opus Tertium," ch. xii.

Without mathematical instruments no science can be mastered ; and these instruments are not to be found among the Latins, and could not be made for two or three hundred pounds. And besides, better tables are indispensably requisite, for although the certifying of tables is done by instruments, yet this cannot be accomplished unless there be an immense number of instruments, and these are hard to use and hard to keep because of rusting, and they cannot be moved from place to place without danger of breaking ; and a man cannot have everywhere and on all occasions new instruments, which yet he ought to have unless he have certified tables. These tables are called *Almanack* or *Tallignum*, in which, once for all, the motions of the heavens are certified from the beginning to the end of the world, without daily labour ; so that a man can find everything in the heavens every day, as we find in the calendar the feast days of the Saints ; and then every day we could consider in the heavens the causes of all things which are renovated in the earth, and seek similar positions [of the heavens] in times past, and discover similar effects. These tables would be worth a king's ransom, and therefore could not be made without vast expense. And I have often attempted the composition of such tables, but could not finish them through failure of the expenses, and the folly of those whom I had to employ. For, first of all, it would be necessary that ten or twelve boys should be instructed in the ordinary canons and mathematical tables ; and when they knew how to work at them, then for a year to discover the motions of each planet singly for every day and every hour, according to all the variations of their motions and other changes in the heavens.

Then there are other instruments and tables of practical geometry, and practical arithmetic, and music, which are of great utility and are indispensably required. But more than any of these it would be requisite to obtain men, who have a good knowledge of optics [1] and its instruments. For this is the science of true vision, and by vision we know all things. This science certifies mathematics and all other things, because astronomical instruments do not work except by vision in accordance with the laws of that science. Nor is it

[1] perspectiva.

wonderful if all things are known by mathematics, and yet all things by the science [optics] because, as I have said before, the sciences are intimately connected, although each has its proper and peculiar province. But this science has not hitherto been read at Paris or among the Latins ; except twice at Oxford in England ; and there are not three persons acquainted with its power. He who pretends to be an authority (of whom I have spoken before) knows nothing of the power of this science, which he would have done had he known it ; nor in his other books has he said anything about it. They are but few who know these things as in the case of mathematics, and are not to be had, except at great expense ; and so likewise are the instruments of this science, which are very difficult, and of greater cost than instruments needed for mathematics.

I say this because I am sorry for his ignorance and that of the generality ; for without these they can know nothing. No author among the ancient masters or the moderns has written about them, but I have laboured at them for ten years, as far as I could find time, and I have examined them narrowly as well as I could, reducing them to writing since the time I received your mandate.

D. The Necessity of Experiment

From the " Opus Tertium," ch. xii.

But besides these sciences is one more perfect than all others, to which all are subject and which in a wonderful way proves them all ; and this is called experimental science, which disregards arguments, because they cannot prove, be they never so strong, unless the conclusion is also found true to experience, as I am setting forth in a dissertation on this science. And this science teaches that the noble conclusions of all the sciences should be tested by experiment ; which in other sciences are either proved by arguments or investigated only by poor [1] and imperfect trials ; and this is its one special privilege, as I am now showing in the Sixth Part of the Opus Majus, in the conclusions of natural philosophy and optics and their truths about the rainbow, about coloured circles round the moon, and about the sun and the stars.

[1] naturales—(?) viles.

And I am setting forth there the immense importance of this science in proving the other sciences. Fools busy themselves about proving statements in the *De Meteoris* of Aristotle and in *Optics*, but quite uselessly. Because here things cannot be proved by argument, but only by experiment. And therefore I place the roots of experiments around these matters ; which none of the Latins can understand, except one, viz. Master Peter.[1]

E. Forecast of Mechanical Inventions

From " De Secretis Operibus Artis et Naturae," ch. iv.

I will tell first, therefore, of the wonderful works of Art and Nature, in order to assign to them afterwards their causes and means ; in these there is nothing of a magical nature. Hence it may be seen that all magic power is inferior to these achievements and unworthy of them. And, first, let us consider the possibilities of unaided art. For first machines of navigation can be constructed, without rowers, as great ships for river or ocean, which are bourne under the guidance of one man at a greater speed than if they were full of men. Also a chariot can be constructed that will move with incalculable speed without any draught animal, as we deem the scythed chariots moved, from which the ancients fought. Also flying machines can be constructed so that a man may sit in the midst of the machine turning a certain instrument, by means of which wings artificially constructed would beat the air, after the manner of a bird flying. Also a machine of small size may be made for raising and lowering weights of almost infinite amount—a machine of the utmost utility. For by means of a machine three fingers in height and of the same, and of even a smaller, bulk a man may deliver himself and his companions from all danger of prison, and may rise on high and sink down again at will. A machine may easily be constructed whereby one man may forcibly draw to himself a thousand men, in spite of themselves ; and other things may be attracted in just the same way. Machines may also be made for going in sea or

---

[1] Petrus de Maharncuris, the obscure scientist of Paris, for whom Bacon had unbounded admiration. *Vide* Pictavet, *Essais*, etc. (Paris, 1913), cap. xii.

14

river down to the bed without bodily danger. For Alexander
the Great made use of these to behold the secrets of the sea,
as is described by Ethicus the Astronomer. These machines
were constructed in ancient times and also, as is certain, in
our own times—all except the flying machine, which I have
never seen, nor have I ever seen a man who had seen one ;
but I know a wise man who has figured out all the details of
the invention. And there are countless other such things
which can be constructed ; such as bridges over rivers without pillars or any such supports, and engineering feats and
unheard-of contrivances.

CHAPTER VI

THE HUNDRED YEARS' WAR

I. THE MILITARY EXPLOITS

EXTRACT FROM FROISSART'S *CHRONICLES*—THE BATTLE OF CREÇY

[Jean Froissart was born at Valenciennes in 1337, and died at Chimay about 1410. His father, named Thomas, appears to have been a painter by trade ; and Jean was from an early age destined for the Church, in spite of the fact that, as he himself tells us in some of his verses, his youthful inclinations were anything but ecclesiastical. Hunting, music, feasting, dancing, wine, and women held a very large place in his life. In spite of this he devoted some time to study, in which his prodigious powers of memory stood him in good stead. At the age of twenty he was requested by Robert de Namur, Lord of Beaufort, to write a history of the wars of his time. Accordingly he

wrote the first part of his great *Chronicle*, covering the years
1326–1340, and drawing most of his information from the writings
of Jehan Le Bel, canon of St. Lambert of Liége. After this he
came to England and entered the service of Philippa of Hainault,
Edward III.'s queen. His visit to England seems to have been
due to a desire to forget in foreign travel the disappointment of
an unsuccessful love affair. In spite of a good reception by the
Queen, he soon returned home ; but came back in 1362, and was
appointed clerk of the Queen's chapel and secretary to the
Queen. In 1364 he visited Scotland and spent some days with
Earl Douglas. He followed the Black Prince to Bordeaux in
1366, and accompanied him for a short distance on his Spanish
expedition in aid of Pedro the Cruel. The Prince, however,
ordered him to return to England. In 1368 he went to Italy
in the suite of Lionel, Duke of Clarence, and took part in company with Chaucer and Petrarch in the fêtes given at Milan to
celebrate the marriage of Lionel and the daughter of Galeazzo
Visconti. After the death of Queen Philippa in 1369, he decided
not to return to England, and to settle down instead in his
native land. But his adventurous spirit gave him no rest.
He soon attached himself as clerk and secretary to Wenceslaus,
Duke of Brabant, and when Wenceslaus died in 1384 he entered
the service of Guy, Count of Blois, who encouraged him to
continue his *Chronicle*, and gave him the means to travel in
search of material. Froissart's *Chronicle* is not to be regarded
as serious history ; but rather as a brilliant and superficial
picture of the pageantry of war in the fourteenth century. It
enables one to see the world from the standpoint of medieval
knight and noble during the heyday of chivalry.

The following extract is made from a translation of Froissart's
Chronicle by Thomas Johnes of Hafod, published 1803–4. A
useful volume of selections from this translation is published in
the Scott Library (Walter Scott Ltd.). An older and finer
translation of Froissart is that made by Lord Berners in the
reign of Henry VIII. But the English is, of course, archaic and
in some places difficult, perhaps, for a modern reader to follow.
A very handy edition of this translation, slightly abridged and
with modernized spelling, is published in the Globe Series
(Macmillan & Co. Ltd.).]

WHEN the king had finished his business in Caen, and
had sent his fleet to England, loaded with cloths,
jewels, gold and silver plate, and a quantity of other
riches, and upwards of sixty knights, with three hundred
able citizens, prisoners, he then left his quarters and continued his march as before, his two marshals on his right and
left, burning and destroying all the flat country. He took

the road to Evreux, but found he could not gain anything there, as it was well fortified. He went on towards another town called Louviers, which was in Normandy, and where there were many manufactories of cloth ; it was rich and commercial. The English won it easily, as it was not enclosed ; and having entered the town, it was plundered without opposition. They collected much wealth there ; and, after they had done what they pleased, they marched on into the county of Evreux, where they burnt everything except the fortified towns and castles, which the king left unattacked, as he was desirous of sparing his men and artillery.[1] He therefore made for the banks of the Seine, in his approach to Rouen, where there were plenty of men-at-arms from Normandy, under the command of the Earl of Harcourt, brother to sir Godfrey, and the Earl of Dreux.

The English did not march direct towards Rouen, but went to Gisors, which has a strong castle, and burnt the town. After this they destroyed Vernon, and all the country between Rouen and Pont-de-l'Arche : they then came to Mantes and Meulan, which they treated in the same manner, and ravaged all the country round about. They passed by the strong castle of Roulleboise, and everywhere found the bridges on the Seine broken down. They pushed forward until they came to Poissy, where the bridge was also destroyed ; but the beams and other parts of it were lying in the river. The king remained here five days, whilst they were repairing the bridge, so that his army might pass over without danger. His marshals advanced very near to Paris, and burnt St. Germain-en-Laye, la Montjoie, St. Cloud, Boulogne, near Paris, and Bourg la Reine. The Parisians were much alarmed, for Paris at that time was not enclosed. King Philip upon this began to stir, and having ordered all the pent-houses in Paris to be pulled down, went to St. Denis, where he found the king of Bohemia, the lord John of Hainault, the Duke of Lorraine, the Earl of Flanders, the Earl of Blois, and great multitudes of barons and knights, ready to receive him. When the Parisians learnt that the king was on the point of quitting Paris, they came to him, and falling on their knees, said, " Ah, sire, and noble king, what are you about to do to leave your fine city of Paris ? " The king

[1] " artillery," in the old sense of missile-throwing engines, arrows, etc. It is doubtful whether Edward had any cannon with him.

replied : "My good people, do not be afraid ; the English will not approach you nearer than they have done." He thus spoke in answer to what they had said, that "Our enemies are only two leagues off ; as soon as they shall know you have quitted us, they will come hither directly ; and we are not able to resist them ourselves, nor shall we find any to defend us. Have the kindness, therefore, sire, to remain in your good city of Paris, to take care of us." The king replied : "I am going to St. Denis, to my army, for I am impatient to pursue the English, and am resolved to fight with them at all events."

The King of England remained at the nunnery of Poissy to the middle of August, and celebrated there the feast of the Virgin Mary.[1] He sat at table in his scarlet robes without sleeves, trimmed with furs and ermines. He afterwards took the field, and his army marched as before : sir Godfrey de Harcourt, one of his marshals, had the command of the vanguard, with five hundred men-at-arms, and about thirteen hundred archers. By accident, he fell in with a large party of the citizens of Amiens on horseback, who were going to king Philip at Paris, in obedience to his summons. He immediately attacked them with those under his command ; but they made a good defence as they were very numerous and well armed, and had four knights from Amiens with them. The engagement lasted a long time, and many were slain at the onset ; but at last those from Amiens were overthrown, killed, or taken prisoners. The English seized all their baggage and arms, and found many valuables ; for they were going to the king excellently well equipped, and had but just quitted their city. Twelve hundred were left dead on the spot. The King of England entered the country of Beauvais, destroying all the flat country, and took up his quarters in a rich abbey called St. Messien, near to Beauvais, where he lodged one night. The morrow, as he was on the march, he by chance turned his head round and saw the abbey all in flames ; upon which he instantly ordered twenty of those who had set fire to it to be hung, as he had most strictly forbidden that any church should be violated or monastery set on fire. He passed near Beauvais without attacking it, for he was anxious to be as careful of his men and artillery as possible, and

[1] *i.e.* the Feast of the Assumption B.V.M., 15th August.

took up his quarters at a small town called Milly. The two marshals passed so near to Beauvais, that they advanced to attack it and skirmish with the townsmen at the barriers, and divided their forces into three battalions ; this attack lasted until the afternoon ; for the town was well fortified and provided with everything, and the bishop was also there, whose exertions were of more service than those of all the rest. When the English found they could not gain anything, they set fire to the suburbs, which they burnt quite close to the gates of the town, and then came, towards evening, to where the king was.

The next day, the king and his whole army marched forward, burning and wasting all the country as they went, and lay that night at a village called Grandvillier. On the morrow, he passed near to Argis ; his scouts not finding any one to guard the castle, he attacked and burnt it, and passing on, destroyed the country, and came to Poix, which was a handsome town with two castles. The lords of both were absent, and no one was there but two handsome daughters of the lord of Poix, who would have been soon violated, if two English knights, sir John Chandos and lord Basset, had not defended them. In order more effectually to guard them, they brought them to the king, who, as in honour bound, entertained them most graciously ; he inquired whither they would wish to go. They answered, to Corbie, to which place they were conducted in safety. The King of England lay that night in the town of Poix. The inhabitants of Poix, as well as those of the castles, had a conference with the marshals of the army, in order to save the town from being plundered and burnt. They offered to pay, as a ransom, a certain number of florins the ensuing day, as soon as the army should have marched off. On the morrow morning, the king and army departed, except some few, who remained behind, by orders of the marshals, to receive the ransom from townsmen. When the inhabitants were assembled together, and considered the small number of the English who were left with them, they resolved to pay nothing, told them so, and directly fell upon them. The English defended themselves gallantly, and sent after the army for succour. When lord Reginald Cobham and sir Thomas Holland, who commanded the rear-guard, were told of this, they cried out, " Treason ! treason ! " and

returned back to Poix, where they found their countrymen
still engaged with the townsmen. Almost all the inhabitants
were slain, the town burnt, and the two castles razed to the
ground. The English then followed the king's army, which
was arrived at Airaines, where he had ordered the troops
to halt, and to quarter themselves for that night, strictly
commanding, under pain of death, that no harm should be
done to the town or inhabitants, by theft or otherwise ; for
he wished to remain there a day or two, in order to gain
information where he could best cross the river Somme,
which he was under the necessity of doing, as you will
shortly hear.

I wish now to return to king Philip, whom we left at
St. Denis with his army, which was increasing every day.
He marched off with it, and pushed forward until he came
to Coppigny les Guises, which is three leagues distant from
Amiens, where he halted. The king of England, who was
still at Airaines, was much embarrassed how to cross the
Somme, which was wide and deep, as all the bridges had
been broken down, and their situations were well guarded by
men-at-arms. The two marshals, at the request of the king,
followed the course of the river, in order if possible to find a
passage for the army ; they had with them a thousand men-
at-arms and two thousand archers. They passed by Lompre,
and came to Pont de Remy, which they found defended by
numbers of knights, squires, and people of the country.
The English dismounted, and attacked the French from the
very dawn of the morning until near ten o'clock ; but the
bridge was so well fortified and guarded, that they could
not gain anything ; so they departed, and went to a large
town called Fontaines-sur-Somme, which they completely
plundered and burnt, as it was quite open. They next came
to another town, called Long, in Ponthieu ; but they could
not gain the bridge, so well was it guarded. They then rode
on to Pecquigny, but found the town, castle, and bridge so
well garrisoned that it was impossible to pass. In this manner
had the king of France ordered all the bridges and fords of
the river Somme to be guarded, to prevent the king of England from crossing it with his army ; for he was resolved to
force them to fight when he should see the most favourable
opportunity, or else to starve them.

The two marshals, having thus in vain followed the

course of the Somme, returned to the king of England, and
related to him that they were unable to find a passage anywhere.   That same evening, the king of France took up his
quarters at Amiens, with upwards of one hundred thousand
men.   The king of England was very pensive ; he ordered
mass before sunrise, and his trumpets to sound for decamping.
All sorts of people followed the marshals' banners, according
to the orders the king had issued the preceding day ; and
they marched through the country of Vimeu, drawing near
to the good town of Abbeville.   In their march, they came
to a town where a great number of the country people had
assembled, trusting to some small fortifications which were
thrown up there ; but the English conquered the town, as
soon as they came to it, and all that were within.   Many of
the townsmen and those from the adjoining country were
slain or taken prisoners.   The king lodged, that night, in
the great hospital.

The king of France set out from Amiens, and came to
Airaines about noon : the English king had quitted it about
ten o'clock.   The French found there provisions of all sorts ;
meat on the spits, bread and pastry in the ovens, wine in
barrels, and even some tables ready spread, for the English
had left it in very great haste.   The king of France fixed
his quarters there, to wait for his nobles and their retinue.
The king of England was in the town of Oisemont.   When
his two marshals returned in the evening, after having
overrun the country as far as the gates of Abbeville, and to
St. Valery, where they had had a smart skirmish, the king
of England summoned a council, and ordered many prisoners,
whom his people had made in the districts of Ponthieu and
Vimeu, to be brought before him.

The king, most courteously, asked if any of them knew
a ford below Abbeville, where he and his army could pass
without danger, and added, " Whoever will show us such
a ford shall have his liberty, and that of any twenty of his
fellow-soldiers whom he may wish to select."   There was
among them a common fellow whose name was Gobin Agace,
who answered the king, and said, " Sir, I promise you, under
peril of my life, that I will conduct you to such a place, where
you and your whole army may pass the river Somme without
any risk.   There are certain fordable places where you may
pass twelve men abreast twice in the day, and not have

water above your knees ; but when the tide is in, the river is full and deep, and no one can cross it ; when the tide is out, the river is so low that it may be passed, on horseback or on foot, without danger. The bottom of this ford is very hard, of gravel and white stones, over which all your carriages may safely pass, and from thence is called Blanchetaque. You must therefore set out early, so as to be at the ford before sunrise." " Friend," replied the king, " if I find what thou hast just said to be true, I will give thee and all thy companions their liberty ; and I will besides make thee a present of a hundred nobles." The king gave orders for every one to be ready to march at the first sound of his trumpet and to proceed forward.

The king of England did not sleep much that night, but, rising at midnight, ordered his trumpet to sound. Very soon everything was ready ; and, the baggage being loaded, they set out from the town of Oisemont about daybreak, and rode on, under the guidance of Gobin Agace, until they came to the ford of Blanchetaque, about sunrise ; but the tide was at that time so full they could not cross. The king, however, determined to wait there for those of his army who were not yet come up ; and he remained until after ten o'clock, when the tide was gone out. The king of France, who had his scouts all over the country, was informed of the situation of the king of England : he imagined he should be able to shut him up between Abbeville and the Somme, and thus take him prisoner, or force him to fight at a disadvantage. From the time of his arrival at Amiens, he had ordered a great baron of Normandy, called sir Godemar du Fay, to guard this ford of Blanchetaque, which the English must cross, and nowhere else. Sir Godemar had set out, in obedience to this order, and had with him, in the whole, one thousand men-at-arms and six thousand foot, with the Genoese. He had passed St. Ricquier in Ponthieu, and from thence came to Crotoy, where this ford was ; he had collected, in his march, great numbers of the country people. The townsmen of Abbeville had also accompanied him, excellently well appointed : they had arrived at the passage before the English. They were, in all, fully twelve thousand men : among them were two thousand who had jackets, resembling waggoner's frocks, called *torviquiaux*.

On the arrival of the English army, sir Godemar du Fay

drew up his men on the banks of the river, to defend and guard the ford. The king of England, however, did not for this give up his intention of crossing ; but, as soon as the tide was sufficiently gone out, he ordered his marshals to dash into the water, in the names of God and St. George. The most doughty and the best mounted leaped in first ; and, in the river, the engagement began ; many on both sides were unhorsed into the water : there were some knights and squires, from Artois and Picardy, in the pay of sir Godemar, who in hopes of preferment, and to acquire honour, had posted themselves at this ford, and they appeared to be equally fond of tilting in the water as upon dry land.

The French were drawn up in battle array, near the narrow pass leading to the ford ; and the English were much annoyed by them as they came out of the water to gain the land ; for there were among them Genoese cross-bowmen who did them much mischief. On the other hand, the English archers shot so well together that they forced the men-at-arms to give way. At this ford of Blanchetaque many gallant feats of arms were performed on each side ; but, in the end, the English crossed over, and, as they came on shore, hastened to the fields. After the king, the prince, and the other lords had crossed, the French did not long keep in the order they were in, but ran off for the fastest. When sir Godemar du Fay found his army was discomfited, he saved himself as quickly as he could, and many with him ; some making for Abbeville, others for St. Ricquier. The infantry, however, could not escape ; and there were numbers of those from Abbeville, Arras, Montreuil, and St. Ricquier, slain or taken prisoners : the pursuit lasted more than a league. The English had scarcely gained the opposite bank, when some of the light horse of the French army, particularly those belonging to the king of Bohemia and sir John of Hainault, advanced upon the rear, took from them some horses and accoutrements, and slew several on the bank who were late in crossing. The king of France had set out from Airaines that morning, thinking to find the English on the banks of the Somme ; when news was brought to him of the defeat of sir Godemar and his army, he immediately halted, and demanded from his marshals what was to be done : they answered, " You can only cross the river by the bridge of Abbeville, for the tide is now in at Blanchetaque." The king of France, therefore, turned back, and took up his quarters at Abbeville. The king of England, when he had crossed the Somme, gave thanks to God for it, and began his march in the same order as he had done before. He called to him Gobin Agace, gave him his freedom without ransom, as well as that of his companions, and ordered the hundred nobles of gold to be given him, and also a good horse. The king continued his march, thinking to take up his quarters at a good and large town called Noyelle, situated hard by ; but when he was informed that it belonged to the countess d'Aumarle, sister to the late Robert D'Artois, he sent to assure the inhabitants, as well as all the farmers belonging to her, that they should not be hurt. He marched farther on ; but his two marshals rode to Crotoy, near the sea ; they took the town, and burnt it. In the harbour they found many ships, and other vessels, laden with wines, from Poitou, Saintonge, and la Rochelle ; they ordered the best to be carried to the English army : then one of the marshals pushed forward, even as far as the gates of Abbeville, and returned by St. Ricquier, following the sea-shore to the town of St. Esprit de Rue.

These two battalions of the marshals came, on a Friday in the afternoon, to where the king was ; and they fixed their quarters, all three together, near Creçy, in Ponthieu. The king of England, who had been informed that the king of France was following him, in order to give him battle, said to his people : " Let us post ourselves here ; for we will not go farther before we have seen our enemies. I have good reason to wait for them on this spot ; as I am now upon the lawful inheritance of my lady-mother, which was given her as her marriage-portion ; and I am resolved to defend it against my adversary, Philippe de Valois." On account of his not having more than an eighth part of the forces which the king of France had, his marshals fixed upon the most advantageous situation ; and the army went and took possession of it. He then sent his scouts towards Abbeville, to learn if the king of France meant to take the field this Friday ; but they returned, and said they saw no appearance of it ; upon which he dismissed his men to their quarters, with orders to be in readiness by times in the morning, and to assemble in the same place. The king of France remained all Friday in Abbeville, waiting for more troops. He sent his marshals, the lord of St. Venant, and lord Charles of Montmorency, out of Abbeville, to examine the country, and get some certain intelligence of the English. They returned, about vespers, with information that the English were encamped on the plain. That night the king of France entertained at supper, in Abbeville, all the princes and chief lords. There was much conversation relative to war ; and the king entreated them, after supper, that they would always remain in friendship with each other ; that they would be friends without jealousy, and courteous without pride. The king was still expecting the earl of Savoy, who ought to have been there with a thousand lances, as he had been well paid for them at Troyes in Champagne, three months in advance.

The king of England, as I have mentioned before, encamped this Friday in the plain ; for he found the country abounding in provisions ; but, if they should have failed, he had plenty in the carriages which attended on him. The army set about furbishing and repairing their armour ; and the king gave a supper that evening to the earls and barons of his army, where they made good cheer. On their taking leave the king remained alone with the lords of his bed-chamber ; he retired into his oratory, and, falling on his knees before the altar, prayed to God, that if he should combat his enemies on the morrow, he might come off with honour. About midnight he went to his bed ; and, rising early the next day, he and the prince of Wales heard mass and communicated. The greater part of his army did the same, confessed, and made proper preparations. After mass the king ordered his men to arm themselves, and assemble on the ground he had before fixed on. He had enclosed a large park near a wood, on the rear of his army, in which he placed all his baggage-waggons and horses ; and this park had but one entrance : his men-at-arms and archers remained on foot.

The king afterwards ordered, through his constable and his two marshals, that the army should be divided into three battalions. In the first he placed the young prince of Wales, and with him the earls of Warwick and Oxford, sir Godfrey de Harcourt, the lord Reginald Cobham, lord Thomas Holland, lord Strafford, lord Mauley, the lord Delaware, sir John Chandos, lord Bartholomew Burgherst, lord Robert Neville, lord Thomas Clifford, the lord Bourchier, the lord Latimer, and many other knights and squires whom I cannot name.   There might be, in this first division, about eight hundred men-at-arms, two thousand archers, and a thousand Welshmen.   They advanced in regular order to their ground, each lord under his banner and pennon, and in the centre of his men.   In the second battalion were the earl of Northampton, the earl of Arundel, the lords Roos, Willoughby, Basset, Saint Albans, sir Lewis Tufton, lord Multon, the lord Lascels, and many others ; amounting, in the whole to about eight hundred men-at-arms, and twelve hundred archers.   The third battalion was commanded by the king, and was composed of about seven hundred men-at-arms, and two thousand archers.

The king then mounted a small palfrey, having a white wand in his hand, and attended by his two marshals on each side of him, he rode a foot's pace through all the ranks, encouraging and entreating the army that they would guard his honour and defend his right.   He spoke this so sweetly, and with such a cheerful countenance, that all who had been dispirited were directly comforted by seeing and hearing him.   When he had thus visited all the battalions, it was near ten o'clock ; he retired to his own division, and ordered them all to eat heartily, and drink a glass after.   They ate and drank at their ease ; and, having packed up pots, barrels, etc., in the carts, they returned to their battalions, according to the marshal's orders, and seated themselves on the ground, placing their helmets and bows before them, that they might be the fresher when their enemies should arrive.

That same Saturday the king of France rose betimes, and heard mass in the monastery of St. Peter's in Abbeville, where he was lodged ; having ordered his army to do the same, he left that town after sunrise.   When he had marched about two leagues from Abbeville, and was approaching the enemy, he was advised to form his army in order of battle, and to let those on foot march forward, that they might not be trampled on by the horses.   The king upon this sent off four knights, the lord Moyne of Bastleberg, the lord of Noyers, the lord of Beaujeu, and the lord of Aubigny, who rode so near to the English that they could clearly distinguish their position.   The English plainly perceived they were come to reconnoitre them ; however, they took no notice of it, but suffered them to return unmolested. When the king of France saw them coming back, he halted his army ; and the knights pushing through the crowds, came near the king, who said to them, " My lords, what news ? " They looked at each other without opening their mouths ; for neither chose to speak first. At last the king addressed himself to the lord Moyne, who was attached to the king of Bohemia, and had performed very many gallant deeds, so that he was esteemed one of the most valiant knights in Christendom. The lord Moyne said, " Sir, I will speak, since it pleases you to order me, but under the correction of my companions. We have advanced far enough to reconnoitre your enemies. Know then, that they are drawn up in three battalions, and are waiting for you. I would advise, for my part (submitting, however, to better counsel), that you halt your army here, and quarter them for the night ; for before the rear shall come up, and the army be properly drawn out, it will be very late, your men will be tired and in disorder, whilst they will find your enemies fresh and properly arrayed. On the morrow, you may draw up your army more at your ease, and may reconnoitre at leisure on what part it will be most advantageous to begin the attack ; for be assured they will wait for you." The king commanded that it should so be done ; and the two marshals rode, one towards the front, and the other to the rear, crying out, " Halt banners, in the name of God and St. Denis." Those that were in the front halted ; but those behind said they would not halt until they were as forward as the front. When the front perceived the rear pressing on, they pushed forward : and neither the king nor the marshals could stop them, but they marched on without any order until they came in sight of their enemies. As soon as the foremost rank saw them, they fell back at once, in great disorder, which alarmed those in the rear, who thought they had been fighting. There was then space and room enough for them to have passed forward, had they been willing so to do ; some did so, but others remained shy. All the roads between Abbeville and Creçy were covered with common people, who, when they were come within three leagues of their enemies, drew their swords, bawling out, " Kill, kill " ; and with them were many great lords that were eager to make show of their courage. There is no man, unless he had been present, that can imagine, or describe truly, the confusion of that day ; especially the bad management and disorder of the French, whose troops were out of number. What I know, and shall relate in this book, I have learnt chiefly from the English, who had well observed the confusion they were in, and from those attached to sir John of Hainault, who was always near the person of the king of France.

The English, who were drawn up in three divisions, and seated on the ground, on seeing their enemies advance rose undauntedly up, and fell into their ranks. That of the prince was the first to do so, whose archers were formed in the manner of a portcullis, or harrow, and the men-at-arms in the rear. The earls of Northampton and Arundel, who commanded the second division, had posted themselves in good order on his wing, to assist and succour the prince if necessary.

You must know that these kings, earls, barons, and lords of France did not advance in any regular order, but one after the other, or any way most pleasing to themselves. As soon as the king of France came in sight of the English, his blood began to boil, and he cried out to his marshals, " Order the Genoese forward, and begin the battle, in the name of God and St. Denis." There were about fifteen thousand Genoese cross - bowmen ; but they were quite fatigued, having marched on foot that day six leagues, completely armed, and with their cross-bows. They told the constable they were not in a fit condition to do any great things that day in battle. The Earl of Alençon, hearing this, said, " This is what one gets by employing such scoundrels, who fall off when there is any need for them." During this time a heavy rain fell, accompanied by thunder and a very terrible eclipse of the sun ; and before this rain a great flight of crows hovered in the air over all those battalions, making a loud noise. Shortly afterwards it cleared up, and the sun shone very bright ; but the Frenchmen had it in their faces, and the English in their backs. When the Genoese were somewhat in order, and approached the English, they set up a loud shout, in order to frighten them ; but they remained quite still, and did not seem to attend to it. They then set up a second shout, and advanced a little forward ; but the English never moved. They hooted a third time, advancing with their cross-bows presented, and began to shoot. The

English archers then advanced one step forward, and shot their arrows with such force and quickness that it seemed as if it snowed. When the Genoese felt these arrows, which pierced their arms, heads, and through their armour, some of them cut the strings of their cross-bows, others flung them on the ground, and all turned about and retreated, quite discomfited. The French had a large body of men-at-arms on horseback, richly dressed, to support the Genoese. The king of France, seeing them thus fall back, cried out, " Kill me those scoundrels ; for they stop up our road, without any reason." You would then have seen the above-mentioned men-at-arms lay about them, killing all they could of these runaways.

The English continued shooting as vigorously and quickly as before ; some of their arrows fell among the horsemen, who were sumptuously equipped, and, killing and wounding many, made them caper and fall among the Genoese, so that they were in such confusion they could never rally again. In the English army there were some Cornish and Welshmen on foot, who had armed themselves with large knives ; these, advancing through the ranks of the men-at-arms and archers, who made way for them, came upon the French when they were in this danger, and, falling upon earls, barons, knights, and squires, slew many, at which the king of England was afterwards much exasperated. The valiant king of Bohemia was slain there. He was called Charles of Luxembourg ; for he was the son of the gallant king and emperor, Henry of Luxembourg : having heard the order of the battle, he inquired where his son, the lord Charles, was ; his attendants answered that they did not know, but believed he was fighting. The king said to them, " Gentlemen, you are all my people, my friends and brethren-at-arms this day ; therefore, as I am blind, I request of you to lead me so far into the engagement that I may strike one stroke with my sword." The knights replied they would directly lead him forward ; and in order that they might not lose him in the crowd, they fastened all the reins of their horses together, and put the king at their head, that he might gratify his wish, and advanced towards the enemy. The lord Charles of Bohemia, who already signed his name as king of Germany, and bore the arms, had come in good order to the engagement ; but when he perceived that it was likely to turn out against the

15

French he departed, and I do not well know what road he took. The king, his father, had ridden in among the enemy, and made good use of his sword ; for he and his companions had fought most gallantly. They had advanced so far that they were all slain ; and on the morrow they were found on the ground, with their horses all tied together.

The earl of Alençon advanced in regular order upon the English, to fight with them ; as did the earl of Flanders, in another part. These two lords, with their detachments, coasting as it were the archers, came to the prince's battalion, where they fought valiantly for a length of time. The king of France was eager to march to the place where he saw their banners displayed, but there was a hedge of archers before him. He had that day made a present of a handsome black horse to sir John of Hainault, who had mounted on it a knight of his called sir John de Fuselles, that bore his banner ; which horse ran off with him, and forced his way through the English army, and, when about to return, stumbled and fell into a ditch and severely wounded him ; he would have been dead if his page had not followed him round the battalions, and found him unable to rise ; he had not, however, any other hindrance than from his horse, for the English did not quit the ranks that day to make prisoners. The page alighted, and raised him up ; but he did not return the way he came, as he would have found it difficult from the crowd. This battle, which was fought on the Saturday between la Broyes and Creçy, was very murderous and cruel ; and many gallant deeds of arms were performed that were never known. Towards evening, many knights and squires of the French had lost their masters ; they wandered up and down the plain, attacking the English in small parties ; they were soon destroyed, for the English had determined that day to give no quarter or hear of ransom from any one.

Early in the day some French, Germans, and Savoyards had broken through the archers of the prince's battalion, and had engaged with the men-at-arms ; upon which the second battalion came to his aid, and it was time, for otherwise he would have been hard pressed. The first division, seeing the danger they were in, sent a knight in great haste to the king of England, who was posted upon an eminence, near a windmill. On the knight's arrival, he said, " Sir, the earl of Warwick, the lord Stafford, the lord Reginald Cobham,

and the others who are about your son, are vigorously attacked
by the French ; and they entreat that you would come to
their assistance with your battalion, for, if their numbers
should increase, they fear he will have too much to do."
The king replied, " Is my son dead, unhorsed, or so badly
wounded that he cannot support himself ? " " Nothing of
the sort, thank God," rejoined the knight ; " but he is in so
hot an engagement that he has great need of your help."
The king answered, "Now, sir Thomas, return back to those
that sent you and tell them from me, not to send again for
me this day, or expect that I shall come, let what will happen,
as long as my son has life ; and say that I command them
to let the boy win his spurs ; for I am determined, if it please
God, that all the glory and honour of this day shall be given
to him, and to those into whose care I have entrusted him."
The knight returned to his lords, and related the king's
answer, which mightily encouraged them, and made them
repent they had ever sent such a message.

It is a certain fact, that sir Godfrey de Harcourt, who was
in the prince's battalion, having been told by some of the
English that they had seen the banner of his brother engaged
in the battle against him, was exceedingly anxious to save
him ; but he was too late, for he was left dead on the field
and so was the earl of Aumarle, his nephew. On the other
hand, the earls of Alençon and Flanders were fighting lustily
under their banners, and with their own people ; but they
could not resist the force of the English, and were there slain,
as well as many other knights and squires that were attending
on or accompanying them. The earl of Blois, nephew to
the king of France, and the duke of Lorraine, his brother-in-
law, with their troops, made a gallant defence ; but they
were surrounded by a troop of English and Welsh, and slain
in spite of their prowess. The earl of St. Pol and the earl
of Auxerre were also killed, as well as many others. Late
after vespers, the king of France had not more about him
than sixty men, every one included. Sir John of Hainault,
who was of the number, had once remounted the king ; for
his horse had been killed under him by an arrow ; he said
to the king, " Sir, retreat whilst you have an opportunity,
and do not expose yourself so simply ; if you have lost this
battle, another time you will be the conqueror." After he
had said this, he took the bridle of the king's horse, and led

him off by force ; for he had before entreated of him to retire. The king rode on until he came to the castle of la Broyes, where he found the gates shut, for it was very dark. The king ordered the governor of it to be summoned ; he came upon the battlements, and asked who it was that called at such an hour ? The king answered, " Open, open, governor ; it is the fortune of France." The governor, hearing the king's voice, immediately descended, opened the gate, and let down the bridge. The king and his company entered the castle ; but he had only with him five barons, sir John of Hainault, the lord Charles of Montmorency, the lord of Beaujeu, the lord of Aubigny, and the lord of Montfort. The king would not bury himself in such a place as that, but having taken some refreshments, set out again with his attendants about midnight, and rode on, under the direction of guides who were well acquainted with the country, until, about daybreak, he came to Amiens, where he halted. This Saturday the English never quitted their ranks in pursuit of any one, but remained on the field, guarding their position, and defending themselves against all who attacked them. The battle was ended at the hour of vespers.

When, on this Saturday night, the English heard no more hooting, or shouting, nor any more crying out to particular lords or their banners, they looked upon the field as their own, and their enemies as beaten. They made great fires, and lighted torches because of the obscurity of the night. King Edward then came down from his post, who all that day had not put on his helmet, and, with his whole battalion, advanced to the prince of Wales, whom he embraced in his arms and kissed, and said, " Sweet son, God give you good perseverance : you are my son, for most loyally have you acquitted yourself this day ; you are worthy to be a sovereign. The prince bowed down very low, and humbled himself, giving all honour to the king his father.[1] The English, during the night, made frequent thanksgivings to the Lord, for the happy issue of the day, and without rioting ; for the king had forbidden all riot or noise. On the Sunday morning, there was so great a fog that one could scarcely see the distance of half an acre. The king ordered a detachment from the army, under the command of the two marshals, consisting of about five hundred lances and two thousand

[1] Cf. the humility of Chaucer's Knight in the " Prologue," p. 279.

archers, to make an excursion and see if there were any bodies
of French collected together. The quota of troops, from
Rouen and Beauvais, had, this Sunday morning, left Abbeville and St. Ricquier in Ponthieu, to join the French army,
and were ignorant of the defeat of the preceding evening:
they met this detachment, and, thinking they must be
French, hastened to join them.

As soon as the English found who they were, they fell
upon them ; and there was a sharp engagement ; but the
French soon turned their backs, and fled in great disorder.
There were slain in this fight in the open fields, under hedges
and bushes, upwards of seven thousand ; and had it been
clear weather, not one soul would have escaped.

A little time afterwards, this same party fell in with the
archbishop of Rouen, and the great prior of France, who were
also ignorant of the discomfiture of the French ; for they
had been informed that the king was not to fight before
Sunday. Here began a fresh battle ; for those two lords
were well attended by good men-at-arms ; however, they
could not withstand the English, but were almost all slain,
with the two chiefs who commanded them ; very few escaping.
In the course of the morning, the English found many Frenchmen, who had lost their road on the Saturday, and had lain
in the open fields, not knowing what was become of the king,
or their own leaders. The English put to the sword all
they met ; and it has been assured to me for fact, that of
foot soldiers, sent from the cities, towns, and municipalities,
there were slain, this Sunday morning, four times as many
as in the battle of the Saturday.

This detachment, which had been sent to look after the
French, returned as the king was coming from mass, and
related to him all that they had seen and met with. After
he had been assured by them that there was not any appearance of the French collecting another army, he sent to have
the numbers and condition of the dead examined.

He ordered on this business, lord Reginald Cobham,
lord Stafford, and three heralds to examine their arms, and
two secretaries to write down all the names. They took
much pains to examine all the dead, and were the whole day
in the field of battle, not returning but just as the king was
sitting down to supper. They made to him a very circum-
stantial report of all they had observed, and said they had

found eighty banners, the bodies of eleven princes, twelve
hundred knights, and about thirty thousand common men.

The English halted there that day, and on the Monday
morning prepared to march off. The king ordered the
bodies of the principal knights to be taken from the ground,
and carried to the monastery of Mountenay, which was hard
by, there to be interred in consecrated ground. He had it
proclaimed in the neighbourhood that he should grant a
truce for three days, in order that the dead might be buried.
He then marched on, passing by Montreuil-sur-mer.

II. THE WAR AND THE CHURCH

A. The First Statute of Praemunire, 1353

[*Statutes of the Realm*, vol. i. p. 329. Praemunire makes it
treason to appeal to the Pope against the King. A second Act
of Praemunire was passed in 1393.]

Our lord the king, by the assent and prayer of the great
men, and the commons of his realm of England, at his great
council holden at Westminster, on Monday next after the
feast of St. Matthew the apostle, the twenty-seventh year of his
reign of England, and of France the fourteenth, in amendment
of his said realm, and maintenance of the laws and usages,
has ordained and established these things under-written :

First, because it is shown to our lord the king, by the
grievous and clamorous complaints of the great men and
commons aforesaid, how that divers of the people be, and
have been drawn out of the realm to answer for things, whereof
the cognizance pertains to the king's court ; and also that
the judgments given in the same court be impeached in another
court, in prejudice and disherison of our lord the king, and
of his crown, and of all the people of his said realm, and to
the undoing and destruction of the common law of the same
realm at all times used.[1]

Whereupon, good deliberation being had with the great
men and others of his said council, it is assented and accorded
by our lord the king, and the great men and commons aforesaid, that all the people of the king's allegiance, of whatso-

---

[1] en prejudice et desheritson nostre seigneur le Roi et de sa corone,
et de tout le poeple de son dit roialme, et in defesance et anientissement
de la commune lei de meisme le roialme usee de tout temps.

ever condition they be, which shall draw any out of the realm in plea, whereof the cognizance pertains to the king's court, or of things whereof judgments be given in the king's court, or which do sue in any other court, to defeat or impeach the judgments given in the king's court, shall have a day, within the space of two months, by warning to be made to them in the place where the possessions be, which are in debate, or otherwise where they have lands or other possessions, by the sheriffs or other the king's ministers, to appear before the king and his council, or in his chancery, or before the king's justices in his places of the one bench or the other, or before other the king's justices which to the same shall be deputed, to answer in their proper persons to the king, of the contempt done in this behalf.

And if they come not at the said day in their proper persons to be at the law, they, their procurators, attorneys, executors, notaries, and maintainers, shall from that day forth be put out of the king's protection, and their lands, goods, and chattels forfeited to the king, and their bodies, wheresoever they may be found, shall be taken and imprisoned, and ransomed at the king's will : And upon the same a writ shall be made to take them, by their bodies, and to seize their lands, goods, and possessions, into the king's hands ; and if it be returned that they be not found, they shall be put in exigent, and outlawed.

Provided always, that at what time they come before they be outlawed, and will yield themselves to the king's prison to be justified by the law, and to receive that which the court shall award in this behalf, that they shall be thereto received ; the forfeiture of lands, goods, and chattels abiding in force, if they do not yield themselves within the said two months, as afore is said.

[Six other clauses on a variety of subjects follow.]

B. Letter of Pope Gregory XI. to Archbishop Sudbury and the Bishop of London, directing proceedings against Wycliffe, 1377

[This letter is one of five papal Bulls signed by Gregory XI. on May 22, 1377, against Wycliffe. Another cites this one, and directs that if Wycliffe cannot be arrested, a public writ should be posted at Oxford and elsewhere, summoning him to appear at

Rome within three months to answer for the propositions objected to, and to receive sentence. A third letter directs them to warn the king etc. of the enormity and political danger of Wycliffe's tenets, and to require them to help to prevent these errors from spreading. *Vide* Gee and Hardy, *Documents Illustrative of English Church History*, p. 105 ; and Wilkins, *Concilia*, iii. 116.]

GREGORY, bishop, servant of the servants of God, to our venerable brethren the Archbishop of Canterbury and the Bishop of London, greeting and apostolic blessing. The realm of England, so glorious for its power, and the abundance of its resources, but more glorious for the piety of faith, and radiant for its renown in the sacred page, was wont to produce men gifted with the true knowledge of the Holy Scriptures of profound ripeness, famous for their devotion, champions of the orthodox faith, who used to instruct not only their own but other peoples in the truest lessons, guiding them into the path of the Lord's commandments, and as we infer from the result of the events of old, the prelates of the said kingdom set on the watch-tower of their solicitude, undertaking their own watch with earnest care, did not suffer any error to arise that might infect their sheep, but if tares did spring up from the sowing of the Enemy of man, they forthwith plucked them up, and so the pure grain grew continually meet to be stored in the Lord's garner. But, alas, it now is clear that in this selfsame realm, watchful by office, but careless through negligence, they do not compass the city, whilst enemies enter into it to prey on the most precious treasure of men's souls ; whose sly entries and open attacks are noted in Rome, though at a distance so far removed, before resistance is made to them in England. We have heard forsooth with much grief by the intimation of many credible persons that John Wycliffe, rector of the church of Lutterworth, in the diocese of Lincoln, professor of the sacred page—would he were not a master of errors !—is said to have rashly broken forth into such detestable madness that he does not fear to assert, profess, and publicly proclaim in the aforesaid realm, certain propositions and conclusions, erroneous and false, and in conflict with the faith, which endeavour to subvert and weaken the stability of the entire Church (and of which some, albeit with certain change of terms, appear to breathe the perverse opinions and the unlearned doctrine of Marsiglio of Padua and John of Jandun, of condemned memory, whose book was reprobated and condemned by Pope John XXII. of happy memory, our predecessor), malevolently infecting with them some of the faithful in Christ, and causing them to swerve from the Catholic faith, outside which is no salvation.

Now for these errors so started, they not having been extirpated, or at all events no opposition which we know of having been offered, but your eyes conniving at their propagation or toleration, you and some of the prelates of England, when you ought to be pillars of the Church and vigilant defenders of the said faith, for that you pass them by so negligently with a certain connivance, ought to be covered with due shame, to be full of compunction, and to feel the sting of your own consciences. Wherefore we—being unwilling, as in duty bound, that an evil so pernicious (which unless cut off, or pulled up by the roots, might, which God forbid, insinuate itself into the souls of very many to their destruction by its fatal poison) should proceed under cover of dissimulation—commission and command you, our brethren, by apostolic writings, that, after receiving these presents, you, or one of you, shall secretly inform yourselves of the said propositions and conclusions, a copy of which we send you enclosed under our Bull, and if you find it so to be, you shall endeavour to have the aforesaid John arrested by our authority, and committed to prison, and receive his confession touching the same propositions or conclusions. And that confession, and whatsoever the said John shall state or write upon the allegation and proof of the same propositions and conclusions, and everything you do in the premises, you shall close up under your own seals and disclose to none, and send to us by a trusty messenger. And you shall keep the said John in prison [1] under safe custody until you receive further commands from us in this matter, restraining all gainsayers by ecclesiastical censure without appeal ; and for this, calling in, if need be, the help of the secular arm : notwithstanding the Bull of Boniface VIII., our predecessor, of happy memory, wherein it is provided " that no one be summoned to judgment outside his city or diocese, save in certain special cases, and in those not beyond one day's journey from the limit of his diocese," or " that no judges delegated from the Apostolic See presume to summon any

[1] vinculis.

persons beyond one day's journey from the limit of their diocese," and concerning two days' journey, in a general council, and exemptions, and other privileges, constitutions, and apostolic letters to the Preachers, the Minorites, the Hermits of St. Augustine, and of St. Mary of Mount Carmel, and to any others of the Mendicants, or to any other orders and places, or to special persons, or to any chapters and convents of the same, general or special, of whatsoever tenors they may be, and also the statutes and customs of the same orders and places to the contrary—whereby the effect of the presents should in any wise be hindered or postponed, even if full and express mention ought to be made in our letters of them and their entire tenors and word by word; or if to the aforesaid John, or to any others, in common or individually, indulgence has been granted by the said see, that they cannot be personally arrested or interdicted or suspended or excommunicated by apostolic letters not making full and express mention and word for word of such indulgence.

Given at Rome, in Sta. Maria Maggiore, the 11th [before] kalends of June [the 22nd day of May], in the seventh year of our Pontificate.

C. Wycliffe Propositions condemned at London, 1382

[The following propositions, drawn up under the direction of Archbishop Courtney, were condemned by the Convocation of Canterbury in a session held at Blackfriars, in May 1382. *Fasciculi Zizaniorum*, pp. 277–282 (Rolls Series).]

Heretical Conclusions repugnant to the Church's Determination [1]

1. THAT in the Sacrament of the altar the material substance of bread and wine remains after consecration. 2. That accidents remain not without a subject in the same sacrament. 3. That Christ is not in the Sacrament of the altar essentially, truly, and really, in His corporal presence. 4. That if bishop or priest be in mortal sin he cannot ordain, consecrate, or baptize. 5. That if a man be properly repentant all outward confession is superfluous or useless for

----
[1] Cf. Gower's *Confessio Amantis*, pp. 259 sqq.

him.   6. To affirm constantly that it was not set down in
the Gospel that Christ instituted the Mass.   7. That God
ought to obey the Devil.   8. That if the pope be an abandoned or evil man, and so a member of the Devil, he has not
power over the faithful of Christ granted him by any, save
perhaps by Cæsar.   9. That after Urban VI. no one is to be
regarded as pope, but we must live like the Greeks under our
own laws.   10. To assert that it is contrary to Holy Scripture
that ecclesiastical men should have temporal possessions.

Erroneous Conclusions repugnant to the Church's Determination

11. That no prelate ought to excommunicate any unless
he first knows that he is excommunicate of God.   12. That
if he excommunicates he is thereby a heretic or excommunicate.   13. That a prelate excommunicating a clerk who
appealed to the king and the council of the realm is thereby
a traitor to God, king, and realm.   14. That those who
cease to preach or hear the word of God or the Gospel
preached on account of the excommunication of men are
excommunicate, and on the day of judgment will be held
traitors to God.   15. To assert that it is lawful to any
deacon or priest to preach the word of God without the
authority of the Apostolic See, or a Catholic bishop, or
some other sufficiently sure.   16. To assert that no one
is civil lord, bishop, or prelate while he is in mortal sin.
17. That temporal lords can at their will take away temporal
goods from ecclesiastics habitually sinful, or that the public
may at their will correct sinful lords.   18. That tithes are
pure alms, and that parishioners can withhold them for the
sins of their curates, and confer them at pleasure on others.
19. That special prayers restricted to one person by prelates
or religious do no more avail the same person, other things
being equal, than general prayers.   20. That the very fact
of a man entering any private religion makes him more
foolish and unfit for performing God's commandment.
21. That holy men endowing private religions, as well of
possessioners as of mendicants, have sinned in so endowing.
22. That the religious living in private religions is not of
the Christian religion.   23. That friars are bound to get their
living by the labour of their hands and not by mendicancy.

24. That he who gives alms to friars or to a preaching friar is excommunicate, and he who takes them.

D. LETTERS PATENT AGAINST THE LOLLARDS, 1384

[Patent Roll, 8 Richard II., pt. i.]

THE king to all to whom etc. greeting. Know ye that whereas lately the venerable Father William, archbishop of Canterbury, primate of all England, informed us by his petition, exhibited to us, that very many conclusions contrary to sacred doctrine, and notoriously redounding to the subversion of the Catholic faith and the Holy Church and his province, in divers places within the province aforesaid, have been openly and publicly, yet damnably, preached, of which conclusions some were by sentence, and wholesomely, declared and condemned as heresies, but others as errors, by the Church, good and mature deliberation being first had thereon by the common counsel of the archbishop himself, and of very many of his suffragans, doctors of theology, and other clerks learned in the Holy Scriptures. Whereupon we—supplication being made to us by the same archbishop, that we would deign to stretch forth the arm of our royal power for the due restraint and punishment of those who with an obstinate mind should henceforth wish to preach or maintain the conclusions aforesaid—being moved by zeal for the Catholic faith, of which we are and wish to be defenders in all things as we are bound, being unwilling in any wise to tolerate such heresies or errors springing up, have within the limit of our power granted authority and licence by our letters patent to the archbishop aforesaid and his suffragans, to arrest all and singular those who should wish secretly or openly to preach or maintain the aforesaid conclusions so condemned, wherever they may be found, and commit them, at pleasure, to their own prisons or to the prisons of others, to be kept in the same until they repent of the wickedness of their errors and heresies, or until it be otherwise provided, concerning such arrested persons by us or our counsel. We now, from zeal for the same faith, willing to provide for the restraint and due punishment of all those who would perchance preach or maintain henceforth the aforesaid conclusions or any others whatsoever containing heresy or error within the province of York, do grant and commit like authority and licence to the venerable Father Alexander, archbishop of York, and each of his suffragans throughout their dioceses, by the tenor of the presents, specially commanding thereupon and enjoining all and singular our liege ministers and subjects, of whatsoever estate or condition they may be, who are held to us by faith and allegiance, that they do not favour, counsel, or aid in any manner the maintainers or preachers of such conclusions so condemned, or their households, under forfeiture of all things which can be forfeited in that event, but obey, be obedient to, and intendent upon the aforenamed archbishop of York and his suffragans and ministers in the execution of the presents ; so that, without disturbance, due and open publication may be made against such conclusions and their maintainers, in order that the defence of the Catholic faith may be better established.

In witness whereof etc. Witness the king at Westminster on the 8th of December.

E. The Second Statute of Provisors, 1390

[13 Richard II., Stat. 2]

[In 1351 a statute was made forbidding provision. In 1390 the following Act was passed, which recites, in full, the statute of 1351, and contains additional safeguards against provision. In 1391 a proposal, supported by the king and the Duke of Lancaster, to repeal this statute was rejected by Parliament (*Statutes of the Realm*, ii. 69).]

II. ITEM, whereas the noble King Edward, the grandfather of our lord the king that now is, at his Parliament holden at Westminster on the Octave of the Purification of Our Lady, the five-and-twentieth year of his reign, caused to be rehearsed that statute made at Carlisle in the time of King Edward, son of King Henry, touching the estate of the Holy Church of England ; the said grandfather of the king that now is, by the assent of the great men of his realm, being in the same Parliament, holden the said five-and-twentieth year, to the honour of God and of Holy Church, and of all his realm, did ordain and establish, that the free elections to archbishoprics, bishoprics, and all other dignities and benefices

elective in England, should hold from thenceforth in the
manner as they were granted by his progenitors, and by the
ancestors of other lords, founders ; and that all prelates and
other people of Holy Church, which had advowsons of any
benefices of the gift of the king, or of his progenitors, or of
other lords and donors, should freely have their collations
and presentments ; and thereupon a certain punishment
was ordained in the same statute for those who accept any
benefice or dignity contrary to the said statute made at
Westminster the said twenty-fifth year, as is aforesaid ; which
statute our lord the king has caused to be recited in this
present Parliament at the request of his Commons in the
same Parliament, the tenor whereof is such as hereafter
follows :

"Whereas of late in the Parliament of Edward of good
memory, king of England, grandfather of our lord the king
that now is, in the twenty-fifth year of his reign, holden at
Carlisle, the petition heard, put before the said grandfather
and his council in the said Parliament by the commonalty
of the said realm, containing : That whereas the Holy Church
of England was founded in the estate of prelacy,[1] within the
realm of England, by the said grandfather and his progenitors,
and the earls, barons, and other nobles of his said realm, and
their ancestors, to inform them and the people of the law of
God, and to make hospitalities, alms, and other works of
charity, in the places where the churches were founded for the
the souls of the founders,[2] their heirs, and all Christians ; and
certain possessions, as well in fees, lands, rents, as in advowsons, which extend to a great value, were assigned by the
founders [3] to the prelates and other people of the Holy Church
of the said realm, to sustain the same charge, and especially
of the possessions which were assigned to archbishops,
bishops, abbots, priors, religious, and all other people of Holy
Church, by the kings of the said realm, earls, barons, and
other great men of his realm ; the same kings, earls, barons,
and other nobles, as lords and advowees, have had and
ought to have the custody of such voidances, and the presentments and collations of the benefices being of such
prelacies.

[1] estoit founde en lestat de prelacie . . .
[2] es leiux ou les Esglises furent founduz per les almes des foundors . . .
[3] foundors.

And the said kings in times past were wont to have the greatest part of their council, for the safeguard of the realm, when they had need, of such prelates and clerks so advanced ; the pope of Rome, accroaching to him the seignories of such possessions and benefices,[1] does give and grant the same benefices to aliens, who never dwelt in England, and to Cardinals, who could not dwell here, and to others as well aliens as denizens, as if he had been patron or advowee of the said dignities and benefices, as he was not of right by the law of England ; whereby if these should be suffered, there would scarcely be any benefice within a short time in the said realm, but that it should be in the hands of aliens and denizens by virtue of such provisions, against the good will and disposition of the founders of the same benefices ; and so the elections of archbishops, bishops, and other religious should fail, and the alms, hospitalities, and other works of charity, which should be done in the said places, should be withdrawn, the said grandfather, and other lay-patrons, in the time of such vacancies, should lose their presentments, the said council should perish, and goods without number should be carried out of the realm, to the annulling of the estate of the Holy Church of England, and disherison of the said realm, and in offence and destruction of the laws and rights of his realm, and to the great damage of his people, and in subversion of all the estate of all his said realm, and against the good disposition and will of the first founders, by the assent of the earls, barons, and other nobles, and of all the said commonalty, at their instant request, the damage and grievances aforesaid being considered in the said full Parliament, it was provided, ordained, and established, that the said oppressions, grievances, and damages in the same realm from henceforth should not be suffered in any manner.

And now it is shown to our lord the king in this present Parliament holden, on the Octave of the Purification of Our Lady, the five-and-twentieth year of his reign of England, and the twelfth of France, by the grievous complaint of all the commons of his realm, that the grievances and mischiefs aforesaid do daily abound, to the greater damage and destruction of all the realm of England, more than ever were

[1] le Pope de Rome accrochant a luy la Seignorie de tielx possessions et benefices . . .

before, viz. that now anew our holy father the pope, by procurement of clerks and otherwise, has reserved, and does daily reserve to his collation generally and especially, as well archbishoprics, bishoprics, abbeys, and priories, as all other dignities and other benefices of England, which are of the advowson of people of Holy Church, and gives the same as well to aliens as to denizens, and takes of all such benefices the first-fruits, and many other profits, and a great part of the treasure of the said realm is carried away and dispended out of the realm, by the purchases of such graces aforesaid ; and also by such privy reservations, many clerks, advanced in this realm by their true patrons, which have peaceably holden their advancements by long time, are suddenly put out ; whereupon the said Commons have prayed our lord the king, that since the right of the crown of England, and the law of the said realm is such, that upon the mischiefs and damages which happen to his realm, he ought, and is bound by his oath, with the accord of his people in his Parliament thereof, to make remedy and law, for the removing of the mischiefs and damages which thereof ensue, that it may please him to ordain remedy for them.

Our lord the king, seeing the mischiefs and damages before mentioned, and having regard to the said statute made in the time of his said grandfather, and to the causes contained in the same ; which statute holds always its force, and was never defeated, repealed, nor annulled in any point, and insomuch as he is bound by his oath to cause the same to be kept as the law of his realm, though that by sufferance and negligence it has been since attempted to the contrary ; also having regard to the grievous complaints made to him by his people in divers his Parliaments holden heretofore, willing to ordain remedy for the great damages and mischiefs which have happened, and daily do happen to the Church of England by the said cause ; by the assent of all the great men and commonalty of the said realm, to the honour of God, and profit of the said Church of England, and of all his realm, has ordered and established : that the free elections of archbishops, bishops, and all other dignities and benefices elective in England, shall hold from henceforth in the manner as they were granted by the king's progenitors, and the ancestors of other lords, founders.

And that all prelates and other people of Holy Church,

which have advowsons of any benefices of the king's gift, or
of any of his progenitors, or of other lords and donors, to do
divine service, and other charges thereof ordained, shall have
their collations and presentments freely to the same, in the
manner as they were enfeoffed by their donors. And in case
that reservation, collation, or provision be made by the
court of Rome, to any archbishopric, bishopric, dignity, or
other benefice, in disturbance of the free elections, collations,
or presentations aforenamed, that, at the same time of the
vacancy as such reservations, collations, and provisions
ought to take effect, our lord the king and his heirs shall have
and enjoy, for the same time, the collations to the archbishoprics, bishoprics, and other dignities elective which be
of his advowson, such as his progenitors had before that free
election was granted ; seeing that the election was first
granted by the king's progenitors upon a certain form and
condition, as to demand licence of the king to choose, and
after the election to have his royal assent, and not in other
manner. Which conditions not being kept, the thing ought
by reason to resort to its first nature.

And if any such reservation, provision, or collation be
made of any house of religion of the king's advowson, in
disturbance of free election, our sovereign lord the king, and
his heirs, shall have, for that time, the collation to give this
dignity to a convenient person. And in case that collation,
reservation, or provision be made by the court of Rome to
any church, prebend, or other benefice, which is of the
advowson of people of Holy Church, whereof the king is
advowee paramount immediate, that at the same time of
the voidance, at which time the collation, reservation or
provision ought to take effect as is aforesaid, the king and
his heirs shall thereof have the presentation or collation for
that time—and so from time to time, whensoever such
people of Holy Church shall be disturbed of their presentments or collations by such reservations, collations, or provisions, as is aforesaid. Saving to them the right of their
advowsons and their presentments, when no collation or
provision by the Court of Rome is made thereof, or where
that the said people of Holy Church shall or will, to the same
benefices, present or make collation ; and that their presentees may enjoy the effect of their collations or presentments. And in the same manner every other lord, of what

16

condition he be, shall have the collations or presentments to the houses of religion which are of his advowson, and other benefices of Holy Church which pertain to the same houses. And if such advowees do not present to such benefices within the half-year after such voidances, nor the bishop of the place give the same by lapse of time within a month after half a year, that then the king shall have thereof the presentments and collations, as he has of others of his own advowson demesne.

And in case that the presentees of the king—or the presentees of other patrons of Holy Church, or of their advowees, or they to whom the king, or such patrons or advowees aforesaid, have given benefices pertaining to their presentments or collations—be disturbed by such provisors, so that they may not have possession of such benefices by virtue of the presentments or collations to them made, or that they which are in possession of such benefices be impeached upon their said possessions by such provisors, then the said provisors, their procurators, executors, and notaries, shall be attached by their bodies, and brought in to answer ; and if they be convicted, they shall abide in prison without being let to mainprize or bail, or otherwise delivered, till they have made fine and ransome to the king at his will, and satisfaction to the party that shall feel himself grieved. And nevertheless before that they be delivered, they shall make full renunciation, and find sufficient surety that they will not attempt such things in time to come, nor sue any process by themselves, nor by others, against any man in the said court of Rome, nor in any part elsewhere, for any such imprisonments or renunciations, nor any other thing depending of them. And in case that such provisors, procurators, executors, or notaries be not found, that the exigent shall run against them by due process, and that writs shall go forth to take their bodies wherever they be found, as well at the king's suit, as at the suit of the party.

And that in the meantime the king shall have the profits of such benefices so occupied by such provisors, except abbeys, priories, and other houses, which have colleges or convents, and in such houses the colleges or convents shall have the profits ; saving always to our lord the king, and to all other lords, their old right."

And this statute shall hold good as well as to reserva-

tions, collations, and provisions made and granted in times
past against all them which have not yet obtained corporal
possession of the benefices granted to them by the same
reservations, collations, and provisions, as against all others
in time to come. And this statute ought to hold place and
to begin at the said octave.

Our lord the king that' now is, of the assent of the
great men of his realm, being in this present Parliament,
has ordained and established, that for all archbishoprics,
bishoprics, and other dignities and benefices elective, and
all other benefices of Holy Church, which began to be void
in deed the twenty-ninth day of January, the thirteenth year
of the reign of our lord King Richard that now is, or after,
or which shall be void in time to come within the realm of
England, the said statute, made the said twenty-fifth year,
shall be firmly held for ever, and put in due execution from
time to time in all manner of points. And if any do accept
a benefice of Holy Church contrary to this statute, and that
duly proved, and be beyond the sea, he shall abide exiled
and banished out of the realm for ever, and his lands and
tenements, goods and chattels shall be forfeited to the king ;
and if he be within the realm, he shall be also exiled and
banished, as is aforesaid, and shall incur the same forfeiture,
and take his way, so that he be out of the realm within six
weeks next after such acceptation. And if any receive any
such person banished coming from beyond the sea, or being
within the realm after the said six weeks, having knowledge
thereof, he shall be also exiled and banished, and incur
such forfeiture as is aforesaid. And that their procurators,
notaries, executors, and summoners have the pain and
forfeiture aforesaid.

Provided nevertheless, that all they for whom the
pope, or his predecessors, have provided any archbishopric,
bishopric, or other dignity, or other benefices of Holy Church,
of the patronage of people of Holy Church, in respect of any
voidance before the said twenty-ninth day of January, and
thereof were in actual possession before the same twenty-
ninth day, shall have and enjoy the said archbishoprics,
bishoprics, dignities, and other benefices peaceably for their
lives, notwithstanding the statutes and ordinances aforesaid.
And if the king send by letter, or in other manner, to the
court of Rome, at the entreaty of any person, or if any other

send or sue to the same court, whereby anything is done contrary to this statute, touching any archbishopric, bishopric, dignity, or other benefice of Holy Church within the said realm, if he that makes such motion or suit be a prelate of Holy Church, he shall pay to the king the value of his temporalties for one year ; and if he be a temporal lord, he shall pay to the king the value of his lands and possessions not moveable for one year ; and if he be another person of a more mean estate, he shall pay to the king the value of the benefice for which suit is made, and shall be imprisoned for one year.

And it is the intent of this statute, that of all dignities and benefices of Holy Church, which were void in deed the said twenty-ninth day of January, which are given, or to which it is provided by the apostolic see before the same twenty-ninth day, that to whom such gifts or provisions be made, may freely, of such gifts and provisions, sue execution without offence of this statute. Provided always, that of no dignity or benefice which was full the said twenty-ninth day of January, shall any man, because of any collation, gift, reservation, and provision, or other grace of the apostolic see, not executed before the said twenty-ninth day, sue thereof execution, upon the pains and forfeitures contained in this present statute.

Also, it is ordained and established, that if any man bring or send within the realm, or the king's power, any summons, sentences, or excommunications, against any person, of what condition soever he be, for the cause of making motion, assent, or execution of the said Statute of Provisors, he shall be taken, arrested, and put in prison, and forfeit all his lands and tenements, goods and chattels for ever, and incur the pain of life and member. And if any prelate make execution of such summons, sentences, or excommunications, that his temporalties be taken and abide in the king's hands, till due redress and correction be thereof made. And if any person of less than a prelate of what condition soever he be, make such execution, he shall be taken, arrested, and put in prison, and have imprisonment, and make fine and ransom at the discretion of the council of our said lord the king.

The King's Writ directing Proclamation of the Statute

The King to the Sheriff of Kent, greeting. We command you, firmly enjoining, that without delay you cause to be read and on our behalf publicly proclaimed and to be firmly kept and observed according to the form of the statutes and ordinances aforesaid, certain statutes and ordinances by us, with the assent of the nobles and commonalty of our realm of England, made in our last Parliament holden at Westminster, which we send you under our great seal in open form, within your county, in places where it may be most expedient. And this under instant peril you shall in no wise omit. Witness the king at Westminster the fifteenth day of May. [The like writs are directed to the several sheriffs throughout England.]

F. THE SECOND STATUTE OF PRAEMUNIRE, 1393

[The first Act of Praemunire was passed in 1353. The following Act, passed in 1393, amplified the previous Act. *Statutes of the Realm*, ii. 84.]

V. ITEM, whereas the Commons of the realm in this present Parliament have showed to our redoubted lord the king, grievously complaining, that whereas the said our lord the king, and all his liege people, ought of right, and of old time were wont, to sue in the king's court, to recover their presentments to churches, prebends, and other benefices of Holy Church, to the which they had right to present, the cognizance of plea, of which presentment belongs only to the king's court of the old right of his crown, used and approved in the time of all his progenitors kings of England ; and when judgment shall be given in the same court upon such a plea and presentment, the archbishops, bishops, and other spiritual persons which have institution to such benefice within their jurisdiction, are bound, and have made execution of such judgments by the king's commandment by all the time aforesaid without interruption (for another lay person cannot make such execution), and also are bound of right to make execution of many other of the king's commandments, of which right the crown of England has been peaceably seised, as well in the time of our said lord the king that now is, as in the time of all his progenitors till this day :

But now of late divers processes are made by the holy father the pope, and censures of excommunication upon certain bishops of England, because they have made executions of such commandments, to the open disherison of the said crown and destruction of our said lord the king, his law, and all his realm, if remedy be not provided.

And also it is said, and a common clamour is made, that the said holy father the pope has ordained and purposed to translate some prelates of the same realm, some out of the realm, and some from one bishopric to another within the same realm, without the king's assent and knowledge, and without the assent of the prelates, which so shall be translated, which prelates be much profitable and necessary to our said lord the king, and to all his realm ; by which translations if they should be suffered, the statutes of the realm would be defeated and made void ; and his said liege sages of his council, without his assent, and against his will, carried away and gotten out of his realm, and the substance and treasure of the realm shall be carried away, and so the realm be destitute as well of council as of substance, to the final destruction of the same realm ; and so the crown of England, which has been so free at all times, that it has been in no earthly subjection, but immediately to God in all things touching the royalty of the same crown, and to none other, should be submitted to the pope, and the laws and statutes of the realm by him defeated and avoided at his will, to the perpetual destruction of the sovereignty of our lord the king, his crown, and his royalty, and of all his realm, which God defend.

And, moreover, the Commons aforesaid say, that the said things so attempted are clearly against the king's crown and his royalty, used and approved from the time of all his progenitors ; wherefore they and all the liege commons of the same realm will stand with our said lord the king, and his said crown and his royalty, in the cases aforesaid, and in all other cases attempted against him, his crown, and his royalty in all points, to live and to die.

And, moreover, they pray the king, and require him by way of justice, that he would examine all the lords in the Parliament, as well spiritual as temporal, severally, and all the estates of the Parliament, how they think of the cases aforesaid, which be so openly against the king's crown, and in derogation of his royalty, and how they will stand in the same

cases with our lord the king, in upholding the rights of the
said crown and royalty.

Whereupon the Lords temporal so demanded, have
answered every one by himself, that the cases aforesaid are
clearly in derogation of the king's crown, and of his royalty,
as it is well known, and has been for a long time known,
and that they will be with the same crown and royalty in
these cases especially, and in all other cases which shall be
attempted against the same crown and royalty in all points
with all their power.

And, moreover, it was demanded of the Lords spiritual
there being, and the procurators of others being absent, their
advice and will in all these cases ; which lords, that is to say,
the archbishops, bishops, and other prelates—being in the
said Parliament severally examined, making protestations
that it is not their mind to deny nor affirm that our holy
father the pope may not excommunicate bishops, nor that
he may make translations of prelates after the law of Holy
Church—answered and said, that if any executions of processes made in the king's court, as before were made, by any,
and the censures of excommunications be made against any
bishops of England, or any other of the king's liege people,
for that they have made execution of such commandments ;
and that if any executions of such translations be made of
any prelates of the same realm, which prelates be very
profitable and necessary to our said lord the king, and to his
said realm, or that the sage people of his council, without
his assent, and against his will, be removed and carried out
of the realm, so that the substance and treasure of the realm
may be consumed—that the same is against the king and his
crown, as it is contained in the petition before named.

And likewise the same procurators, every one by himself
examined upon the said matters, have answered and said in
the name of and for their lords, as the said Lords spiritual
will and ought to be with the king in these cases in lawfully
maintaining his crown, and in all other cases touching his
crown and his royalty, as they are bound by their allegiance.

Whereupon our said lord the king, by the assent aforesaid,
and at the request of his said Commons, has ordained and
established, that if any purchase or pursue, or cause to be
purchased or pursued, in the court of Rome, or elsewhere,
any such translations, processes, and sentences of excom-

munication, bulls, instruments, or any other things whatsoever, which touch our lord the king, against him, his crown, and royalty, or his realm, as aforesaid, and they which bring the same within the realm, or receive them, or make thereof notification, or any other execution whatsoever within the same realm or without, that they, their notaries, procurators, maintainers, abettors, favourers, and counsellors, shall be put out of the king's protection, and their lands and tenements, goods and chattels, forfeited to our lord the king ; and that they be attached by their bodies, if they may be found, and brought before the king and his council, there to answer to the cases aforesaid, or that process be made against them by " Praemunire facias," in manner as it is ordained in other statutes concerning provisors, and others who sue, in any other court, in derogation of the royalty of our lord the king.[1]

G. The Lollard Conclusions, 1394

[These Conclusions are said to have been presented in full Parliament by the Lollards in a little book about the year 1394 ; they are printed in the *Fasciculi Zizaniorum*, in the Rolls Series. Foxe has translated them in his *Acts and Monuments*, iii. 203, from a source not specified.]

1. That when the Church of England began to go mad after temporalities, like its step-mother the Roman Church, and churches were authorized by appropriation in divers places, faith, hope, and charity began to flee from our Church, because pride, with its doleful progeny of mortal sins, claimed this under title of truth. This conclusion is general, and proved by experience, custom, and manner or fashion, as you shall afterwards hear.

2. That our usual priesthood which began in Rome, pretended to be of power more lofty than the angels, is not that priesthood which Christ ordained for His apostles. This conclusion is proved because the Roman priesthood is bestowed with signs, rites, and pontifical blessings, of small virtue, nowhere exemplified in Holy Scripture, because the bishop's ordinal and the New Testament scarcely agree, and we cannot see that the Holy Spirit, by reason of any such signs, confers the gift, for He and all His excellent gifts cannot consist in

---

[1] qui seuent en autry Courte en derogacion de la regalie nostre seigneur le Roy.

any one with mortal sin. A corollary to this is that it is a grievous play for wise men to see bishops trifle with the Holy Spirit in the bestowal of orders, because they give the tonsure in outward appearance in the place of white hearts ; and this is the unrestrained introduction of antichrist into the Church to give colour to idleness.

3. That the law of continence enjoined to priests, which was first ordained to the prejudice of women, brings sodomy into all the Holy Church, but we excuse ourselves by the Bible because the decree says that we should not mention it, though suspected. Reason and experience prove this conclusion : reason, because the good living of ecclesiastics must have a natural outlet, or worse ; experience, because the secret proof of such men is that they find delight in women, and when thou hast proved such a man mark him well, because he is one of them. A corollary to this is that private religions and the originators or beginning of this sin would be specially worthy of being checked, but God of His power with regard to secret sin sends open vengeance in His Church.

4. That the pretended miracle of the sacrament of bread drives all men, but a few, to idolatry, because they think that the Body of Christ which is never away from heaven could by power of the priest's word be enclosed essentially in a little bread which they show the people ; but God grant that they might be willing to believe what the evangelical doctor [1] says in his *Trialogus* (iv. 7), that the bread of the altar is habitually the Body of Christ, for we take it that in this way any faithful man and woman can by God's law perform the sacrament of that bread without any such miracle. A final corollary is that although the Body of Christ has been granted eternal joy, the service of Corpus Christi, instituted by Brother Thomas Aquinas, is not true, but is fictitious and full of false miracles. It is no wonder ; because Brother Thomas, at that time holding with the pope, would have been willing to perform a miracle with a hen's egg ; and we know well that any falsehood openly preached turns to the disgrace of Him who is always true and without defect.

5. That exorcisms and blessings performed over wine, bread, water, and oil, salt, wax, and incense, the stones of the altar, and church walls, over clothing, mitre, cross, and

[1] John Wycliffe.

pilgrims' staves, are the genuine performance of necromancy rather than of sacred theology. This conclusion is proved as follows, because by such exorcisms creatures are honoured as being of higher virtue than they are in their own nature, and we do not see any change in any creature which is so exorcized, save by false faith which is the principal characteristic of the Devil's art. A corollary : that if the book of exorcizing holy water, read in church, were entirely trustworthy, we think truly that the holy water used in church would be the best medicine for all kinds of illnesses—sores, for instance ; whereas we experience the contrary day by day.

6. That king and bishop in one person, prelate and judge in temporal causes, curate and officer in secular office, puts any kingdom beyond good rule. This conclusion is clearly proved because the temporal and spiritual are two halves of the entire Holy Church. And so he who has applied himself to one should not meddle with the other, for no one can serve two masters. It seems that hermaphrodite or ambidexter would be good names for such men of double estate. A corollary is that we, the procurators of God in this behalf, do petition before Parliament that all curates, as well superior as inferior, be fully excused and should occupy themselves with their own charge and no other.

7. That special prayers for the souls of the dead offered in our Church, preferring one before another in name, are a false foundation of alms, and for that reason all houses of alms in England have been wrongly founded. This conclusion is proved by two reasons : the one is that meritorious prayer, and of any effect, ought to be a work proceeding from deep charity, and perfect charity leaves out no one, for " Thou shalt love thy neighbour as thyself." And so it is clear to us that the gift of temporal good bestowed on the priesthood and houses of alms is a special incentive to private prayer which is not far from simony. For another reason is that special prayer made for men condemned is very displeasing to God. And although it be doubtful, it is probable to faithful Christian people that founders of a house of alms have for their poisonous endowment passed over for the most part to the broad road. The corollary is : effectual prayer springing from perfect love would in general embrace all whom God would have saved, and would do away with that

well-worn way or merchandise in special prayers made for
the possessionary mendicants and other hired priests, who
are a people of great burden to the whole realm, kept in
idleness ; for it has been proved in one book, which the
king had, that a hundred houses of alms would suffice in all
the realm, and from this would rather accrue possible profit
to the temporal estate.

8. That pilgrimages, prayers, and offerings made to
blind crosses or roods, and to deaf images of wood or stone,
are pretty well akin to idolatry and far from alms, and
although these be forbidden and imaginary, a book of error
to the lay folk, still the customary image of the Trinity is
specially abominable.   This conclusion God clearly proves,
bidding alms to be done to the needy man because they are
the image of God, and more like than wood or stone ; for
God did not say, " Let us make wood or stone in our likeness
and image," but man ; because the supreme honour which
clerks call " latria " appertains to the Godhead only ; and
the lower honour which clerks call " dulia " appertains to
man and angel and to no inferior creature.   A corollary is
that the service of the cross, performed twice in any year in
our church, is full of idolatry, for if that should, so might the
nails and lance be so honoured ; then would the lips of Judas
be relics indeed if any were able to possess them.   But we
ask you, pilgrim, to tell us when you offer to the bones of
saints placed in a shrine in any spot, whether you relieve the
saint who is in joy, or that almshouse which is so well endowed and for which men have been canonized, God knows
how.   And to speak more plainly, a faithful Christian
supposes that the wounds of that noble, whom men call
St. Thomas, were not a case of martyrdom.

9. That auricular confession which is said to be so
necessary to the salvation of a man, with its pretended
power of absolution, exalts the arrogance of priests and
gives them opportunity of other secret colloquies which we
will not speak of ; for both lords and ladies attest that, for
fear of their confessors, they dare not speak the truth.   And
at the time of confession there is a ready occasion for assig-
nation that is for " wooing," and other secret understandings
leading to mortal sins.   They themselves say that they are
God's representatives to judge of every sin, to pardon and
cleanse whomsoever they please.   They say that they have

the keys of heaven and of hell, and can excommunicate and
bless, bind and loose, at their will, so much so that for a
drink, or twelve pence, they will sell the blessing of heaven
with charter and close warrant sealed with the common seal.
This conclusion is so notorious that it needs not any proof.
It is a corollary that the pope of Rome, who has given himself
out as treasurer of the whole Church, having in charge that
worthy jewel of Christ's passion together with the merits of
all saints in heaven, whereby he grants pretended indulgence
from penalty and guilt, is a treasurer almost devoid of
charity, in that he can set free all that are prisoners in hell at
his will, and cause that they should never come to that place.
But in this any Christian can well see there is much secret
falsehood hidden in our Church.

10. That manslaughter in war, or by pretended law of
justice for a temporal cause, without spiritual revelation, is
expressly contrary to the New Testament, which indeed
is the law of grace and full of mercies.   This conclusion is
openly proved by the examples of Christ's preaching here
on earth, for he specially taught a man to love his enemies,
and to show them pity, and not to slay them.   The reason is
this, that for the most part, when men fight, after the first
blow, charity is broken.   And whoever dies without charity
goes the straight road to hell.   And beyond this we know
well that no clergyman can by Scripture or lawful reason
remit the punishment of death for one mortal sin and not for
another ; but the law of mercy, which is the New Testament,
prohibits all manner of manslaughter, for in the Gospel :
" It was said unto them of old time, Thou shalt not kill."
The corollary is that it is indeed robbery of poor folk when
lords get indulgences from punishment and guilt for those
who aid their army to kill a Christian people in distant lands
for temporal gain, just as we too have seen soldiers who run
into heathendom to get them a name for the slaughter of
men ; much more do they deserve ill thanks from the King
of Peace, for by our humility and patience was the faith
multiplied, and Christ Jesus hates and threatens men who
fight and kill, when He says : " He who smites with the
sword shall perish by the sword."

11. That the vow of continence made in our Church by
women who are frail and imperfect in nature, is the cause
of bringing in the gravest horrible sins possible to human

nature, because, although the killing of abortive children before they are baptized and the destruction of nature by drugs are vile sins, yet connexion with themselves or brute beasts or any creature not having life surpasses them in foulness to such an extent as that they should be punished with the pains of hell. The corollary is that, widows and such as take the veil and the ring, being delicately fed, we could wish that they were given in marriage, because we cannot excuse them from secret sins.

12. That the abundance of unnecessary arts practised in our realm nourishes much sin in waste, profusion, and disguise. This, experience and reason prove in some measure, because nature is sufficient for a man's necessity with few arts. The corollary is that, since St. Paul says : " having food and raiment, let us be there with content," it seems to us that goldsmiths and armourers and all kinds of arts not necessary for a man, according to the apostle, should be destroyed for the increase of virtue ; because although these two arts were exceedingly necessary in the old law, the New Testament abolishes them and many others.

This is our embassy, which Christ has bidden us fulfil very necessary for this time for several reasons. And although these matters are briefly noted here they are, however, set forth at large in another book, and many others besides, at length in our own language, and we wish that these were accessible to all Christian people. We ask God then of His supreme goodness to reform our Church, as being entirely out of joint, to the perfectness of its first beginning.

H. Extracts from the " Confessio Amantis " of John Gower

[John Gower was born about 1325, and probably spent much of his early life travelling in France. He afterwards settled down in England as a country gentleman. During his latter years his works made him well known at the court of Richard II. and of Henry IV. He became blind in 1400, and died in 1408, at the Priory of St. Mary Ovaries, Southwark. He was at one time a friend of Chaucer, who originated the appellation "Moral Gower," and who afterwards seems to have quarrelled with him. Gower wrote in three languages. The *Speculum Meditantis* is a poem in French ; and the *Vox Clamantis* is in Latin elegiacs. The

Confessio Amantis is Gower's only English poem. The whole
of it has been edited with introduction and notes by G. C.
Macaulay in three volumes (Cambridge University Press).]

PROLOGUE (lines 193 sqq.), THE CORRUPTION OF THE CHURCH

To thinke upon the daies olde,
The life of clerkes to beholde,
Men sein how that they weren tho
Ensample and reule of alle tho
Whiche of wisdom the vertu soughten
Unto the god ferst thei besoughten
As to the substance of her Scole,
That thei ne scolden noght befole   200
Her wit upon none erthly werkes,
Which were ayein the stat of clerkes,
And that thei myghten fle the vice
Which Simon hath in his office,
Whereof he taketh the gold in honde,
For thi-lke tyme I understonde
The Lumbard made non eschange
The bisschopriches forto change,
Ne yet a lettre for to sende
For dignite ne for Provende,   210
Or cured withouten cure.
The cherche keye in aventure
Of armes and of brigantaille
Stod nothing thanne upon bataille ;
To fyhte or for to make cheste
It thoghte hem thanne noght honeste ;
Bot of simplesce and pacience
Thei maden thanne no defence :
The court of worldly regalie

Line 195. *tho*: then.   196. *tho*: those.   201. *Her*: their.
204. *Simon*: *i.e.* Simon Magus (Acts viii. 18), from whose name the
word simony is derived.   207. *Lumbard*: Lombard bankers were
used as intermediaries in seeking ecclesiastical preferment.   209.
lettre: *i.e.* some papal provision or perhaps some letter addressed to
the Pope requesting preferment.   210. *Provende*; prebend.   212
sqq. "The authority of the Church" (symbolized by the key) " did
not then lie at the mercy of armed bands or depend upon the issue
of battle."   213. *brigantaille*: bands of irregular troops.   215. *cheste*:
strife.   218. *defence*: prohibition.

To hem was thanne no baillie ;   220
The vein honour was noght desired,
Which hath the proude herte fyred ;
Humilite was tho witholde,
And Pride was a vice holde.
Of holy cherche the largesse
Yaf thanne and dede gret almesse
To povere men that hadden nede :
Thei were ek chaste in word and dede,
Wherof the poeple ensample tok ;
Her lust was al upon the bok.   230
Or forto preche or forto preie,
To wisse men the ryhte weie
Of such as stode of trowthe unhered.
Lo, thus was Petres barge stiered
Of hem that thilke tyme were,
And thus came ferst to mannes Ere
The feith of Crist and alle goode
Thurgh hem that thanne weren goode
And sobre and chaste and large and wyse.
Bot now men sein is otherwise,   240
Simon the cause hath undertake,
The worldes swerd in honde to take ;
And that is wonder natheles,
Whan Crist him self hath bode pes
And set it in his testament,
And now that holy Cherche is went,
Of that here lawe positif
Hath set to make werre and strif
For worldes good, which may noght laste.
God wot the cause to the laste   250
Of every right and wrong also ;
But whil the lawe is reuled so
That clerkes to the warre entende,
I not how that thei scholde amende
The woful world in othre thinges.

Line 220. *baillie* : charge or government of a thing. The line,
therefore, means " was no charge of theirs," *i.e.* did not come under
their authority.   232. *wisse* : instruct.   233. *unhered* : unin-
structed.   236. *Ere* : ear.   244. *bode pes* : commanded peace.
247. *lawe positif* : lex positiva, that which is not morally binding
intrinsically, but only so because it is enjoined by the authority of
Holy Church.   254. *not* : know not.

To make pes between the kynges
After the law of charite,
Which is the propre duete
Belongende unto the presthode
Bot as it thenkth to the manhode,   260
The hevene is ferr, the world is nyh,
And veine gloire is ek so slyh,
Which coveitise hath now withholde,
That they non other thing beholde,
But only that they myhten winne.
And thus the werres thei beginne,
Whereof the holi cherche is taxed,
That in the point as it is axed
The disme goth to the bataille,
As thogh Crist myhte noght availe   270
To don hem riht be other weie.
In to the swerd the cherche keie
Is torned and the holy bede
Into cursinge, and every stede
Which scholde stonde upon the feith
And to this cause an Ere leyth
Astoned is of the quarele.
That scholde be the worldes hele
Is now, men sein, the pestilence
Which hath exiled pacience   280
Fro the clergie in special :
And that is schewed overal,
In eny thing whan thei ben grieved.
Bot if Gregoire be believed,
As it is in the bokes write,
He doth us somdel forto wite
The cause of thilke prelacie,
Wher god is noght of compaignie :
For every werk as it is founded
Schal stonde or elles be confounded ;   290
Who that only for Cristes sake

Line 260. *thenkth to the manhode* : seems to men.   268. *in the point,*
etc. ; the allusion is to the warlike Despencer, Bishop of Norwich, and
his campaign of 1385.   273. *bede* ; prayer.   278. *That scholde be* ; the
Great Schism of the Papacy has caused that which should have been a
blessing to the world to be a source of war and strife.   284. *Gregoire* :
St. Gregory the Great, author of the *Regula Pastoralis*, etc., dealing
particularly with the conduct of the clergy.

Desireth cure forto take,
And noght for pride of thilke astat,
To bere a name of a prelat,
He schal by resoun do profit
In holy cherche upon the plit
That he hath set his conscience ;
Bot in the worldes reverence
Ther ben of suche manie glade,
Whan thei to thilke astat ben made   300
Noght for the merite of the charge,
Bot for thei wolde hemself descharge
Of poverte and become grete ;
And thus for pompe and for beyete
The Scribe and ek the Pharisee
Of Moises upon the see
In the chaiere on high ben set ;
Whereof the feith is ofte let,
Which is betaken hem to kepe.
In Cristes cause alday thei slepe,   310
Bot of this world is noghte foryete ;
For wel is him that now may gete
Office in court to ben honoured.
The stronge coffre hath al devoured
Under the keye of avarice
The tresor of the benefice,
Whereof the povere schulden clothe
And ete and drinke and house bothe ;
The charite goth al unknowe,
For thei no grein of pite sowe :   320
And slouthe kepeth the libraire
Which longeth to the Saintuaire ;
To studie upon the worldes lore
Sufficeth now withoute more ;
Delicacy his swete toth
Hath fostred so that it fordoth
Of abstinence al that ther is.
And forto loken over this,
If Ethna brenne the clergie,
Al openly to mannes ye   330

Line 293. *thilke* ; that same.   308. *let* : hindered.   311. *is noghte*
foryete : "there is no forgetting."   329. *Ethna* : Mount Etna, the fire
of the volcano being compared with the fire of envy.   330. *ye* : eye.

17

At Avynoun thexperience
Therof hath yove an evidence,
Of that men sen hem so divided.
And yet the cause is noght decided ;
Bot it is seid and evere schal,
Between tuo stoles lyth the fal,
Whan that men wenen best to sitte :
In holy cherche of such a slitte
Is for to rewe un to ous alle ;
God grante it mote wel befalle　　　　　　　340
Towardes him which hath the trowthe.
Bot ofte is sen that muchel slowthe,
Whan men ben drunken of the cuppe,
Doth mochel harm, whan fyr is uppe,
Bot if somewho the flamme stanche ;
And so to speke upon this branche,
Which proud Envie hath mad to springe,
Of Scisme, causeth forto bringe
This new Secte of Lollardie,
And also many an heresie　　　　　　　　350
Among the clerkes in hemselve.
It were betre dike and delve
And stonde upon ryhte feith,
Than knowe al that the Bible seith
And erre as somme clerkes do.

.　　.　　.　　.　　.　　.　　.

BOOK III. (lines 2485 sqq.), ARE CRUSADES LAWFUL ?

Lover : Mi fader, understonde it is,
That ye have seid ;　bot over this
I prei you tell me nay or yei,
To passe over the grete See
To werre and sle the Sarazin,
Is that the lawe ?
Confessor :　　　　Sone myn,　　　　2490
To preche and soffre for the feith
That have I herd the gospel seith ;
Bot forto slee, that hiere I noght.

Line 331. *Avynoun* : Avignon, the dwelling-place of the Pope during the " Babylonish Captivity."　　339. *Is for to rewe*, etc. : impersonal expression, " there is cause for us all to be sorry."

Crist with his oghne deth hath boght
Alle othre men, and made hem fre,
In token of parfit charite ;
And after that he tawhte himselve.
Whan he was ded, these othre twelve
Of hise Apostles wente aboute
The holi feith to prechen oute,   2500
Wherof the deth in sondri place
Thei soffre, and so God of his grace
The feith of Crist hath mad aryse :
Bot of this wolde in other wise
Be werre have broght in the creance,
It hadde yit stonde in balance.
And that may proven in the dede ;
For what man the Croniqes rede,
Fro ferst that holi cherche hath weyved
To preche, and hath the swerd received,   2510
Wherof the werres ben begonne,
A gret partie of that was wonne
To Cristes feith stant now miswent :
Godd do therof amendement,
So as he wot what is the best.

BOOK V. (lines 1803 sqq.), LOLLARDY

Now were it good that thou forthi,
Which thurgh baptisme properly
Art unto Cristes feith professed,
Be war that thou be noght oppressed
With Anticristes lollardie.
For as the Jewes prophecie
Was set of god for avantage,
Riht so this newe tapinage   1810
Of lollardie goth aboute
To sette Cristes feith in doute.
The seintz that weren ous tofore,
By whom the feith was ferst upbore,
That holi cherche stod relieved,

Line 2509. *weyved* : omitted to.   1807. Cf. Wycliffe Propositions
condemned at London, 1382, p. 234 ; also the Letters Patent against
the Lollards, p. 236, etc.   1810. *tapinage* : noise, disturbance.
1813. " The saints that were before us,"

Thei oghten betre be believed,
Than these, whiche that men knowe
Noght holy, thogh thei feigne and blowe
Here lollardie in mennes Ere.
Bot if thou wolt live out of fere,   1820
Such newe lore, I rede, eschuie,
And hold forth riht the weie and suie,
As thine Ancestres dede er this :
So schalt thou noght believe amis.

. . . .

BOOK VI. (lines 1285 sqq.), SORCERY AND WITCHCRAFT

And thus to telle of him in soth,
Ful many a wonder thing he doth,
That were betre to be laft,
Among the whiche is wicchecraft.
That som men clepen Sorcerie
Which forto winne his druerie   1290
With many a circumstance he useth,
Ther is no point which he refuseth.
The craft which that Saturnus fond,
To make prickes in the sond,
That Geomance cleped is,
Fulofte he useth it amis ;
And of the flod his Ydromance,
And of the frye the Piromance,
With questions echon of tho
He tempteth ofte, and ek also   1300
Aeremance in juggement
To love he bringeth of his assent :
For these craftes, as I finde,
A man mai do be weie of kinde,
Be so it be of good entente.
Bot he goth al an other wente ;

Line 1290. *druerie* : courtship.   1294. *prickes in the sond* :
Geomancy seems to have been done originally by marks made on
sand or earth and later by casual dots on paper. In this and the
following lines are mentioned the four usual kinds of divination, by
the four elements ; Geomancy by earth, Hydromancy by water,
Aeromancy by air, and Pyromancy by fire.   1306 sqq. Gower seems
here to derive much of his matter from a treatise ascribed to Albertus
Magnus, called *Speculum Astronomiae*.

For rathere er he scholde faile,
With Nigromance he wole assaile
To make his incantacioun
With hot fumigacioun.   1310
Thilke art which Spatula is hote,
And used is of comun rote
Among Paiens, with that craft ek
Of which is Auctor Thosz the Grek.
He worcheth on and on be rowe :
Razel is noght to him unknowe,
Ne Salomones Candarie,
His Ydeae, his Eutonye ;
The figure and the bok withal
Of Balamuz, and of Gheubal   1320
The seal, and therupon thymage
Of Thebith, for his avantage
He takth, and somwhat of Gibiere,
Which helplich is to this matiere.
Babilla with hire Sones sevene,
Which hath renonced to the hevene,
With Cernes bothe square and rounde,
He traceth ofte upon the grounde
Makende his invocacioun ;
And for full enformacioun   1330
The Scole which Honorius
Wrot, he poursuieth : and lo, thus
Magique he useth forto winne
His love, and spareth for no sinne.
And over that of his Sotie,

Line 1308. *Nigromance* ; necromancy, the supposed art of raising
spirits of the dead, also black magic, *i.e.* magic of a harmful kind as
opposed to white magic which was harmless.   1314. *Thosz the Grek* :
Thoth, the Hermes of Egyptian mythology, the reputed inventor of
many arts and sciences—particularly of magic.   Many books of magic
were attributed to him.   1316. *Razel* ; Rasiel the angel, who according
to the legend in the Talmud, was the tutor of Adam after the Creation.
A book of magic was attributed to him.   1317. *Salomones* ; In the
Speculum Astronomiae, three books—*De Novem Candariis, De Arte
Eutonica*, and *De Arte Ideica*—are attributed to Solomon.   1320.
Balamuz, etc. ; In the *Speculum Astronomiae* is mentioned a book of
Belenus de Opere Horarum, also the seal of Gheubal.   1322. *Thebith* :
Thabet, son of Corah, a distinguished Arab mathematician to whom
were attributed certain works on Astrology and Magic that were
current in Latin.   1323. *Gibiere* : Geber, an Arab mathematician
and reputed magician, *floruit* A.D. 776.

Riht as he secheth Sorcerie
Of hem that ben Magiciens,
Riht so of the Naturiens
Upon the Sterres from above
His weie he secheth unto love,   1340
Als fer as he hem understondeth.
In many a sondry wise he fondeth :
He makyth ymage, he makth sculpture,
He makth writinge, he makth figure,
He makth his calculacions,
He makth his demonstracions ;
His houres of Astronomie
He kepeth as for that partie
Which longeth to thinspeccion
Of love and his affeccion ;   1350
He wolde into the helle seche
The devel himselve to beseche,
If that he wist forto spede,
To gete of love his lusti mede :
Wher that he hath his herte set,
He bede nevere fare bet
Ne wite of other hevene more.

.   .   .   .

I. The Act " De Haeretico Comburendo," 1401

[Letters Patent against the Lollards had been issued in 1382
and 1384, but the following Act was the earliest step taken by
Parliament to suppress Lollardy. The Act was expanded by
2 Henry V., Stat. 1, cap. 7. *Statutes of the Realm*, ii. 125.]

XV. WHEREAS it is showed to our sovereign lord the king on
behalf of the prelates and clergy of his realm of England in
this present Parliament, that although the Catholic faith,
founded upon Christ, and by His Apostles and the Holy
Church sufficiently determined, declared and approved, has
been hitherto by good and holy and most noble progenitors
of our sovereign lord the king in the said realm, amongst all
the realms of the world, most devoutly observed, and the
English Church by his said most noble progenitors and
ancestors, to the honour of God and of the whole realm aforesaid, laudably endowed and in her rights and liberties sus-

tained, without that that the same faith or the said Church
was hurt or grievously oppressed, or else disturbed by
any perverse doctrine or wicked, heretical, or erroneous
opinions :

Yet nevertheless divers false and perverse people of a
certain sect, damnably thinking of the faith of the sacraments of the Church and the authority of the same, and,
against the law of God and of the Church, usurping the
office of preaching, do perversely and maliciously, in divers
places within the said realm, under the colour of dissembled
holiness, preach and teach in these days, openly and privily,
divers new doctrines and wicked, heretical, and erroneous
opinions contrary to the same faith and blessed determina-
tions of the Holy Church.

And of such sect and wicked doctrine and opinions, they
make unlawful conventicles and confederacies, they hold
and exercise schools, they make and write books, they do
wickedly instruct and inform people, and, as much as they
may, excite and stir them to sedition and insurrection, and
make great strife and division among the people, and do
daily perpetrate and commit enormities horrible to be heard,
in subversion of the said Catholic faith and doctrine of the
Holy Church, in diminution of God's honour, and also in
destruction of the estate, rights, and liberties of the said
English Church ; by which sect and wicked and false preachings, doctrines, and opinions of the said false and perverse
people, not only the greatest peril of souls, but also many
more other hurts, slanders, and perils, which God forbid,
might come to this realm, unless it be the more plentifully
and speedily helped by the king's majesty in this behalf,
namely :

Whereas the diocesans of the said realm cannot by their
jurisdiction spiritual, without aid of the said royal majesty,
sufficiently correct the said false and perverse people, nor
refrain their malice, because the said false and perverse
people go from diocese to diocese, and will not appear before
the said diocesans, but the same diocesans and their jurisdiction spiritual and the keys of the church, with the censures
of the same, do utterly disregard and despise, and so they
continue and exercise their wicked preachings and doctrines,
from day to day, to the utter destruction of all order and rule
of right and reason.

Upon which novelties and excesses above rehearsed, the prelates and clergy aforesaid, and also the Commons of the said realm being in the same Parliament, have prayed our sovereign lord the king, that his royal highness would vouchsafe in the said Parliament to provide a convenient remedy : the same our sovereign lord the king—graciously considering the premises, and also the laudable steps of his said most noble progenitors and ancestors, for the conservation of the said Catholic faith, and sustentation of God's honour and also the safeguard of the estate, rights, and liberties of the said English Church, to the praise of God, and merit of our said sovereign lord the king, and prosperity and honour of all his said realm, and for the eschewing of such dissensions, divisions, hurts, slanders, and perils, in time to come, and that this wicked sect, preachings, doctrines, and opinions should from henceforth cease and be utterly destroyed—by the assent of the estates and other discreet men of the realm, being in the said Parliament, has granted, established, and ordained from henceforth firmly to be observed : That none within the said realm, or any other dominions, subject to his royal majesty, presume to preach, openly or privily, without the licence of the diocesan of the same place first required and obtained curates in their own churches, and persons hitherto privileged, and other of the canon law granted, only except. And that none, from henceforth, preach, hold, teach, or instruct anything, openly or privily, or make or write any book contrary to the Catholic faith or determination of the Holy Church, nor that any of such sect and wicked doctrines and opinions shall make any conventicles, or in any wise hold or exercise schools. And also that none from henceforth in any wise favour such preacher, or maker of any such and the like conventicles, or holding or exercising schools, or making or writing such books, or so teaching, informing, or exciting the people, nor them, nor any of them, maintain or in any wise sustain.

And that all and singular having such books or any writings of such wicked doctrine and opinions, shall really, with effect, deliver, or cause to be delivered, all such books and writings to the diocesan of the same place within forty days from the time of the proclamation of this ordinance and statute. And if any person or persons, of whatsoever kind, estate, or condition he or they be, from henceforth do or attempt against the royal ordinances and statute aforesaid, in the premises or in any of them, or such books, in form aforesaid, do not deliver, then the diocesan of the same place, in his diocese, such person or persons, in this behalf defamed or evidently suspected, and every of them, may, by the authority of the said ordinance and statute, cause to be arrested, and under safe custody in his prisons to be detained, till he or they of the articles laid to him or them in this behalf, canonically purge him or themselves, or else such wicked sect, preachings, doctrines, and heretical and erroneous opinions abjure, according as the laws of the Church do require ; so that the said diocesan, by himself or his commissaries, do openly and judicially proceed against such persons so arrested and remaining under his safe custody to all effect of the law, and determine that same business, according to the canonical decrees, within three months after the said arrest, any lawful impediment ceasing.

And if any person, in any case above expressed, be, before the diocesan of the place, or his commissaries, canonically convicted, then the same diocesan may cause to be kept in his prison the said person so convicted according to the manner of his default, and after the quality of the offence, according, and as long as, to his discretion shall seem expedient, and moreover put the same person to pay a pecuniary fine to the lord the king, except in cases where he, according to the canonical decree, ought to be left to the secular court, according as the same fine shall seem competent to the diocesan, for the manner and quality of the offence, in which case the same diocesan shall be bound to certify the king of the same fine in his exchequer by his letters patent sealed with his seal to the effect that such fine, by the king's authority may be required and levied to his use of the goods of the same person so convicted.

And if any person within the said realm and dominions, upon the said wicked preachings, doctrines, opinions, schools, and heretical and erroneous informations, or any of them, be, before the diocesan of the same place, or his commissaries, convicted by sentence, and the same wicked sect, preachings, doctrines, and opinions, schools and informations, do refuse duly to abjure, or by the diocesan of the same place, or his commissaries, after abjuration made by the same person, be pronounced relapsed, so that according to the holy canons he ought to be left to the secular court, whereupon credence shall be given to the diocesan of the same place, or to his commissaries in this behalf—then the sheriff of the county of the same place, and the mayor and sheriff or sheriffs, or mayor and bailiffs of the city, town, or borough of the same county nearest to the same diocesan or the said commissaries, shall be personally present in preferring of such sentences, when they, by the same diocesan or his commissaries, shall be required : and they shall receive the same persons and every one of them, after such sentence promulgated, and them, before the people, in a high place [1] cause to be burnt, that such punishment may strike fear to the minds of others, whereby no such wicked doctrine and heretical and erroneous opinions, nor their authors and favourers in the said realm and dominions, against the Catholic faith, Christian law, and determination of the Holy Church be sustained (which God forbid), or in any wise suffered. In which all and singular the premises concerning the said ordinance and statute, the sheriffs, mayors, and bailiffs of the said counties, cities, boroughs, and towns shall be attending, aiding, and supporting, to the said diocesan and his commissaries.

J. The Royal Writ for the Burning of Sawtre, 1401

[Whilst the Bill de Haeretico was before Parliament, Convocation instituted proceedings against Sawtre. On February 24 he was degraded by that assembly, and on February 26 the following royal writ was issued for his execution. Close Roll, 2 Henry IV., pt. i.]

The king to the mayor and sheriffs of London, greeting. Whereas the venerable father Thomas, archbishop of Canterbury, Primate of all England, and legate of the Apostolic See, with the consent and advice of his fellow-bishops [2] and suffragan brethren,[3] and also of all the clergy of his province, in his provincial council assembled, the order of his right in this respect having been duly observed in everything, has by his definitive sentence pronounced and declared William Sawtre, formerly chaplain—who was condemned for heresy, and who aforetime abjured, in form of law, and has now relapsed unto the aforesaid heresy—to be

---

[1] eminenti. [2] co-episcoporum.
[3] confratrum suffraganeorum.

a manifest heretic, and decreed that he should be degraded, and for that cause has actually [1] degraded him from all his position and clerical privilege, and has decreed that the same William be left to the secular court, and has actually left him according to the laws and canonical sanctions enacted in that behalf, and Holy Mother Church has nothing further to do in the premises : We therefore—zealous for justice and a cherisher of the Catholic faith, willing to maintain and defend Holy Church, and the rights and liberties of the same, and to extirpate radically such heresies and errors from our realm of England, to the utmost of our power, and to punish with condign chastisement heretics so convicted, and considering that such heretics so convicted and condemned in the form aforesaid ought to be burnt in the flames, according to law divine and human, and the canonical institutes customary therein—as straitly as we are able, firmly enjoining, command you that the aforesaid William, being in your custody, be committed to the fire in any public and open place, within the liberty of the city aforesaid, by reason of the premises, and that you cause him to be actually [1] burnt in the same fire, in detestation of such crime, and to the manifest example of other Christians ; and this you shall in no wise omit under instant peril. Witness ourself at Westminster the 26th day of February.

By the king himself and the council of Parliament.

[1] realiter.

CHAPTER VII

THE BLACK DEATH

I. THE STATUTE OF LABOURERS, 1349

[*Statutes of the Realm*, vol. i. p. 307, *anno* 23° Edwardi III., 1349. This was a royal ordinance, not an Act of Parliament like the Second Statute of Labourers of 1351.]

EDWARD, by the grace of God, etc., to the reverend father in Christ William, by the same grace archbishop of Canterbury, Primate of all England, greeting. Because a great part of the people and especially of the workmen and servants has now died in that pestilence, some, seeing the straits of the masters and the scarcity of servants, are not willing to serve unless they receive excessive wages, and others, rather than through labour gain their living, prefer to beg in idleness [1] : We, considering the grave inconveniences which might come from the lack especially of ploughmen and such labourers, have held deliberation and treaty concerning this with the prelates and nobles and other learned men sitting by us ; by whose Consentient Counsel we have seen fit to ordain : that every man and woman of our kingdom of England, of whatever condition, whether bond or free, who is able bodied and below the age of sixty years, not living by trade nor carrying on a fixed craft, nor having of his own the means of living, or land of his

[1] Cf. *Piers Plowman*, Prologue, p. 300.

own with regard to the cultivation of which he might occupy
himself, and not serving another,—if he, considering his
station, be sought after to serve in a suitable service, he shall
be bound to serve him who had seen fit so to seek after him ;
and he shall take only the wages, liveries, meed or salary
which, in the places where he sought to serve, were accustomed
to be paid in the twentieth year of our reign of England, or
the five or six common years next preceding. Provided,
that in thus retaining their service, the lords are preferred
before others of their bondsmen or of their land tenants :
so, nevertheless that such lords thus retain as many as shall
be necessary and not more ; and if any man or woman
being thus sought after in service will not do this, the fact
being proven by two faithful men before the sheriffs or the
bailiffs of our lord the King, or the constables of the town
where this happens to be done,—straightway through them,
or some one of them, he shall be taken and sent to the next
jail, and there he shall remain in strict custody until he shall
find surety for serving in the aforesaid form.

And if a reaper or mower, or other workman or servant,
of whatever standing or condition he be, who is retained in
the service of anyone, do depart from the said service before
the end of the term agreed, without permission or reasonable
cause, he shall undergo the penalty of imprisonment, and
let no one, under the same penalty, presume to receive or
retain such a one in his service. Let no one, moreover, pay
or permit to be paid to anyone more wages, livery, meed or
salary than was customary as has been said ; nor let anyone
in any other manner exact or receive them, under penalty
of paying to him who feels himself aggrieved from this,
double the sum that has been paid or promised, exacted or
received, and if any such person be not willing to prosecute,
then it [the sum] is to be given to any one of the people who
shall prosecute in the matter ; and such prosecution shall
take place in the court of the lord of the place where such
case shall happen. And if the lords of the towns or manors
presume of themselves or through their servants in any way
to act contrary to this our present ordinance, then in the
Counties, Wapentakes and Trithings suit shall be brought
against them in the aforesaid form for the triple penalty
[of the sum] thus promised or paid by them or their servants ;
and if perchance, prior to the present ordinance, anyone

shall have covenanted with anyone thus to serve for more wages, he shall not be bound by reason of the said covenant to pay more than at another time was wont to be paid to such person ; nay, under the aforesaid penalty he shall not presume to pay more.

Likewise saddlers, skinners, white tawyers, cordwainers, tailors, smiths, carpenters, masons, tilers, shipwrights, carters and all other artisans and labourers shall not take for their labour and handiwork more than what, in the places where they happen to labour, was customarily paid to such persons in the said twentieth year and in the other common years preceding, as has been said ; and if any man take more, he shall be committed to the nearest jail in the manner aforesaid.

Likewise let butchers, fishmongers, hostlers, brewers, bakers, pulters and all other vendors of any victuals, be bound to sell such victuals for a reasonable price, having regard for the price at which such victuals are sold in the adjoining places : so that such vendors may have moderate gains, not excessive, according as the distance from the places from which such victuals are carried may seem reasonably to require ; and if anyone sell such victuals in another manner, and be convicted of it in the aforesaid way, he shall pay the double of that which he received to the party injured, or in default of him, to another who shall be willing to prosecute in this behalf ; and the mayor and bailiffs of the cities and boroughs, merchant towns, and others, and of the maritime ports and places shall have power to inquire concerning each and every one who shall in any way err against this, and to levy the aforesaid penalty for the benefit of those at whose suit such delinquents shall have been convicted ; and in case that the said mayor and bailiffs shall neglect to carry out the aforesaid, and shall be convicted of this before justices to be assigned by us, then the same mayor and bailiffs shall be compelled by the same justices, to pay to such wronged person or to another prosecuting in his place, the treble of the thing thus sold, and nevertheless, on our part too, they shall be grievously punished.

And because many sound beggars do refuse to labour so long as they can live from begging alms, giving themselves up to idleness and sins, and, at times, to robbery and other crimes—let no one, under the aforesaid pain of imprisonment, presume, under colour of piety or alms, to give anything to such as can very well labour, or to cherish them in their sloth—so that thus they may be compelled to labour for the necessaries of life.

II. THE SECOND STATUTE OF LABOURERS, 1351

[From *Statutes of the Realm*, vol. i. p. 311, 25° Edward III., Stat. 2, 1351. Statutes in the Parliament holden at Westminster, in the Octave of the Purification of the Blessed Virgin Mary ; in the year of the reign of Our Sovereign Lord Edward, King of England and of France, to wit of. England the twenty-fifth, and of his reign of France the twelfth.]

WHEREAS late against the Malice of Servants, which were idle and not willing to serve after the Pestilence, without taking excessive wages,[1] it was ordained by our Lord the King, and by the assent of the Prelates, Earls, Barons and other of his Council, that such manner of servants, as well men as women, should be bound to serve, receiving salary and wages accustomed in the places where they ought to serve in the Twentieth Year of the Reign of the King that now is, or five or six years before ; and that the same servants refusing to serve in such manner should be punished by imprisonment of their bodies, as in the said Statute is more plainly contained : Whereupon Commissions were made to divers People in every county to inquire and punish all them which offended against the same : And now forasmuch as it is given the King to understand in this present Parliament, by petition of the Commonalty, that the said servants having no regard to the said ordinance, but to their ease and singular covetise, do withdraw themselves to serve great men and other, unless they have Livery and Wages to the double or treble of that they were wont to take the said Twentieth Year, and before, to the great damage of the great men, and impoverishing of the said Commonalty, whereof the said Commonalty prayeth remedy : wherefore in the said Parliament by the assent of the said Prelates, Earls and Barons, and other great men of the same Commonalty there assembled, to refrain the malice of the said servants, be ordained and established the things underwritten :

First, that carters, ploughmen, drivers of the plough, shepherds, swineherds, deies,[2] and all other servants shall

[1] Cf. p. 268; also *Piers Plowman*, Prologue, p. 300.   [2] dairy-women.

take liveries and wages accustomed in the Twentieth Year, or Four Years before ; so that in the country where wheat was wont to be given, they shall take for the bushel ten pence, or wheat at the will of the giver, till it be otherwise ordained. And they shall be allowed to serve by a whole year, or by other usual terms and not by the day ; and that none pay in the time of sarcling or hay-making but a penny the day ; and a mower of meadows for the acre five pence, or by the day five pence ; and reapers of corn in the first week of August two pence, and the second three pence, and so till the end of August. and less in the country where less was wont to be given, without meat or drink, or other courtesie to be demanded, given, or taken ; and that all workmen bring openly in their hands to the merchant towns their instruments, and there shall be hired in a common place and not privy.

Item, that none take for the threshing of a quarter of wheat or rye over iid. ob.[1] and the quarter of barley, beans, pease, and oats, id. ob.,[2] if so much were wont to be given ; and in the country, where it is used to reap by certain sheaves, and to thresh by certain bushels, they shall take no more nor in other manner than was wont the said xxth year and before ; and that the same servants be sworn two times in the year before lords, stewards, bailiffs and constables of every town to do and hold these ordinances ; and that none of them go out of the town, where he dwelleth in the Winter, to serve the Summer, if he may serve in the same town, taking as before is said. Saving that the people of the Counties of Stafford, Lancaster and Derby, and people of Craven, and of the Marches of Wales, and Scotland, and other places may come in time of August, and labour in other counties and safely return, as they were wont to do before this time ; and that those who refuse to make such oath, or to perform that they be sworn to, or have taken upon them, shall be put in the stocks by the said lords, stewards, bailiffs and constables of the towns by three days or more, or sent to the next gaol there to remain, till they will justify themselves. And that stocks be made in every town by such occasion betwixt this and the Feast of Pentecost.

Item, that carpenters, masons and tilers, and other workmen of houses, shall not take by the day for their work, but

[1] twopence halfpenny.   [2] three halfpence.

in manner as they were wont, that is to say : a master carpenter iiid. and another iid. A master free mason [1] iiiid. and other masons iiid. and their servants id. ob.[2] Tylers iiid. and their knaves id. ob.[2] and other coverers of fern and straw iiid. and their knaves id. ob.[2] Plasterers and other workers of mud walls, and their knaves, by the same manner without meat or drink, is. from Easter to St. Michael ; and from that time less, according to the rate and discretion of the justices, which should be thereto assigned : and that they that make carriage by land or by water, shall take no more for such carriage to be made, than they were wont the said xxth year, and iiii years before.

Item, that cordwainers and shoemakers shall not sell boots nor shoes nor such other thing touching their mystery, in any other manner than they were wont the said xxth year ; item that goldsmiths, sadlers, horsesmiths, spurriers, tanners, carriers, tanners of leather, taylors and other workmen, artificers and labourers, and all other servants here not specified, shall be sworn before the justices, to do and use their Crafts and offices in the manner as they were wont to do the said xxth year, and in the time before, without refusing the same because of this ordinance ; and if any of the said servants, labourers, workmen or artificers, after such oath made, come against this ordinance, he shall be punished by fine and ransome, and imprisonment after the discretion of the justices.

. . . .

[Summary of Remainder of the Statute

Stewards and bailiffs shall certify offenders to the justices. The justices shall inquire and punish. Hostelers and victuallers subject to inquiry. Excess of wages received to be refunded. Sheriffs, constables, etc., shall take nothing of servants for fees etc. Justices shall inquire thereof. Forfeitures shall be applied in aid of the subsidy for the time being. Sessions of justice shall be held quarterly or oftener. Punishment of abettors. Of servants flying from one country to another.]

[1] free stone mason.
[2] *i.e.* three halfpence.

III. THE POPULATION OF ENGLAND AS RECORDED IN THE POLL-TAX ACCOUNTS OF 1377 AND 1381

[Only those liable to poll-tax are included in these figures. Children under fourteen in 1377 and under fifteen in 1381 are not included. The relative sizes of towns and counties should be compared with those gathered from *Domesday Book*. The figures are derived from the Lord Treasurer's Remembrancer's Enrolled Accounts. From Oman, *The Great Revolt of 1381*, Appendix II., pp. 162 sqq., by kind permission of Sir Charles Oman and Oxford University Press.]

	51 Edw. III. (1377).	4 Rich. II. (1381).
Comitatus [1] Bedford	20,339	14,895
Comitatus [1] Berks	22,723	15,696
Comitatus Bucks.	24,672	17,997
Comitatus Cantabrigiae (Cambridge) .	27,350	24,324
villa [2] de Cantebr' (Cambridge) . .	1,902	1,739
Comitatus Cornubiae (Cornwall) .	34,274	12,056
Comitatus Cumbriae (Cumberland) . .	11,841	4,748
civitas Karliol (Carlisle). . . .	678	no separate return
Comitatus Derby.	23,243	15,637
villa de Derby	1,046	no separate return
Comitatus Devon	45,635	20,656
civitas [3] Exon (Exeter)	1,560	1,420
villa de Dertemuth (Dartmouth) . .	506	no separate return
Comitatus Dorset	34,241	19,507
Comitatus Essex	47,962	30,748
villa de Colchestr'	2,955	1,609
Comitatus Gloucestriae	36,730	27,857
villa Gloucestriae	2,239	1,446
villa de Bristoll	6,345	5,652
Comitatus Hereford	15,318	12,659
civitas Hereford	1,403	no separate return
Comitatus Hertford	19,975	13,296
Comitatus Hunts.	14,169	11,299
Comitatus Kent	56,307	43,838
civitas Cantuar. (Canterbury) . .	2,574	2,123
civitas Roffen (Rochester) . . .	570	no separate return

[1] *comitatus* : county.   [2] *villa* : town.   [3] *civitas* : city.

	51 Edw. III. (1377).	4 Rich. II. (1381).
Comitatus Lancastriae	23,880	8,371
Comitatus Leycestriae	31,730	21,914
villa de Leycester	2,101	1,708
Comitatus Lincoln :		
Lindesey	47,303	30,235
Kesteven	21,566	15,734
Holand	18,592	13,795
civitas Lincoln	3,412	2,196
clausum de Lincoln.	157	no separate return
villa de Stamford	1,218	do.
villa de Boston	2,871	do.
villa de Grymesby	no separate return	562
Comitatus Middlesex	11,243	9,937
civitas London.	23,314	20,397
Comitatus Norffolk	88,797	66,719
civitas Norwyci (Norwich) . . .	3,952	3,833
villa de Lenne (King's Lynn) . .	3,127	1,824
villa de Jernemuth (Yarmouth) . .	1,941	no separate return
Comitatus Northamptoniae . . .	40,225	27,997
villa Northamp'	1,477	1,518
Comitatus Northumbriae	14,162	return missing
villa Novi Castri super Tynam (Newcastle-on-Tyne)	2,647	1,819
Comitatus Nottingham	26,260	17,442
villa de Nottingham	1,447	1,266
villa de Newark	1,178	no separate return
Comitatus Oxon	24,981	20,588
villa Oxon (Oxford)	2,357	2,005
Comitatus Roteland (Rutland). . .	5,994	5,593
Comitatus Salopiae (Shropshire) . .	23,574	13,041
villa Salopiae (Shrewsbury) . . .	2,082	1,618
villa de Lodelowe (Ludlow) . . .	1,172	no separate return
Comitatus Somerset	54,603	30,384
civitas Bathon (Bath)	570	297
civitas Welles	901	487
Comitatus Stafford	21,465	15,993
civitas Lychfeld (Lichfield) . . .	1,024	no separate return
Comitatus Suffolk	58,610	44,635
villa Gippewici (Ipswich) . . .	1,507	963
villa Sti Edmundi (Bury St. Edmunds)	2,445	1,334

	51 Edw. III. (1377).	4 Rich. II. (1381).
Comitatus Surrey	18,039	12,684
villa de Southwerk	no separate return	1,059
Comitatus Sussex	35,326	26,616
civitas Cicestriae (Chichester) . .	869	787
Comitatus Southampton (Hampshire) .	33,241	22,018
Insula Vecta (Isle of Wight) . .	4,733	3,625
villa de Suthampton	1,152	1,051
Comitatus Warrewici (Warwickshire) .	25,447	20,481
villa de Coventre	4,817	3,947
Comitatus Westmoreland	7,389	3,859
Comitatus Wigorniae (Worcestershire) .	14,542	12,043
civitas Wigorn (Worcester) . . .	1,557	932
Comitatus Wyltes (Wiltshire) . . .	42,599	30,627
civitas Novi Sarum (Salisbury) . .	3,226	2,708
Comitatus Eboraci (Yorkshire). . .	..	..
Estrithing (East Riding) . . .	38,238	25,184
Westrithing (West Riding) . . .	48,149	23,029
Northrithing (North Riding). . .	33,185	15,690
civitas Eboraci (York)	7,248	4,015
villa de Beverley	2,663	no separate return
villa de Scardeburg (Scarborough) .	no separate return	1,480
villa de Kyngeston super Hull (Hull) .	1,557	1,124
Totals .	1,355,201	896,481

IV. EXTRACTS FROM THE PROLOGUE OF CHAUCER'S *CANTERBURY TALES*

[Geoffrey Chaucer, the son of John Chaucer, a citizen and vintner of London, was born about 1340. The first certain information about him concerns his service in the household of Elizabeth de Burgh, Countess of Ulster, wife of Lionel, Duke of Clarence, the third son of Edward III. In 1359, he served in France and was taken prisoner. The fact that the king contributed the comparatively large sum of £16 towards his ransom shows that he was regarded, both by captors and ransomers, as a person of some importance. In 1367, in consideration of his past and future services, Edward III. granted him a pension of twenty marks per annum. It is probable that about the year 1366, Chaucer married a lady named Philippa ; and if, as has been thought, this lady is to be identified with Philippa Roet, the sister of Catherine Swynford the marriage would account for Chaucer's close association with John of Gaunt. In 1369, Chaucer again served in the French War, and in 1372 he was sent on a diplomatic mission to Genoa. On his return to England his affairs prospered greatly. Thus, for instance, on St. George's Day, 1374, the king, then at Windsor, granted him a pitcher of wine daily. The following June he was appointed Comptroller of Customs, etc., in the Port of London. The same month John of Gaunt granted him and his wife a pension of £10 for good services rendered by them " to the said Duke, his consort, and his mother the queen." In 1377 he was sent on a diplomatic mission to Flanders. In 1378 he was sent on another diplomatic mission—this time to Milan and other towns in Northern Italy. John of Gaunt continued to treat him with the greatest favour. On three successive New Year's Days (1380–82) he presented Chaucer's wife with a silver cup and cover. In 1386 Chaucer sat in Parliament as Knight of the Shire for Kent ; and supported Richard II. against the Duke of Gloucester's party. Consequently when Gloucester's party gained the upper hand Chaucer was deprived of many of his lucrative posts and reduced to great financial distress. In 1389 he had a brief spell of prosperity, being appointed Clerk of the King's Works in connection with buildings at Westminster, the Tower of London, and other places. The triumph of his opponents soon caused him to lose his appointments, and he was again plunged in penury and died 25th October 1400.

The plan of the *Canterbury Tales* took shape about the years 1386–88. It is possible that Chaucer himself made the pilgrimage to Canterbury in 1385, and based his " Prologue " to some extent on his own experience. However this may be, there is no need to enlarge upon its value as an historical document for the study of social, religious, and economic conditions in the later half of the thirteenth century. Chaucer's connexion with John of Gaunt, the great supporter of Wycliffe in his attacks on Church property, may perhaps account for his scornful description of many ecclesiastical personages in the " Prologue." But the corruptions of the Church after the Black Death are painted in colours almost as dark in *Piers Plowman*, the works of Gower, and other contemporary documents.

A handy edition of *Chaucer's Works*, with introduction, short notes, and glossary, is that by Pollard, Heath, Liddle and McCormick in the Globe Edition (Macmillan & Co. Ltd., 1923).]

SELECTIONS FROM THE PROLOGUE

[(*a*) *Lines* 43 *sqq.*]

A KNIGHT ther was, and that a worthy man,
That fro the tyme that he first bigan
To riden out, he loved chivalrye,
Trouthe and honour, fredom and curteisie.
Ful worthy was he in his lordes werre,
And therto hadde he riden (no man ferre)
As wel in Cristendom as hethenesse,
And ever honoured for his worthinesse.   50
    At Alisaundre he was, whan it was wonne ;
Ful ofte tyme he hadde the bord bigonne
Aboven alle naciouns in Pruce.
In Lettow hadde he reysed and in Ruce,
No Cristen man so ofte of his degree.
In Gernade at the sege eek hadde he be
Of Algezir, and riden in Belmarye.
At Lyeys was he, and at Satalye,
Whan they were wonne ; and in the Grete See
At many a noble aryve hadd he be   60
At mortal batailles hadde he been fiftene,
And foughten for our feith at Tramissene
In listes thryes, and ay slayn his fo.

Line 47. *worthy* : distinguished. For current ideals of chivalry, cf.
Froissart, pp. 214 sqq. *werre* : war.   48. *ferre* : further.   51.
Alisaundre ¡ Alexandria was won by Pierre de Lusignan, King of
Cyprus, in 1365.   It was, however, immediately afterwards abandoned.
52. *hadde the bord bigonne* : "had been placed at the head of the
table." It was the chivalrous custom to compliment the most
valiant knight present at a banquet by placing him at the head of
the table.   53. *Pruce* : Prussia, the land held by the knights of the
Teutonic Order who were waging war against the heathen of Lithuania
(Lettow) and Russia (Ruce).   56. *Gernade* : Granada, in the
south of Spain, which continued to be held by the Moors till the year
1492.   57. *Algezir* : Algeciras, on the south coast of Spain, near
Gibraltar.   It was taken from the Moorish king of Spain in 1344 after
a long siege in which several Englishmen played a conspicuous part.
Belmarye : One of the Moorish kingdoms in North Africa.   58. *Lyeys* :
the modern Ayas in Armenia.   Pierre of Lusignan, King of Cyprus,
led an expedition thither and captured it in 1367.   *Satalye* ; a town on
the south coast of Asia Minor, the modern Adalia.   It was captured
by Pierre of Lusignan in 1352.   59. the *Grete See* : the Mediterranean.   60. *aryve* : disembarkation of troops.   62. *Tramissene* :
the modern Themcen in Algeria.   63. *listes* : ground enclosed for a
tournament.

This ilke worthy knight had been also
Somtyme with the Lord of Palatye,
Ageyn another hethen in Turkye :
And evermore he hadde a sovereyn prys.
And though that he were worthy, he was wys,
And of his port as meke as is a mayde.
He never yet no vileinye ne sayde   70
In al his lyf, un-to no maner wight.
He was a verray parfit gentil knight.
But for to tellen yow of his array,
His hors weren gode, but he was nat gay.
Of fustian he wered a gypoun
Al bismotered with his habergeoun ;
For he was late y-come from his viage,
And wente for to doon his pilgrimage.
    With him ther was his sone, a yong SQUYER,
A lovyere, and a lusty bacheler,   80
With lokkes crulle, as they were leyd in presse.
Of twenty yeer of age he was, I gesse.
Of his stature he was of evene lengthe,
And wonderly deliver, and greet of strengthe.
And he had been somtyme in chivachye,
In Flaundres, in Artoys, and Picardye,
And born him wel, as of so litel space,
In hope to stonden in his lady grace.
Embrouded was he, as it were a mede
Al ful of fresshe floures, whyte and rede.   90
Singinge he was, or floytinge, al the day ;
He was as fresh as is the month of May.
Short was his goune, with sleeves longe and wyde.
Wel coude he sitte on hors, and faire ryde.
He coude songes make and wel endyte,
Juste and eek daunce, and wel purtreye and wryte.
So hote he lovede, that by nightertale

Line 65. *Palatye* : Palathia, in Asia Minor. It was held by Christian barons, who sometimes had to pay tribute to the Turk. 71. *no maner wight* : nobody whatever. 74. *hors* : horses. 75. *gypoun* : a short vest or doublet. 76. *bismotered* : dirtied. *habergeon* : a small hauberk or coat of mail. 81. *crulle* : curly. 84. *deliver* : active. 85. *chivachye* : a military expedition. 86. *Flaundres, Artoys, and Picardye* : provinces in north-east France. 95. *endyte* : compose. 96. *purtreye* : portray. 97. *nightertale* : night-time.

He sleep namore than dooth a nightingale.
Curteys he was, lowly, and servisable,
And carf biforn his fader at the table.   100
    A YEMAN hadde he, and servaunts namo. . . .

.   .   .   .

[*Lines* 118 *sqq.*]
There was also a Nonne, a PRIORESSE,
That of hir smyling was ful simple and coy :
Hir gretteste ooth was but by sëynt Loy ;   120
And she was cleped madame Eglentyne.
Ful wel she song the service divyne,
Entuned in hir nose ful semely ;
And Frensh she spak ful faire and fetisly,
After the scole of Stratford atte Bowe,
For Frensh of Paris was to hir unknowe.
At mete wel y-taught was she with-alle ;
She leet no morsel from hir lippes falle,
Ne wette hir fingres in hir sauce depe.
Wel coude she carie a morsel, and wel kepe,   130
That no drope ne fille up-on hir brest.
In curteisye was set ful muche hir lest.
Hir over lippe wyped she so clene,
That in hir coppe was no ferthing sene
Of grece, whan she dronken hadde hir draughte.
Ful semely after hir mete she raughte,
And sikerly she was of greet disport,
And ful plesaunt, and amiable of port,
And peyned hir to countrefete chere
Of court, and been estatlich of manere,   140
And to ben holden digne of reverence.
But, for to speken of hir conscience,
She was so charitable and so pitous,
She wolde wepe, if that she sawe a mous

Line 101. *Yeman* : a servant of the next degree above a groom.
namo : no more.   120. *sëynt Loy* : Saint Eligius, who on one famous
occasion refused to swear.   To swear by this saint may mean, therefore, not to swear at all. Cf., however, the Friar's Tale, D. 1564.
124. *fetisly* : excellently.   125. *Stratford atte Bowe* ; in Middlesex.
The Benedictine nunnery there was probably a girls' school.   126.
Frensh of Paris ; probably a sly hit at the Anglo-French spoken in
Chaucer's day.   132. *lest* ; pleasure.   134. *ferthing* : a morsel
(originally " a fourth part "). *sene* ; to be seen.   136. *raughte* :
reached.   137. *sikerly* ; surely.   139. *chere* ; manner, appearance.   140. *estatlich* ; stately, dignified.   141. *digne* : worthy.

Caught in a trappe, if it were deed or bledde.
Of smale houndes had she, that she fedde
With rosted flesh, or milk and wastel-breed.
But sore weep she if oon of hem were deed,
Or if men smoot it with a yerde smerte :
And al was conscience and tendre herte. 150
Ful semely hir wimpel pinched was ;
Hir nose tretys ; hir eyen greye as glas ;
Hir mouth ful smal, and ther-to softe and reed ;
But sikerly she hadde a fair forheed ;
It was almost a spanne brood, I trowe ;
For, hardily, she was nat undergrowe.
Ful fetys was hir cloke, as I was war.
Of smal coral aboute hir arm she bar
A peire of bedes, gauded al with grene ;
And ther-on heng a broche of gold ful shene, 160
On which ther was first write a crowned A,
And after, *Amor vincit omnia*.
Another NONNE with her hadde she,
That was hir chapeleyne, and PREESTES THREE.
A MONK ther was, a fair for the maistrie,
An out-rydere, that lovede venerie ;
A manly man, to been an abbot able.
Ful many a deyntee hors hadde he in stable :
And, whan he rood, men mighte his brydel here
Ginglen in a whistling wind as clere, 170

Line 147. *wastel-breed* : bread made of cake flour. " Wastel " is
the same word as the modern French " gâteau," cake. 149. *men* :
indefinite pronoun. *smerte* : smartly. 151. *wimpel* : covering for
the neck, wimple. 152. *tretys* : well-made, long and well-shaped.
157. *fetys* : neat, well-made. *war* : aware. 159. *A peire of bedes* : a
set of beads, *i.e.* a rosary. *gauded*, etc. : the gawdies were the greater
beads of the rosary. These stood each for a Paternoster, whereas the
smaller beads stood for Ave Marias. The gawdies in this rosary were
coloured green. 160. *shene* : beautiful. 162. *Amor vincit omnia* :
from Virgil's *Eclogues*, x. 69, " Love overcomes all things." 164.
chapeleyne : a woman chaplain was not unusual in the smaller nunneries.
Preestes three : three priests. The nunnery of St. Mary, Winchester,
had as many as twenty-six priests attached to it at the time of the
Dissolution of the Monasteries. 165. *a fair for the maistrie* : a fair one
above all others. The Latin expression " *pro magisterio* " was used
similarly of medicines that were particularly good. 166. *out-rydere* :
an officer of a monastery, whose duty was to look after the manors
belonging to it. *venerie* : hunting. 170. *ginglen* : jingle. It was the
custom of men of fashion to have their horses' bridles hung with bells.

And eek as loude as dooth the chapel-belle
Ther as this lord was keper of the celle.
The reule of seint Maure or of seint Beneit,
By-cause that it was old and som-del streit,
This ilke monke leet olde thinges pace,
And held after the newe world the space.
He yaf nat of that text a pulled hen,
That seith, that hunters beth nat holy men ;
Ne that a monk, whan he is cloisterlees,
Is lykned til a fish that is waterlees ;   180
This is to seyn, a monk out of his cloistre.
But thilke text held he nat worth an oistre ;
And I seyde, his opinioun was good.
What sholde he studie, and make hymselven wood,
Upon a book in cloistre alwey to poure,
Or swinken with his handes, and laboure,
As Austin bit ?   How shal the world be served ?
Lat Austin have his swink to him reserved.
Therefore he was a pricasour aright ;
Grehoundes he hadde, as swifte as fowel in flight ;   190
Of priking and of hunting for the hare
Was al his lust, for no cost wolde he spare.
I seigh his sleves purfiled at the hond
With grys, and that the fyneste of a lond ;
And, for to festne his hood under his chin,
He hadde of gold y-wroght a curious pin :
A love-knotte in the gretter ende ther was.
His heed was balled, that shoon as any glas,
And eek his face, as he had been anoint.
He was a lord ful fat and in good point ;   200

Line 172. *Ther as* : where. *keper of the celle* : prior of a small
religious house, subordinate to a greater one.   173. *Maure* : St.
Maurus (A.D. 510–584), a disciple of St. Benedict and Abbot of Glafeuil,
which was afterwards called after him, St. Maur-sur-Loire.   *Beneit* :
St. Benedict, the famous Abbot of Monte Cassino, whose " Rule "
laid down the form of monastic discipline that became almost universal
in the Latin Church.   174. *som-del* : something.   175. *ilke* : same.
177. *yaf* : gave.   *that text* : the reference is probably to some version
of the *Life of St. Anthony* attributed to St. Athanasius.   184. *wood* :
mad.   186. *swinken* : work.   187. *Austin* : St. Augustine of Hippo.
188. *swink* : work.   189. *pricasour* : a hard rider.   192. *lust* :
pleasure.   193. *seigh* : saw.   *purfiled* : trimmed with fur.   194.
grys : costly grey fur.   200. *in good point* : cf. French embonpoint,
stoutness.

His eyen stepe, and rollinge in his heed,
That stemed as a forneys of a leed ;
His botes souple, his hors in greet estat.
Now certeinly he was a fair prelat ;
He was nat pale as a for-pyned goost.
A fat swan loved he best of any roost.
His palfrey was as broun as is a berye.
   A FRERE [1] ther was, a wantown and a merye,
A limitour, a ful solempne man.
In alle the ordres foure is noon that can   210
So muche of daliaunce and fair langage ;
He hadde maad ful many a mariage
Of yonge wommen, at his owne cost.
Un-to his ordre he was a noble post.
Ful wel biloved and famulier was he
With frankeleyns over-al in his contree,
And eek with worthy wommen of the toun :
For he had power of confessioun,
As seyde him-self, more than a curat,
For of his ordre he was licentiat.   220
Ful swetely herde he confessioun,
And plesaunt was his absolucioun ;
He was an esy man to geve penaunce
Ther as he wiste to han a good pitaunce ;
For unto a povre ordre for to give
Is signe that a man is wel y-shrive.
For if he gaf, he dorste make avaunt,
He wiste that a man was repentaunt.
For many a man so hard is of his herte,
He may nat wepe al-thogh him sore smerte.   230
Therfore, in stede of weping and preyeres,

Line 201. *stepe* : bright.   202. *stemed* : shone. *forneys of a leed* : the furnace under a cauldron.   205. *for-pyned* : wasted by torture. 209. *limitour* : one licensed to beg within a certain district of defined limits.   210. *ordres foure* : these were the Dominicans, Franciscans, Carmelites, and Augustines.   212–13. *He hadde maad*, etc. : probably means that he had paid sums of money to get women, who had been his concubines, married.   219. *curat* : parish priest.   220. *licentiat* : licensed to hear confessions everywhere. This privilege granted to friars often made the position of the parish priest a difficult one.   224. *pitaunce* : portion of food.   226. *y-shrive* : confessed, shriven.

[1] Cf. Extract from the Rule of St. Francis, p. 96 ; also *Piers Plowman*, Prologue, p. 301.

Men moot geve silver to the povre freres.
His tipet was ay farsed ful of knyves
And pinnes, for to geven yonge wyves.
And certeinly he hadde a mery note ;
Wel coude he singe and pleyen on a rote.
Of yeddinges he bar utterly the prys.
His nekke whyt was as the flour-de-lys ;
Ther-to he strong was as a champioun.
He knew the tavernes wel in every toun,   240
And everich hostiler and tappestere
Bet than a lazar or a beggestere ;
For un-to swich a worthy man as he
Accorded nat, as by his facultee,
To have with sike lazars aqueyntaunce.
It is nat honest, it may nat avaunce
For to delen with no swich poraille,
But al with riche and sellers of vitaille.
And over-al, ther as profit sholde aryse,
Curteys he was, and lowly of servyse.   250
Ther nas no man no-wher so vertuous.
He was the beste beggere in his hous ;
[And yaf a certeyn ferme for the graunt ;
Noon of his bretheren cam ther in his haunt ;]
For thogh a widwe hadde noght a sho,
So plesaunt was his ' *In principio*,'
Yet wolde he have a ferthing, er he wente.
His purchas was wel bettre than his rente.
And rage he coude, as it were right a whelpe.
In love-dayes ther coude he muchel helpe.   260
For there he was nat lyk a cloisterer,
With a thredbar cope, as is a povre scoler,
But he was lyk a maister or a pope.
Of double worsted was his semi-cope,

Line 233. *tipet* : hood.   236. *rote* : a small harp, or a kind of
fiddle.   237. *yeddinges* : popular songs.   241. *tappestere* : bar-
maid.   242. *beggestere* : beggar-woman.   246. *avaunce* : profit.
247. *poraille* : from the Anglo-French " poverail," poor folk, rabble.
256. *In principio* : from the first verse of St. John's Gospel, " In
principio erat verbum," which the limitours were accustomed to
recite at every house on their rounds.   258. *purchas* : proceeds of
begging.   260. *love-dayes* : days fixed for settling differences
amongst neighbours by arbitration without recourse to the law courts.
264. *semi-cope* : a short cloak.

That rounded as a belle out of the presse.
Somewhat he lipsed, for his wantownesse,
To make his English swete up-on his tonge ;
And in his harping, whan that he had songe,
His eyen twinkled in his heed aright,
As doon the sterres in the frosty night.   270
This worthy limitour was cleped Huberd.
    A MARCHANT was ther with a forked berd,
In motteley, and hye on horse he sat,
Up-on his heed a Flaundrish bever hat ;
His botes clasped faire and fetisly.
His resons he spak ful solempnely,
Souninge alway th'encrees of his winning.
He wolde the see were kept for any thing
Bitwixe Middelburgh and Orewelle.[1]
Wel coude he in eschaunge sheeldes selle.   280
This worthy man ful wel his wit bisette ;
Ther wiste no wight that he was in dette,
So estatly was he of his governaunce,
With his bargaynes, and with his chevisaunce.
For sothe he was a worthy man with-alle,
But sooth to seyn, I noot how men him calle.
    A CLERK ther was of Oxenford also,[2]
That un-to logik hadde longe y-go.
As lene was his hors as is a rake,
And he nas nat right fat, I undertake ;   290
But loked holwe, and ther-to soberly.
Ful thredbar was his overest courtepy ;
For he had geten him yet no benefyce,
Ne was so worldly for to have offyce.

Line 272. *forked berd* : the fashionable middle-class .method of dressing the beard. 273. *motteley* : a motley or parti-coloured garb. 277. *souninge* : sounding like, or tending to. 278. *were kept* : *i.e.* kept clear of privateers. 279. *Middelburgh* : the canal port on the island of Walcheren, Holland. *Orewelle* : the modern Harwich. 280. *sheeldes* : French crowns, worth about 3s. 4d. ; so called because stamped with a shield on one side. 284. *chevisaunce* : agreement for borrowing money. 288. *longe y-go* : had devoted himself for a long time. 292. *overest courtepy* : his outer cloak.

---

[1] Cf. the Libel of English Policy, p. 365.
[2] Cf. pp. 145 sqq. ; also. the *Paston Letters*, p. 330 ; also the *Stonor Papers*, p. 363.

For him was lever have at his beddes heed
Twenty bokes, clad in blak or reed,
Of Aristotle and his philosophye,
Than robes riche, or fithele, or gay sautrye.
But al be that he was a philosophre,
Yet hadde he but litel gold in cofre ;   300
But al that he mighte of his freendes hente,
On bokes and on lerninge he it spente,
And bisily gan for the soules preye
Of hem that gaf him wher-with to scoleye.
Of studie took he most cure and most hede.
Noght o word spak he more than was nede,
And that was seyd in forme and reverence,
And short and quik, and ful of hy sentence.
Souninge in moral vertu was his speche,
And gladly wolde he lerne, and gladly teche.   310

.   .   .   .

[(*b*) *Lines* 411 *sqq.*]

With us ther was a Doctour of Phisik,[1]
In al this world ne was ther noon him lyk
To speke of phisik and of surgerye ;
For he was grounded in astronomye.
He kepte his pacient a ful greet del
In houres, by his magik naturel.
Wel coude he fortunen the ascendent
Of his images for his pacient.
He knew the cause of everich maladye,
Were it of hoot or cold, or moiste, or drye,   420

Line 295. *him was lever* : he would prefer.   298. *fithele* : fiddle.
sautrye : a kind of harp.   299. *philosophre* : a play on the word
" philosopher " ; which was used also in the sense of alchemist, one
who sought to transmute the baser metals into gold.   301. *hente* :
get.   304. *scoleye* : to attend college, to study.   308. *sentence* :
meaning, wisdom, judgment.   309. *Souninge* : cf. line 277, tending
to.   415. *kepte* : observed.   416. *houres* : *i.e.* astrological hours.
417. *fortunen the ascendent* : *i.e.* choose a favourable moment, when
a sign of the Zodiac was in position, for making images wherewith
to cure his patients.   420. *hoot*, etc. : according to Galen and
later medical writers these were the four fundamental " humours "
which were united in varying proportions to make up each man's
" complexion " or temperament.

---

[1] Cf. the *Stonor Letters*, p. 362.

And where engendered, and of what humour ;
He was a verrey parfit practisour.
The cause y-knowe, and of his harm the rote,
Anon he yaf the seke man his bote.
Ful redy hadde he his apothecaries,
To sende him drogges and his letuaries,
For ech of hem made other for to winne ;
His frendschipe nas nat newe to bigynne.
Wel knew he th'olde Esculapius,
And Deiscorides, and eek Rufus,   430
Old Ypocras, Haly, and Galien ;
Serapion, Razis, and Avicen ;
Averrois, Damascien, and Constantyn ;
Bernard, and Gatesden, and Gilbertyn.

Line 424. *bote* : remedy.   426. *letuaries* : electuaries, remedies.
429. *Esculapius* : the classical deity of medicine, to whom many
medical works had come to be ascribed.   430. *Deiscorides* : a
physician of the second century A.D., born in Cilicia. *Rufus* : a
physician of Ephesus of the time of the Emperor Trajan. He wrote
chiefly on anatomy.   431. *Ypocras* : Hippocrates of Cos (*circa* 460–
360 B.C.), often called " the father of medicine." Many medical works
bearing his name are still extant. *Haly* : an eleventh-century Arab
physician, who wrote a commentary on Galen. *Galien* : Galen, born
at Pergamos, 130 A.D., the physician of the Emperor Marcus Aurelius.
His works were the greatest treasury of medieval medicine, both
Christian and Muhammedan.   432. *Serapion* : There were three
great medical writers of this name. *Razis* : a famous Arabian physician
of Spain in the tenth century. *Avicen* : Avicenna, the celebrated
Arabian physician and philosopher, born near Bokhara in A.D. 980.
He was a great student of mathematics, logic, medicine, and theology.
After holding the office of physician to several famous Muhammedan
princes, he died at Hammedan in 1037. Amongst his voluminous works
are a commentary on the *Metaphysics* of Aristotle and his famous
Canon, which was the supreme authority on medical science during the
Middle Ages.   433. *Averrois* : Averroes, or Ibn Rosht, an Arabian
scholar who lived in Spain and Morocco, A.D. 1126–98. He was famous
as a physician and a philosopher, and a great translator of the works of
Aristotle. His most famous medical treatise was the " Collyget " or
" Kulligat," *i.e.* the Total. He suffered much from his fellow-Muham-
medans owing to his heretical views on religion. *Damascien* : John of
Damascus, a Muhammedan physician and philosopher of the ninth
century A.D. *Constantyn* : Constantinus Afer, a twelfth-century
Benedictine monk, born at Carthage, and belonging to the famous
monastery of Monte Cassino. He took a leading part in founding
the great medical school of Salerno.   434. *Bernard* : a professor
of medicine at Montpellier, a contemporary of Chaucer. *Gatesden* :
court physician under Edward II., fellow of Merton, Oxford, author
of a medical treatise called *Rosa Anglica*. *Gilbertyn* : Gilbertus

Of his diete mesurable was he,
For it was of no superfluitee,
But of greet norissing and digestible.
His studie was but litel on the Bible.
In sangwin and in pers he clad was al,
Lyned with taffata and with sendal ;   440
And yet he was but esy of dispence ;
He kepte that he wan in pestilence.
For gold in phisik is a cordial,
Therfore he lovede gold in special.
    A good WYF was ther of bisyde BATHE,
But she was som-del deef, and that was scathe.
Of clooth-making she hadde swiche an haunt,
She passed hem of Ypres and of Gaunt.
In al the parisshe wyf ne was ther noon
That to th' offring bifore hir sholde goon ;   450
And if ther dide, certeyn, so wrooth was she,
That she was out of alle charitee.
Hir coverchiefs ful fyne were of ground ;
I dorste swere they weyeden ten pound
That on a Sonday were upon hir heed.
Hir hosen weren of fyn scarlet reed,
Ful streite y-teyd, and shoos ful moiste and newe.
Bold was hir face, and fair, and reed of hewe.
She was a worthy womman al hir lyve,
Housbondes at chirche-dore she hadde fyve,   460
Withouten other companye in youthe ;
But therof nedeth nat to speke as nouthe.
And thryes hadde she been at Jerusalem ;

Anglicus, one of the earliest English writers on medicine, *floruit*
A.D. 1250.
    Line 439. *pers* : bluish-grey.   440. *sendal* : fine silk.   442.
pestilence : the Black Death of 1349, followed by the lesser pestilences
of 1362, 1369, 1376.   443. *cordial* : gold was regarded as a sovereign
remedy for disease, if taken in the proper form.   448. *Ypres* and
Gaunt : the great cloth markets of the Low Countries.   450. *offring* :
on certain occasions the congregation used to go to the altar at Mass
with their offerings of bread and wine.   They would go up one by one,
in order of precedence—men first, then women.   453. *ground* :
texture.   454. *ten pound* : a satire on the gigantic ladies' head-
dresses which were fashionable at this period.   460. *chirche-dore* :
the marriage service began in the church porch before the celebration
of the nuptial Mass.   It was in the church porch, too, that marriage
settlements were usually made.

She hadde passed many a straunge streem ;
At Rome she hadde been, and at Boloigne,
In Galice at seint Jame, and at Coloigne.
She coude muche of wandring by the weye :
Gat-tothed was she, soothly for to seye.
Up-on an amblere esily she sat,
Y-wimpled wel, and on hir heed an hat.   470
As brood as is a bokeler or a targe ;
A foot-mantel aboute hir hipes large,
And on hir feet a paire of spores sharpe.
In felawschip wel coude she laughe and carpe.
Of remedyes of love she knew perchaunce,
For she coude of that art the olde daunce.
    A good man was ther of religioun,
And was a povre PERSOUN of a town ;
But riche he was of holy thoght and werk.
He was also a lerned man, a clerk,   480
That Cristes gospel trewely wolde preche ;
His parisshens devoutly wolde he teche.
Benigne he was, and wonder diligent,
And in adversitee ful pacient ;
And swich he was y-preved ofte sythes.
Ful looth were him to cursen for his tythes,
But rather wolde he yeven, out of doute,
Un-to his povre parisshens aboute
Of his offring, and eek of his substaunce.
He coude in litel thing han suffisaunce.   490
Wyd was his parisshe, and houses fer a-sonder,
But he ne lafte nat, for reyn ne thonder,
In siknes nor in meschief, to visyte

Line 465. *Boloigne* : Boulogne, where was a famous statue of the
Blessed Virgin.   466. *seint Jame* : the shrine of St. James of
Compostella at Santiago in Galicia, one of the most frequented resorts
of medieval pilgrims. *Coloigne* : Cologne, where a famous relic, the
bones of the magi, was venerated by pilgrims. The city was also
one of the greatest trading centres in the world at this time.   468.
Gat-tothed : either " gap-toothed " or " goat-toothed,' *i.e.* lascivious.
470. *Y-wimpled* : decked with a wimple.   472. *foot-mantel* : an
outer riding skirt.   474. *carpe* : chatter.   475. *remedyes of love* :
the allusion is to Ovid's *Remedia Amoris*.   476. *daunce* : custom.
485. *sythes* : times.   486. *cursen* : the parish priest had to collect
the tithes due to him, and refusal to pay might be punished by lesser
excommunication.   489. *offring* : voluntary gifts. *substaunce* : his
private fortune, or his regular income.

The ferreste in his parisshe, muche and lyte,
Up-on his feet, and in his hand a staf.
This noble ensample to his sheep he yaf,
That first he wroghte, and afterward he taughte ;
Out of the gospel he tho wordes caughte ;
And this figure he added eek ther-to,
That if gold ruste, what shal iren do ?   500
For if a preest be foul, on whom we truste,
No wonder is a lewed man to ruste ;
And shame it is, if a preest take keep,
A shiten shepherde and a clene sheep.
Wel oghte a preest ensample for to yive,
By his clennesse, how that his sheep shold live.
He sette nat his benefice to hyre,
And leet his sheep encombred in the myre,
And ran to London, un-to seynt Poules,
To seken him a chaunterie for soules.   510
Or with a bretherhed to been withholde ;
But dwelte at hoom, and kepte wel his folde,
So that the wolf ne made it nat miscarie ;
He was a shepherde and no mercenarie.
And though he holy were, and vertuous,
He was to sinful man nat despitous,
Ne of his speche daungerous ne digne,
But in his teching discreet and benigne.
To drawen folk to heven by fairnesse
By good ensample, was his bisinesse :   520
But it were any persone obstinat,
What-so he were, of heigh or lowe estat,
Him wolde he snibben sharply for the nones.
A bettre preest, I trowe, that nowher noon is.
He wayted after no pompe and reverence,
Ne maked him a spyced conscience,
But Cristes lore, and his apostles twelve,
He taughte, and first he folwed it himselve.

Line 502. *lewed* : ignorant or lay.   503. *take keep* : pay
heed.   504. *shiten* : foul.   509. *seynt Poules* : *i.e.* he did not
go to St. Paul's, London, to make an easy living by singing
masses for the souls of those who had left an endowment for the
purpose. There were thirty-five chantries at St. Paul's served by
fifty-four priests.   511. *bretherhed* : a religious fraternity.   514.
mercenarie : hireling.   523. *snibben* : reprove.   526. *spyced* :
seasoned, *i.e.* corrupt.

With him ther was a PLOWMAN, was his brother,

·   ·   ·   ·   ·   ·   ·

[*Lines* 545 *sqq.*]

The MILLER was a stout carl, for the nones,
Ful big he was of braun, and eek of bones ;
That proved wel, for over-al ther he cam,
At wrastling he wolde have alwey the ram.
He was short-sholdred, brood, a thikke knarre,
Ther nas no dore that he nolde heve of harre,   550
Or breke it, at a renning, with his heed.
His berd as any sowe or fox was reed,
And ther-to brood, as though it were a spade.
Up-on the cop right of his nose he hade
A werte, and ther-on stood a tuft of heres,
Reed as the bristles of a sowes eres ;
His nose-thirles blake were and wyde ;
A swerd and bokeler bar he by his syde ;
His mouth as greet was as a greet forneys.
He was a janglere and a goliardeys,   560
And that was most of sinne and harlotryes.
Wel coude he stelen corn, and tollen thryes ;
And yet he hadde a thombe of gold, pardee.
A whyt cote and a blew hood wered he.
A baggepype wel coude he blowe and sowne.
And ther-with-al he broghte us out of towne.

·   ·   ·   ·   ·   ·   ·

[*Lines* 587 *sqq.*]

The REVE was a sclender colerik man,
His berd was shave as ny as ever he can.
His heer was by his eres round y-shorn.
His top was dokked lyk a preest biforn.   590
Ful longe were his legges, and ful lene,
Y-lyk a staf, ther was no calf y-sene.

Line 548. *ram* : a ram was often offered as a prize at wrestling
matches.   549. *thikke knarre* : a thick knot, *i.e.* a strong muscular
fellow.   550. *nolde* ; would not.   *heve of harre* : heave off its hinges.
554. *cop* : top.   557. *nose-thirles* : nostrils.   560. *janglere* : loud
talker.   *goliardeys* : buffoon.   562. *tollen thryes* : take three times
the toll due.   563. *thombe of gold* : an allusion to the proverb, " An
honest miller has a golden thumb."

Wel coude he kepe a gerner and a binne ;
Ther was noon auditour coude on him winne.
Wel wiste he, by the droghte, and by the reyn,
The yelding of his seed, and of his greyn.
His lordes sheep, his neet, his dayerye,
His swyn, his hors, his stoor, and his pultrye,
Was hoolly in this reves governing,
And by his covenaunt gaf the rekening,   600
Sin that his lord was twenty yeer of age ;
Ther coude no man bringe him in arrerage.
Ther nas baillif, ne herde, ne other hyne,
That he ne knew his sleighte and his covyne ;
They were adrad of him, as of the deeth.
His woning was ful fair up-on an heeth,
With grene treës shadwed was his place.
He coude bettre than his lord purchace.
Ful riche he was astored prively,
His lord wel coude he plesen subtilly,   610
To geve and lene him of his owne good,
And have a thank, and yet a cote and hood,
In youthe he lerned hadde a good mister ;
He was a wel good wrighte, a carpenter.
This reve sat up-on a ful good stot,
That was al pomely grey, and highte Scot.
A long surcote of pers up-on he hade,
And by his syde he bar a rusty blade.
Of northfolk was this reve, of which I telle,
Bisyde a toun men clepen Baldeswelle.   620
Tukked he was, as is a frere, aboute,
And ever he rood the hindreste of our route.
 A SOMNOUR was ther with us in that place,
That hadde a fyr-reed cherubinnes face,

Line 597. *neet* : cattle. 598. *stoor* : stock. 602. *bringe him in arrerage* : prove him a defaulter. 603. *hyne* : hind, farm-servant. 604. *sleighte* : craft. *covyne* : deceit. 605. *the deeth* : the Black Death. 613. *mister* : "mystery," *i.e.* trade or craft (mastery). 615. *stot* : a cob. 616. *pomely* : dappled. 617. *surcote* : overcoat. *pers* : blue or bluish-grey. 621. *tukked*, etc. : *i.e.* his surcote was tucked up under his girdle very much as was a friar's cassock. 623. *Somnour* : the apparitor, whose business it was to summon accused persons before the Courts Christian—usually the Archdeacon's court. 624. *cherubinnes* : highly coloured. Brilliantly illuminated books were called "Cherubici libri." Cherubs were usually painted red and seraphs blue.

For sawcefleem he was, with eyen narwe.
As hoot he was, and lecherous, as a sparwe ;
With scalled browes blake, and piled berd ;
Of his visage children were aferd.
Ther nas quik-silver, litarge, ne brimstoon,
Boras, ceruce, ne oille of tartre noon,   630
Ne oynement that wolde clense and byte,
That him mighte helpen of his whelkes whyte,
Nor of the knobbes sittinge on his chekes.
Wel loved he garleek, oynons, and eek lekes,
And for to drinken strong wyn, reed as blood.
Than wolde he speke, and crye as he were wood.
And whan that he wel dronken hadde the wyn,
Than wolde he speke no word but Latyn.
A fewe termes hadde he, two or three,
That he had lerned out of som decree ;   640
No wonder is, he herde it al the day ;
And eek ye knowen wel, how that a jay
Can clepen " Watte," as well as can the pope.
But who-so coude in other thing him grope,
Thanne hadde he spent al his philosophye ;
Ay " *Questio quid iuris* " wolde he crye.
He was a gentil harlot and a kinde ;
A bettre felawe sholde men noght finde.
He wolde suffre, for a quart of wyn,
A good felawe to have his concubyn   650
A twelf-month, and excuse him atte fulle :
Ful prively a finch eek coude he pulle.
And if he fond o-wher a good felawe,
He wolde techen him to have non awe,
In swich cas, of the erchedeknes curs,
But-if a mannes soule were in his purs ;
For in his purs he sholde y-punisshed be.
" Purs is the erchedeknes helle " seyde he.
But wel I woot he lyed right in dede ;

Line 625. *sawcefleem* : pimpled.   627. *scalled* : scabby.   *piled* :
plucked, thin.   629. *litarge* : white lead.   630. *ceruce* : a kind of
white lead, ceruse.   630. *oille of tartre* : cream of tartar (potassium
bitartarate).   632. *whelkes* : pimples.   636. *wood* : mad.   643.
Watte : Walter.   644. *grope* : probe, try.   646. *Questio quid iuris* :
the question is, what is the law on this point.   647. *harlot* : fellow,
rascal, of either sex.   652. *pulle a finch* : plunder a fool.   655.
erchedeknes : archdeacon's.

Of cursing oghte ech gilty man him drede—   660
For curs wol slee, right as assoilling saveth—
And also war him of a *significavit.*
In daunger hadde he at his owne gyse
The yonge girles of the diocyse,
And knew hir counseil, and was al hir reed.
A gerland hadde he set up-on his heed,
As greet as it were for an ale-stake ;
A bokeler hadde he maad him of a cake.
   With him ther rood a gentil PARDONER
Of Rouncival, his freend and his compeer,   670
That streight was comen fro the court of Rome.
Ful loude he song, " Com hider, love, to me."
This somnour bar to him a stif burdoun,
Was never trompe of half so greet a soun.
This pardoner hadde heer as yelow as wex,
But smothe it heng, as dooth a strike of flex ;
By ounces henge his lokkes that he hadde,
And ther-with he his shuldres overspradde ;
But thinne it lay, by colpons oon and oon ;
But hood, for jolitee, ne wered he noon,   680
For it was trussed up in his walet.
Him thoughte, he rood al of the newe jet ;
Dischevele, save his cappe, he rood al bare.
Swiche glaringe eyen hadde he as an hare.
A vernicle hadde he sowed on his cappe.

Line 662. *significavit* : the opening word of a writ for imprisoning
an excommunicate person.   663. *daunger* : jurisdiction.   *gise* :
fashion, manner.   664. *girles* : young persons, of both sexes.   665.
reed : counsel.   667. *ale-stake* : a pole projecting horizontally from
the wall of an ale-house after the manner of a modern inn sign.
The pole was ornamented with a bush of ivy-leaves or a " garland " ;
cf. the old proverb, " Good wine needs no bush."   670. *Rouncival* :
A Hospital " Beatae Mariae de Rouncyvalle in Charing London " is
mentioned in Dugdale's *Monasticon*, vol. ii. p. 433. This is probably
the house to which the pardoner belonged. The parent house, Ronce-
vaux, was in Navarre.   673. *bar* . . . *stif burdoun* : put in a strong
base.   677. *ounces* : small pieces.   679. *colpons* : shreds.   682.
jet : fashion.   683. *dischevele* : with hair loose.   685. *vernicle* : a
miniature of a famous picture of Our Lord preserved in the Church
of St. Silvesto, Rome, and known as St. Veronica's handkerchief.
The legendary origin of the picture is that St. Veronica's house stood
on the way to Calvary. Seeing Our Lord pass by to be crucified, she
gave Him her kerchief to wipe His face ; and when He returned it to
her the kerchief was found to retain a perfect likeness of His features.

His walet lay biforn him in his lappe,
Bret-ful of pardoun come from Rome al hoot.
A voys he hadde as smal as hath a goot.
No berd hadde he, ne never sholde have,
As smothe it was as it were late y-shave ;   690
I trowe he were a gelding or a mare.
But of his craft, fro Berwik into Ware,
Ne was ther swich another pardoner.
For in his male he hadde a pilwe-beer,
Which that, he seyde, was our lady veyl :
He seyde, he hadde a gobet of the seyl
That sëynt Peter hadde, whan that he wente
Up-on the see, till Jesu Crist him hente.
He hadde a croys of latoun, ful of stones,
And in a glas he hadde pigges bones.   700
But with thise relikes, whan that he fond
A povre person dwelling up-on lond,
Up-on a day he gat him more moneye
Than that the person gat in monthes tweye.
And thus, with feyned flaterye and japes,
He made the person and the peple his apes.
But trewely to tellen, atte laste,
He was in chirche a noble ecclesiaste.
Wel coude he rede a lessoun or a storie,
But alderbest he song an offertorie ;   710
For wel he wiste, whan that song was songe,
He moste preche, and wel affyle his tonge,
To winne silver, as he ful wel coude ;
Therefore he song so meriely and loude.

V. EXTRACTS FROM THE *VISION OF PIERS THE PLOWMAN*

[This is a long poem written in alliterative verse, after the manner
of Early English poetry. It, therefore, has the appearance of
much greater antiquity than Chaucer's works. It exists in
three main versions. The earliest, known as the A. text, is

In the thirteenth century it was customary to make a pilgrimage to
Rome for the express purpose of seeing this picture.
      Line 694. *male* : wallet. *pilwe-beer* : pillow case.   699. *latoun* :
brass of a fine kind. *stones* : set with precious ones.   702. *up-on*
lond : in the country.

shown by internal evidence to have been written about the year 1362. About 1377 this was expanded into the very much longer B. text. Finally, about 1390, or perhaps a few years later, a revision of the B. text was published in the form known as the C. text. The extracts here given are taken from the B. text.

The authorship of the *Vision* is a matter of considerable dispute. The old view, based on a fifteenth-century memorandum to a MS. of the C. text and on certain apparently biographical details—chiefly in the B. and C. texts—is that the author of all these versions was a certain William Langland, who is variously stated to have been born at Cleobury Mortimer, in Shropshire, or at Shipton-under-Wychwood, in Oxfordshire. It has been deduced from the B. text that he received minor orders, was nicknamed "Long Will," owing to his tall stature, found his way to London at an early age, was married to a wife named "Kitty," and had a daughter named "Calote." He lived a life of great poverty and gloomy discontent, earning a meagre and precarious livelihood by singing "placebos" and "diriges" at rich men's funerals, and copying out legal documents and the like.

This view of the authorship has been seriously shaken by modern research. Professor Manly of Chicago, in the *Cambridge History of English Literature*, vol. ii., attributes the *Vision* to five different writers ; and scholars have not yet arrived at a final verdict on the question. It may be that Langland was only one editor who produced one of the versions of the work. It seems unlikely that he was both the author of the A. text and the reviser of the B. and C. texts. For, in the first place, certain textual derangements of the A. text have been accepted by the editor of the B. text, in a manner which would be almost inconceivable in the original author. Secondly, there is a noticeable difference of mood and outlook in the various versions. Finally, the distance of time between the publication of the A. text and the C. text would give Langland a very long life— were he the producer of both—particularly when it is realized that the A. text bears the marks of the work of a middle-aged man.

Whoever wrote the poems, their value as historical documents for the social and religious life of the later fourteenth century is immense. They are the work, not of a courtly artist like Chaucer, but of idealists and social reformers, men speaking out of the abundance of their discontent with things as they were after the Black Death. They are filled with a passionate sincerity, a great love of righteousness and a hatred of evil. They are quite impartial in their condemnation of the vices of all classes and orders of men ; but their aim is to exhort men to a change of heart rather than a change of political or ecclesiastical institutions.

The poem is not an easy one to understand, owing to the fact that it is not one vision, nor even two, but a series of visions dissolving one into the other without any more attempt at coherence—of completion even in the dream-integer, such as it is—than actual dreams exhibit. It would seem as if the author, whether owing to his mysticism and its accompanying vagueness, or to his satiric intent, and the wholesome sense of danger which accompanied that, deliberately avoided rounding off his chapters and driving home his meanings.[1]

The following is the general scheme of the poem according to the B. text:

PROLOGUE: THE FIELD FULL OF FOLK'

The dreamer, wandering on the Malvern Hills, falls asleep beside a stream and sees in a vision a vast plain full of people plying their daily tasks.

PASSUS I.: THE VISION OF HOLY CHURCH

A lovely lady in linen clothes, who is Holy Church, explains the meaning of the field full of folk, and of the deep dungeon on one side (Hell) and of the high tower (Heaven) on the other side of the field.

PASSUS II.: MEED AND FALSEHOOD

The dreamer wishes to hear of Falsehood as well as Truth. Accordingly " Meed the Maid " is introduced, representing both reward in the good sense, and bribery, etc., in the bad. She is about to marry Favel or Falsehood. The pair set out to be married in London under the escort of Simony and Civil Law. But Soothness anticipates them, and tells Conscience, who tells the King. Consequently, when Meed's companions reach the entrance to the court they hear the King speak in wrath of their doings and flee terrified in all directions.

PASSUS III.: MEED AND CONSCIENCE

Meed stands her ground weeping and is taken before the King. She has a crowd of friends at court owing to her largesse, and the King decides that she shall marry Conscience. Conscience refuses, owing to his abhorrence of the bad kind of Meed, viz. bribery.

PASSUS IV.: MEED AND REASON

Conscience, at the request of the King, fetches Reason, who supports Conscience. The King is convinced by Reason, whom he requests to remain with him for ever.

[1] Saintsbury's *Short Introduction to English Literature* (Macmillan & Co.), p. 133.

Passus V. : The Seven Deadly Sins

Reason exhorts divers persons to repent of their evil lives. They do so and make their confession. Among them is Gluttony, whose confession is one of the most famous and brightly coloured passages of the poem, the description of a London tavern and the bibbers there. Finally, all the repentant sinners decide to set out in search of Truth. Only at the end of this " passus " does the personage who gives his name to the poem, Piers the Plowman, make his appearance. He is a floating, dream-like character, at one time a simple ploughman who digs and delves and cannot leave his work ; at another time the guide to Truth, having a wife and children, whose names are curious anticipations of the later Puritan nomenclature ; finally, in the last Passus, he appears as Christ Himself, opposing the venal priests of the day, and teaching a better way to salvation.

Passus VI. : The Vision of Piers the Plowman

Piers offers to guide the pilgrims to the shrine of Truth, after he has ploughed his half-acre of land. Meanwhile he gives them all work to do. Many of them shirk their tasks, but are soon brought to their senses by Hunger, who at first is satisfied with coarse fare, but afterwards, when the harvest comes, gorges himself with all the delicacies of the season—an allegory on the spendthrift peasantry of the day.

Passus VII. : Piers the Plowman's Pardon

Piers receives a full pardon from Truth as a reward for his honest life. A similar remission is given to many classes of men ; but merchants and lawyers are only granted a partial remission of the pains of Purgatory. A priest examines the pardon and finds that it only declares : " Those who have done good shall go into everlasting life ; but those who have done evil into everlasting punishment." The priest and Piers dispute so hotly as to the value of the pardon that the sleeper awakes and comes to the conclusion that " dowel " will avail at the Day of Judgment far more than pardons, indulgences, and provincial letters.

The full text of the A., B., and C. versions of the poem are contained in Professor Skeat's *William Langland's Piers the Plowman and Richard the Redeless* (Oxford University Press, 2 vols.). The B. text is edited by Skeat in the Clarendon Press Series (Oxford University Press), also by J. F. Davies (University Tutorial Press). A useful volume on the poem as an historical document is Chadwick's *England in the Age of Piers Plowman* (Cambridge University Press).

In the following extracts two Middle English letters are used.
þ (thorn) is approximately equivalent to TH. ʒ was originally
merely a variant of the Anglo-Saxon G, but by the fourteenth
century it had become equivalent to Y or (before a consonant)
to GH.]

PROLOGUE

IN a somer seson . whan soft was the sonne,
I shope me in shroudes . as I a shepe were,
In habite as an heremite . vnholy of workes,
Went wyde in þis world . wondres to here.
Ac on a May mornyng . on Maluerne Hulles,
Me byfel a ferly . of fairy me thouʒte ;
I was wery forwandred . and went me to reste
Vnder a brode banke . bi a bornes side,
And as I lay and lened . and loked in þe wateres,
I slombred in a slepyng . it sweyued so merye.   10
   Thanne gan I to meten . a marueilouse sweuene,
That I was in a wildernesse . wist I neuer where.
As I bihelde in-to þe est . an hiegh to þe sonne,
I seigh a toure on a toft . trielich ymaked,
A depe dale binethe . a dongeon þere-inne,
With depe dyches and derke . and dredful of sight ;
A faire felde ful of folke [1] . fonde I there bytwene,
Of alle maner of men . þe mene and þe riche,
Worchyng and wandryng . as þe worlde asketh.
Some putten hem to þe plow . pleyed ful selde,   20
In settyng and in sowyng . swonken ful harde,
And wonnen that wastours . with glotonye destruyeth.
   And some putten hem to pruyde . apparailed hem þere-
after,
In contenaunce of clothyng . comen disgised.
   In prayers and in penance . putten hem manye,
Al for loue of owre Lorde . lyueden ful streyte,

Line 2. *shope me in shroudes* ; " clad myself in a rough garb."
as I a shepe were : as if I were a shepherd.   3. *vnholy of workes* :
i.e. leading a worldly life.   6. *ferly* : a wondrous thing.   9. *lened* :
reclined.   11. *meten* : to measure.   *sweuene* : dream.   14. *trielich* :
exquisitely.   20. *pleyed* : took their ease.   21. *swonken* : worked.
23. *putten hem to pruyde* : " ran after fashion."   24. *contenaunce* :
parade.   *disgised* : decked out.   26. *lyueden* : lived.

---

[1] Cf. the " felde ful of folke " with Chaucer's band of pilgrims,
pp. 278 sqq.

In hope forto haue . heueneriche blisse ;
As ancres and heremites . that holden hem in here selles,
And coueiten nought in contre . to kairen aboute,
For no likerous liflode ; her lykam to plese. 30
　　And somme chosen chaffare . they cheuen the bettere,
As it semeth to owre sy3t . that suche men thryueth ;
And somme murthes to make . as mynstralles conneth,
And geten gold with here glee . giltles, I leue.
Ac iapers and iangelers . Iudas chylderen,
Feynen hem fantasies . and foles hem maketh,
And han here witte at wille . to worche, 3if þei sholde—
That Poule precheth of hem . I nel nought preue it here—
Qui turpiloquium loquitur . is Luciferes hyne.
　　Bidders and beggeres . fast aboute 3ede, 40
With her bely and her bagges . of bred ful ycrammed,
Fayteden for here fode . fou3ten atte ale.
In glotonye, God it wote . gon hij to bedde,
And risen with ribaudye . tho Roberdes knaues ;
Slepe and sori sleuthe . seweth hem eure.
　　Pilgrymes and palmers . pli3ted hem togidere
To seke seynt Iames . and seyntes in Rome.
Thei went forth in here wey . with many wise tales,
And hadden leue to lye . al here lyf after.
I seigh somme that seiden . þei had ysou3t seyntes ; 50
To eche a tale þat þei tolde . here tonge was tempred to lye
More þan to sey soth . it semed bi here speche.
　　Heremites on an heep . with hoked staues,
Wenten to Walsyngham . and here wenches after ;

Line 28. *ancres* : anchorites.　*holden hem in here selles* ⁱ keep to
their cells.　　29. *contre* : country.　*kairen* : wander.　　30. *For no
likerous liflode* : "for any dainty food."　　31. *chaffare* : to trade.
cheuen : to thrive.　　34. *giltles* : honestly.　*leue* : believe.　　35.
iapers : jesters.　*iangelers* : chatter-boxes, buffoons.　　36. *Feynen
hem fantasies* : give reins to their loose fancies.　　39. *Qui turpiloquium
loquitur* : he who speaketh lewdly.　*hyne* : servant.　　40. *bidders* :
mendicants.　　42. *fayteden* ; played the humbug, begged under false
pretences.　*atte ale* : at the alehouse, over their cups.　　44. *tho* :
those.　*Roberdes knaues* : Robert's servants, *i.e.* robbers.　"Roberts-
men" was a common name for wandering brigands.　　45. *seweth hem
eure* : they ever pursue.　　46. *Pilgrymes and palmers* : a pilgrim had a
dwelling-place to which he returned at the end of his pilgrimage.　A
palmer had no fixed dwelling-place and spent his whole life travelling
from shrine to shrine.　　47. *seynt Iames* ; *i.e.* St. James of Compostella, one of the most famous resorts of medieval pilgrims.　　54.
Walsyngham ; in Norfolk.　The shrine of the Blessed Virgin Mary

Grete lobyes and longe . that loth were to swynke.
Clotheden hem in copis . to ben knowen fram others.
And shopen hem heremites . here ese to haue.
  I fonde pere freris . alle þe foure ordres,
Preched þe peple . for profit of hem-seluen,
Glosed þe gospel . as hem good lyked,   60
For coueitise of copis . construed it as þei wolde.
Many of þis maistres freris . mowe clothen hem at lykyng,
For here money and marchandise . marchen togideres.
For sith charite haþ be chapman . and chief to shryue lordes
Many ferlis han fallen . in a few ȝeris.
But holychirche and hij . holde better togideres,
The moste myschief on molde . is mountyng wel faste.
  þere preched a pardonere . as he a prest were,
Brouȝte forth a bulle . with bishopes seles,
And seide þat hym-self myȝte . assoilen hem alle,   70
Of falshed, of fastyng . of vowes ybroken.
  Lewed men leued hym wel . and lyked his wordes,
Comen vp knelyng . to kissen his bulles ;
He bonched hem with his breuet . and blered here eyes,
And rauȝte with his ragman . rynges and broches ;
Thus þey geuen here golde . glotones to kepe.

  .   .   .   .
Were þe bischop yblissed . and worth bothe his eres,
His seel shulde nouȝt be sent . to deceyue þe peple.
Ac it is nauȝt by þe bischop . þat þe boy precheth,   80
For the parisch prest and þe pardonere . parten þe siluer,

there was one of the most famous resorts of pilgrims in the fourteenth
and fifteenth centuries.
  Line 55. *swynke* : labour.   56. *copis* : hoods or cloaks.   57.
shopen hem : shaped themselves as, clothed themselves as.   58.
foure ordres : *i.e.* the Franciscans, Dominicans, Augustines, and Carmelites.   60. *as hem good lyked* : according to their liking.   61.
coueitise of copis : "desire for copes," *i.e.* as presents.   62. *maistres
freris* : lordly friars.   64. *For sith . . . lordes* : "for since charity
has become a huckster and chief in shriving lords."   65. *ferlis* :
wondrous things.   66. *but* : unless. *hij* : they.   67. *the moste
. . . faste* : "the direst evils on earth will grow apace."   68.
pardonere : cf. Chaucer's "Prologue," 686–87.   70. *assoilen* : absolve.
74. *he bonched . . . eyes* : "he banged them with his brief and made
their eyes water."   75. *rauȝte* : got. *ragman* : roll. The word was
used of any legal document with seals attached, and even of a tedious
story. Hence the modern English "rigmarole."   78. *yblissed* :
"blessed," and so "pious."   80. *by þe bischop* : *i.e.* by the bishop's
permission. *boy* : knave.

That þe poraille of þe parisch . sholde haue, ȝif þei nere.
Persones and parisch prestes . pleyned hem to þe bischop,
Pat here parisshes were pore . sith þe pestilence tyme,
To haue a lycence and a leue . at London to dwelle,
And syngen þere for symonye . for siluer is swete.
Bischopes and bachelers . bothe maistres and doctours,
þat han cure vnder Criste . and crounyng in tokne
And signe þat þei sholden . shryuen here paroschienes,
Prechen and prey for hem . and þe pore fede,   90
Liggen in London . in lenten an elles.
Somme seruen þe kyng . and his siluer tellen
In cheker and in chancerye . chalengen his dettes
Of wardes and wardmotes . weyues and streyues.
And some seruen as seruantz . lordes and ladyes,
And in stede of stuwardes . sytten and demen.
Here messe and here matynes . and many of here oures
Arn don vndeuoutlych ; . drede is at þe laste,
Lest Crist in consistorie . acorse ful manye.
I parceyued of þe power . þat Peter had to kepe,   100
To bynde and to vnbynde . as þe boke telleth,
How he it left wiþ loue . as owre Lorde hight,
Amonges foure vertues . þe best of alle vertues,
þat cardinales been called . and closyng ȝatis,
þere Crist is in kyngdome . to close and to shutte,
And to opne it to hem . and heuene blisse shewe.

Line 82. *poraille*: poor. *ȝif þei nere*: "if they were not"; *i.e.*
but for them.   83. *pleyned hem*: complained.   84. *sith þe pestilence
tyme*: *i.e.* the Black Death of 1348–49. Further outbreaks occurred
in 1361–62, 1369, 1375–76.   86. *syngen þere*: the reference is to the
chantries of St. Paul's, where priests made money by singing masses for
the souls of the departed: cf. Chaucer's "Prologue" (507).   87.
bachelers: novices, or bachelors of arts of the Universities. *maistres*:
i.e. masters of arts.   88. *crounyng*: the Roman tonsure of the crown
of the head, by which clergy were distinguished.   91. *liggen*: "lie,"
i.e. "lodge." *elles*: at other times.   93. *cheker*: the Exchequer,
so called from the squared (or checked) top of the table upon which
accounts were verified. *chalengen*: make claim for.   94. *wardmotes*:
ward-moots, *i.e.* the meeting of a ward. *weyues*: goods without a
legal owner.   96. *demen*: pronounce judgment.   97. *here*: their.
99. *consistorie*: an ecclesiastical court. The term is here used, of
course, of the final judgment of the Last Day. *acorse*: curse or excommunicate.   102. *hight*: named.   104. *cardinales*: the four
cardinal virtues are Temperance, Justice, Prudence, and Fortitude.
105. *þere Crist is in kyngdome*: "where Christ is king."   106. *to
hem*: "to people," indefinite pronoun.

Ac of þe cardinales atte court . þat cauȝt of þat name,
And power presumed in hem . a pope to make,
To han þat power þat Peter hadde . inpugnen I nelle ;
For in loue and letterure . þe eleccioun bilongeth,　　　110
For-þi I can and can nauȝte . of courte speke more.
　　þanne come þere a kyng . knyȝthod hym ladde,
Miȝt of þe comunes . made hym to regne,
And þanne cam kynde wytte . and clerkes he made,
For to conseille þe kyng . and þe comune saue.
The kyng and knyȝthode . and clergye bothe
Casten þat þe comune . shulde hem-self fynde.
þe comune contreued . of kynde witte craftes,
And for profit of alle þe poeple . plowmen ordeygned,
To tilie and trauaile . as trewe lyf askeþ.　　　120
þe kynge and þe comune . and kynde witte þe thridde
Shope lawe and lewte . eche man to knowe his owne.
　　þanne loked vp a lunatik . a lene þing with-alle,
And knelyng to þe kyng . clergealy he seyde ;
" Crist kepe þe, sire kyng . and þi kyngriche,
And leue þe lede þi londe . so leute þe louye,
And for þi riȝtful rewlyng . be rewarded in heuene ! "
　　And sithen in þe eyre an hiegh . an angel of heuene
Lowed to speke in Latyn— . for lewed men ne coude
Iangle ne iugge . þat iustifie hem shulde,　　　130
But suffren and seruen— . for-þi seyde þe angel :
" *Sum rex, sum princeps . neutrum fortasse deinceps ;*

Line 107. *cauȝt* : received.　109. *nelle* : will not.　110. *in loue . . . bilongeth* : depends on love and learning.　111. *for-þi* : therefore.　*courte* : *i.e.* the Papal court : cf. line 107.　112. *ladde* : guided.　114. *kynde wytte* : " mother wit," natural intelligence.　117. *casten* : planned, contrived.　*shulde hem-self fynde* : " should provide food for them all."　" Hemself " includes all the aforementioned classes.　118. *contreued of kynde witte craftes* : " crafts that could be pursued by the exercise of natural intelligence."　122. *lewte* : loyalty.　123. *lunatik* : the author thus refers in all probability to himself here.　124. *clergealy* : like a scholar.　125. *kyngriche* : kingdom.　126. *leue . . . louye* " grant thee to rule thy land so that loyalty may love thee."　127–28. *And sithen . . . Latyn* : " and then in the air on high, an angel of heaven stooped to speak in Latin."　130. *Iangle* : discuss.　131. *for-þi* : therefore. 132–38. *Sum rex . . . de pietate metas* : the lines have been translated as follows :
" (You say) I am a king, I am a prince (but you will be) neither
　　perhaps hereafter.
O thou who dost administer the special laws of Christ the King,

O qui iura regis . Christi specialia regis,
Hoc quod agas melius . iustus es, esto pius !
Nudum ius a te . vestiri vult pietate ;
Qualia vis metere . talia grana sere.
Si ius nudatur . nudo de iure metatur ;
Si seritur pietas . de pietate metas ! "
    . Thanne greued hym a goliardeys . a glotoun of wordes,
And to þe angel an hei3 . answerd after :   140
" Dum rex a regere . dicatur nomen habere,
Nomen habet sine re . nisi studet iura tenere."
    And þanne gan alle þe comune . crye in vers of Latin,
To þe kynges conseille . construe ho-so wolde :
" Precepta regis . sunt nobis vincula legis."
    Wiþ þat ran þere a route . of ratones at ones,
And smale mys myd hem . mo þen a þousande,
And comen to a conseille . for here comune profit ;
For a cat of a courte . cam whan hym lyked,
And ouerlepe hem ly3tlich . and lau3te hem at his wille,   150
And pleyde wiþ hem perilouslych . and possed hem aboute.
" For doute of dyuerse dredes . we dar nou3te wel loke,
And 3if we grucche of his gamen . he wil greue vs alle,
Cracche vs, or clowe vs . and in his cloches holde,
That vs lotheth þe lyf . or he lete vs passe.
My3te we wiþ any witte . his wille withstonde,
We my3te be lordes aloft . and lyuen at owre ese."

That thou mayest do this the better, as thou art just, be merciful !
Naked justice desires to be clothed by thee with mercy.
Whatever crops thou wouldst reap, such be sure to sow.
If justice is stripped bare, let bare justice be reaped by thee ;
If pity be sown, mayest thou reap of pity ! "
    Line 139. *greued hym* : " grew angry." *goliardeys* : the word is
derived from Golias, a name applied by the thirteenth-century satirist,
Walter Map, to an imaginary bishop. It came to mean an educated
jester or buffoon.   140. *an hei3* : on high.   141-42. These lines
may be rendered :
" While a king is said to have his name from ruling
He has the name without the thing unless he strive to keep the laws."
    Line 145. *Precepta . . . legis* : " the precepts of the king are for
us the bonds of law."   146 sqq. In this version of the ancient fable
the rats are citizens and commoners of the wealthier class ; the mice
are the humbler folk ; the cat is Edward III. or possibly John of Gaunt,
and the kitten is Edward's grandson, afterwards Richard II.   146.
ratones : rats.   150. *ouerlepe hem ly3tlich* : " caught them easily."
lau3te hem at his wille : " Seized them at will."   153. *grucche* :
grumble.   154. " Scratch us or claw us or hold us in his clutches."

A raton of renon . most renable of tonge,
Seide for a souereygne . help to hym-selue :
" I haue ysein segges," quod he . " in þe cite of London 160
Beren biȝes ful briȝte . abouten here nekkes,
And some colers of crafty werk ; . vncoupled þei wenden
Boþe in wareine and in waste . where hem leue lyketh,
And otherwhile þei aren elles-where . as I here telle ;
Were þere a belle on here beiȝ . bi Ihesu, as me thynketh,
Men myȝte wite where þei went . and awei renne !
And riȝt so," quod þat ratoun . " reson me sheweth,
To bugge a belle of brasse . or of briȝte syluer,
And knitten on a colere . for owre comune profit,
And hangen it vp-on þe cattes hals . þanne here we 170
    mowen
Where he ritt or rest . or renneth to playe ;
And ȝif him list for to laike . þenne loke we mowen,
And peren in his presence . þer-while hym plaie liketh,
And ȝif him wrattheth, be ywar . and his weye shonye."
    Alle þis route of ratones . to þis reson þei assented.
Ac þo þe belle was ybouȝt . and on þe beiȝe hanged,
þere ne was ratoun in alle þe route . for alle þe rewme of
    Fraunce,
þat dorst haue ybounden þe belle . aboute þe cattis nekke,
Ne hangen it aboute þe cattes hals . al Engelonde to
    wynne ;
And helden hem vnhardy . and here conseille feble, 180
And leten here laboure lost . and alle here longe studye.
    A mous þat moche good . couthe, as me thouȝte,
Stroke forth sternly . and stode biforn hem alle,
And to þe route of ratones . reherced þese wordes :
" Thouȝ we culled þe catte . ȝut sholde þer come another,
To cracchy vs and al owre kynde . þouȝ we croupe vnder
    benches.
For-þi I conseille alle þe comune . to lat þe catte worthe,
And be we neuer so bolde . þe belle hym to shewe ;
For I herde my sire seyn . is seuene ȝere ypassed,

Line 158. *renable* ; ready, glib.   160. *segges* ; men, people.
161. *biȝes* : rings or collars.   163. *wareine* : a warren is a place
where certain game rights exist.   Hunting hounds were not allowed
to go uncoupled in another person's warren.   168. *bugge* : to buy.
169. *knitten* ; knit or hang.   170. *hals* ; neck.   172. *laike* : play.
173. *peren* : appear.   174. *wrattheth* ; grow wrathful.   186. *croupe* :
creep.   187. *lat þe catte worthe* : let the cat be.

20

þere þe catte is a kitoun . þe courte is ful elyng ;   190
þat witnisseth holiwrite . who so wil it rede :

Ve terre vbi puer rex est, &c.

For may no renke þere rest haue . for ratones bi ny3te ;
þe while he caccheþ conynges . he coueiteth nou3t owre
        caroyne,
But fet hym al with venesoun . defame we hym neuere.
For better is a litel losse . þan a longe sorwe,
þe mase amonge vs alle . þou3 we mysse a schrewe.
For many mannus malt . we mys wolde destruye,
And also 3e route of ratones . rende mennes clothes,
Nere þat cat of þat courte . þat can 3ow ouerlepe ;
For had 3e rattes 3owre wille . 3e couthe nou3t reule 3owre-
        selue.   200
I sey for me," quod þe mous . " I se so mykel after,
Shal neuer þe cat ne þe kitoun . bi my conseille be greued,
Ne carpyng of þis coler . þat costed me neure ;
And þou3 it had coste me catel . biknowen it I nolde,
But suffre as hym-self wolde . to do as hym liketh,
Coupled and vncoupled . to cacche what thei mowe.
For-þi vche a wise wi3te I warne . wite wel his owne."
    What þis meteles bemeneth . 3e men þat be merye,
Deuine 3e, for I ne dar . bi dere God in heuene !
    3it houed þere an hondreth . in houues of selke,   210
Seriauntz it semed . þat serueden atte barre,
Plededen for penyes . and poundes þe lawe,
And nou3t for loue of owre Lorde . vnlese here lippes onis.
þow my3test better mete þe myste . on Maluerne Hulles,
þan gete a momme of here mouthe . but money were
        shewed
    Barones an burgeis . and bonde-men als
I sei3 in þis assemble . as 3e shul here after :

Line 190. *elyng* : wretched.   192. *Ve . . . est*, etc. : " woe to
thee, O land, where king is a child."   192. *renke* : man.   193. *he
caccheþ conynges* : " he (*i.e.* the cat) catcheth conies."   *caroyne* :
carrion.   196. *þe mase . . . schrewe* : " the confusion that would
arise amongst us all, even though we do lose a tyrant."   199. *nere* :
were there not.   203. *ne carpyng*, etc. : " nor shall there be any
more talk about the collar that would never have cost me anything."
204. *biknowen it I nolde* : " I would not confess it," or " I would
have nothing to do with it."   207. *vche a* : each.   208. *meteles* :
dream.   210. *houed* : hovered about.   *houues* : coifs.   211. *seriauntz* : Sergeants-at-Law.

Baxsteres and brewesteres . and bocheres manye,
Wollewebsteres . and weueres of lynnen,
Taillours and tynkeres . and tolleres in marketes,   220
Masons and mynours . and many other craftes ;
Of alkin libbyng laboreres . lopen forth somme,
As dykers and delueres . þat doth here dedes ille.
And dryuen forth þe dere day . with " Dieu vous saue, Dame
    Emme ! "
Cokes and here knaues . crieden, " Hote pies, hote !
Gode gris and gees . gowe dyne, gowe ! "
Tauerners vn-til hem . tolde þe same :
" White wyn of Oseye . and red wyn of Gascoigne,
Of þe Ryne and of þe Rochel . þe roste to defye."
Al þis sei3 I slepyng . and seuene sythes more.   230

PASSUS I

Passus Primus de Visione[1]

What this montaigne bymeneth . and þe merke dale,
And þe felde ful of folke . I shal 3ow faire schewe.
A loueli ladi of lere . in lynnen yclothed,
Come down fram a castel . and called me faire,
And seide, " Sone, slepestow . sestow þis poeple,
How bisi þei ben . abouten þe mase ?
þe moste partie of þis poeple . þat passeth on þis erthe,
Haue þei worschip in þis worlde . þei wilne no better ;
Of other heuene þan here . holde þei no tale."
    I was aferd of her face . þei3 she faire were,   10
And seide, " Mercy, Madame . what is þis to mene ? "
" þe toure vp þe toft," quod she . " Treuthe is þere-inne,
And wolde þat 3e wrou3te . as his worde techeth
For he is fader of feith . fourmed 3ow alle,   ;

Line 218. *baxsteres and brewesteres* : female bakers and brewers ;
cf. The Consuetudinary of Winchester, p. 128.   220. *tolleres* : collectors
of tolls.   222. *of alkin*, etc. : "of labourers of every kind living
there came forward some."   224. *þe dere day* : " the livelong day."
" *Dieu . . . Emme* " : " God save you, Lady Emma," the refrain of
a popular song.   226. *gris* : porkers. *gowe dyne* : "let's go and
dine."   228. *Oseye* : Alsace.   229. *defye* : digest.   230. *sythes* :
times.   2. *faire schewe* : " show clearly."   3. *lere* : face.   6.
abouten þe mase : " in this confused throng."   12. *vp þe toft* :
" upon the knoll."   13. *wolde þat 3e wrou3te* : " meant you to work."

[1] *The Vision of Holy Church.*

Bothe with fel and with face . and ȝaf ȝow fyue wittis
Forto worschip hum þer-with . þe while þat ȝe ben here.
And þerfore he hyȝte þe erthe . to help ȝow vchone
Of wollen, of lynnen . of lyflode at nede,
In mesurable manere . to make ȝow at ese.
  " And comaunded of his curteisye . in comune þree þinges ;
Arne none nedful but þo . and nempne hem I thinke,   21
And rekne hem bi resoun . reherce þow hem after :
That one is vesture . from chele þe to saue,
And mete atte mele . for myseise of þi-selue,
And drynke whan þow dryest . ac do nouȝt out of resoun,
That þow worth þe werse . when þow worche shuldest.

.   .   .   .

[*Lines* 27–33]
For-þi drede delitable drynke . and þow shalt do þe bettere ;
Mesure is medcyne . þouȝ þow moche ȝerne.
It is nauȝt al gode to þe goste . þat þe gutte axep,
Ne liflode to þi likam . þat leef is to þi soule.
Leue not þi likam . for a lyer him techeth,
That is þe wrecched worlde . wolde þe bitraye ;
For þe fende and þi flesch . folweth þe to-gidere,   40
This and þat seeth þi soule . and seith it in þin herte ;
And for þow sholdest ben ywar . I wisse þe þe beste."
  " Madame, mercy," quod I . " me liketh wel ȝowre wordes,
Ac þe moneye of þis molde . þat men so faste holdeth,
Telle me to whom, madame . þat tresore appendeth ? "
  " Go to þe gospel," quod she . " þat God seide hym-seluen,
Tho þe poeple hym apposed . wiþ a peny in þe temple,
Whether þei shulde þer-with . worschip þe kyng Sesar.
And God axed of hem . of whome spake þe lettre,
And þe ymage ilyke . þat þere-inne stondeth ;   50
' *Cesaris*,' þei seide . ' we sen hym wel vchone.'
' *Reddite Cesari*,' quod God . ' þat *Cesari* bifalleth,

Line 15. *fel* : skin.   17. *hyȝte* ; named.   *to help ȝow vchone* : to
provide you each one with.   18. *lyflode* : sustenance.   19. *mesurable manere* : in a moderate degree.   21. " there are none needful
but these, and I will name them."   24. " *for myseise of þi-selue* :
" against discomfort of thyself," *i.e.* to allay the pangs of hunger.
37. *likam* ; body.   40. *fende* ; fiend, devil.   44. *moneye of þis
molde* : money of this earth.   47. *hym apposed wiþ* ; " tried to
pose Him with."   50. *ilyke* ; likewise.   51. *vchone* ; each one.
52. *Reddite Cesari* ; render unto Caesar.

Et que sunt dei, deo . or elles ʒe done ille.'
For riʒtful reson . shulde rewle ʒow alle,
And kynde witte be wardeyne . ʒowre welthe to kepe,
And tutour of ʒoure tresore . and take it ʒow at nede,
For housbonderye and hij . holden togideres."
þanne I frained hir faire . for hym þat hir made,
" That dongeoun in þe dale . þat dredful is of siʒte,
What may it be to mene . madame, I ʒow biseche ? "   60
" þat is þe castel of care . who-so cometh þerinne
May banne þat he borne was . to body or to soule.
þerinne wonieth a wiʒte . þat Wronge is yhote,
Fader of falshed . and founded it hym-selue.
Adam and Eue . he egged to ille,
Conseilled Caym . to kullen his brother ;
Iudas he iaped . with Iuwen siluer,
And sithen on an eller . honged hym after.
He is letter of loue . and lyeth hem alle,
That trusten on his tresor . bitráyeth he sonnest."   70
   Thanne had I wonder in my witt . what womman it were,
Pat such wise wordes . of holy writ shewed ;
And asked hir on þe hieʒe name . ar heo þennes ʒeode,
What she were witterli . þat wissed me so faire.
   " Holicherche I am," quod she . " þow ouʒtest me to
      knowe,
I vnderfonge þe first . and þe feyth tauʒte,
And brouʒtest me borwes . my biddyng to fulfille,
And to loue me lelly . þe while þi lyf dureth."
   Thanne I courbed on my knees . and cryed hir of grace,
And preyed hir pitousely . prey for my synnes,   80
And also kenne me kyndeli . on Criste to bileue,
That I miʒte worchen his wille . þat wrouʒte me to man.
" Teche me to no tresore . but telle me þis ilke,

Line 57. *hij* : they.   58. *frained* : asked.   *for hym . . . made* :
" by Him that made her."   62. *banne* : curse.   *borne to body or to
soule* : " born a body or a soul."   63. *wonieth a wiʒte* : " dwelleth a
man."   *yhote* : called.   67. *iaped* : beguiled.   68. *an eller* : an elder
tree, upon which, according to tradition, Judas was hanged; cf.
Shakespeare, *Love's Labour's Lost*, v. iii. 606.   69. *letter* : hinderer.
73. *And asked . . . þennes ʒeode* ; " and asked her by the High Name
(of God) ere she went away."   74. *wissed* ; counselled.   76.
vnderfonge ; received.   77. *brouʒtest me borwes* : " thou gavest me
sureties " (*i.e.* sponsors).   78. *lelly* : loyally, faithfully.   79.
courbed : bent, kneeled.   81. *kenne* : teach.   82. *wrouʒte me to
man* ; made me man.

How I may saue my soule . þat seynt art yholden ? "
" Whan alle tresores aren tried," quod she . " trewthe is
    þe best ;
I do it on *deus caritas* . to deme þe soþe ;
It is as derworth a drewery . as dere God hym-seluen.

Line 84. *þat seynt art yholden* : thou who art considered holy.
86. *Deus caritas* : God is love.   87. " It is as dearly loved treasure
as dear God Himself."

CHAPTER VIII

THE DECLINE OF MEDIEVAL CIVILIZATION

I. A Selection from the *Paston Letters*—
1. Agnes to William Paston (before 1440).
2. Robert Repps to John Paston, 1st November 1440.
3. Margaret to John Paston, 28th September 1443.
4. John Northwood to Viscount Beaumont, between 1440 and 1450.
5. Margaret Paston to John Paston, 12th March 1449.
6. William Lomner to John Paston, 5th May 1450.
7. John Crane to John Paston, 6th May 1450.
8. Sir John Fastolf to Sir Thomas Howys, Parson of Castlecomb, 27th May 1450.
9. J. Wingfield to John Paston, Esq., between 1450 and 1460.
10. Richard Calle to John Paston, 29th December, between 1450 and 1460.
11. Margaret Paston to John Paston, 5th November 1452.
12. Agnes Paston to John Paston, 29th June 1454.
13. Elizabeth Clere to John Paston, 29th June 1454.
14. James Gresham to John Paston, 28th October 1455.
15. Errands to London of Agnes Paston, 28th January 1457.
16. Margaret Paston to John Paston, before 1459.
17. William Worcester to Master Paston, 2nd September, before 1459.
18. Margaret Paston to John Paston, before 1459.
19. Friar John Brackley to John Paston, Esq., 1459.
20. Margaret Paston to John Paston, about 1461.
21. John Paston to Margaret Paston, between 1461 and 1465.
22. John Paston to Margaret Paston, between 1460 and 1470.
23. Margaret Paston to Sir John Paston, 9th July 1468.
24. Sir John Paston to John Paston, Esq., at Caister, 9th November 1468.
25. John Paston, Esq., to Sir John Paston, May 1469.
26. Sir John Paston to Margaret Paston and John Paston, Esq., 1469 or 1474.

I. A SELECTION FROM THE *PASTON LETTERS*

[The *Paston Letters* consist of upwards of one thousand letters, most of them written by, or to, particular members of the family of Paston during the fifteenth century. The letters were carefully preserved in the Paston family for several generations, till the death of the Earl of Yarmouth, their lineal descendant, in the reign of George II. (1732), terminated the male line of the family. After passing through the hands of several antiquaries the letters were published by Sir John Fenn in four volumes during the years 1787–89. A fifth volume completing the series was published by the Master of Downing College, Cambridge, in 1823. The letters were again edited, together with many others subsequently discovered, by James Gairdner, and published 1872–75. A new edition was published in four volumes in 1900 (Archibald Constable & Co. Ltd.).

Among the *Paston Letters* are many documents of considerable importance in connexion with the political history of the fifteenth century. But the chief interest of the letters as a whole lies in the abundance of material they contain for reconstructing the social, economic, and cultural conditions of one of the most obscure centuries of English History. They serve well to illustrate the decay of the medieval state, the lawlessness of the country even before the outbreak of the Wars of the Roses, and the rapid increase of liveries and maintenance.

The pedigree of the Paston family, shown on p. 314, will assist the understanding of the letters.]

1. To my worshipful husband, William Paston, be this letter taken.

DEAR HUSBAND, I recommend me to you, &c. Blessed be God I send you good tidings of the coming and the bringing home of the gentlewoman [1] that ye weeten (know) of from Reedham this same night, according to appointment that ye made there for yourself.

And as for the first acquaintance between John Paston and the said gentlewoman, she made him gentle cheer in gentle wise, and said he was verily your son; and so I hope there shall need no great treaty between them.

The parson of Stockton told me if ye would buy her a gown, her mother would give thereto a goodly fur; the gown needeth for to be had; and of colour it would be a goodly blue, or else a bright sanguine.

I pray you to buy for me two pipes of gold. Your stews [2] do well. The Holy Trinity have you in governance.

Written at Paston in haste the Wednesday next after "Deus qui errantibus"; [3] for default of a good secretary, &c.

Yours,

AGNES PASTON.

PASTON,
Wednesday, before 1440. 18 H. VI.

2. To my right reverend and right honourable master, John Paston, be this given.

SALVETE, &c. Tidings, the Duke of Orleans [4] hath made his oath upon the sacrament, and used it, never for to bear arms against England, in the presence of the king and all the lords, except my Lord of Gloucester; and in proving (as a proof

---

[1] Margaret Mauteby, afterwards wife of John Paston, Esq.
[2] Fish-ponds.
[3] The Third Sunday after Easter. These words are the beginning of the Collect for that Sunday.
[4] He had been taken prisoner at Agincourt, 25th October 1415.

PEDIGREE OF THE PASTON FAMILY

CLEMENT PASTON of Paston, —m.— BEATRICE, daughter of John de Somerton.
died 1419.   She died before 1419.

Sir WILLIAM PASTON, born 1378, educated as a lawyer and became a judge of the Common Pleas. He died 13th August 1444. *m.* AGNES, daughter and co-heiress of Sir Edmund Berry, of Harlingbury Hall, Hertfordshire. She died 1479.

- JOHN PASTON, Esq., born 1420. Studied in the Inner Temple, was one of the executors of Sir John Fastolf. His estates were seized by Edward IV. and he was committed to the Fleet. He died 26th May 1466. *m.* MARGARET, daughter and heiress of John Mauteby, Esq.

- EDMUND PASTON, Esq., born 1425.

- WILLIAM PASTON, who had disputes with his nephews concerning their estates.

- CLEMENT PASTON, born 1442. Was in London under the care of Master Grenefield in 1457.

- ELIZABETH, born about 1429.

- Sir JOHN PASTON, born about 1440. He took possession of his father's estates by a warrant from Edward IV. dated 6th July 1466. He performed many gallant exploits in the French Wars and was the King's champion at Eltham. He died, unmarried, 15th November 1479.

- JOHN PASTON, Esq., a soldier in the French Wars, succeeded his brother as head of the family in 1479. Became High Sheriff of Norfolk in 1485, made a knight banneret at Stoke in 1487; died 1503. *m.*, about 1477, MARGERY, daughter of Thomas Brews of Stinton Hall. She died in 1479.

- WILLIAM, at Eton, 1467.

- ANNE PASTON, *m.* William Yelverton.

- EDMUND, at Calais, 1473.

- MARGERY, *m.* Richard Calle.

- WALTER, graduated at Oxford, 1479.

- CHRISTOPHER PASTON, born 1478, and probably died in infancy.

- Sir WILLIAM PASTON, an eminent Counsellor-at-Law, born about 1480, died 1554. *m.* BRIDGET, daughter of Sir Henry Heydon of Baconsthorpe.

that) my said Lord of Gloucester agreed never to his deliverance, when the mass began he took his barge, &c.

God give grace the said Lord of Orleans be true, for this same week shall be towards France.

Also Frenchmen and Picards a great number came to Arfleet,[1] for to have rescued it ; and our lords with their small puissance manly beat them, and put them to flight, and, blessed be our Lord, have taken the said city of Arfleet ; [1] the which is a great jewel to all England, and especially to our Country.

Moreover there is one come into England, a knight out of Spain, with a kerchief of pleasaunce [2] enwrapped about his arm ; the which knight will run a course with a sharp spear for his sovereign lady's sake, whom either Sir Richard Wodvile, or Sir Christopher Talbot, shall deliver, to the worship of England and of themselves by God's grace.

Farthemore ye be remembered, that an esquire of Suffolk, called John Lyston, recovered, in assize of "novel disseisin," 700 marks (£466. 13s. 4d.) in damages against Sir Robert Wingfield, &c. In avoiding of the payment of the said 700 marks, the said Sir Robert Wingfield subtlely hath outlawed the said John Lyston in Nottinghamshire, by the virtue of which outlawry all manner of chattel to the said John Lyston appertaining are accrued unto the king, &c. And anon (as soon) as the said outlawry was certified, my Lord Treasurer granted the said 700 marks to my Lord of Norfolk for the arrears of his sowde [3] whilst he was in Scotland. And according to this assignment aforesaid, tallies (were) delivered, &c. And my Lord of Norfolk hath released the same 700 marks to Sir Robert Wingfield.

And here is great heaving and shoving by my Lord of Suffolk and all his counsel for to espy how this matter came about, &c. Sir, I beseech (you) recommend me unto my mistress your mother, to my mistress your wife, and to my mistress your sister, et omnibus aliis quorum interest, &c.

Sir, I pray you, with all my heart, hold me excused that I write thus homely and briefly unto you, for truly convenable (competent) space sufficed me not.

---

[1] Harfleur in Normandy.

[2] A richly embroidered handkerchief presented by his lady, in whose honour he tilted.

[3] pay.

No more, at this time, but the Trinity have you in protection, &c., and when your leisure is, resort again unto your college, the Inner Temple, for there be many which sore desire your presence, Welles and others, &c.

Written on the Feast of All Saints, between mass and matins calamo festinante, &c.

Yours,

ROBERT REPPS.

All-Saints-Day,
Tuesday, 1 *November* 1440.   19 H. VI.

3. *To my right worshipful husband, John Paston, dwelling in the Inner Temple at London, in haste.*

RIGHT WORSHIPFUL HUSBAND, I recommend me to you, desiring heartily to hear of your welfare, thanking God of your amending of the great disease that ye have had, and I thank you for the letter that ye sent me, for by my troth my mother and I were nought in heart's ease from the time that we wist (knew) of your sickness, till we wist verily of your amending.

My mother behested (vowed) another image of wax of the weight of you, to our Lady of Walsingham, and she sent four nobles (£1. 6s. 8d.) to the four orders of friars at Norwich to pray for you, and I have behested to go on pilgrimage to Walsingham and to St. Leonard's [1] for you ; by my troth I had never so heavy a season as I had from the time that I wist of your sickness, till I wist of your amending, and yet my heart is in no great ease, nor nought shall be, till I weet that ye be very whole.   Your father and mine was this day sev'night at Beccles, for a matter of the Prior of Bromholm, and he lay at Gelderstone that night, and was there till it was nine of the clock and the other day.   And I sent thither for a gown, and my mother said that I should none have than till I had been there-anon, and so they could none get.

My father Garneys [2] sent me word that he should have been here the next week and my Emme [3] also, and play them here with their hawks, and they should have me home with them ; and so God help me, I shall excuse me of my going

---

[1] The Church of the Priory of St. Leonard's at Norwich—a famous resort of pilgrims.
[2] probably her godfather.   [3] uncle.

thither if I may, for I suppose that I shall readilier have tidings from you here than I should have there. I shall send my mother a token that she took (brought to) me for I suppose that the time is come that I should send it her, if I keep the behest that I have made ; I suppose I have told you what it was ; I pray you heartily that (ye) will vouchsafe to send me a letter as hastily as ye may, if writing be none disease (pain) to you, and that ye will vouchsafe to send me word how your sore do. If I might have had my will, I should have seen you ere this time ; I would ye were at home, if it were your ease, and your sore might be as well looked to here as it is there (where) ye be now, lever (rather) than a new gown though it were of scarlet. I pray you if your sore be whole, and so that ye may endure to ride when my father come to London, that ye will ask leave and come home when the horse should be sent home again, for I hope ye shall be kept as tenderly here as ye be at London. I may none leisure have to do write half a quarter so much as I should say to you if I might speak with you. I shall send you another letter as hastily as I may. I thank you that ye would vouchsafe to remember my girdle and that ye would write to me at the time, for I suppose that writing was none ease to you. Almighty God have you in his keeping, and send you health. Written at Oxnead, in right great haste, on St. Michael's even.

Yours,

M. PASTON.

OXNEAD,
Saturday, 28th September 1443.　22 H. VI.

My mother greet you well, and sendeth you God's blessing and hers ; and she prayeth you, and I pray you also, that ye be well dieted of meat and drink, for that is the greatest help that ye may have now to your healthward. Your son fareth well, blessed be God !

4. *To my worshipful and reverend Lord John Viscount Beaumont.*[1]

RIGHT WORSHIPFUL, and my reverend and most special Lord, I recommend me unto your good grace in the most humble

[1] He was afterwards killed at the battle of Northampton in 1460, fighting on the Lancastrian side.

and lowly wise that I can or may, desiring to hear of your prosperity and welfare, as to my most singular joy and special comfort.

And if it please your Highness, as touching the sudden adventure that fell lately at Coventry, please it your Lordship to hear, that on Corpus Christi even last passed, between eight and nine of the clock at afternoon, Sir Humphrey Stafford had brought my master, Sir James of Ormond, toward his inn from my Lady of Shrewsbury and returned from him towards his inn, he met with Sir Robert Harcourt coming from his mother's towards his inn, and passed Sir Humphrey ; and Richard his son came somewhat behind, and when they met together they fell in hands together, and Sir Robert smote him a great stroke on the head with his sword, and Richard with his dagger hastily went toward him, and as he stumbled, one of Harcourt's men smote him in the back with a knife ; men wot (know) not who it was readily ; his father heard (a) noise and rode toward them, and his men ran before him thither-ward ; and in the going down off his horse, one, he wot not who, behind him, smote him on the head with an edged tool ; men know not with us, with what weapon, that he fell down, and his son fell down before him as good as dead ; and all this was done, as men say, in a Pater-noster while.

And forthwith Sir Humphrey Stafford's men followed after, and slew two men of Harcourt's, one Swynerton and Bradshawe, and more be hurt, some be gone, and some be in prison in the jail at Coventry.

And before the coroner of Coventry, upon the sight of the bodies there be indicted as principals for the death of Richard Stafford, Sir Robert Harcourt and the two men that be dead, and for the two of Harcourt's that be dead, there be indicted two men of Sir Humphrey's as principals ; and as yet there hath been nothing found before the justice of the peace of Coventry of this riot, because the sheriff of Warwickshire is dead, and they may not sit unto the time there be a new sheriff ; and all this mischief fell because of an old debate that was between them for taking of a distress, as it is told.

And Almighty Jesu preserve your high estate, my special Lord, and send you long life and good health.

Written at Coventry on Tuesday next after Corpus
Christi day, &c.
By your own poor servant,

JOHN NORTHWOOD.

COVENTRY,
Tuesday after Corpus Christi day,
between 1440 *and* 1450. 18 & 28 H. VI.

5. *To my right worshipful master, John Paston, be this delivered in haste.*

RIGHT WORSHIPFUL HUSBAND, I recommend me to you,
desiring heartily to hear of your welfare, &c. (then follows
some common business about his farms and tenants).

.   .   .   .

William Rutt, the which is with Sir John Heveningham,
came home from London yesterday, and he said plainly to
his master, and to many other folks, that the Duke of Suffolk
is pardoned, and hath his men again waiting upon him, and
is right well and at ease and merry, and is in the king's good
grace, and in the good conceit of all the lords, as well as
ever he was.

There have been many enemies against Yarmouth and
Cromer, and have done much harm, and taken many Englishmen, and put them in great distress, and greatly (heavily)
ransomed them ; and the said enemies have been so bold
that they come up to the land, and play them on Caister
Sands and in other places, as homely as (as much at home
as if) they were Englishmen ; folks be right sore afraid that
they will do much harm this summer, but if (unless) there
be made right great purveyance against them.

Other tidings know I none at this time ; the blissful
Trinity have you in his keeping.

Written at Norwich on Saint Gregory's day.
Yours,

M. PASTON.

NORWICH,
St. Gregory's Day,
Thursday, 12*th of March,* 1449. 28 H. VI.

6. *To the right worshipful John Paston, at Norwich.*

RIGHT WORSHIPFUL SIR, I recommend me to you, and am
right sorry of that I shall say, and have so washed this little

bill with sorrowful tears, that uneths (scarcely) ye shall read it.

As on Monday next after May day (4th of May) there came tidings to London, that on Thursday before (30th of April) the Duke of Suffolk came unto the coasts of Kent full near Dover with his two ships and a little spinner ; the which spinner he sent with certain letters, by certain of his trusted men, unto Calais ward, to know how he should be received ; and with him met a ship called Nicholas of the Tower with other ships waiting on him, and by them that were in the spinner the master of the Nicholas had knowledge of the duke's coming.

When he espied the duke's ships, he sent forth his boat to weet what they were, and the duke himself spoke to them, and said, he was by the king's commandment sent to Calais ward, &c., and they said he must speak with their master ; and so he, with two or three of his men, went forth with them in their boats to the Nicholas ; and when he came, the master bade him, " Welcome, traitor," as men say.

And further the master desired to weet if the shipmen would hold with the duke, and they sent word they would not in no wise ; and so he was in the Nicholas till Saturday (2nd May) next following.

Some say he wrote much thing to be delivered to the king, but that is not verily known.

He had his confessor with him, &c., and some say he was arraigned in the ship on their manner upon the Impeachments, and found guilty, &c.

Also he asked the name of the ship, and when he knew it, he remembered Stacy that said, if he might escape the danger of the Tower he should be safe, and then his heart failed him, for he thought he was deceived.

And in the sight of all his men he was drawn out of the great ship into the boat, and there was an axe and a stock, and one of the lewdest (meanest) of the ship bade him lay down his head, and he should be fairly ferd (dealt) with, and die on a sword ; and took a rusty sword and smote off his head within (in less than) half a dozen strokes, and took away his gown of russet, and his doublet of velvet mailed, and laid his body on the sands of Dover : and some say his head was set on a pole by it ; and his men set on the land by (with) great circumstance and prey (parade and robbery).

And the sheriff of Kent doth watch the body, and (hath) sent his under-sheriff to the judges to weet what to do ; and also to the king (to know) what shall be done.

Further I wot not, but thus far is it, if the process be erroneous let his counsel reverse it, &c.

Also for all the other matters they sleep, and the fryar also, &c. Sir Thomas Keriel [1] is taken prisoner and all the leg-harness, and about 3000 Englishmen slain.

Matthew Gooth (? Gough) with 1500, fled, and saved himself and them. And Peris Brusy was chief captain, and had 10,000 Frenchmen and more, &c.

I pray you let my mistress, your mother, know these tidings, and God have you all in his keeping.

I pray you (that) this bill may recommend me to my mistresses, your mother and wife, &c.

James Gresham hath written to John of Dam, and recommendeth him, &c.

Written in great haste at London, the 5th day of May, &c.

By your wife,[2]

WILLIAM LOMNER.

LONDON,
Tuesday, 5th of May 1450. 28 H. VI.

7. To my right worshipful cousin, John Paston, of Norwich, Esq.

RIGHT WORSHIPFUL SIR, I recommend me unto you in the most goodly wise that I can ; and forasmuch as ye desired of me to send you word of divers matters here, which have been opened in the parliament openly, I send you of them such as I can.

First most especial, that for very truth upon Saturday that last was, the Duke of Suffolk was taken in the sea, and there he was beheaded, and his body with the appurtenance set at land at Dover ; and all the folks that he had with him were set to land, and had none harm.

Also the king hath somewhat granted to have the resumption again, in some but not in all, &c.

Also if ye purpose to come hither to put up your bills, ye may come now in a good time, for now every man that hath

---

[1] He had been defeated and captured at the battle of Formigny, 18th April 1450.

[2] Lomner often acted as amanuensis to Margaret Paston, and probably subscribed himself thus from force of habit.

21

any they put them in, and so may ye if ye come, with God's grace to your pleasure.

.   .   .   .   .

Furthermore, upon the 4th day of this month, the Earl of Devonshire came hither with 300 men well beseen (provided), &c. and upon the morrow after, my Lord of Warwick, with 400 and more, &c.

Also as it is noised here, Calais shall be besieged within this seven days, &c.

God save the king, and send us peace, &c.

Other tidings be there none here, but Almighty God have you in his keeping.

Written at Leicester, the 6th day of May.

JOHN CRANE.

LEICESTER, *Wednesday, 6th of May,* 1450.   28 H. VI.

8. *To my trusty and well-beloved friend, Sir Thomas Howys, Parson of Castlecomb.*

TRUSTY AND WELL-BELOVED FRIEND, I greet you well. [Here follow some orders respecting his affairs at Caister.] And I pray you send me word who dare be so hardy to kick against you in my right ; and say (to) them on my half (behalf) that they shall be quyt (requited), as far as law and reason will ; and if they will not dread nor obey that, then they shall be quyt by Blackbeard or Whitebeard, that is to say, by God or the devil ; and therefore I charge you, send me word whether such as have been mine adversaries before this time continue still in their wilfulness, &c.

Item, I hear ofttimes many strange reports of demenys [1] of the governance of my place at Caister and other places, as in my chatell approving in my wines, the keeping of my wardrobe and clothes, the avail (use, profit) of my conies at Hellesdon, &c., and approvement of my lands ; praying you heartily, as my full trust is in you, to help reform it. And that ye suffer no vicious man at my place of Caister (to) abide, but well governed and diligent, as yet will answer to it.

Almighty God keep you. Written at London, the 27th day of May, in the 28th year of the reign of King Henry VI.

JOHN FASTOLF, Knight.

LONDON, *Wednesday, 27th of May,* 1450.
28 H. VI.

---

[1] Probably " misdemeanours."

9. *To my well-beloved brother, John Paston, Esq.*

BROTHER PASTON, I recommend me unto you, praying you that ye take the labour to speak with Thomas Ratcliff of Framsden (in Suffolk) for the deliverance of part of an house which lyeth in his wood at Framsden, which house the owner hath carried part thereof to Orford, which, so departed, the remanent, that remaineth there in his wood, shall do him little good, and it shall hurt greatly the workmen and the owner thereof also, which is my tenant, and the house should be set upon the ground.

I write unto you in this behalf, because I understand he will be much advised by you, and if he do anything at my request I shall do as much that shall please him ; and also the poor man shall give him two nobles, or twenty shillings rather than fail ; I pray you be as good a mean for him as ye may in this behalf as my very trust in you, and I shall be ready at all times to do that may be to your pleasure, I trust to Jesu, who have you in his keeping, and send you joy of all your ladies.

Written at Letheringham, this Tuesday in Whitsun week.
Your brother and friend,
J. WYNGFIELD.

Tuesday, May or June,
between 1450 and 1460.

10. *To my right reverend and most worshipful master, my master, John Paston.*

RIGHT WORSHIPFUL AND MY MOST REVEREND MASTER, I recommend me unto your good mastership ; like you to weet that on Childermas day [1] there were much people at Norwich at the shire (the county court), because it was noised in the shire that the under-sheriff had a writ to make a new election, wherefore the people was grieved because they had laboured so often, saying to the sheriff that he had the writ, and plainly he should not away unto the time the writ were read. The sheriff answered and said that he had no writ, nor wist who had it : hereupon the people peaced (became peaceable), and stilled unto the time the shire was done, and after that

[1] 28th December. The day was considered by superstitious people to be an unfortunate one.

done, the people called upon him, "kill him, head him," and so John Damme, with help of others, gat him out of the shire-house, and with much labour brought him into Spurrier Row, and there the people met against him, and so they avoided (withdrew) him into an house, and kept fast the door unto the time the mayor was sent for, and the sheriff, to strengthen him, and to convey him away, or else he had been slain ; wherefore divers of the thrifty men came to me, desiring that I should write unto your mastership to let you have understanding of the guiding of the people, for they be full sorry of this trouble ; and that it please you to send them your advice how they shall be guided and ruled, for they were purposed to have gathered an hundred or two hundred of the thriftiest men, and to have come up to the king to let the king have understanding of their mocking.

And also the people fear them sore of you, and of Master Berney, because ye come not home.

Please you that ye remember the bill I sent you at Hallow-mas [1] for the place and lands at Beighton which Cheeseman had in his farm for five marks (£3. 6s. 8d.) ; there will no man have it above forty-six shillings and eight pence, for Alblaster and I have done as much thereto as we can, but we cannot go above that, and yet we cannot let it so for this year without they have it for five or six years ; I wrote to your mastership hereof but I had none answer, wherefore I beseech you that I may have answer of this by twelfth (6 January) for and (if) we have an answer of this by that time we shall enfeoff him with all, &c.

My right worshipful and my most reverend master, Almighty Jesu preserve you and send you the victory of your enemies, as I trust to Almighty Jesu ye shall.

Written at Norwich on St. Thomas's Day after Christmas Day.

Your poor servant and beadsman,

RICHARD CALLE.[2]

NORWICH, ST. THOMAS BECKET,
29th December between 1450 *and* 1460.
29 *and* 39 H. VI.

[1] 1st November.
[2] He afterwards married Margery Paston, to the intense disgust of the Paston family.   See subsequent letters.

11. *To my right worshipful husband, John Paston, be this delivered in haste.*

RIGHT WORSHIPFUL HUSBAND, I commend me to you, I pray you that ye will do buy two dozen trenchers, for I can none get in this town ; also I pray you that ye will send me a book with chardeqweyns [1] that I may have of in the morning, for the air be not wholesome in this town, therefore I pray you heartily let John Suffield bring it home with him.

No more, but the blessed Trinity have you in his keeping, and send you good speed in all your matters.   Written on St. Leonard's even.

My uncle Philip commends him to you, and he hath been so sick since that I came to Reedham, that I wend (weened—thought) he should never have escaped it, nor not is like to do but if (unless) he have ready help, and therefore he shall into Suffolk this next week, to mine aunt, for there is a good physician, and he shall look to him.

My Lady Hastyngs told me that Heydon hath spoken to Jeffrey Boleyn of London, and is agreed with him that he should bargain with Sir John Fastolf to buy the manor of Blickling as it were for himself, and if Boleyn buy it in truth Heydon shall have it.

I came to Norwich on Soulmas day (2nd of November).

Yours,

MARGARET PASTON.

NORWICH,
5th November 1452.   32 H. VI.

12. *To John Paston be this letter delivered.*

SON, I greet you well, with God's blessing and mine, and I let you weet that my cousin Clere writted (wrote) to me that she spake with Scroope after that he had been with me at Norwich, and told her what cheer that I had made him ; and he said to her he liked well by the cheer that I made him.

He had such words to my cousin Clere, that, less than (unless) ye made him good cheer and gave him words of comfort at London, he would no more speak of the matter.

My cousin Clere thinketh that it were a folly to forsake him less than ye know of one other as good or better ; and

---

[1] *Either* quince-jam *or* artichoke leaves, which were called " chards."

I have assayed your sister,[1] and I found her never so willing to none as she is to him ; if it be so that his land stand clear.

I sent you a letter by Brawnton for silk, and for this matter before my cousin Clere wrote to me, the which was written on the Wednesday next after Midsummer Day.

Sir Harry Inglose is right busy about Scroope for one of his daughters.

I pray you forget not to bring me my money from Orwellberry, as ye come from London, either all or a great part ; the due debt was at Christmas last past, nothing allowed, £7. 14s. 8d. and at this Midsummer it is £5. more ; and though I allow him all his asking, it is but £1. 6s. 6d. less, but I am not so advised yet. As for the friar, he hath been at Saint Benet's, and at Norwich, and made great boast of the suit that he hath against me, and bought many boxes, to what intent I weet never ; it is well done to beware at London, in dread if he bring any syse (writ of assize) at St. Margaret's (20th July) time.

I can no more, but Almighty God be our good Lord, who have you ever in keeping. Written at Oxnead in great haste, on the Saturday next after Midsummer.

By your mother,
AGNES PASTON.

OXNEAD,
Saturday, 29th June 1454.
32 H. VI.

13. *To my cousin, John Paston, be this letter delivered.*

TRUSTY AND WELL-BELOVED COUSIN, I commend me to you, desiring to hear of your welfare and good speed in your matters, the which I pray God send you to his plesaunce (pleasure) and to your heart's ease.

Cousin, I let you weet that Scroope hath been in this country to see my cousin your sister,[2] and he hath spoken with my cousin your mother, and she desireth of him that he should show you the indentures made between the knight that hath his daughter and him, whether that Scroope, if he were married and fortuned to have children, if those

---

[1] Elizabeth Paston, for whom many marriage alliances were arranged.
[2] Elizabeth Paston.

children should inherit his land, or his daughter, the which is married.

Cousin, for this cause take good heed to his indentures, for he is glad to show you them, or whom ye will assign with you ; and he saith to me he is the last in the tayle (entail) of his livelihood the which is three hundred and fifty marks (£233. 6s. 8d.) and better, as Watkin Shipdam saith, for he hath taken a compt (an account) of his livelihood divers times ; and Scroope saith to me if he be married and have a son and heir, his daughter that is married shall have of his livelihood fifty marks (£33. 6s. 8d.) and no more ; and therefore, cousin, meseemeth he were good for my cousin your sister with that (without that) ye might get her a better ; and if ye can get a better I would advise you to labour it in as short time as ye may goodly, for she was never in so great sorrow as she is nowadays, for she may not speak with no man, whosoever come, ne not (neither) may see nor speak with my man, nor with servants of her mother's, but that she beareth her an hand otherwise than she meaneth ; and she hath since Easter the most part been beaten once in the week or twice, and sometimes twice on a day, and her head broken in two or three places. Wherefore, cousin, she hath sent to me by Fryar Newton in great counsel, and prayeth me that I would send to you a letter of her heaviness, and pray you to be her good brother, as her trust is in you ; and she saith if ye may see by his evidences that his children and hers may inherit and she to have reasonable jointure, she hath heard so much of his birth and his conditions, that and (if) ye will she will have him, whether that her mother will or will not, notwithstanding it is told her his person is simple (plain) for she saith men shall have the more dainty (deyute) of her, if she rule her to him as she ought go do.

Cousin, it is told me there is a goodly man in your inn, of the which the father died lately, and if ye think that he were better for her than Scroope, it would be laboured, and give Scroope a goodly answer, that he be not put off till ye be sure of a better ; for he said when he was with me but if (unless) he have some comfortable answer of you he will no more labour in this matter, because he might not see my cousin your sister, and he saith he might have seen her and she had been better than she is ; and that causeth him to deem that her mother was not well willing ; and so have I sent my

cousin your mother word ; wherefore, cousin, think on this
matter, for sorrow oftentime causeth women to beset them
otherwise than they should do, and if she were in that case,
I wot well ye would be sorry : cousin, I pray you burn this
letter, that your men nor none other men see it ; for and (if)
my cousin your mother knew that I had sent you this letter,
she should never love me. No more I write to you at this
time, but Holy Ghost have you in keeping. Written in haste,
on Saint Peter's day, by candle light.

By your cousin,
E<small>LIZABETH</small> C<small>LERE</small>.[1]

St. Peter's Day,
Saturday, 29th of June 1454.
32 H. VI.

14. *To my right worshipful master, John Paston, at Norwich, be this delivered.*

P<small>LEASE</small> it your mastership to weet (here follows an account
of some law business, &c.).

Here be many marvellous tales of things that shall fall
this next month, as it is said ; for it is talked that one Doctor
Grene a priest hath kalked (calculated), and reporteth that
before St. Andrew's day next coming shall be the greatest
battle that was since the battle of Shrewsbury,[2] and it shall
fall between the Bishop's Inn of Salisbury [3] and Westminster Bars ; [4] and there shall die seven lords, whereof three
should be bishops. All this and much more is talked and
reported. I trust to God it shall not fall so.

Also there is great variance between the Earl of Devonshire and the Lord Bonvile, as hath been many day, and
much debate is like to grow thereby ; for on Thursday (23rd
of October) at night last passed, the Earl of Devonshire's son
and heir came, with sixty men of arms, to Radford's Place in
Devonshire, which was of counsel with my Lord Bonvile ;
and they set an house on fire at Radford's gate, and cried and
made a noise as though they had been sorry for the fire ; and
by that cause Radford's men set open the gates and yede

---

[1] Widow of Robert Clere of Ormesby. She died 1492.

[2] This battle was fought 22nd July 1403.

[3] Situated in the Strand, near the site of the present Salisbury Street.

[4] Probably the gate of London facing towards Westminster.

(went) out to see the fire ; and forthwith the Earl's son afore-said entered into the place, and entreated Radford to come down of his chamber to speak with them, promising him that he should no bodily harm have ; upon which promise he came down, and spoke with the said Earl's son : in the mean-time his meny (servants) rob his chamber, and rifled his hutches, and trussed such as they could get together and carried it away on his own horses : then the Earl's son said, " Radford, thou must come to my lord, my father." He said he would, and bade one of his men make ready his horse to ride with them ; which answered him that all his horses were taken away : then he said to the Earl's son, " Sir, your men have robbed my chamber, and they have mine horses, that I may not ride with you to my lord your father, wherefore I pray you let me ride, for I am old, and may not go."

It was answered him again that he should walk forth with them on his feet ; and so he did till he was a flight shot or more from his place, and then he was . . . softly, for cause he might not go fast, and when they were thus departed he turned . . . forthwith came nine men again upon him and smote him on the head and felled . . . of them cut his throat.

This was told to my Lord Chancellor this forenoon . . . messengers, as come of purpose out of the same country. This matter is taken greatly . . . passed at two after mid-night rode out of London as it is said more than . . . the best wise. Some say it was to ride toward my Lord of York, and some . . . so much rumour is here, what it meaneth I wot not, God turn it . . . at Hertford, and some men are afraid that he is sick again, I pray God . . . my Lords of York, Warwick, Salisbury, and others are in purpose to convey him . . . &c.

The said Nicholas Crome, bearer hereof, shall tell you such tidings . . . in haste at London on Saint Simon's day and Jude.

Your poor
JAMES GRESHAM.

LONDON,
Tuesday, 28th of October, 1455.
34 H. VI.

15. *Errands to London of Agnes Paston, the 28th day of January 1457, the year of King Henry VI. the 36th.*

To pray Greenfield to send me faithfully word by writing how Clement Paston hath done his endeavour in learning.

And if he hath not done well, nor will not amend, pray him that he will truly belash (whip) him till he will amend ; and so did the last master, and the best that ever he had at Cambridge.[1]

And say (tell) Greenfield, that if he will take upon to bring him into good rule and learning, that I may verily know he doth his endeavour, I will give him 10 marks (£6. 13s. 4d.) for his labour, for I had lever (rather) he were fairly buried than lost for default.

Item, to see how many gowns Clement hath, and they that he bare, let them be raised (let them have a new nap set upon them).

He hath a short green gown. And a short musterdevelers gown (which) were never raised.

And a short blue gown, that was raised, and made of a side gown when I was last at London.

And a side russet gown furred with beaver was made this time two years.

And a side murray gown was made this time twelvemonth.

Item, to do make me (get made for me) six spoons of eight ounces of troy weight, well fashioned and double gilt.

And say (tell) Elizabeth Paston that she must use herself to work readily, as other gentlewomen do, and somewhat to help herself therewith.

Item, to pay the Lady Pole 26s. and 8d. for her board.

And if Greenfield have done well his devoir to Clement, or will do his devoir, give him the noble (6s. 8d.).

AGNES PASTON.

16. *To my right worshipful husband, John Paston.*

RIGHT WORSHIPFUL HUSBAND, I recommend me to you, and pray you to get some crossbows and wyndacs [2] (windlasses) to bind them with and quarrels,[3] for your houses here be so

---

[1] For university life, cf. pp. 145 sqq. ; also Chaucer's " Clerk of Oxenford," pp. 285 sqq. ; also the *Stonor Papers*, p. 363.

[2] Grappling-irons with which the bow-string was drawn home.

[3] An arrow with a square head.

low that there may none man shoot out with no long bow, though we had never so much need.

I suppose ye should have such things of Sir John Fastolf if ye would send to him ; and also I would ye should get two or three short pole-axes to keep with (in) doors, and as many jackets and (if) ye may.

Partrich and his fellowship are sore afraid that ye would enter again upon them, and they have made great ordinance within the house, and it is told me they have made bars to bar the doors crosswise, and they have made wickets on every quarter of the house to shoot out at, both with bows and with hand-guns : and the holes that be made from hand-guns they be scarce knee high from the plancher (floor), and of such holes be made five, there can none man shoot out at them with no hand-bows.

Purry fell in fellowship with William Hasard at Quarles's, and told him that he would come and drink with Partrich and with him, and he said he should be welcome, and after noon he went thither for to espy what they dedyn (had done), and what fellowship they had with them ; and when he came thither the doors were fast sperred (bolted) and there were none folks with them but Maryoth, and Capron and his wife, and Quarles's wife, and another man in a black yed (went) somewhat halting, I suppose by his words that it was Norfolk of Gimmingham ; and the said Purry espied all these foresaid things.

And Maryoth and his fellowship had much great language that shall be told you when ye come home.

I pray you that ye will vouchsafe to do buy for me one lb. of almonds and one lb. of sugar, and that ye will do buy some frieze to make of your children's gowns, ye shall have best cheap and best choice of Hays's wife as it is told me. And that ye will buy a yard of broad cloth of black for one hood for me of 44d. or four shillings a yard, for there is neither good cloth nor good frieze in this town. As for the children's gowns and (if) I have them, I will do them maken (have them made).

The Trinity have you in his keeping, and send you good speed in all your matters.

MARGARET PASTON.

No date, but before 1459.
37 H. VI.

17. *To my Master Paston, H.R.*

AFTER due recommendation with my simple service preceding, please your mastership to weet, that as to such remembrance that ye desire me to continue forth, to the uttermost I shall, with good will, so as my master will license me, as oft as I can, the officer to have leisure to be with me, for ye know well I cannot do it alone, &c.

And whereas ye of your pleasure write me or call me Master Worcester, I pray and require you forget that name of mastership, for I am not amended by my master of a farthing in certainty, but of wages of household in common entent comme nous plaira,[1] by Worcester or Botoner I have five shillings yearly, all costs borne, to help to pay for bonnets that I lose ; I told so my master [2] this week, and he said (told) me yesterday, he wished me to have been a priest so I had been disposed to have given me a living by reason (means) of a benefice, that another man must give it, as the bishop, but (if) he would ; and so I indure inter egenos ut servus ad aratrum.

Forgive me, I write to make you laugh ; and our Lord bring my master into a better mood for others as (well as) for me. At Caister the 2nd day of September.

I pray you displeasure not your servant be so long, for my master letted him.

Your

W. WORCESTER.

CAISTER, *2nd of September, before* 1459.
38 H. VI.

18. *To my right worshipful husband, John Paston, be this delivered in haste.*

RIGHT WORSHIPFUL HUSBAND, I recommend me to you, desiring to hear of your welfare ; praying you to weet that Sir Thomas Howes hath purveyed four dormants (beams) for the drawte chamber, and the malthouse, and the brewery, whereof he hath bought three, and the fourth, that shall be the longest and greatest of all, he shall have from Heylesdon, which he saith my master Fastolf shall give me, because my

---

[1] As much as we please.
[2] Sir John Fastolf.

chamber shall be made therewith. As for the laying of the said dormants, they shall be laid this next week because of the malthouse, and as for the remanent I trow it shall abide till ye come home, because I can neither be purveyed of posts nor of boards not yet.

I have taken the measure in the drawte chamber, there as ye would your coffers and your cowntewery [1] should be set for the while, and there is no space beside the bed, though the bed were removed to the door, for to set both your board and your coffers there, and to have space to go and sit beside ; wherefore I have purveyed that ye shall have the same drawte chamber that ye had before, thereas ye shall ly to yourself ; and when your gear is removed out of your little house, the door shall be locked, and your bags laid in one of the great coffers, so that they shall be safe, I trust.

Richard Charles and John Dow have fetched home the child from Rockland Tofts, and it is a pretty boy; and it is told me that Will is at Blickling with a poor man of the town ; a young woman that was some time with Burton of this town sent me word thereof ; I pray you send me word if ye will that anything that ye will be done to him ere ye come home. Richard Charles sendeth you word that Willes hath been at him here, and offered him to make him estate in all things according to their indenture, and if he do the contrary ye shall soon have word.

My mother prayeth you for to remember my sister,[2] and to do your part faithfully ere ye come home to help to get her a good marriage ; it seemeth by my mother's language that she would never so fain to have be delivered of her as she will now.

It was told here that Knivet, the heir, is for to marry ; both his wife and child be dead, as it was told here ; wherefore she would that ye should inquire whether it be so or no, and what his livelihood is, and if ye think that it be for to do, to let him be spoken with thereof.

I pray you that ye be not strange of writing of letters to me betwixt this and that ye come home, if I might I would have every day one from you.   The blessed Trinity have you

---

[1] Probably desks or writing-tables.
[2] Elizabeth Paston, for whom they had not yet succeeded in arranging marriage.

in his keeping. Written at Norwich on the Tuesday next after the conversion (of) Saint Paul. (25 January.)

By yours,

MARGARET PASTON.

NORWICH,
Tuesday, January, sometime before 1459.
38 H. VI.

19. *Carissimo suo magistro, Johanni Paston, Armigroe.*

Jesus, Maria, &c.

RIGHT REVEREND MASTER AND MOST TRUSTY FRIEND IN EARTH, as lowly as I can or may I recommend me, &c.

Sir, in faith I was sore afraid that ye had a great letting, that ye came not on Wednesday to meet, &c. by my faith and (if) ye had been here ye should have had right good cheer, &c. ; and have fared right well after your pleasure, &c., with more, &c.

Sir John Tatteshall is at one with Heydon, &c., and Lord Scales hath made a loveday [1] with the prior and Heydon in all matters, except the matter of Snoring, &c. And the said prior spake masterly to the jurors, &c., and told them and (if) they had dreaded God and hurt of their souls, they would have some instruction of the one party as well as of the other, but they were so bold, they were not afraid, for they found no bones to say in their verdict as Thomas Todenham and John Heydon would, &c.

A lewd doctor of Ludgate preached on Sunday fort'night at Paul's, charging the people that no man should pray for these lords traytors, &c., and he had little thank, as he was worthy, &c., and for his lewd demeaning his brethren are had in the less favour at London, &c., Dr. Pinchbeck and Dr. Westhawe, great preachers and parsons at London, be now late made monks of Charter-house at Sheen, one at the one place and another at the other place, &c.

The chancellor is not good to these lords, &c., for he feareth the Earl of March will claim by inheritance the Earldom of Ha . . . &c., of which matter I heard great speech in Somersetshire, &c.

---

[1] A day on which arbitrations were made and quarrels between neighbours settled ; cf. Chaucer's Prologue to the *Canterbury Tales*, p. 284. For the Friars, cf. also pp. 96 sqq. ; and *Piers Plowman*, p. 301.

Wyndham, Heydon, Todenham, Blake, W. Chamber-
leyne, and Wentworth have late commissions to take for
traytors and send to the next gaol all persons fautorers
(favourters) and well-willers to the said lords, &c. Master
Radcliff and ye have none of commissions directed to you,
&c., for ye be holden favourable, &c.

Wyndham & Heydon be named here causers of these
commissions, &c.

On Monday last at Cromer was the oar and the books of
registry of the admiralty taken away from my Lord Scales's
men by a great multitude of my Lord Roos's men, &c. the
Lord Scales is to my Lord Prince, &c. to wait on him, &c.
he saith, per Deum sanctum, as we say here, he shall be
admiral, or he shall lye thereby, &c., by my faith here is a
coisy (unsettled) word (world). Walsham of Chancery that
never made leasing (lying) told me that Bocking was with
my Lord Chancellor this term, but I asked not how many
times, &c.

As I have written to you often before this, " Facite vobis
amicos de mammona iniquitatis " (Luke xvi. 9).

Thomas Todenham, Johannes Heydon, et J. Wyndham
cum caeteris magistri Fastolf fallacibus famulis magnam
gerunt ad vos invidiam, quod excelleritis eos in bonis, &c.
Judas non dormit, &c. " Noli zelare facientes iniquitatem
quoniam tanquam fenum velociter arescent, et quemadmodum
olera herbarum cito per Dei gratiam decident." Ideo sic in
Psalmo, " Spera in Domino et fac bonitatem, et pasceris in
divitiis ejus et delectare in Domino et dabit tibi petitiones
cordia tui " (Psalm xxxvii. 1, 2, 3, 4). " Et aliter. Jacta
cogitatum tuum in domino, & ipse te enutriet " (Psalm lv.
22). " Utinam inquit apostolus abscindantur qui vos
conturbant," &c. (Gal. v. 12). " Et alibi, cavete vos a
malis et importunis hominibus " (2 Thess. iii. 2).

Precor gratiosum Deum qui vos et me creavit et
suo pretioso sanguine nos redemit, vos vestros et vestra
gratiose conservet in prosperis, et gratiosius dirigat in
agendis.[1]

Scriptum, Walsham feria 4ta in nocte cum magna

---

[1] I pray gracious God, who created you and me and redeemed
us with His precious blood, that He would graciously preserve
you and yours in prosperity and graciously direct you in your
deeds.

festinatione, &c. Utinam iste mundus malignus transiret et concupiscentia ejus. Vester ad vota promptissimus.

Frater JOHANNES BRACKLEY,[1]
Minorum Minimus.

WALSHAM, NORFOLK,
Wednesday, 1459. 38 H. VI.

20. *To my right worshipful husband, John Paston, be this delivered in haste.*

RIGHT WORSHIPFUL HUSBAND, I recommend me to you, desiring heartily to hear of your welfare, praying you that ye will send me word in haste how ye be agreed with Witchingham and Inglos for that matter ye spake to me of at your departing, for if I should purvey either wood or hay it should be bought best cheap betwixt this and Saint Margaret's mass (20th July), as it is told me. As for Appleyard he come not yet to this town since he come from London ; I have sent to Sir Bryse to let me have knowledge when he cometh to town, and he hath promised that I shall have knowledge, and when he cometh I shall do your commandment. My mother bade me send you word that Waryn Herman hath daily fished her water all this year, and therefore she prayeth you to do therefore, while ye be at London, as ye think best. Church of Burlingham was taken and brought to the castle yesterday by the bishop's men, and all his goods be seized for that he oweth to the bishop ; and the said Church saith, as for that he hath said of them that he hath appealed before this time, he will avow it, and abide thereby ; and saith that he will appeal one that hath more nobles than they have all that he hath spoken of yet, and that shall avail the king more than they have all that he hath spoken of yet, but what he is he will not name till he know more. I trow but if (unless) there be the great labour made against him, he is like to have great favour of them that have been his supporters ; men think, that have spoken with him, that he hopeth to have good help ; I pray God that the truth might be known.

I pray you that ye will vouchsafe to send me another sugar-loaf, for my old is done ; and also that ye will do make

---

[1] John Brackley was born in 1418. He entered the House of Friars Minor at Norwich, became famous as a preacher, and was made Chaplain to Sir John Fastolf.

(have made) a girdle for your daughter, for she hath need thereof. The blessed Trinity have you in his keeping.

Written at Norwich, in haste, on the Tuesday next before Saint Thomas's day.

Paper is dainty.[1]

Yours,

MARGARET PASTON.

NORWICH,
Tuesday and of June or beginning of July, about 1461.
1 Ed. IV.

21. *To my cousin, Margaret Paston.*

MINE OWN DEAR SOVEREIGN LADY, I recommend me to you, and thank you of the great cheer that ye made me here to my great cost and charge and labour. No more at this time, but that I pray you ye will send me hither two ells of worsted for doublets, to happe me this cold winter and that ye inquire where William Paston bought his tippet of fine worsted, which is almost like silk, and if that be much finer than ye should buy me after seven or eight shillings, then buy me a quarter and the nail thereof for collars, though it be dearer than the other, for I would make my doublet all worsted for worship of Norfolk, rather than like Gonner's doublet.

Item, as for the matter of the nine score pounds asked by my Lady of Bedford [2] for the manor of West Thurrock, whereas Sir Thomas Howes saith that he hath no writing thereof, but that Sir John Fastolf purchased the said manor, and paid certain money in earnest, and afterwards granted his bargain to the Duke Bedford, and so the money that he took was for the money that he had paid ; peradventure Sir Thomas Howes hath writing thereof, and knoweth it not ; for if there be any such money paid upon any bargain he shall find it in Kyrtling's books, that was Sir John Fastolf's receiver, and it was about such time as the Duke of Bedford was last in England, which, as it is told me, was the eighth year of King Harry V. (1420) or the eighth year of King

---

[1] The only complaint of a shortage of paper in the Paston Letters. The letter is written on a piece nearly square, out of which a quarter had been cut before the letter was written.

[2] Jaqueline of Luxembourg, second wife of John, Duke of Bedford. Afterwards in 1435 she married Sir Thomas Woodville. She died in 1472.

22

Harry VI. (1429) ; and the sum that he paid for the said bargain was 300 marks (£200). Also, he shall find the twenty-second year of King Harry (VI.), or there about (1443), in the accounts of one of Fastolf's receivers at London, that there was taken of Sir Thomas Tyrell, and of the Duchess of Exeter,[1] that was wife to Sir Lewis Johnes, farmer of the said manor, certain money for repayment of part of the said 300 marks. Also he shall find in years after that, or that year, or thereabouts, that Sir John Fastolf received money of my Lord Rivers that now is, by the name of Richard Wydvile, for his own debt due to Sir John Fastolf; wherefore, if Sir Thomas be true to his master, let him do his devoir to make that Worcester, which is upheld by him with the dead's goods, be true to his master, or else it is time for Sir Thomas to forsake him, and help to punish him, or men must say that Sir Thomas is not true ; and moreover let Sir Thomas examine what he can find in this matter that I sent him word of, which matter he shall find in the said receiver's books if he list to seek it.

Item, on the day after your departing I received letters by William Roos from your sons to me, and to you, and to Richard Calle, &c.

Item, I shall tell you a tale.

Pampyng and I have picked your male [2]
And taken out pieces [3] five,
For upon trust of Calle's promise we may soon unthrive,
And if Calle bring us hither twenty pound,
Ye shall have your pieces again, good and round ;
Or else if he will not pay you the value of the pieces, there
To the post do nail his ear,
Or else do him some other wrongs,
For I will no more in his default borrow ;
And but if (unless) the receiving of my livelihood be better plied,
He shall Christ's hour and mine clean tried ; [4]
And look ye be merry and take no thought,
For this rhyme is cunningly wrought.
My Lord Percy [5] and all this house
Recommend them to you, dog, cat, and mouse,

---

[1] Probably Margaret, widow of Thomas Beaufort, Duke of Exeter.
[2] Trunk or portmanteau.   [3] Pieces of money.
[4] A suggested reading of this obscure line is : " He shall Christ's curse and mine clean bide."   [1461.
[5] Son of the Earl of Northumberland, who was killed at Towton in

And wish ye had been here still,
For they say ye are a good gill.[1]
No more to you at this time,
But God him save that made this rhyme.

Written the   of Saint Mathe,
   By your true and trusty husband,

J. P.

February, between 1461 *and* 1465.
   1 & 5 E. IV.

22. *To Mistress Margaret Paston, be this delivered.*

PLEASE it you to weet that I send you by Barker, the bearer
hereof, three treacle pots of Geane [2] as my apothecary
sweareth unto me, and moreover that they were never
undone since they came from Geane, whereof ye shall take
as many as pleaseth you, nevertheless my brother John sent
to me for two, therefore I must beseech you that he may
have at the least one ; there is one pot that is marked under
the bottom two times, with these letters M.P., which pot I
have best trust unto, and next him to the wryghe (? twisted)
pot, and I mistrust most the pot that hath a krott (? a
crack, or peice chipt off) above on the top, lest that he hath
been undone ; and also the other two pots be printed with
the merchant's mark two times on the covering, and that
other pot is but once marked but with one print ; notwithstanding I had like oath and promise for one as well as for all.
JOHN PASTON.

Between 1460 *and* 1470.
   1 & 10 E. IV.

23. *To Sir John Paston, Knight, be this delivered in haste.*

I GREET you well, and send you God's blessing and mine ;
letting you weet that Blickling of Heylesdon came from
London this week, and he is right merry, and maketh his
boast that within this fortnight at Heylesdon should be
both new lords and new officers ; and also this day was
brought me word from Caister, that Rysing of Fretton
should have heard said in divers places there, as he was in
Suffolk, that Fastolf of Conghawe maketh all the strength

---

[1] An agreeable companion.   [2] Treacle of Genoa.

that he may, and proposeth him to assault Caister, and to enter there if he may, insomuch that it is said that he hath a five score men ready, and sendeth daily spies to understand what fellowship keep the place ; by whose power, or favour, or supportation, that he will do this I know not, but ye wot well that I have been affrayed (frightened) there before this time, when that I had other comfort than I have now ; and I cannot well guide nor rule soldiers, and also they set not by a woman as they should set by a man ; therefore I would ye should send home your brothers or else Daubeney to have a rule, and to take in such men as were necessary for the safeguard of the place, for if I were there, without I had the more sadder (graver) or worshipful persons about me, and there come a meny [1] of knaves and prevailed in their intent, it should be to me but a villainy. And I have been about my livelihood to set a rule therein, as I have written to you, which is not yet all performed after mine desire, and I would not go to Caister till I had done ; I will no more days make thereabout if I may, therefore in any wise send somebody home to keep the place, and when that I have done and performed that I have begun I shall purpose me thither-ward if I should do there any good, and else I had lever (rather) be thence.

I have sent to Nicholas and such as keep the place, that they should take in some fellows to assist and strength them till ye send home some other word, or some other man to govern them that be therein, &c.

I marvel greatly that ye send me no word how that ye do, for your elmyse (enemies) begin to wax right bold, and that putteth your friends both in great fear and doubt, therefore purvey that they may have some comfort that they be no more discouraged, for if we lose our friends it shall (be) hard in this troublesome world to get them again.

The blessed Trinity speed you in your matters, and send you the victory of your elmyse (enemies), to your heart's ease and their confusion.

Written at Norwich, the Saturday next before Relic Sunday,[2] in haste.

I pray you remember well the matters that I wrote to you for in the letter that ye had by James Gresham's man,

[1] A following.
[2] The Sunday fortnight after Midsummer's Day.

and send me an answer thereof by the next man that cometh, &c.

By your mother,

MARGARET PASTON.

NORWICH,
Saturday, 9th of July, 1468.
8 E. IV.

24. *To my right well-beloved brother, John Paston, Esq., being at Caister or to John Daubeney there, be this letter delivered.*

RIGHT WELL-BELOVED BROTHER, I commend me to you ; letting you weet that I have waged, for to help you and Daubeney to keep the place at Caister four well assured and true men to do all manner of thing what that they be desired to do in safeguard or inforcing (strengthening) of the said place ; and moreover they be proved men, and cunning (expert) in the war and in feats of arms, and they can well shoot both guns and cross-bows, and amend and string them, and devise bulwarks, or any things that should be a strength to the place, and they will as need is keep watch and ward, they be sad (serious) and well-advised men, saving one of them, which is bald, and called William Peny, which is as good a man as goeth on the earth saving a little, he will, as I understand be a little copschotyn (high-crested) but yet he is no brawler but full of courtesy, much upon (much like) James Halman ; the other three be named Peryn Sale, John Chapman, Robert Jack's Son (Jackson), saving that as yet they have none harness come, but when it cometh it shall be sent to you, and in the mean while I pray you and Daubeney to purvey them some.

Also a couple of beds they must needs have, which I pray you by the help of my mother to purvey for them till that I come home to you ; ye shall find them gentlemanly comfortable fellows, and that they will and dare abide by their tackling, and if ye understand that any assault should be towards ; I send you these men, because that men of the country there about you should be frayed (frightened) for fear of loss of their goods ; wherefore if there were any such thing towards, I would ye took of men of the country but few, and that they were well assured men, for else they might discourage all the remanent.

And as for any writing from the king, he hath promised that there shall come none, and if there do his unwarys (with his privity), your answer may be this how the king hath said, and so to delay them till I may have word, and I shall soon purvey a remedy.

I understand that ye have been with my Lord of Norfolk now of late, what ye have done I wot not ; we see that he shall be here again this day. Moreover I trow John Alford shall not long abide with my lord ; I shall send you tidings of other things in haste, with the grace of God, who, &c. Written on Wednesday next before St. Martin.

JOHN PASTON.

I fear that Daubeney is not all there (altogether) best stored to continue household long ; let him send me word in haste, and I will relieve him to my power, and ere long too I hope to be with you.

Roger Ree is sheriff of Norfolk, and he shall be good enough. The escheator I am not yet ascertained of.

Also, that these men be at the beginning entreated as courteously as ye can.

Also, I pray you to send me my flower [1] by the next messenger that cometh.

Also, as for my Lord Fitzwalter's obligation I know none such in mine adward as yet.

Also, the obligation of the Bishop of Norwich's obligation, I never saw it that I remember, wherefore I would and pray my mother to look it up.

Also, as for the Bible,[2] that the master hath, I wend the utmost price had not past five marks (£3. 6s. 8d.) and so I trow he will give it, weet I pray you.

Also, as for Sir William Barber and Sir William Falgate, I would, if they can purvey for themselves, full fain be discharged of them.

LONDON,
Wednesday, 9th November 1468.
8 E. IV.

[1] His device or cognisance ; or, possibly, flour for baking.

[2] This must mean some manuscript copy. Only one printed edition of the Bible was in existence at this time. It would have been worth much more than the sum mentioned.

25. *To Sir John Paston, Knight.*

SIR, pleaseth it to understand that I conceive, by your letter
which ye sent me by Juddy, that ye have heard of Richard
Calle's labour which the maketh by our ungracious sister's
assent, but whereas they write that they have very good will
therein, saving your reverence, they falsely lie of it for they
never spake to me of that matter, nor none other body in
their name.   Lovell asked me once a question whether that
I understood how it was betwixt Rd. Calle and my sister ;
I can think that it was by Calle's means, for when I asked
him whether Calle desired him to move me that question or
not, he would have gotten it away by hums and by haas,
but I would not so be answered ; wherefore at the last he
told me that his eldest son desired him to spere (inquire)
whether that Richard Calle were sure of her or not, for he
said that he knew a good marriage for her, but I wot he lied,
for he is whole with Richard Calle in that matter ; wherefore to that intent that he nor they should pick no comfort
of me, I answered him that and (if) my father, whom God
assoil ! were alive, and had consented thereto, and my
mother, and ye both, he should never have my good will
for to make my sister to sell candle and mustard in Framlingham, and thus, with more which were too long to write to
you, we departed (parted).

And whereas it pleaseth you in your letter to cry me
mercy for that ye sent me not such gear as I sent you money
for ; I cry you mercy that I was so lewd (rude) to encumber
you with any so simple a matter, considering the great
matters and weighty that ye have to do ; but need compelled
me, for in this country is no such stuff as I sent to you for.

Also, whereas it pleaseth you to send to Richard Calle to
deliver me money, so God help me I will none ask him for
myself, nor none had I of him, nor of none other man but of
mine own since ye departed, but that little that I might
forbear (spare) of mine own I have delivered to Daubeney
for household, and paid it for you in men's wages, and therefore whoever sendeth you word that I have spent you any
money since ye went hence, they must give you another
reckoning, saving in meat, and drink, for I eat like an horse,

---

[1] Margery Paston, who afterwards married Richard Calle, to the
intense disgust of her family.

of purpose to eat you out at the doors, but that needeth not for you come not within them, wherefore so God help me, the fellowship here thinks that ye have forgotten us all, wherefore and (if) anything be ill ruled when ye come home wyte (blame) yourself for default of oversight.

Also I understand for very certain, and it is sent me so word out of my lord's house, that this Pentecost (Whitsuntide) is my lord's counsel at Framlingham, and they purpose this week and the next to hold courts here at Caister, and at all other manors that were Sir John Fastolf's, purchased of Yelverton, and of Sir Thomas Howys, whom God assoil, and how that my demeaning should be it is too late to send you for advice, wherefore and (if) I do well I ask no thank, and if I do ill I pray you lay the default on over little wit, but I purpose to use the first point of hawking, to hold fast and (if) I may ; but so God help me, and (if) they might pull down the house on our heads I wyte (blame) them not, which I trust to God to keep them from ; for by God that bought me, the best earl in England would not deal so with my lord and my lady as ye do, without making of some means to them ; so God help me, whosoever advise you to do so he is not your friend ; and I may I trust to God to see you about Midsummer or before, for in good faith I ween ye purpose you that it shall be Easter ere ye come home, for all your servants here ween that ye purpose no more to deal with them, but to leave them here in hostage to my Lord of Norfolk.

Also, Sir, I pray you purvey what inn [1] that my brother Edmund [2] shall be in, for he loseth sore his time here I promise you ; I pray you send me word by the next messenger that cometh, and I shall either send him or bring him up with me to London.

Also, Sir, we poor sans deniers (moneyless men) of Caister have broken three or four steel-bows, wherefore we beseech you and there be any maker of steel-bows in London which is very cunning, that ye will send me word, and I shall send you the bows that be broken, which be your own great bow, and Robert Jackson's bow, and John Pampyng's bow ; these three have cast so many calvys that they shall never cast quarrels (square-headed arrows) till they be new made.

[1] Inn of Court.
[2] Edmund Paston became a soldier and was in the garrison of Calais in 1473.

I pray you find the means that my lord may have some reasonable mean proffered, so that he and my lady may understand that ye desire to have his good lordship ; I promise you it shall do you ease and your tenants both, and God preserve (you).

JOHN PASTON.

CAISTER,
Whitsuntide, May 1469. 9 E. IV.
(Whitsunday was on the 21st May in 1469.)

26. *To my mother, and to my brother John Paston.*

BROTHER, it is so that the king shall come into Norfolk in haste, and I wot (know) not whether that I may come with him or not ; if I come, I must do make a livery of twenty gowns, which I must pick out by your advice ; and as for the cloth for such persons as be in that country, if it might be had there at Norwich or not I wot not ; and what persons I am not remembered.

If my mother be at Caister, as there shall be no doubt, for the keeping of the place while the king is in that country, that I may have the most part [1] at Caister.

And whether ye will offer yourself to wait upon my Lord of Norfolk or not, I would ye did that best were to do ; I would do my lord pleasure and service, and so I would ye did, if I wist (thought) to be sure of his good lordship in time to come. He shall have two hundred in a livery blue and tawny, and blue on the left side, and both dark colours.

I pray you send me word and your advice by Juddy of what men, and what horse I could be purveyed of, if so be that I must needs come ; and of your advice in all things by writing, and I shall send you hastily other tidings. Let Sorrell [2] be well kept.

1469 or 1474.   JOHN PASTON, knight.

27. *To Sir John Paston, Knight.*

I GREET you well, letting you weet that your brother and his fellowship stand in great jeopardy at Caister, and lack victuals, and Daubeney and Berney be dead, and divers other greatly hurt, and they fail gunpowder and arrows, and the place (is) sore broken with guns of the other party, so that but (unless)

---

[1] The strongest party.   [2] A horse.

they have hasty help they be like to lose both their lives and the place, to the greatest rebuke to you that ever came to any gentleman, for every man in this country marvelleth greatly that ye suffer them to be so long in so great jeopardy without help or other remedy.

The duke [1] hath been more fervently set (determined) thereupon, and more cruel, since that Writtill, my Lord of Clarence's man, was there, than he was before : and he hath sent for all his tenants from every place, and others, to be there at Caister on Thursday next coming, that there is then like to be the greatest multitude of people that came there yet ; and they purpose then to make a great assault, for they have sent for guns to Lynn and other places by the sea's side, that, with their great multitude of guns with other shot and ordnance, there shall be no man dare appear in the place, they shall hold them so busy with their great (number of) people that it shall not lie in their power within to hold it against them without God help them or (they) have hasty succour from you ; therefore, as ye will have my blessing, I charge you and require you that ye see your brother be holpen in haste, and if ye can have none mean rather desire writing from my Lord of Clarence if he be at London, or else of my Lord Archbishop of York, to the Duke of Norfolk, that he will grant them that be in the place their lives and their goods, and in eschewing of insurrections with other inconveniences that be like to grow within the shire of Norfolk, this troublous were (tumultuous world), because of such conventicles and gatherings within the said shire, for cause of the said place, they shall suffer him to enter upon such appointment or other like, taken by the advice of your counsel there at London if ye think, as I can suppose, that the Duke of Norfolk will not agree to this because he granted this afore, and they in the place would not accept it, then I would the said messenger should with the said letters bring from the said Lord of Clarence, or else my lord archbishop, to my Lord of Oxford other letters to rescue them forthwith, though the said Earl of Oxford should have the place during his life for his labour ; spare not this to be done in haste if ye will have their lives, and be set by (esteemed) in Norfolk, though ye should lose the best manor of all for the rescuse (rescue). I had lever (rather) ye lost the livelihood than

---

[1] The Duke of Norfolk.

their lives ; ye must get a messenger of the lords, or some other notable man, to bring these letters ; do your devoir now, and let me send you no more messengers for this matter, but send me by the bearer hereof more certain comfort than ye have done by all other that I have sent before ; in any wise let the letters that shall come to the Earl of Oxford, come with the letters that shall come to the Duke of Norfolk, that if he will not agree to the one, that ye may have ready your rescuse that it need no more to send, therefore God keep you.

Written the Tuesday next before Holy Rood day, in haste.

By your mother,

MARGARET PASTON.

NORWICH,

Tuesday, 12th of September 1469.

10 E. IV.

28. *To John Paston, Esquire, being at Norwich, be this letter delivered.*

I COMMEND me to you, letting you weet, &c. (Here follows an account of bills, and receipts, &c., of no consequence.)

Item, as for Mistress Katherine Dudley I have many times recommended you to her, and she is nothing displeased with it ; she rekkythe not how many gentlemen love her, she is full of love ; I have betyn (enforced) the matter for you, your unknowledge (without your knowledge) as I told her ; she answered me that she would (have) no one this two years, and I believe her : for I think she hath the life that she can hold her content with. I trow she will be a sore labouring woman this two years for the meed of her soul.

And Mistress Gryseacress is sure to Selenger (St. Leger) with my Lady of Exeter,[1] a foul loss.

Item, I pray you speak with Harcourt of the abbey, for a little clock which I sent him by James Gresham to mend, and that ye would get it of him, and (if) it be ready, and send it me ; and as for money for his labour, he hath another clock of mine, which Sir Thomas Lyndes, God have his soul ! gave

---

[1] Anne, daughter of Richard, Duke of York. She married the Duke of Exeter in 1462, and after his death married Sir Thomas St. Leger. She died in 1475.

me ; he may keep that till I pay him ; this clock is my lord archbishop's, but let not him weet of it, and that it (be) easily carried hither by your advice.

Also as for oranges I shall send you a serteyn by the next carrier, and as for tidings the bearer hereof shall inform you ; ye must give credence to him.

As for my good speed, I hope well, I am offered yet to have Mistress Anne Hawte, and I shall have help enough as some say.

(Here follows an account of some disputes between Sir William Yelverton, and Sir John Paston, his uncle William, &c., of no consequence.)

Item, it is so that I am half in purpose to come home within a month hereafter, or about Midlent, or before Easter, under your correction, if so be that ye deem that my mother would help me to my costs, ten marks (£6. 13s. 4d.) or there-abouts. I pray you feel her disposition and send me word.

Item, I cannot tell you what will fall of the world, for the king verily is disposed to go into Lincolnshire, and men wot not what will fall thereof, nor thereafter, they ween my Lord of Norfolk shall bring 10,000 men.

Item, there is come a new little Turk, which is a well-visaged fellow of the age of forty years ; and he is lower than Manuel by an handful, and lower than my little Tom by the shoulders, and more little above his pap ; and he hath, as he said to the king himself, three or four children (sons) each one of them as high and as likely as the king himself and he is legged right enough.

Item, I pray you show, or read to my mother, such things as ye think are for her to know after your discretion ; and to let her understand of the article of the treaty between Sir William Yelverton and me.

Item, my Lord of Warwick, as it is supposed, shall go with the king into Lincolnshire ; some men say that his going shall do good, and some say that it doth harm.

I pray you ever have an eye to Caister, to know the rule there, and send me word, and whether my wise lord and my lady be yet as sotted upon it (as fond of it) as they were ; and whether my said lord resorteth thither as often as he did or not ; and of the disposition of the country.

Circa 1470.   JOHN PASTON, knight.

*29. To Mrs. Margaret Paston, or to John Paston, Esquire,
her son, in haste.*

RIGHT WELL-BELOVED BROTHER, I commend me to you,
letting you weet that I am in welfare, I thank God, and have
been ever since that I spake last with you ; and marvel for
that ye sent never writing to me since ye departed ; I heard
never since that time any word out of Norfolk ; ye might at
Bartholomew fair [1] have had messengers enough to London,
and if ye had sent to Wykes he should have conveyed it to
me.   I heard yesterday that a Worsted man of Norfolk, that
sold worsteds at Winchester, said that my Lord of Norfolk
and my lady were on pilgrimage at our lady [2] on foot, and so
they went to Caister ; and that at Norwich one should have
had large language to you, and called you traitor, and picked
many quarrels to you ; send me word thereof ; it were well
done that ye were a little surer of your pardon than ye be ;
advise you, I deem ye will hereafter else repent you.

I understand that Bastard Fauconbridge [3] is either headed
or like to be, and his brother both ; some men say he would
have deserved it and some say nay.

I purpose to be at London the first day of the term, send
me word whether ye shall be there or not.

Item, I would weet whether ye have spoken with my Lady
of Norfolk or not, and of her disposition and the household's
to me and to you wards, and whether it be a possible (thing)
to have Caister again and their good wills, or not.

And also I pray you understand what fellowship and
guiding is in Caister ; and have a spy resorting in and out,
so may ye know the secrets amongst them.

There is much ado in the North, as men say ; I pray you
beware of your guiding, and in chief of your language, so
that from henceforth by your language no man perceive that
ye favour any person contrary to the king's pleasure.

I understand that the Lord Rivers hath licence of the
king to go to Portugal [4] now within this sev'nnight.

I pray you recommend me to my mother, and beseech

---

[1] Bartholomew Fair in Smithfield.   [2] Our Lady of Walsingham.
[3] Thomas Nevil, illegitimate son of Lord Fauconberg.   After
fighting for the Lancastrians he was reconciled to Edward IV. in May
1471, but was executed the following September.
[4] On a pilgrimage.

her of her blessing on my behalf. (Here follow some directions about payments of money.)

Item, I pray you send me word if any of our friends or well-willers be dead, for I fear that there is great death in Norwich and in other borough towns in Norfolk ; for I ensure you, it is the most universal death that ever I wist in England ; for by my truth, I cannot hear by pilgrims that pass the country, nor none other man that rideth or goeth any country, that any borough town in England is free from that sickness ; God cease it when it please him.

Wherefore, for God's sake, let my mother take heed to my young brethren that they be not in none place where that sickness is reigning, nor that they disport not with none other young people which resorteth where any sickness is ; and if there be any of that sickness dead or enfect (infected) in Norwich, for God's sake let her send them to some friend of hers into the country, and do ye the same by mine advice ; let my mother rather remove her household into the country.

Even now Thyrston brought me word from London that it was Doctor Allen that caused your trouble that ye had at Norwich ; and that John Pampyng rode for a discharge for you, and that he hath sped well, but how that, wot I not ; if ye be clear out of Doctor Allen's danger keep you there, and hereafter ye may scoff as well at his carte (? cost) ; I pray you send me word of all the form of his dealing with you.

I had almost spoken with Mrs. Anne Hawte, but I did not, nevertheless this next term I hope to take one way with her or other ; she is agreed to speak with me, and she hopeth to do me ease as she saith.

I pray you send me word how ye do with my Lady Elizabeth Bourchier, ye have a little chafed it but I cannot tell how ; send me word whether ye be in better hope or worse.

I hear say that the Earl of Oxford's brethren be gone out of sanctuary. Sir Thomas Fulforth [1] is gone out of sanctuary, and a great fellowship fetched him, a three score, and they say that within five miles of London he was 200 men, and no man weeteth (knoweth) where he is become not yet. The Lords Hastings and Howard be in Calais and have it peaceably ; and Sir Walter Wrottesly and Sir Jeffrey Gate be coming thence, and will be at London this day as it is said.

[1] He was beheaded at Bristol in 1461.

Written at Waltham beside Winchester the day next Holyrood day.[1]

JOHN PASTON, knight.

15th of September, 1471.
11 E. IV.

30. *To his well-beloved John Paston, Esquire, at Norwich,
or to Mrs. Margaret, his mother.*

I COMMEND me to you, letting you weet that, &c. (Here follows an account that the Duchess of Suffolk and Duke of Norfolk intend again commencing appeals against Sir John Paston and his brother &c. concerning Caister, &c.) I would fain have the measure where my father lieth at Bromholm,[2] both the thickness and compass of the pillar at his head, and from that the space to the altar, and the thickness of that altar, and imagery of timber work ; and what height the arch is to the ground of the aisle, and how high the ground of the choir is higher than the ground of the aisle.

Item; I pray you let the measure by packthread be taken, or else measured by yard, how much is from the north gate where the brigg was at Gresham to the south wall, and in like form from the east side to the west ; also the height of the east wall, and the height of the south-east tower from the ground, if ye may easily. Also what breadth every tower is within the wall, and which tower is more than other within. Also how many foot, or what breadth each tower taketh within each corner of the quadrate overthwart the doors, and how many tailor's yards is from the mote side, where the brigg was, to the highway, or to the hedge all along the entry, and what breadth the entry is between the dikes.

I pray you, if ye have a leisure in any wise, see this done yourself if ye may, or else if Pampyng do it, or who that ye think can do it ; I would spend 20d., or as ye seem (more if you think proper), to have the certain of everything herein.

And as for my father's tomb I charge you see it yourself, and when I speak with you I will tell you the causes why that I desire this to be done.

As for tidings, the king and the queen and much other

---

[1] 14th September.
[2] John Paston, the father, was buried at the Priory Church, Bromholm in 1466.

people are ridden and gone to Canterbury, never so much people seen in pilgrimage heretofore at once as men say.

Also it is said that the Earl of Pembroke [1] is taken unto Bretagne ; and men say that the king shall have delivery of him hastily ; and some say that the king of France will see him safe, and shall set him at liberty again.

Item, Thomas Fauconbridge his head was yesterday set upon London Bridge looking into Kent ward ; and men say that his brother was sore hurt, and escaped to sanctuary to Beverley.

Sir Thomas Fulforth escaped out of Westminster with 100 spears as men say, and is into Devonshire, and there he hath stricken off Sir John Crokker's head and killed another knight of the Courtenays as men say ; I would ye had your very (absolute) pardon at once ; wherefore I pray you fail not to be at London within four days after Saint Faith's ; [2] ye shall do good in many things, and I pray you send me word hereof by the next messenger ; and if it come to Mrs. Elizabeth Higgens, at the Black Swan, she shall convey it to me, for I will not fail to be there at London again within this six days.

Mrs. Elizabeth hath a son, and was delivered within two days after Saint Bartholomew ; [3] and her daughter A. H.[4] was, the next day after, delivered of another son, as she saith eleven weeks ere her time ; it was christened John, and is dead, God save all ; no more till I speak with you.

Written at London on Michaelmas even,

JOHN PASTON, knight.

Item, I pray you let some witty fellow, or else yourself, go to the towns there as (where) these two women dwell, and inquire whether they be married since and again or not, for I hold the hoorys (whores) wedded ; and if they be, then the appeals were abated thereby. I remember not their names, ye know them better than I. Also in the sheriff's books there may ye find of them.

LONDON,
Saturday, 28th of September 1471.
11 E. IV.

[1] Jasper Tudor, half-brother of Henry VI. and uncle of Henry, Earl of Richmond, who became King Henry VII.
[2] 5th October.   [3] 24th August.   [4] Possibly Anne Hawte.

31. *To my right worshipful brother, Sir John Paston, knight.*

RIGHT WORSHIPFUL SIR, I recommend me to you ; letting you weet that your desire, as for the knights of the shire was an impossible (thing) to be brought about ; for my Lord of Norfolk[1] and my Lord of Suffolk[2] were agreed more than a fortnight ago to have Sir Robert Wyngfield and Sir Richard Harcourt, and that knew I not till it was Friday last past. I had sent ere I rode to Framlingham to warn as many of your friends to be at Norwich, as this Monday, to serve your intent as I could ; but when I came to Framlingham and knew the appointment that was taken for the two knights, I sent warning again to as many as I might, to tarry at home ; and yet there came to Norwich this day as many as their costs drew to 9s. 1½d. paid and reckoned by Peacock and R. Capron ; and yet they did but break their fast and departed ; and I thanked them in your name, and told them that ye would have no voice as this day, for ye supposed not to be in England when the parliament should be ; and so they came not at the Shire-house, for if they had it was thought, by such as be your friends here, that your adversaries would have reported that ye had made labour to have been one, and that ye could not bring your purpose about.

I sent to Yarmouth, and they have promised also to Doctor Aleyn and John Russe to be (burgesses) more than three weeks ago.

James Arblaster hath written a letter to the bailiff of Maldon in Essex to have you a burgess there ; how Jude shall speed let him tell you when ye speak together.

Sir, I have been twice at Framlingham since your departing ; but now the last time the council was there, I saw your letter which was better than well endited. R. C. was not at Framlingham when the council was there but I took my own advice, and delivered it to the council with a proposition therewith, as well as I could speak it ; and my words were well taken, but your letter a thousand fold better ; when they had read it they showed it to my lady[3] ; and after that my lady had seen it I spoke with my lady,[3] offering to my

---

[1] John Mowbray.   [2] John De La Pole.
[3] Elizabeth, Duchess of Norfolk.

lord and her your service, and besides that, ye to do my lord
a pleasure [1] and her a better, so as ye might depart without
any sum specified ; she would not tell in that matter, but
remitted me again to the council, for she said and she spoke
in it till my lord and the council were agreed, they would lay
the weight of all the matter on her, which should be reported
to her shame ; but this she promised, to be helping so it were
first moved by the council ; then I went to the council and
offered before them your service to my lord, and to do him a
pleasure, for the having again of your place and lands in
Caister £40., not speaking of your stuff nor thing else ; so
they answered me your offer was more than reasonable, and
if the matter were theirs, they said, they wist (knew) what
conscience would drive them to, they said they would move
my lord with it, and so they did ; but then the tempest arose,
and he gave them such an answer that none of them all would
tell it me ; but when I asked an answer of them they said ;
" And (if) some lords or greater men moved my lord with it,
the matter were yours ; " (keep counsel). And with this
answer I departed, but Sir W. Brandon, Southwell, Tymperley,
Harry Wentworth, W. Gurney, and all other of council understand that ye have wrong ; insomuch that they moved me
that ye should take a recompense of other land to the value,
but they would not avow the offer ; for I answered them, if
they had right they would have offered no recompense ; discover not this, but in my reason and (if) my lord chamberlain [2]
would send my lady a letter with some privy token between
them, and also to move my Lord of Norfolk when he cometh
to the parliament, certainly Caister is yours.

If ye miss to be burgess of Maldon, and my lord chamberlain will, ye may be in another place ; there be a dozen towns
in England that choose no burgess which ought to do it, ye
may be set in for one of those towns and (if) ye be friended.
Also in no wise forget not in all haste to get some goodly
ring (at the) price of 20s., or some pretty flower of the same
price, and not under, to give to Jane Rodon ; for she hath
been the most special labourer in your matter, and hath
promised her good will forth (in future) ; and she doth all
with her mistress. And (if) my lord chamberlain will he may
cause my Lord of Norfolk to come up sooner to the parliament

[1] *i.e.* make my Lord a present.
[2] William, Lord Hastings.

than he should do, and then he may appoint with him for you ere the farm corn be gathered. I proffered but £40., and if my lord chamberlain proffer my lady the remanent I can think it shall be taken ; my lady must have somewhat to buy her a coverchief besides my lord.

A supper that I paid for, where all the council was at Framlingham, 2s. 3d. and my costs at Framlingham, twice lying there by eight days, with 9s. 1½d. for costs of the country at Norwich draweth about 20s. I trow more. By our Lady if it be less stand to your harms, and sic remanet £5. 13s. 4d.

I ask no more good of you for all the service that I shall do you while the world standeth, but a goss hawk,[1] if any of my lord chamberlain's men or yours go to Calais, or if any be to get in London ; that is a mewed hawk, for she may make you sport when ye come into England a dozen years hence ; and to call upon you hourly, nightly, daily, dinner, supper, for this hawk, I pray no more but my brother (Edmund), J. Pampyng, Thyrston, J. Myryel, W. Pitt, T. Platting, Jude, Little Jack, Master Botoner, and W. Wood to boot, to which persons I pray you to commend me and if all these list (be disposed) to speak to you of this matter when Sir George Browne, W. Knyvet, R. Hyde, or any folk of worship and of my acquaintance be in your company, so that they may help forth (for all is little enough, and ye be not very well willing) I shall so purvey for them, and ever ye come to Norwich, and they with you, that they shall have as dainty victuals and as great plenty thereof for 1d. as they shall have of the treasurer of Calais for 15d., and ye peradventure a pye of Wymondham to boot ; now think on me good lord, for if I have not an hawk I shall wax fat for default of labour, and dead for default of company by my troth. No more, but I pray God send you all your desires, and me my mewed goss hawk in haste, or rather than fail a soar hawk [2] there is a grocer dwelling right over against the Well with two Buckets, a little from Saint Helen's, hath ever hawks to sell.

Written at Norwich the 21st day of September, in the 12th year of Edward IV.

JOHN PASTON.

[1] A " gosshawk " was the first and most highly esteemed kind of hawk.

[2] A hawk previous to the time that she had mewed her feathers.

Rather than fail, a tarssel [1] proved will occupy the time till I come to Calais.

NORWICH,
Monday, 21st of September 1472.
12 E. IV.

32. To my worshipful cousin, John Paston, be this bill delivered, &c.

COUSIN, I recommend me unto you, thanking you heartily for the great cheer ye made me and all my folks the last time that I was at Norwich ; and ye promised me that ye would never break the matter to Margery [2] unto such time as ye and I were at a point. But ye have made her such (an) advocate for you, that I may never have rest night or day for calling and crying upon to bring the said matter to effect, &c.

And, cousin, upon Friday is Saint Valentine's Day, and every bird chuseth him a make (mate) ; and if it like you to come on Thursday at night, and so purvey you that ye may abide there till Monday, I trust to God that ye shall so speak to mine husband ; and I shall pray that we shall bring the matter to a conclusion, &c.

> For, cousin, "it is but a simple oak,
> That's cut down at the first stroke,"

for ye will be reasonable I trust to God, which have you ever in his merciful keeping, &c.

By your cousin,
DAME ELIZABETH BREWS,
Otherwise shall be called by God's grace.[3]

Between the 9th and 14th of February, 1476–77.
16 E. IV.

33. To his worshipful brother, John Paston, be this delivered in haste.

RIGHT REVEREND AND WORSHIPFUL BROTHER, after all duties of recommendation I recommend me to you, desiring to hear

---

[1] Tiercel, i.e. the male of the gosshawk, so called because a third (tierce) less than the female.

[2] Daughter of Sir Thomas and Elizabeth Brews, of Stinton Hall.

[3] i.e. not cousin but cn.

of your prosperity and welfare, which I pray God long to continue to his pleasure and to your heart's desire ; letting you weet that I received a letter from you, in the which letter was 8d. with the which I should buy a pair of slippers.

Farthermore certifying you as for the 13s. 4d. which ye sent by a gentleman's man for my board, called Thomas Newton, was delivered to mine hostess, and so to my creancer (creditor), Mr. Thomas Stevenson ; and he heartily recommended him to you ; also ye sent me word in the letter of 12 lb. of figgs [1] and 8 lb. of raisins ; I have them not delivered, but I doubt not I shall have, for Alweder told me of them, and he said that they came after in another barge.

And as for the young gentlewoman, I will certify you how I first fell in acquaintance with her ; her father is dead, there be two sisters of them, the elder is just wedded ; at which wedding I was with mine hostess, and also desired (invited) by the gentleman himself, called William Swan, whose dwelling is in Eton. So it fortuned that mine hostess reported on me otherwise than I was worthy,[2] so that her mother commanded her to make me good cheer, and so in good faith she did ; she is not abiding where she is now, her dwelling is in London ; but her mother and she came to a place of hers five miles from Eton where the wedding was, for because it was nigh to the gentleman which wedded her daughter ; and on Monday next coming, that is to say, the first Monday of Clean Lent, her mother and she will go to the pardon at Sheene,[3] and so forth to London, and there to abide in a place of hers in Bow Churchyard ; and if it please you to inquire of her, her mother's name is Mistress Alborow, the name of the daughter is Margaret Alborow, the age of her is, by all likelyhood, eighteen or nineteen years at the farthest ; and as for the money and plate, it is ready whensoever she were wedded ; but as for the livelihood, I trow (I believe) not till after her mother's decease, but I cannot tell you for very certain, but you may know by inquiring.

And as for her beauty, judge you that when you see her, if so be that ye take the labour ; and specially behold her hands, for and if it be as it is told me, she is disposed to be thick.

---

[1] Food for Lent.
[2] *i.e.* beyond what I was worthy of.
[3] Now called Richmond.

And as for my coming from Eton, I lack nothing but versifying, which I trust to have with a little continuance.

> Quare, Quomodo. Non valet hora, valet mora.
> Unde di
> Arbore jam videas exemplum. Non die possunt
> Omnia suppleri, sed tu illa mora.

And these two verses aforesaid be of mine own making,

No more to you at this time, but God have you in his keeping.

Written at Eton the even of Saint Mathias [1] the Apostle, in haste, with the hand of your brother.

WILLIAM PASTON, junior.

ETON,

Wednesday, 23rd of February, 1478–9.

18 E. IV.

34. *The Inventory of English books, of John (Paston), made the 5th day of November, in the . . . . year of the reign of Edward IV.*

1. A Book had of my hostess at the George, ... of the Death of Arthur, beginning at Cassibelan.
   Guy Earl of Warwick.
   King Richard Cœur de Lyon.
   A Chronicle to Edward the III. Price   .

2. Item, a Book of Troilus, which William Br . . . . hath had near ten years, and lent it to Dame . . . .
   Wyngfeld, and there I saw it. . . . . worth   .

3. Item, a black Book, with the Legend of Lad . . . . . sans Mercy.
   The Parliament of Birds.
   The Temple of Glass.
   Palatyse and Scitacus.
   The Meditations of . . . . .
   The Green Knight . . . . worth   .

4. Item, a Book in print of the Play of the . . .

5. Item, a Book lent Midleton, and therein is—
   Belle Dame sans Mercy.
   The Parliament of Birds.

[1] 24th February.

Ballad of Guy and Colbrond,
. . . . of the Goose, the . . . . .
The Disputation between Hope and Despair.
. . . . . . Merchants.
The Life of Saint Chrystopher.

6. A red Book that Percival Robsart gave me ; of the
Meeds of the Mass .
The Lamentation of Child Ipotis.
A Prayer to the Vernicle, called the Abbey of the Holy
Ghost

7 Item, in quires, Tully de Senectute, in whereof there is
no more clear writing.

8. Item, in quires, Tully or Cypio [1] (Scipio) de Amicitia,
left with William Worcester . . . . . . worth   .

9. Item, in quires, a Book of the Policy of In . . . . .

10. Item, in quires, a Book de Sapientia, wherein the second
person is likened to Sapience.

11. Item, a Book de Othea (Wisdom), text and gloss, worth
in quires Memorandum ; mine old Book of Blazonings
of Arms.
Item, the new Book portrayed and blazoned.
Item, a Copy of Blazonings of Arms, and the . . . names
to be found by Letter (alphabetically).
Item, a Book with Arms portrayed in paper.
Memorandum ; my Book of Knighthood ; and the
manner of making of Knights ; of Justs, of Tourna-
ments ; fighting in Lists ; paces holden by Soldiers ;
and Challenges ; Statutes of War ; and de Regimine
principum . . . . worth   .
Item, a Book of new Statutes from Edward the IV.

5th of November. E. IV.

II. EXTRACTS FROM THE *STONOR PAPERS*

[With the exception of the *Paston Letters*, the most extensive
correspondence of the fifteenth century that has come down to
us is the *Stonor Letters and Papers*. These consist of more than
three hundred documents, chiefly letters written, or received, by
members of the Stonor family, which had been established at
Stonor, in Oxfordshire, about five miles north of Henley, as

[1] Perhaps a mistake for " Somnium Scipionis."

early as the thirteenth century. *The Stonor Letters and Papers,
1290–1483*, were edited from the original documents in the Public
Record Office by C. L. Kingsford in 1919 in two volumes (Camden
Society, Third Series, vols. xxix. and xxx.). The following
extracts are given in slightly modernized English.]

1. *A Weaver's Bill for Cloth to Mistress Stonor,*
21st December 1468.

ITEM to my mistress Stonor xvi yards of broad cloth, white
xid.
Item also vi yards of fine cloth xd. ob.[1]
Item also xvi yards of roset [2] of fine broad xid. ob.[1]
Item also vii yards of kersey that was made of the same
roset [2] xd.
Item also xiv yards of coarse roset broad, xid.
Item also xii yards of fine * * * re blue vd.
Item also xii ells of roset [2] kersey xd.
Sum xviis. xd.[3]

Everything reckoned between William Demnyst, Weaver
of Watlington, for weaving all manner of cloth, saving a white
piece, the which is at the fuller's. And this reckoning unto
Saint Thomas next afore Christmas in the IXth year of King
Edward the IVth paid.

2. *Sir William Sandes to Sir William Stonor.*

(Probably written *circ.* 1478–80)

RIGHT WORSHIPFUL AND TRUSTY COUSIN, I commend me
unto you in as hearty wise as I can and as a gentleman not
greatly acquainted with you, trusting in time to come to be
better acquainted with you. Sir, if it please you, I understand ye have a farmer at Penyton Meyse, the which as I
understand for his wilful disposition and negligent rule in
the same is both against the welfare of your mother and your
hereafter, for as I both hear and in part know he is a troublous
fellow not only with your tenants but as well with other
gentlemen's tenants in likewise : and so by this means he

---

[1] Halfpenny.
[2] Russet, coarse homespun cloth often of a reddish-brown colour
and mostly worn by the peasantry.
[3] There is some mistake in this total.

getteth himself but little love among them. And as I understand sometime as I walk in my recreation I may see that in
your woods he hath made great waste and destruction the
which should cause a great displeasure to me if it were done
in my woods as it is in yours, as ye may have larger understanding of this on your next coming into the country :
whereupon, if it please you, if case be that ye have made
no grant of the said farm, such favour as ye may I pray you
to show the * * * man, the which cometh with your Chaplain,
parson and curate of the said Penyton, and I trust he shall
deserve ut * * * to you after his power so that he may have
your good mastership : and as for his truth and such covenants
as he shall make with you, if ye desire me, I dare be bound
for him for his truth, and for such covenants that he maketh
I will find sufficient surety besides to perform in his behalf.
And upon this I have desired your parson to ride to you
with him to give you information of him ; what he is. And as
he knoweth right well he is for you and such a man as shall
please you and all your tenants and others also, of whose
coming I wot well they will be right glad. And Jesus preserve
you both body and soul.

Written at Andover on Corpus Christi day, hastily.

W. SANDES, Knight.

To my trusty and well beloved Cousin Sir William Stonor
this letter be delivered.

3. *Annys Wydeslade to Sir William Stonor.*

[This letter was written early in 1480 by Annys, the daughter of
John Wynnard, whose property lay in Devon and Cornwall.
She was a widow, and a few months after writing this letter
became Sir William Stonor's second wife.]

RIGHT WORSHIPFUL MASTER, I heartily commend me unto
you with all such service as I can or may : thanking you for
your kindness shown unto me, so poor a woman as I am, and
unto your Mastership undeserved : desiring to hear of your
welfare, the which I pray Almighty God to preserve you to
your most pleasure and heart's desire. May it please you to
have knowledge of my poor welfare : at the making of this
letter I was in good recovery (hele), and I trust God in short
space to be better : for now I am at liberty, whereof I thank

you, in my own house at Exeter. The physician will do his cunning upon me, but undertake me he will not, nor never did none in his life. Comfort in him I find and in my mind I think he will do me good. Furthermore the dealing of my father-in-law ye shall have knowledge of by a bill which Thomas Mathu shall deliver you. A very end between him and me will not be had unto the time of your coming, which I trust will not be long. Methinketh a thousand years gone since I heard any tidings from you. And in good faith ye may say unto me that I am unkind that I wrote not nor sent unto you since your last being at Wideslade. The cause is, for mine excuse, that I have been in Hell, where I had little comfort, but as soon as I came to Exeter then was I in Heaven ; and because that I am now in joy I do send you this letter. Master, it is so that the physician is in hands with me, and he desireth to have me in cure three months, for which cause I pray you to remember your Worship and my poor quest. And as I amend I shall put you in knowledge by the grace of Jesu, who may He keep you."

From your true lover,

ANNYS WYDESLADE.

4. *A Physician's* [1] *Prescription.*

William Goldwyn to John Byrell.

[The prescription was probably intended for the second Lady Stonor in 1480.]

Sirroporum rosarum epatice,[2] mirtillorum, anᵃ [3] ʒiii. endive, compot, berberis, anᵃ ʒiiii. aquarum pocculatarum de stipitibus rosarum, plantaginis, mirtillorum, acedule, anᵃ ʒii. absinthii, foliorum quercus, anᵃ ʒi.ss. endivie commisceantur, etc. etc.

SIR, I recommend me unto you, praying you heartily as I may that ye have the oversight in the serving of this bill, as my trust is in you : for this is for a special Mistress of

---

[1] Cf. Chaucer's " Prologue," p. 286.

[2] Common liverwort.

[3] anᵃ represents the Greek ἀνα, " to the amount of." It is curious to find a Greek word in use as early as this. It is probably a survival from ancient times.

mine. And with the grace of God it shall not be long ere
I see you. And then I purpose to tarry with you. Written
at Stonor the XII day of June.

MR. W. GOLDWYN.

To John Byrell the elder, Apothecary, dwelling in
Bucklers Bury, be this bill delivered.

5. *Thomas Bank to Sir William Stonor.*

[Dr. Thomas Bank was Rector of Lincoln College, Oxford, 1493–
    1509. He wrote this letter on 16th January 1482.]

MAY it please your mastership to understand that I have
been with Dr. Sutton, our Commissary, and I did show him
how your mastership both was and is disposed to the
university,[1] as in finding and relieving of divers scholars to
the same and also by relieving of many other such as come
to your mastership at divers times in the year, like as Mr.
Eadmunde, Mr. Flynte, Mr. Kyckall, and I with other more
did relate : of whom I desired the commissary to inquire
your worshipful and gentle behaviour to them, and to each
one of them, because I would that he should give more
credence to my information. Also, Sir, I was with my Lord
Edward [2] and Master Stanley,[3] and informed them in like
wise, and did show both to my Lord Edward and Master
Stanley, and to master commissary, the dealing and the
behaviour of certain scholars against your mastership and
your servants, especially when they come to the University
for such necessities as ye have to do there : and then my
Lord Edward and Master Stanley desired the commissary
at their instance to see a remedy, so that your servants
might both come and go to and from the University in safeguard of their bodies : and the commissary said that he
would do as much as he might by the virtue of his office to
provide a remedy ; notwithstanding all this, meseems the

---

[1] For university life, cf. pp. 145 sqq. ; also Chaucer's " Clerk of
Oxenford," pp. 285 sqq. ; also the *Paston Letters*, p. 330.

[2] One of the younger sons of John de la Pole, Duke of Suffolk.
He was studying at Oxford at this time.

[3] James, son of Sir Thomas Stanley, afterwards Earl of Derby.
He was Bishop of Ely 1506–15. (*N.B.* the deference paid to these
young nobles. It is characteristic of the period of the Wars of the
Roses.)

most sure way is your own way, to send for them by privy seals. Cawey is beneficed in Oxford : he may not flee. Sir, I said to the commissary that ye would send for them by privy seals, unless the University did see a remedy : and the commissary said if ye did so he could not blame you, insomuch as they will not be ruled. No more, save I beseech Jesu preserve you and yours evermore, Amen. From Oxford the xvi day of January.

Your servant and bedeman,
THOMAS BANK.

CHAPTER IX

THE END OF THE MIDDLE AGES

I. THE LIBEL OF ENGLISH POLICY

[The date of this important political poem is shown by internal evidence to be 1436. It is published in *Political Songs and Poems relating to English History*, by Thomas Wright, vol. ii. pp. 157–205, 1861 (Rolls Series, 14b). The poem is here given in its entirety, with the exception of four sections forming the eleventh and twelfth "Chapitles."]

HERE BEGINNETH THE PROLOGE OF THE PROCESSE OF THE LIBELLE OF ENGLYSHE POLYCYE, EXHORTYNGE ALL ENGLANDE TO KEPE (GUARD) THE SEE ENVIROUN (AROUND), AND NAMELYE THE NARROWE SEE, SHEWYNGE WHATE PROFETE COUMETH THEREOF AND ALSO WORSHYPE AND SALVACIOUN TO ENGLANDE AND TO ALLE ENGLYSHE MENNE.

THE trewe processe of Englysh polycye,
  Of utterwarde to kepe thys regne [1] in rest
  Of oure England, that no man may denye,
Nere say of soth but one of the best
Is thys, that who seith southe, northe, est and west,
Cheryshe marchandyse, kepe thamyralte,
That we bee maysteres of the narowe see.[2]

[1] Kingdom.
[2] Cf. Chaucer's "Merchant," p. 285.

For Sigesmonde [1] the grete emperoure,
Whyche yet regneth, whan he was in this londe
Wyth kynge Herry the V[te], prince of honoure
Here moche glorye as hym thoughte [2] he founde ;
A myghty londe, whyche hadde take on honde
To werre in Ffraunce and make mortalite
And evere welle kept rounde about the see.

And to the kynge thus he seyde, " My brothere "
Whan he perecyved too townes Calys [3] and Dovere,
" Of alle your townes to chese of one and othere
To kepe the see and sone to come overe
To werre oughtwardes and your regne to recovere,
Kepe these two townes, Sire, and your magesté.
As your tweyne eyne [4] to kepe the narowe see."

Ffor if this see be kepe in tyme of werre,
Who cane here pass withoughte daungere and woo ?
Who may eschape, who may myschef dyfferre ?
What marchandye may for by be agoo ?
Ffor nedes hem muste take truse every ffo [5]
Fflaundres, and Spayne, and othere, trust to me
Or ellis hyndered all for thye narowe see.

Therfore I caste me by a lytele wrytinge
To shewe att eye thys conclusione,
Ffor concyens [6] and for myne acquytynge [7]
Agenst God [8] and ageyne abuyson,
And cowardyse and to oure enmyes confusione ;
Ffor iiij thynges our noble sheweth to me,
Kyng, shype, and swerde, and power of the see.

Where bene our shippes ? where bene oure swerdes become ?
Oure enmyes bid for the shippe set a shepe.
Allas ! Oure reule halteth, hit it benome ;
Who dare weel say that lordeshyppe shulde take kepe ?
I wolle asaye, thoughe myne herte gynne to wepe,
To do thys werke, yf we wole ever the, [9]
Ffor verry shame, to kepe aboute the see.

---

[1] The Emperor Sigismund of Luxembourg (1411–37.)
[2] *hym thoughte* : it seemed to him.   [3] Calais.   [4] Two eyes.
[5] " For every enemy will be compelled to make peace."
[6] Conscience.   [7] Acquittal.   [8] On God's part.   [9] Flourish.

Shalle any prynce, what so be hys name,
Wheche hathe nobles moche lyche oures,
Be lorde of see, and Fflemmyngis to oure blame
Stoppe us, take us, and so make fade the floures
Of Englysshe state, and disteyne oure honoures ?
Ffor cowardyse, allas ! hit shulde so be ;
Therfore I gynne to wryte now of the see.

Of the commodytes of Spayne and of Fflaundres.
The ffyrste Chapitle.

Knowe welle alle men that profites certayne,
Commodytes called, commynge out of Spayne,
And marchandy, who so wylle wete what that is,
Bene fygues, raysyns, wyne bastarde, and dates ;
And lycorys, Syvyle Oyle, and grayne,
Whyte Castelle sope, and wax, is not in vayne ;
Iren, wolle, wadmole, gotefet, kydefel also,
Ffor poynt-makers fulle nedefulle be the ij ;
Saffron, quiksilver, whiche arne Spaynes marchandy,
Is into Fflaundres shypped fulle craftylye
Unto Bruges, as to here staple fayre,
The haven of Sluse here havene for here repayre,
Whiche is cleped Swyn, thaire shyppes gydynge,
Where many wessell and fayre arne abydynge.
But these merchandes, wyth there shyppes greet,
And such chaffare as they bye and gette
By the weyes, most nede take one honde
By the costes to passe of our Englonde.
Betwyxt Dover and Calys, thys is no doute,
Who can weelle ellis suche mater bringe aboute.
And whenne these seyde marchauntz discharged be
Of marchaundy in Fflaundres neere the see,
Than they be charged agayn wyth marchaundy
That to Fflaundres bougeth full rychelye ;
Ffyne clothe of Ipre, that named better than oure is,
Cloothe of Curtryke, fyne cloothe of alle coloures,
Moche ffustyane and also lynen cloothe.
But ye Fflemmyngis, yf ye be nor wrothe,
The grete substaunce of youre cloothe, at the fulle,
Ye wot ye make hit of your Englissh wolle.
Thanne may hit not synke in mannes brayne,
But that hit most, this marchaundy of Spayne,

But ought and inne by oure costes passe ;
He that seyde nay, in wytte was lyche an asse.
Thus if thys see werre kepte, I dare well sayne,
Wee shulde have pease with the growndes tweyne.
Ffor Spayne and Fflaundres is as yche othere brothere.
And nethere may well lyve wythowght othere.
The may not lyven to, mayntene there degrees,
Wythought oure Englysshe commodytees,
Wolle and tynne ; for the wolle of Englonde
Susteyneth the comons Fflemmyngis I understonde.
Thane yf Englonde wolde hys wolle restreyne
Ffrome Fflaundres, thys ffoloweth in certayne,
Fflaundres of nede must wyth us have pease
Or ellis he is distroyde, wythowght lees.
Also yef Fflaundres thus distroyed bee,
Some marchaundy of Spayne wolle nevere ithe ;
Ffor distroyed hit is, and, as in cheffe,
The wolle of Spayne hit cometh not to presse,
But if it be toseed and menged well
Amonges Englysshe wolle the gretter delle.
Ffor Spayneshe wolle in Fflaundres draperd is,
And ever hath be, that men have mynde of this ;
And yet woolle is one of the cheffe marchaundy
That longeth to Spayne, who so woll aspye ;
Hit is of lytelle valeue, trust unto me,
Wyth Englysshe wolle but if it menged be.
Thus if the see be kepte, then herkene hedere,
Yff these ii londes comene not togedere,
So that the fflete of Fflaundres passe nought,
That in the narrowe see he be not brought
Into Rochelle, to feche the fumose wine,
Nor into Britonuse bay for salt so fyne,
What is then Spayne ? what is Fflaundres also ?
As who seyde, nought, the thryfte is ago.
Ffor the lytelle londe of Fflaundres is
But a staple of other longes, iwys,
And alle that growth in Fflaundres, greyne and sede,
May not a moneth ffynde hem mete of brede.
What hath thenne Fflaundres, be Fflemmyngis leffe or lothe,
But a lytelle madere and Flemmyshe cloothe ?
By drapynge of oure woolle in substaunce
Lyvene here comons, this is here governaunce ;

Wythought whyche they may not leve at ease,
Thus moste hem sterve, or wyth us most have pease.

Of the commoditees of Portingalle.   The ij captle.

The marchaundy also of Portyngale
To dyverse londes torne into sale.
Portyngalers wyth us have trought one hande,
Whose marchaundy cometh moche into Englande.
They bene oure ffrendes wyth there commoditez.
And wee Englysshe passed into there countrees.
Here londe hathe oyle, wyne, osey, wex, and greyne ;
Ffygues, reysyns, hony and cordeweyne ;
Dates and salt, hydes and suche marchaundy.
And if they wolde to Fflaundres passe forth bye,
They schulde not be suffrede ones ner twyes,
Ffor supportynge of oure cruelle enmyes ;
That is to saye Fflemmyngis wyth here gyle,
Ffor chaungeable they are in lytelle whyle.
Than I conclude by resons many moo,
Yf wee sufferede nethere ffrende nere ffoo,
What soo enmyes and so supportynge,
Passe for-by us in tyme of werrynge,
Sethe oure ffrendys wolle not bene in causse
Of oure hyndrenge, yf reason lede thy clausse.
Than nede frome Fflaundres pease shulde by to us sought,
And othere londes shulde seche pease, doute nought.
Ffor Fflaundres is staple, as men tell me,
To alle nacyons of Crystianté.

*The commodytés of Pety Brytagne, wyth here revers [1] on
the see.   The iij capitle.*

Fforthermore to wrytene I hame fayne,
Somwhate spekynge of the Lytell Bretayne ;
Commodite therof there is and was,
Salt and wynes, creste clothe,[2] and canvasse ;
And the londe of Fflaundres sekerly
Is the staple of there marchaundy ;
Wheche marchaundy may not passe awey,
But by the coste of Englonde, this is no nay.

[1] *revers* : robbers, pirates.
[2] *Creste clothe* ; a kind of fine linen.

24

And this of Bretayn, who so truth levys,
Are the grettest rovers and the grettest thevys
That have bene in the see many oone yere;
That oure marchauntes have bowght full dere.
Ffor they have take notable gode of oures
On thys seyde see, those false coloured pelours,
Called of Seynt Malouse,[1] and elles where,
Wheche to there duke none obeysaunce will bere.
Wyth suche colours we have bene hindred sore,
And fayned pease is called no werre herefore.
Thus have they bene in dyverse costes manye
Of oure England, mo than reherse can I;
In Northfolke coostes, and othere places aboutte,
And robbed and brente and slayne by many a routte,
And they have also ransonned toune by toune,
That into the regnes of bost have ronne here soune;
Wyche hath bene ruthe unto thys realme and shame;
They that the see shulde kepe are moche to blame,
Ffor Bretayne is of easy reputasyoun,
And seynt Malouse turneth hem to reprobacioun.

*A storie of kynge Edwarde the iij^{de} hys ordynaunce
for Bretayne.*

Here brynge I in a storye to me lente,
What a goode squyere in tyme of parlemente,
Toke unto me welle wretene in a scrowe,
That I have comonde bothe wyth hygh and lowe,
Of whyche all mene accordene in to one,
That hit was done not monye yeris agone,
But when noble kynge Edwarde the thirde
Regned in grace, ryght thus hit betyde.
Ffor he hadde a manere gelozye
To hys marchauntes, and loved hem hartelye.
He felte the weyes to reule well the see,
Whereby marchauntes myght have prosperité,
That fro Harflewe [2] and Hondflewe [3] dyd he makene,
And grete werres that tyme were undertakene
Betwyx the kynge and the duke of Bretayne;
At last to falle to pease bothe were they feyne.
Upon the whyche, made by convencioun,
Oure marchaundys made hem redy boune

[1] St. Malo in Brittany.   [2] Harfleur.   [3] Honfleur.

Towarde Bretayne to lede here marchaundye,
Wenynge hem frendes, and wente forthe boldelye.
But sone anone oure marchaundes were itake,
And wee spede nevere the bettere for treuse sakes.
They loste here goode, here moné, and spendynge ;
But there compleynte come unto the kynge.
Then wex he wrothe, and to the duke he sente,
And compleyned that such harme was hente
By convencions, and pease made so refused.
Whiche duke sent ageyne, and hym excused,
Rehersynge that the mount of Seynte Michele
And Seynt Malouse wolde never a dele
By subject unto his governaunce,
Ner be undere his obeysaunce ;
And so they did withouten hym that dede.
But whan the kynge anone had takene hede,
He in his herte set a jugemente,
Wythoute callynge of ony parlemente,
Or grete tary to take longe avyse,
To fortefye anone he dyd devyse
Of Englysshe townes iij., that is to seye
Dertmouth, Plymmouthe, the third it is Ffoweye,
And gaffe hem helpe and notable puissance,
Wyth insistence set hem in governaunce
Upon Pety Bretayn for to werre,
That gode see-menne wolde no more deferre,
But bete theme home, and that they might not
    route,
To be prysoners, and lernyd hem for to loutte.[1]
And efte the duke an ensample wysse
Wrote to the kynge, as he flyrste did dewysse,
Hym excusynge ; but oure meny wode
Wyth grete poure passed overe the fflode,
And verrie forth unto the dukes londe,
And had neygh destrued free and bonde.
But than the duke knewe that the townes three
Shulde have loste all hys natale cuntree,
Undertoke by sewrté trewe, not false,
Ffor Mount Mychelle and Seinte Malouse als,
And othere partees of the Lytelle Bretaynne,
Whyche to obeye, as seyde was, were nott fayne,

[1] *lernyd . . . loutte* : taught them to bow to his will.

The duke hymselfe for all dyd undertake,
Wyth all hys herte a full pease dyd he make,
So that in all the lyffe tyme of the kynge
Marchaundes hadde pease wythowtene werrynge.
He made a statute for Lumbardes in thys londe,
That they shulde in no wysse take one honde
Here to enhabite, here to charge and to dyscharge,
Butt xl. dayes, nomore tyme had they large.
Thys good kynge, be wytt of suche appreffe [1]
Kepte hys marchauntes and the see fro myscheffe.

*Of the commodites of Scotelonde, and drapynge of her wolle
in Fflaundres.   The iiij chapitle.*

Moreovere of Scotelonde the commoditees
Ar ffelles, hydes, and of wolle the ffleesse.
And alle thesse muste passe bye us aweye
Into Fflaundres by Englonde, soth to saye.
And alle her wolle was draped for to selle
In the townes of Poperynge and of Belle,
Whyche my lorde of Glowcester [2] wyth ire
Ffor here ffalshede sett upon a ffyre.
And yet they of Belle and Poperynge
Cowde never drapere here wolle for any thynge,
But if they hadde Englysshe wolle wythalle.
Oure godely wolle that is so generalle
Nedefulle to hem in Spayne and Scotelonde als,
And othere costis, this sentence is not fals.
Ye worthi marchauntes, I do it upon yow,
I have this lerned, ye wott wele where and howe ;
Ye wotte the staple of that marchaundye
Of this Scotelonde is Fflaundres sekerlye.
And the Scottes bene chargede, knowene at the eye,
Out of Fflaundres wyth lytyll mercerye,
And grete plentee of haburdasshers ware,
And halfe here shippes wyth carte whelys bare,
And wyth barrowes, are laden as in substaunce.
Thus most rude ware be in here chevesaunce ;
So they may not forbere thys Fflemysshe londe.
Therefor if we wolde manly take on honde

---

[1] *appreffe* : contrivance.
[2] Humphrey, Duke of Gloucester, younger brother of Henry V.
He was Protector of England during the minority of Henry VI.

To kepe this see fro Fflaundres and fro Spayne,
And fro Scotelonde, lych as fro Pety Bretayne,
Wee schulde ryght sone have pease for all here bostis ;
Ffor they muste nede passe by oure Englysshe costis.

Of the Commoditees of Pruse, and Hyghe Duche menne,
and Esterlynges.   The v. chapitle.

Now goo wee fforthe to the commoditees
That cometh to Pruse in too manere degrees ;
Ffor too manere peple have suche use,
This is to saye, Highe Duch men of Pruse
And Esterlynges,, whyche myghte not be forborne
Oute of Flaundres, but it were verrely lorne.
Ffor they bringe in the substaunce of the beere
That they drinken fele [1] to goode chepe, not dere.
Ye have herde that twoo Fflemmynges togedere
Wol undertake, or they goo any whethere,
Or they rise onys, to drinke a barille fulle
Of gode berkyne [2] so sore they hale and pulle,
Under the borde they pissen as they sitte ;
This cometh of covenant of a worthy witte.
Wythouten Calise in ther buttere the cakked,
Whan they flede home, and when they leysere lakked
To hold here sege, they went like as a doo ;
Wel was that Fflemmynge that myght trusse and goo.
Ffor fere they turned bake, and hyede fast ;
Mi lorde of Gloucestre made them go agaste
Wyth his commynge, and sought them in here londe,
And brente and slowe as he hadded take on honde ;
So that oure enmyse durste not byde nor stere,
They flede to mewe, they durste no more appere.
Then his meyné seyden that he was dede,
Till we were goo, ther was non better rede.
Ffy ! cowardy knyghthode was aslepe,
As dede their duk yn mew they did hym kepe
Rebukede sore for evere so shamefully
Unto here uttere everlastinge vylany.

After bere and bacon, odre gode commodités usene.

Now bere and bacon bene fro Pruse ibroughte
Into Fflaundres, as loved and fere isoughte ;

[1] *fele* : much.   [2] *berkyne* : beer.

Osmonde,[1] coppre, bow-staffes, stile,[2] and wex.
Peltre-ware [3] and grey,[4] pych, terre, borde, and flex.
And Coleyne threde, fustiane, and canvasse.
Carde, bokeram, of olde tyme thus it wase.
But the Fflemmyngis amonge these thinges dere
In comen loven beste bacon and bere.
Thus arn they hogges, and drynken well ataunt,[5]
Ffare wele, Fflemynge, hay, harys [6] hay, avaunt.
Also Pruse mene make here aventure
Of plate of sylvere, of wegges [7] gode and sure
In grete plenté, whiche they bringe and bye
Oute of londes of Bealme and Hungrye ;
Which is encrese ful grete unto thys londe.
And thei bene laden, I understonde,
Wyth woollen clothe alle manere of coloures,
By dyers craftes ful dyverse that bene oures.
And they aventure ful gretly unto the Baye
Ffor salte, that is nedefulle wythoute naye.
Thus if they wolde not oure frendys bee,
Wee myght lyghtlye stope hem in the see ;
They shulde not passe oure stremes wythoutene leve,
It wolde not be, but if we shulde hem greve.

*Of the Commoditees of the Januays,[8] and here grette
karekkys.[9]   The vj chapitle.*

The Januays comynge in sondre wyses
Into this londe, wyth dyverse marchaundyses,
In grete karrekkis arrayde withouten lake,
Wyth clothes of golde, silke, and pepir blake,
They bringe wyth hem, and of wood grete plenté,
Wolle, oyle, woad aschen, by vessels in the see,
Coton, roche-alum, and gode gold of Jene.[10]
And they will be charged wyth wolle ageyne, I wene.
And wollene clothe of owres of colours alle.
And they aventure, as ofte it dothe byfalle,
Into Fflaundres wyth such thynges as they bye,
That is here cheffe staple sykerlye ;

---

[1] *Osmonde* : a kind of iron.
[2] *stile* : steel.
[3] *Peltre-ware* ; raw-hides.
[4] *grey* ; badger-skins or furs.
[5] *ataunt* : so much.
[6] *harys* : hares.
[7] *wegges* : wedges.
[8] *Januays* : Genoese.
[9] *karekkys* ; large ships or galleons.
[10] *Jene* : Genoa.

And if they wolde be oure fulle ennemyse,
They shulde not passe our stremez with merchaundyse.

The commodités and nycetees of Venicyans and Florentynes,
with there galees.   The vij chapitle.

But the grete galees of Venees and Fflorence
Be wel laden wyth thinges of complacence,
Alle spicerye and of grocers ware,
Wyth swete wynes, alle manere of chaffare,
Apes, and japes [1] and marmusettes taylede,
Nifles,[2] trifles, that litelle have availede,
And thynges wyth whiche they fetely blere oure eye,
Wyth thynges not enduryng that we bye ;
Ffor mocke of this chaffare that is wastable
Mighte be forborne for dere and dyssevable
And that I wene, as for infirmities
In oure Englonde is suche commoditees,
Wuthouten helpe of any othere londe,
Whych by wytte and practike bethe ifounde,
That alle humors might be voyded sure ;
Whych that we gledre wyth oure Englush cure,
That wee shulde have no nede to skamonye [3]
Turbit, euforbe [4] correctid, diagredie,
Rubarde, sené, and yet they bene to nedefulle ;
But I knowe thynges also spedsfulle,
That growene here, as these thynges seyde ;
Lett of this matere no mane be dysmayde,
But that a man may voyde infirmytee
Wythoute degrees fet fro beyonde the see.
And yett there shulde excepte be ony thynge,
It were but sugre, trust to my seyinge.
He that trustith not to my seyinge and sentence,
Lett hym better serche experience.
In this mater I wole not ferthere prese,
Whoso not beleveth, let hum leve and cease.
Thus these galeise for this lykynge ware,
And etynge ware, bere hens oure beste chaffare,
Clothe, wolle, and tynne, whiche, as I seyde beforne,
Oute of this londe werste myghte be forborne.

[1] *japes* : tricks.   [2] *Nifles* : nick-nacks.
[3] *skamonye* : scammony, a plant used medicinally.
[4] *euforbe* : a plant, purge.

Ffor eche other londe of necessité
Have grete nede to by some of the thre ;
And wee resseyve of hem into this cooste
Ware and chaffare that lyghtlye wol be loste.
And wolde Jhesu that oure lordis wolde
Considre this wel, both yonge and olde ;
Namelye olde, that have experience,
That myghte the yonge exorten to prudence.
What harme, what hurt, and what hinderance
Is done to us unto youre grete grevaunce,
Of suche londes and of such nacions ?
As experte men knowe by probacions ;
By wretynge as discured oure counsayles,
And false coloure alwey the countertayles
Of oure enmyes, that doth us hinderynge
Unto oure goodes, oure realme, and to the kynge ;
As wysse men have shewed welle at eye,
And alle this is coloured by marchaundrye.

An ensampelle of desceytte.

Also they bere the golde out of thys londe,
And souketh the thryfte awey oute of oure honde,
As the waffore [1] soukethe honye fro the bee
So mynuceth [2] oure commodite.
Now wolle ye here how they in Cotteswolde
Were wont to borrowe, or they schulde be solde,
Here wolle gode, as for yere and yere,
Of clothe and tynne they did in lych [3] manere
And in her galeys schyppe this marchaundye ?
Than sone at Venice of them men wil it bye,
Then utterne [4] there the chaffare be the payse.
And lyghtly als ther they make her reys.
And whan tho gode bene at Venice solde,
Than to carrye her chaunge they ben fulle bolde
Into Fflaundres, whan thei this money have,
They will it profre there sotilté to save,
So Englysshe marchaundis to yeve it out by exchaunge.
To be paid agayn, thei make not straunge,
Here in Englonde, semynge for the better,
At the reseyvinge and syght of the lettir,

[1] *waffore* : wasp.
[2] *mynuceth* : diminishes.
[3] *lych* : like.
[4] *utterne* : they utter.

By iiij pens lesse in the noble rounde,
That is xij pens in the golden pounde.
And yf we wolle have of paymente,
A fulle monythe than moste hym nedes assente,
To viij pens losse, that is shellyngis tweyne
In the Englysshe pounde, what is that to seye,
But iij shyllingis, so that in pounde felle
Ffor hurt and harme harde is wyth hem to delle.
And whenne Englysshe marchaundys have contente
This eschaunge in Englonde of assente,
That these seyde Veneciance have in wone,
And Florentynes, to bere here golde sone
Overe the see into Flaundres ageyne.
And thus they live in Flaundres, sothe to sayne,
And in London, wyth suche chevesaunce
That men call usuré, to oure losse and hinderaunce.

Anothere exemple of disceytte.

Now listen welle how they made us a baleys [1]
Whan they borwed at the towne of Caleys,
As they were wonte, ther wolle that was hem lente,
Ffor yere and yere they schulde make paymente,
And some tyme als too yere and too yere ;
This was fayre lone, but yette wolle ye here
How they to Bruges wolde her wolles carye,
And for hem take paymente wythouten tarye,
And selle it faste for redy money in honde ?
Ffor fifty pounde of money of losse they wolde not wonde
In a thousand pounde, and live therebye.
Tylle the day of paymente easylye,
Some ageyne in exchaunge makynge,
Ffulle lyke usurie, as men make undertakynge.
Than whan thys payment of a thousande pounde
Was welle contente, they shulde have chaffare sounde,
Yff they wolde fro the staple fulle
Reseyve ageyne ther thousande pounde in wolle.
And thus they wolde, if we will beleve,
Wypen our nose with our owne sleve ;
Thow this proverbe be homly and undew,
Yet be liklynesse it is for soth fulle trew.
In Cotteswolde also they ryde aboute,

[1] *baleys* : rod.

And al Englonde, and bien, wythouten doute,
What hem liste, wythe fredome and fraunchise,
More then we Englisshe may getyn in any wyse.
But wolde God that, wythoute lenger delayse,
These galeise were unfraught in xl daies,
And in those xl dayes charged ageyne ;
And that they myght be put to certeyne
To go to oste,[1] as wee ther wyth hem doo.
It were expediente that they did right soo
As we do there ; if the kynge wolde itt,
A ! what worschip wolde falle to Englysse witte !
What profite also to oure marchaundye,
Whiche wolde of nede be cherisshed hartelye !
Ffor I wolde wete why nowe oure navey fayleth,
When many a foo us at oure dorre assayleth,
Now in these dayes, that, if there come a nede,
What navey shulde wee have it is to drede.
In Danemarke ware fulle noble conquerours
In tyme passed, fulle worthy werriours,
Whiche when they had here marchaundes destroyde,
To poverte they felle, thus were they noyede ;
And so they stonde at myscheffe at this daye ;
This lerned I late, welle wryten, this no naye.
Therefore be ware, I can no better wylle,
Yf grace it wole of other mennys perylle ;
Ffor yef marchaundes were cherysshede to here spede,
We were not lykelye to fayle in ony nede.
Yff they be riche, than in prosperité
Schalbe oure londe, lordes, and comonté.
And in worship nowe think I on the sonne
Of marchaundye, Richarde of Whitingdone,
That loode-sterre and chefe chosen ffloure,
Whate hathe by hym oure England of honoure ?
And whate profite hathe bene of his richesse ?
And yet lasteth dayly in worthinesse,
That penne and papere may not me suffice
Him to describe, so high he was of prise ;
Above marchaundis to sette him one of the beste,
I can no more, but God have hym in reste.

---

[1] *to go to oste* : to go to a host, *i.e.* take lodgings at the house of someone who would be surety for them. Foreigners were usually required to do this.

Now the principalle matere.

What reason is it that wee schulde go to oste [1]
In there cuntrees, and in the Englisshe coste
They schulde not so, but have more liberté
Than wee oure selfe ? now, alle so mot I the,
I wolde men shulde to giftis take no hede
That lettith oure thinge publique for to spede ;
Ffor this wee see welle every day at eye,
Geftes and festes stopene oure pollicye.
Now se that fooles bene eyther they or wee,
But evere wee have the warse in this contré.
Therefore lett hem unto oste go here,
Or be we free wyth hem in lyke manere
In these contrés ; and if it wolle not bee,
Compelle them unto oste, and ye shall se
Moche avauntage, and muche profite arise,
Moche more than I write can in any wyse.

Of oure charge and discharge at her martis.

Conseyve welle here that Englysshe men at martis
Be discharged, for alle her craftes and artes,
In the Braban [2] of her marchaundy
In xiiij dayes, and ageyne hastely
In the same dayes xiiij are charged efte ;
And yf they byde lenger alle is berefte,
Anone they schulde forget here godes alle,
Or marchaundry, it schulde no bettere falle.
And wee to martis of Braban charged bene
Wyth Englyssh clothe, fulle gode and feyre to seyne,
Wee bene ageyne charged with merceyre,
Haburdasshere ware, and wyth grocerye.
To wyche martis, that Englisshe men call feyres,
Iche nacion ofte maketh here repayeres,
Englysshe and Frensh, Lumbardes, Januayes,[3]
Cathalones,[4] theder they take there wayes,
Scottes, Spaynardes, Iresshmen they abydes,
Wythe grete plenté bringinge of salte hydes.

[1] *Vide supra*, p. 378, footnote.
[2] *Braban* ; the province of Brabant in the Netherlands.
[3] *Januayes* : Genoese.
[4] *Cathalones* ; Catalans, from Catalonia in N.E. Spain.

And I here saye that wee in Braban lye,
Fflaundres and Seland, wee bye more marchaundy
In comon use, then done alle other nacions ;
This have I herde of marchaundes relacions.
And yff the Englysshe be not in the martis,
They bene febelle, and as noughte bene here partes ;
Ffor they bye more, and fro purse put owte
More marchaundy than alle othere rowte.
Kepte than the see, shyppes schulde not bringe ne feche,
And than the carreys wolde not theder streche ;
And so the martes wolde full evel thee,
If we manly kepte aboute the see.

*Of the commoditees of Braban and Selande [1] and Henaulde,[2]
and marchaundyses caryed by londe to the martes. The
viij capitle.*

Yit marchaundy of Braban and Selande [1]
The madre [3] and woode [4] that dyers take on hande
To dyne with, garleke and onjons,
And salt fysshe als for husbond and comons ;
But they of Holonde at Caleys byene oure felles,[5]
And oure wolles, that Englyshe men hem selles.
And the chefare that Englysshe men do byene
In the martis, that noman may denyene,
Is not made in Braban that cuntré,
It commeth frome out of·Henaulde, not be the see,
But alle by londe by carris,[6] and frome Fraunce,
Burgoyne, Coleyne,[7] Camerete,[8] in substaunce.
Therfore at martis yf there be a restreynte,
Men seyne pleynly, that liste no fables peynte,
Yf Englisshe men be wythdrawene awey,
Is grete rebuke and losse to her affraye.
As though wee sent into the londe of Fraunce
Tenne thousande peple, men of gode puissaunce,
To werre unto her hynderynge multiphary ;
So bene oure Englysshe marchauntes necessary.

[1] *Selande* : Zeeland in Holland.
[2] *Henaulde* : Hainault in Belgium.
[3] *madre* : madder.
[4] *woode* : woad.
[5] *felles* : hides.
[6] *carris* : carts.
[7] *Coleyne* : Cologne.
[8] *Camerete* : (?) Cambrai.

Yf it be thus assay, and we schall weten
Of men experte, by whom I have this wrytene.
Ffor seyde is that this carted marchaundye
Drawethe in valew as moche verralye
As alle the gode that commethe in shippes thedyre,
Whyche Englissche men bye moste nad bring it gedire.
Ffor here martis bene feble, shame to saye,
But Englisshe men thedire dresse here waye.

Conclusion of this deppendinge of kepinge of the see.

Than I conclude, yff nevere so moche by londe
Werre by carres brought unto there honde,
Yff welle the see were kepte in governaunce,
They shulde by see have no delyveraunce,
Wee shulde hem stoppe, and wee shulde hem destroy,
As prysoners wee shulde hem brynge to noy ;
And so wee shulde of oure cruelle enmysse
Make our ffrendes for fere of marchaundysse
Yff they were not suffred for to passe
Into Fflaundres ; but we be frayle as glasse,
And also bretylle, not thought, never abydynge,
But when grace shynethe sone are wee slydynge.
We woll it not reseyve in any wysse ;
That maken luste, envye, and covetysse.
Expoune me this, and ye shall sothe it fynde,
Bere it aweye, and kepe it in youre mynde.

Thenayle of this conclusioun.

Than shulde worshyp unto our noble be,
In feet and forme to lorde and magesté ;
Liche as the seale the gretteste of this londe
On the one syde hathe, as I understonde,
A prince rydynge wyth his swerde idraue,
In the othere syde sittynge, sothe it is in sawe,
Betokenynge goode reule and ponneshynge
In verry ded of Englande by the kynge.
And hit is so, God blessed mote he bee ;
So one lyche wysse I wolde were on the see.
By the noble that swerde schulde have powere,
And the shippes one the see aboute us here.
What nedeth a garlande, whyche is made of ivye,
Shew a tavern wynelesse, also thryve I ;

Yf men were wysely, the Frenshmen and Flemmynge
Shulde bere no state in see by werrynge.

Of Hankyne Lyons.

Thane Hankyne Lyons shulde not be so bolde
To stoppe wyne, and shippes for to holde,
Unto oure shame ; he hadde be betene thens.
Allas ! Allas ! why dede wee these offence,
Ffully to shende the olde Englysshe fames,
And the profites of Englonde, and there names ?
Why is this powere called of covetise
Wyth ffals colours caste beforne oure eyes ?
That if goode men ben called werryours
Wolde take the see for the comon socours,
And purge the see unto oure grete avayle,
And wynne hem gode, and have up the sayle,
And one oure enmyes there lyves to juparte,
So that they myght there pryses well departe,
As reason wolde, justice, and equité,
To make this lande have lordeshyp of the see.

A ffalse coloure in excusyng of prises.

Than shall Lumbardes and othere feyned frendes
Make her chalenges by coloure false of fendes,
And sey there chafare in the shippes is,
And chalenge alle, loke yf this be amisse.
Ffor thus may alle that men have brought to sorowe,
And ben excused and saved by false coloure.
Be ware ye men that bare the grete on honde,
That they destroy the polycye of this londe,
By gifte and goode, and fyne golden clothes,
And silke and othere, sey ye nat this sothe is ?
But if ye hadde verry experience,
That they take mede wythe pryvé violence,
Carpettis, and thynges of price and of pleysaunce,
Whereby stopped shulde be gode governaunce.
And if it were as ye seye unto me,
Than wolde I seye, allas, cupidité !
That they that have here lyves put in drede
Schal be sone oute of wynnynge, al for mede,
And lese here costes, and brought to poverté,
That they shalle nevere have luste to go to see.

Sterynge to an ordinaunce ayens coloure of maynteners and
excusers.

Ffor thys coloure that muste be seyde alofte
And by declared of the grete ful ofte,
That oure seemen wolle by many wysse
Spoylle oure frendys in stede of oure enmyse ;
Ffor whych coloure and Lumbardes mayntenaunce,
The kynge it nedeth to make an ordinaunce,
Wyth his counselle, that may not fayle, I troue,
That frendes shuld frome enmyes welle be knoue,
Oure enmyes taken, and oure frendes spared ;
The remedy of hem muste be declared.
Thus may the see be kept in no selle ;
Ffor if ought be taken, wotte ye weel,
Wee have the strokes, and enmyes have the wynnyng,
But maynteners ar parteners of the synnynge.
Wee lyfe in luste, and byde in covetyse,
This is oure reule to mayntene marchauntyse,
And polycye that we have on the see ;
And, but God helpe, it woll none other bee.

Of the commoditees of Irelonde, and policye and kepynge thereof,
and conquerynge of wylde Iryshe, wyth an incident of
Walys. The ix chapitle.

I caste to speke of Irelonde but a lytelle,
Commoditees yet I wolle entitelle,
Hydes and fish, samon, hake, herynge,
Irish wollen, lynyn cloth, faldynge,
And marternus [1] gode bene here marchaundysse,
Hertys hydes and other of venerye,
Skynnes of otere, squerel, and Irysh are,[2]
Of shepe, lambe, and fox, is here chaffare,
Ffelles of kydde and conyes grete plenté.
So that if Irelond halpe us to kepe the see,
Because the kynge clepid is " rex Angliae,"
And is " dominus " also " Hiberniae,"
Old possessyd by progenitours,
The Yriche men have cause lyke to oures
Oure londe and herres [3] togedre defende,
That none enmye shulde hurte ne offende

---

[1] Furs of the marten.   [2] *are* : hare.   [3] *herres* : theirs.

Yrelonde ne us, but as one comonté
Shulde helpe to kepe welle aboute the see.
Ffor they have havenesse grete and godely bayes,
Sure wyde and depe, of gode assayes,
Att Waterforde and coostis monye one,
And as men seyn in England, be there none
Better havenesse shyppes in to ryde,
Ne more sure for enmyes to abyde.
Why speke I thus so muche of Yrelonde ?
Ffor also muche as I can understonde
It is fertyle for thynge that there do growe
And multiplyen, loke who so lust to knowe ;
So large, so gode, and so comodyouse,
That to declare is straunge and merveylouse.
Ffor of sylvere and golde there is the oore
Amonge the wylde Yrishe, though they be pore ;
Ffor they are rude, and can thereone no skylle ;
So that if we had there pese and gode wylle,
To myne and fyne, and metalle for to pure,
In wylde Yrishe might we fynde the cure.
As in London seyth a juellere,
Whyche brought from thens gold oore to us here,
Whereof was fyned metalle gode and clene,
As the touche, no bettere coude be sene.
Nowe here be ware and hertly take entente,
As ye wolle answere at the laste jugemente,
That for sloughe and for racheshede
Ye remembere, wyth alle youre mighte take hede
To kepe Yrelonde, that it be not loste ;
Ffor it is a boterasse and a poste
Undre England, and Wales another.
God forbede but eche were othere brothere,
Of one ligeaunce dewe unto the kynge.
But I have pité, in gode feythe, of thys thynge,
That I shall saye, wythe avysemente,
I ham aferde that Yrelonde wol be shente ;
It muste awey, it wolle be loste frome us,
But if thow helpe, thow Jhesu graciouse,
And yeve us grace all sloughte to leve bysyde.
Ffor myche thynge in my harte is hyde,
Whyche in anothere tretyse I caste to wrytte,
Made alle onelye for that soyle and sitee

Of fertyle Yerelonde, whyche mythe not be forborne,
But if Englond were nighe as gode as gone.
God forbede that a wylde Yrishe wyrlynge
Shulde be chosene for to be there kynge,
Aftere here conqueste for oure laste puisshaunce,
And hyndere us by other londes allyaunce.
Wyse mene seyne, whyche folyn not me dotyn,
That wylde Yrishe so muche of grounde have gotyne
There upon us, as lyklynesse may be
Lyke as England to cherish two or thre
Of thys oure londe is made comparable,
So wylde Yrish have wonne unto us unable
Yit to defende, and of no powere
That oure grounde there is a lytelle cornere
To alle Yrelonde in trewe comparisone.
It nedeth no more this mater to expone,
Which if it beloste, as Christe Jhesu forbede,
Ffarewelle Wales, than Englond cometh to drede
Ffor alliaunce of Scotelonde and of Spayne,
And other moo, as the Pety Bretayne,
And so have enmyes environ rounde aboute.
I beseche God that some prayers devoute
Mutt lett the seyde apparaunce probable
Thys disposed wythought feyned fable ;
But alle onely for perelle that I see
Thus ymynent as lykely for to be.
And welle I wote that frome hens to Rome,
And, as men sey, in all Christendome,
Ys no grounde ne londe to Yrelond lyche,
So large, so gode, so plenteouse, so riche,
That to this worde " dominus " dothe longe.
Than me semyth that ryght were, and not wronge,
To gete that lond, and it were piteouse
To us to lese thys hyghe name " dominus."
And alle this words " dominus " of name
Shulde have the grounde obeisaunte, wylde and tame.
That name and peple togedere might accorde,
Alle the grounde subjecte to the lorde ;
And that it is possible to be subjecte
Unto the kynge, welle shall it be detect
In the lytelle boke that I of spake ;
I trowe reson alle this wolle undertake.

25

And I knowe welle with Irland how it stant ;
Allas ! fortune begynneth so to stant,
Or ellis grace, that dede is governaunce.
Ffor so mynusshyth partyes of oure puissaunce
In that land, that we lesse every yere
More grounde and more, as well as ye may here.
I herde a man speke to me fulle late,
Whyche was a lorde of ful grete astate,
That expensis of one yere don in Fraunce
Werred on men welle wylled of puissaunce,
Thys seyd grounde of Yrelonde to conquere,
And yit because Englonde myght not forbere
These seyde expensis gedred in one yere,
But in iij yere or iiij gadred up here,
Myght wynne Yrelonde to a fynalle conquest
In one soole yere, to sett us all in reste.
And how sone wolde thys be payde ageyne,
What were it worthe yerely, yf wee not feyne,
I wylle declare, who so luste to looke,
I trowe ful pleynly in my lytele boke.
But covetyse and singularité
Of one profite, envye and cruelté,
Hathe done us harme, and doo us every daye,
And mustres made that shame it is to saye,
Oure money spente alle to lytelle avayle ;
And oure enmyes so gretely done prevayle,
That what harme may falle and overthwarte,
I may unneth wrytte more for sore of herte.

An exhortacion to the kepynge of Walys.

Be ware of Walys, Criste Jhesu mutt us kepe,
That it make not oure childeis childe to wepe,
Ne us also, if it go his waye
By unwarenesse ; seth that many a daye
Men have be ferde of here rebellioun
By grete tokenes and ostentacioun.
Seche the menys wyth a discrete avyse,
And helpe that they rudely not aryse
Ffor to rebelle, that Criste it forbede ;
Loke wele aboute, for, God wote, we have nede,
Unfayllyngly, unfeynynge, and unfeynte,
That concience for slought you not atteynte.

Kepe welle that grounde for harme that may bene used,
Or afore God mutt ye bene accused.

Of the comodious stokfysshe of Yselonde,[1] and kepynge of the
see, namely the narowe see, wyth an incident of the kepynge
of Calyse.   The tenne chapitule.

Of Yseland [1] to wryte is lytelle nede,
Save of stockfische ; yit for sothe in dede
Out of Bristowe, and costis many one,
Men have practised by nedle and by stone
Thiderwardes wythine a lytel whylle,
Within xij yere, and withoute perille,
Gone and commen, as men were wonte of olde
Of Scarborowgh unto the costes colde ;
And now so fele shippes thys yere there were,
That moche losse for unfraught they bare ;
Yselonde myght not make hem to be fraught
Unto the hawys ; this moche harme they caught.
Thene here I ende of the commoditees
Ffor whiche nede is well to kepe the sees ;
Este and weste, sowth and northe they be ;
And chefely kepe the sharpe narrowe see
Betwéne Dover and Caleise, and as thus
That fosse passe not wythought gode wyll of us,
And they abyde oure daunger in the lenghte,
What for oure costis and Caleise in oure strenghte.

An exhortacioun of the sure kepynge of Calise.

And for the love of God and of his blisse,
Cherishe ye Caleise better than it is ;
See well therto, and here the grete compleynte
That trewe men tellen, that woolle no lies paynte ;
And as ye knowe that wrytynge commyth from thens,
Do not to England for sloughte so grete offens,
But that redressed it be for ony thynge,
Lest that a songe of sorow that wee synge.
Ffor lytelle wenythe the fole, who so myght chese,
What harme it were gode Caleise for to lese
What woo it were for alle this Englysshe grounde.
Whiche welle conceyved the emperoure Sigesmounde,

[1] Iceland.

That of all joyes made it one of the moste,
That Caleise was soget unto Englysshe coste.
Hym thoughte it was a jewel most of alle,
And so the same in Latyn did it calle.
And if ye wolle more of Caleise here and knowe,
I caste to writte wythine a litelle scrowe,
Like as I have done beforene by and bye
In othir parties of oure pollicie.
Loke welle how harde it was at the firste to gete,
And by my counselle lyghtly let it not leete.
For if we leese it wyth shame of face
Wylfully, it is for lake of grace.
Howe was the Hareflewe [1] cryed upon, and Rone,[2]
That it were likely for slought to be gone,
How was it warened, and cryed on in Englonde,
I make record wyth this penne in myne honde.
It was warened pleynly in Normandye,
And in England, and I thereone dyd crye,
The worlde was defrauded, it betid ryght soo ;
Ffarewelle Hareflewe ! lewdely it was agoo ;
Now ware Caleise, I can sey no bettere,
My soule discharge I by this presente lettere.

. . . .

HERE ENDITH THE TREWE PROCESSE OF THE LIBELLE OF
ENGLYSSHE POLICIE, EXHORTYNGE ALLE ENGLANDE TO
KEPE THE SEE ENVIROUN, AND NAMELY THE NAROWE
SEE ; SHEWYNGE WHATE WORSHIPE, PROFITE AND
SALVACION COMMETHE THEREOF TO THE REIGNE OF
ENGLONDE, ETC^A.

Go furthe, libelle, and mekely shewe thy face,
Apperynge evere wyth humble contynaunce ;
And pray my lordes the to take in grace
In opposaile, and cherisshynge the avaunce
To hardynesse, if that not variaunce
Thow haste fro troughte by full experience,
Auctours and reasone, yif ought faile in substaunce,
Remitte to heme that yafe the this science.
That sythe it is sothe, in verray feythe,
That the wyse lorde baron of Hungerforde
Hathe the oversene, and verrily he seithe

----

[1] *Harflewe* : Harfleur.   [2] *Rone* : Rouen.

That thow arte trewe, and thus he dothe recorde,
Nexte the gospell ; God wotte, it was his worde,
Whanne he the redde alle over in a nyghte.
Go forthe, trewe booke, and Christe defende thi ryghte.
Explicit libellus de policia conservativa maris.

II. EXTRACTS FROM MORE'S *HISTORY OF KING RICHARD III.*

[Sir Thomas More, the son of Sir John More, judge of the King's Bench, was born in London in 1480. He was educated at Oxford, and at the age of twenty-one entered Parliament. He was one of the greatest humanists of the English Renaissance, the friend of Erasmus and the protégé of Wolsey. He was sent on a variety of diplomatic missions by Henry VIII. and in 1520 became treasurer of the exchequer. In 1523, he was chosen Speaker of the House of Commons, and in 1530 succeeded Wolsey as Lord Chancellor. On the occasion of Henry VIII.'s divorce from Katherine of Arragon he resigned the Seals, and was soon afterwards committed to the Tower for refusing the Oath of Supremacy. He was tried on a charge of treason and, notwithstanding a most eloquent defence, was found guilty and beheaded, 6th July 1535. In the absence of contemporary authorities, his *History of Richard III.* is one of the most important documents for the history of the latter years of the House of York. From his earliest years More moved among men who had played a conspicuous part in the reign of Richard III., and consequently he had every opportunity of gaining the fullest and most reliable information. There is nevertheless a noticeably Lancastrian bias about the book, owing to the fact that the early Tudors, in spite of their union of York and Lancaster, were most ostentatiously Lancastrian—and history is always written in favour of the winning side. Had Richard III. won the battle of Bosworth, a much less repulsive picture of him might have been handed on to posterity. The extracts here printed are taken from the folio edition of Sir Thomas More's works, published in London in 1557. The work was left unfinished and never finally revised. A useful edition of *The Historie of Kyng Rycharde the Thirde* is that edited by J. R. Lumby in the Pitt Press Series (Cambridge University Press. Reprinted 1924).]

A. A DESCRIPTION OF EDWARD IV., RICHARD III., ETC.

HE [Edward IV.] was a goodly parsonage, and very Princely to behold, of hearte couragious, politique in counsaile, in aduersitie nothynge abashed, in prosperitie rather joyfull then prowde, in peace juste and mercifull, in warre sharpe and fyerce, in the fielde bolde and hardye, and nathelesse no farther then wysedome woulde aduenturouse. Whose warres who so well consyder, hee shall no lesse commende hys wysedome where hee voyded, than hys mannehoode where he vainquisshed. He was of visage louelye, of bodye myghtie, stronge, and cleane made : howe bee it in his latter dayes, wyth ouer liberall dyet, sommewhat corpulente and boorelye,[1] and nathelesse not vyncomelye, hee was of youthe greatlye geuen to fleshlye wantonnesse : from whiche healthe of bodye, in greate prosperitye and Fortune, wythoute a specyall grace hardelye refrayneth. Thys faute not greatlye gryeued the people : for neyther could any one mans pleasure stretch and extende to the dyspleasure of verye manye, and was wythoute violence, and ouer that in hys latter dayes lessyd and wel lefte. In whych tyme of hys latter daies thys Realm was in quyet and prosperous estate : no feare of outewarde enemyes, no warre in hande, nor none towarde, but such as no manne looked for ; the people towarde the Prince, not in a constrayned feare, but in a wyllynge and louynge obedyence : amonge them selfe, the commons in good peace. The Lordes whome he knewe at varyaunce, hymselfe in hys deathe bedde appeased. He hadde lefte all gatherynge of money (which is the onelye thynge that withdraweth the heartes of Englyshmenne fro the Prynce) nor anye thynge entended hee to take in hande, by which hee shoulde bee dryeuen theretoo, for hys trybute [2] oute of Fraunce hee hadde before obtayned. And the yere foregoynge hys deathe hee hadde obtayned Barwycke.[3] And al bee it that all the tyme of hys raygne hee was wyth hys people soo benygne, courteyse, and so familyer, that no parte of hys vertues was more estemed ; yet that condicyon in the ende of hys dayes (in which many princes, by a long continued souerainty, decline in to a prowde porte from debonayre behauioure of theyr beginning) meruaylouslye in him grewe and increased ; so farrefoorthe that in the sommer the laste that euer he sawe, hys hyghenesse beeyng

---

[1] burly.

[2] By the Treaty of Picquigny, Louis XI. agreed to pay an annual pension of 50,000 crowns.

[3] In 1482 he gained Berwick-on-Tweed from the Scots.

at Wyndesore in huntynge, sente for the Mayre and Alder-
menne of London to hym.   For none other eraunde, but too
haue them hunte and bee mery with hym, where hee made
them not so statelye, but so frendely and so familier chere,
and sente venson from thence so frelye into the Citye, that
no one thing, in many dayes before, gate hym eyther moe
heartes or more heartie fauoure amonge the common people,
whiche oftentymes more esteme and take for greatter
kindenesse a lyttle courtesye, then a greate benefyte.

So deceased (as I haue said) this noble Kynge, in that
tyme in whiche hys life was moste desyred.   Whose loue of
hys people, and theyr entiere affeccion towarde him, hadde
bene to hys noble children (hauynge in themselfe also as
manye gyftes of nature, as manie Princely vertures, as muche
goodlye towardenesse as theire age coulde receiue) a meruail-
ouse forteresse and sure armoure, if deuision and discencion
of their frendes hadde not vnarmed them, and lefte them
destitu(t)e, and the execrable desire of souerayntee prouoked
him to theire destruccion , which yf either kinde or kindenesse
hadde holden place, muste needes haue bene theire chiefe
defence.   For Richarde the Duke of Gloucester, by nature
theyr Uncle, by office theire protectoure, to theire father
beholden, to them selfe by othe and allegyaunce bownden,
al the bandes broken that binden manne and manne together,
withoute anye respecte of Godde or the worlde, vnnaturallye
contriued to bereue them, not onelye their dignitie, but also
their liues.   But forasmuche as this Dukes demeanoure
ministreth in effecte all the whole matter whereof this booke
shall entreate, it is therefore conueniente, sommewhat to
shewe you ere we farther goe, what maner of manne this
was, that coulde fynde in his hearte so muche mischiefe to
conceiue.

Richarde Duke of Yorke, a noble manne and a mightie,
beganne not by warre, but by lawe, to challenge the crown,
puttyng his claime into the parliamente.   Where hys cause
was eyther for right or fauour so farrefoorth auaunced, that
kinge Henrye his bloode [1] (all bee it he hadde a goodlye
Prince) vtterlye reiected, the crowne was by authoritye of
parliament entayled vnto the Duke of York and his issue
male in remainder immediatelye after the deathe of Kinge
Henrye.   But the Duke not endurynge so longe to tarye,

[1] *i.e.* King Henry's blood.

but entending vnder pretexte of discencion and debate arisynge in the realme, to preuente his time, and to take vppon hym the rule in Kinge Harry his life,[1] was with manye nobles of the realme at Wakefielde [2] slaine, leauinge three sonnes, Edwarde George and Rycharde. Al three as they wer great states of birthe, soo were they greate and statelye of stomacke, gredye and ambicious of authoritie, and impacient of parteners. Edward reuenging his fathers death, depriued king Henrie and attained the crown. George Duke of Clarence was a goodly noble Prince, and at all pointes fortunate, if either his owne ambicion had not set him against his brother, or the enuie of his enemies his brother agaynste hym. For were it by the Queene and the Lordes of her bloode whiche highlye maligned the kynges kinred (as women commonly not of malice but of nature hate them whome theire housebandes loue) or were it a prowde appetite of the Duke himself entendinge to be king, at the lest wise heinous Treason was there layde to his charge, and finallye, wer hee fautye were hee faultlesse, attainted was hee by parliament and judged to the death, and thereupon hastely drouned in a Butte of Malmesey, whose death kyng Edwarde (albeit he commaunded it) when he wist it was done, pitiously bewailed and sorrowfully repented.

Richarde the third sonne, of whom we nowe entreate, was in witte and courage egall with either of them, in bodye and prowesse farre vnder them bothe, little of stature, ill fetured of limmes, croke backed, his left shoulder much higher then his right, hard fauoured of visage, and suche as is in states called warlye, in other menne otherwise, he was malicious, wrathfull, enuious and, from afore his birth, euer frowarde. It is for trouth reported, that the Duches his mother had muche a doe in her trauaile, and that hee came into the worlde with the feete forwarde, as menne bee borne outwarde, and (as the fame runneth) also not vntothed, whither menne of hatred reporte aboue the trouthe, or elles that nature chaunged her course in hys beginninge, whiche in the course of his lyfe many thinges vnnaturallye committed. None euill captaine was hee in the warre, as to whiche his disposicion was more metely then for peace. Sundrye victories hadde hee, and sommetime ouerthrowes, but neuer in defaulte, as for his owne parsone, either of

---

[1] *i.e.* King Harry's life.   [2] 31st December 1460.

hardinesse or polytike order, free was hee called of dyspence, and sommewhat aboue hys power liberall, with large giftes hee get him vnstedfaste frendeshippe, for whiche hee was fain to pil and spoyle in other places, and get him stedfast hatred. He was close and secrete, a deepe dissimuler, lowlye of counteynaunce, arrogant of heart, outwardly coumpinable where he inwardely hated, not letting to kisse whome hee thoughte to kyll; dispitious and cruell, not for euill will alway, but after for ambicion, and either for the suretie or encrease of his estate. Frende and foo was muche what indifferent, where his aduauntage grew, he spared no mans deathe, whose life withstoode his purpose. He slewe with his owne handes king Henry the sixt, being prisoner in the Tower, as menne constantly saye, and that without commaundemente or knowledge of the king, whiche would vndoubtedly, yf he had entended that thinge, haue appointed that boocherly office, to some other then his owne borne brother. Somme wise menne also weene, that his drifte couertly conuayde, lacked not in helping furth his brother Clarence to his death : whiche hee resisted openly, howbeit somwhat (as menne demed) more faintly then he that wer hartely minded to his welth. And they that thus deme, think that he long time in king Edwardes life forethought to be king in case that the king his brother (whose life hee looked that euil dyete shoulde shorten) shoulde happen to decease (as in dede he did) while his children wer yonge. And thei deme, that for thys intente he was gladde of his brothers death the Duke of Clarence, whose life must needes haue hindered hym so entendynge, whither the same Duke of Clarence hadde kepte him true to his nephew the yonge king, or enterprised to be kyng himself. But of al this pointe is there no certaintie, and whoso diuineth vppon coniectures maye as wel shote to farre as to short. Howbeit this haue I by credible informacion learned, that the selfe nighte in whiche kynge Edwarde died, one Mystlebrooke longe ere mornynge came in great haste to the house of one Pottyer dwellyng in Reddecrosse strete without Crepulgate : and when he was with hastye rappyng quickly letten in, hee shewed vnto Pottyer that kynge Edwarde was departed. By my trouthe manne, quod Pottier, then wyll my mayster the Duke of Gloucester bee kynge. What cause hee hadde soo to thynke harde it is to saye, whyther hee being toward him

anye thynge knewe that hee suche thynge purposed, or otherwyse had anye inkelynge thereof : for hee was not likelye
to speake it of noughte.

. . . .

B. Elizabeth Woodville in Sanctuary

In this wise the Duke of Gloucester tooke upon himself the
order and gouernance of the young king, whom with much
honor and humble reuerence he conuayed vppewarde towarde
the citye. But anone the tidinges of this mater came hastely
to the queen, a litle before the midnight folowing, and that
in the sorest wise, that the king her sonne was taken, her
brother her sonne and her other frendes arested, and sent
no man wist whither, to be done with God wot what. With
which tidinges the quene in gret flight and heuines, bewailing
her childes rain, her frendes mischance, and her own infortune,
damning the time that euer shee diswaded the gatheryng of
power aboute the kinge, gate her selfe in all the haste possible
with her yonger sonne and her doughters oute of the Palyce
of Westminster in whiche shee then laye, into the Sainctuarye,
lodginge her selfe and her coumpanye there in the abbottes
place.

Nowe came there one, in likewise not longe after mydde-
nighte, fro the Lorde Chaumberlayn vnto the archbishoppe
of Yorke then Chaunccellor of Englande, to his place not farre
from Westminster. And for that he shewed his seruauntes
that hee hadde tidinges of soo great importaunce, that his
maister gaue him in charge not to forbeare his reste, they
letted not to wake hym, nor hee to admitte this messenger
in to his bedde syde. Of whome hee hard that these Dukes
were gone backe with the Kynges grace from Stonye Strat-
forde vnto Northampton. Notwithstanding, sir, quod hee,
my Lorde sendeth youre Lordeshippe woorde that there is
no feare. For hee assureth you that all shall bee well. I
assure him, quod the Archebishoppe, bee it as well as it will,
it will neuer bee soo well as wee haue seene it. And there-
uppon by and by after the messenger departed, hee caused
in all the haste al his seruauntes to bee called vppe, and so
with his owne householde aboute hym, and euerie manne
weaponed, hee tooke the greate Seale with him, and came
yet beefore daye vnto the Queene. Aboute whome he found
muche heauinesse rumble haste and businesse, carriage and

conueyaunce of her stuffe into Sainctuary, chestes coffers packes fardelles trusses, all on mennes backes, no manne vnoccupyed, somme lading, somme goynge, somme des-charging, somme commynge for more, somme breakinge downe the walles to bring in the nexte waye, and somme yet drewe to them that holpe to carrye a wronge waye. The Quene her self satte alone alowe on the rishes all desolate and dis-mayde, whome the Archebishoppe coumforted in the best manner hee coulde, shewinge her that hee trusted the matter was nothynge soo sore as shee tooke it for.   And that he was putte in good hope and oute of feare by the message sente him from the Lorde Chamberlaine. Ah, woo worthe him, quod she, for hee is one of them that laboureth to destroye me and my bloode.   Madame, quod he, be ye of good chere. For I assure you if thei crowne any other kinge then your sonne, whome they nowe haue with them, we shal on the morowe crowne his brother whome you haue here with you. And here is the greate Seale, whiche in likewise as that noble prince your housebande deliuered it vnto me, so here I delieuer it vnto you, to the use and behoofe of youre sonne, and therewith hee betooke her the greate Seale, and departed home agayne, yet in the dauninge of the daye.   By which tyme hee might in his chaumber window see all the Temmes full of bootes of the Duke of Gloucesters seruantes, watchinge that no manne shoulde go to Sainctuary, nor none coulde passe vnserched.   Then was there greate commocion and murmure as well in other places about, as specially in the city, the people dieurselye diuininge vppon this dealinge. And somme Lordes Knightes, and Gentlemenne either for fauoure of the Quene, or for feare of themselfe, assembled in sundry coumpanies, and went flockmele in harneis ; and manye also, for that they reckened this demeanoure attempted, not so specially againste the other Lordes, as agaynste the kinge hymselfe in the disturbaunce of hys coronacion.   But then by and by the Lordes assembled together at ——— Towarde which meting, the Archebishoppe of York fearing that it wold be ascribed (as it was in dede) to his ouermuch lightnesse, that he so sodainly had yelded vp the great seale to the Quene, to whome the custodye thereof nothing par-tained, without especial commaundement of the kynge, secretely sent for the seale againe, and brought it with him after the customable maner.   And at this meting the lord

Hasting, whose trouth towarde the king no manne doubted nor neded to doubte, perswaded the Lordes to belieue, that the Duke of Gloucester was sure and fastlye faithfull to hys prince, and that the lorde Riuers and lord Richard with the other knightes wer, for maters attempted by them against the dukes of Gloucester and Buckingham, putte vnder arreste for theire surety, not for the Kynges jeopardye; and that thei were also in sauegarde, and there no lenger shoulde remayn, then tyll the matter wer, not by the dukes onelye, but also by all the other Lordes of the Kynges counsayle indifferentelye examyned, and by other discrecions ordered, and eyther judged or appeased. But one thynge hee aduised them beware, that they judged not the matter to farrefoorth, ere they knewe the trueth, nor turnynge theire priuate grudges into the common hurte, yrritinge and prouoking mene vnto anger, and disturbynge the Kynges Coronacion, towardes whiche the Dukes were commynge vppe, that thei mighte paraduenture brynge the matter so farre oute of joynt, that it shold neuer be brought in frame agayne. Whiche stryfe if it shoulde happe, as it were lykelye, to come to a fielde, though both parties were in all other thynges egall, yet shoulde the authoritie bee on that syde where the Kynge is hymselfe. With these parswasions of the Lorde Hastynges, whereof parte hymselfe belieued, of parte he wist the contrarye, these commocions were sommewhat appeased. But specyally by that that the Dukes of Gloucester and Buckingham were so nere, and came so shortelye on with the kynge, in none other maner, with none other voyce or semblaunce, then to his coronacion, causynge the fame to bee blowen about, that these Lordes and knightes whiche were taken hadde contryued the destruccyon of the Dukes of Gloucester and Buckingham, and of other the noble bloode of the realme, to the ende that them selfe woulde alone demeane and gouerne the king at their pleasure. And for the colourable proofe thereof, such of the Dukes seruantes as rode with the cartes of theyr stuffe that were taken (amonge whiche stuffe no meruayle thoughte somme were harneys, whiche at the breakinge vp of that householde muste needes eyther bee broughte awaye or caste awaye) they shewed vnto the people al the waye as they wente, loe here bee the barelles of harneys that this traitours had priuelye conuayed in theyr carryage to destroye the noble lordes with all. This deuise all be it that it made the matter to wise men more vnlykely, well perceyuyng that the intendours of suche a purpose wolde rather haue hadde theyr harneys on theyr backes, then haue bounde them vppe in barrelles, yet muche part of the common people were therewith verye well satisfyed, and said it wer almoise [1] to hange them.

C. The Right of Sanctuary

When the protectoure hadde said, al the counsayl affyrmed that the mocion was good and reasonable, and to the kynge and the Duke his brother honourable, and a thing that should cease greate murmure in the realme, if the mother might be by good meanes enduced to delyuer hym. Whiche thynge the Archebishoppe of Yorke, whome they all agreed also to bee thereto moste conuenyente, tooke vppon hym to moue her, and therein to dooe hys vttermoste deuowre. Howe bee it if shee coulde bee in no wyse entreated with her good wyll to delyuer hym, then thoughte hee and suche other as were of the spiritualtye present, that it were not in anye wyse to be attempted to take him oute agaynste her wil. For it would bee a thynge that shoulde tourne to the greate grudge of all menne and hyghe dyspleasure of Godde, yf the priueledge of that holye place should nowe bee broken. Whiche hadde so manye yeares bee kepte, whyche both Kynges and Popes soo good hadde graunted, so many hadde confirmed, and whiche holye grounde was more then fyue hundred yeare agoe by Saincte Peter his own parsone in spirite, accompanyed with greate multitude of aungelles, by nyghte so specyallye halowed and dedicate to Godde, (for the proofe wherof they haue yet in the Abbay Sainct Peters cope to shewe) that from that tyme hytherwarde, was there neuer so vndeuowte a Kinge, that durst that sacred place violate, or so holye a Bishoppe that durste it presume to consecrate. And therefore (quod the Archebishoppe of Yorke) Godde forbydde that anye manne shoulde, for anye thynge earthlye enterpryse to breake the immunitee and libertye of that sacred Sainctuary, that hath bene the safegarde of so many a good mannes life. And I truste that shee shall bee with reason contented, and all thynge in good maner obtayned. And yf it happen that I brynge it not so to passe, yet shall I towarde

---

[1] charity (almesse).

it so farrefoorth dooe my beste, that ye shall all well percieue that no lacke of my deuoure, but the mothers drede and wommanishe feare shall bee the let.

Womannishe feare, naye womannishe frowardennesse (quod the Duke of Buckyngham). For I dare take it vppon my soule, she well knoweth she needeth no such thyng to feare, either for her sonne or for her selfe. For as for her, here is no manne that will be at warre with women. Woulde God some of the men of her kynne were women too, and then shoulde al bee soone in reste. Howe bee it there is none of her kinne the less loued, for that they bee her kinne, but for their owne euill deseruinge. And nathelesse if we loued neither her nor her kinne, yet were there no cause to thinke that we shoulde hate the kynges noble brother, to whose Grace wee ourselfe bee of kynne. Whose honoure if shee as muche desyred as oure dishonoure, and as muche regarde tooke to his wealthe, as to her owne will, she woulde bee as lothe to suffer him from the kinge, as anye of vs bee. For if shee haue anye witte, (as would Goode she hadde as good will as she hathe shrewde witte) she reckoneth her selfe no wiser than shee thinketh some that bee here, of whose faithe-full mynde she nothing doubteth, but verelye beleueth and knoweth, that they woulde bee as sorye of his harme as her selfe, and yet would haue hym from her yf she byde there. And wee all (I thinke) contente, that bothe bee with her, yf she come thence and bide in suche place where they maie with their honoure bee.

Nowe then yf she refuse in the deliueraunce of hym, to folowe the counsaile of them whose wisdom she knoweth, whose trouth she well trusteth, it is ethe to perceiue, that frowardnesse letteth her, and not feare. But goe to suppose that she feare (as who maye lette her to feare her owne shadowe) the more she feareth to delyuer hym, the more oughte wee feare to leaue him in her handes. For if she caste suche fonde doubtes, that shee feare his hurte ; then wyll she feare that hee shall bee fette thence. For she will soone thinke, that if menne were sette (whiche Godde forbydde) vppon so greate a mischiefe, the saintuarye woulde litle let them. Which good menne mighte, as mee thynketh, without sinne sommewhat less regarde then they do.

Nowe then if she doubte leste hee mighte bee fetched from her, is it not likelye ynoughte that she shall sende him somme

where out of the realme ?   Verely I looke for none other.
And I doubte not but shee nowe as sore myndeth it, as wee
the lette thereof.   And yf she myghte happen to brange
that to passe (as it were no greate maistrye, wee lettinge
her alone) all the worlde woulde saye that wee wer᾽ a wyse
sort of counsaylers aboute a kynge that lette his brother
bee caste awaye vnder oure noses.   And therefore I ensure
you faythfully for my mynde, I wyll rather, maugrye her
mynde, fetche hym awaye, then leaue hym ther, till her
frowardnes or fond feare conuay hym awaye.   And yet will
I breake no Saintuarye therefore.   For verelye sithe the
priuileges of that place, and other lyke, haue bene of long
continued, I am not he that woulde bee aboute to breake
them.   And in good faith if they were nowe to begynne, I
woulde not bee he that shoulde bee aboute to make them.
Yet wyll I not saye naye, but that it is a deede of pitie, that
suche menne, as the sea or theyr euill dettours haue broughte
in pouertye, shoulde haue somme place of libertye, to keepe
their bodies oute of the daunger of their cruell creditours.
And also yf the crowne happen (as it hathe done) to comme
in questyon, whyle eyther parte taketh other as traytours,
I wyll well there bee somme places of refuge for bothe.   But
as for theeues, of whiche these places bee full, and which
neuer fall fro the crafte after thei once falle thereto, it is pitie
the saintuarye shoulde serue them.   And muche more
mannequellers, whome Godde badde to take from the aulter
and kyll them yf theyr murther were wylfull.   And where
it is otherwyse there neede wee not the sayntuaryes that God
appointed in the olde lawe.   For yf eyther necessitie, hys
owne defence, or misfortune drawe hym to that dede, a pardon
serueth, which eyther the law graunteth of course, or the
Kynge of pitie maye.

   Then looke me nowe how few saintuarye menne there
bee, whome any fauourable necessitie compelled to gooe
thyther.   And then see on the tother syde what a sorte
there be commonlye therein, of them whome wylfull vnthrifty-
nesse hathe broughte to nought.

   What a rabble of theues, murtherers and malicious
heyghnous traitours, and that in twoo places specyallye.
The tone at the elbowe of the citie, the tother in the verye
bowelles.   I dare well auowe it, waye the good that they dooe
with the hurte that commeth of them, and ye shall fynde

it muche better to lacke bothe, then haue bothe. And this
I saye, although they were not abused as they nowe bee,
and so longe haue bee, that I feare mee euer they wyll bee
whyle menne bee a fearde to sette theyr handes to the
mendement ; as thoughe Godde and Saincte Peter were the
patrons of vngracious lyuinge.

Nowe vnyhriftes ryote and runne in dette, vppon the
boldenesse of these places ; yea and ryche menne runne
thither with poor mennes goodes, there they builde, there
thei spende and bidde their creditours gooe whistle them.
Mens wyues runne thither with theyr housebandes plate,
and saye thei dare not abyde with theyr housebandes for
beatinge. Theues bryng thyther theyr stollen goodes, and
there lyue thereon. There deuise thei newe roberies, nightlye
they steale out, they robbe and reue and kyll, and come in
again as though those places gaue them not onely a safe
garde for the harme they haue done, but a licence also to
dooe more. Howe bee it muche of this mischiefe, if wyse
menne woulde sette their handes to it, myghte bee amended,
with greate thank of God and no breache of the priueledge.
The residew sith so long agoe I wote neere what Pope and
what Prince, more pyteous then politique, hathe graunted
it and other menne since of a certayne relygious feare haue
not broken it, lette vs take a payne therewith, and lette it a
Goddes name stande in force, as farrefoorth as reason wyll.
Whiche is not fullye so farrefoorth as may serue to lette vs
of the fetchynge foorthe of this noble manne to hys honoure
and wealthe, oute of that place in whiche he neither is, nor
canne bee a Saynctuary manne.

$\cdot \qquad \cdot \qquad \cdot \qquad \cdot \qquad \cdot \qquad \cdot \qquad \cdot$

D. The Execution of Lord Hastings

WHERUPON sone after, that is to wit, on the Friday the —
day of — many Lordes assembled in the Tower, and there
sat in counsaile, deuising the honorable solempnite of the
kinges coronacion, of which the time appointed then so nere
approched, that the pageauntes and suttelties were in making
day and night at Westminster, and much vitaile killed
therfore, that afterward was cast away. These lordes so
sytting togyther comoning of thys matter, the protectour
came in among them, fyrst aboute ix. of the clock, saluting
them curtesly, and excusyng hymself that he had ben from

them so long, saieng merely that he had bene a slepe that
day.   And after a little talking with them, he sayd vnto
the Bishop of Elye, my lord you haue very good strawberies
at your gardayne in Holberne, I require you let vs haue a
messe of them.   Gladly my lord, quod he, woulde God I
had some better thing as redy to your pleasure as that.
And therwith in al the hast he sent hys seruant for a messe of
strauberies.   The protectour sette the lordes fast in comoning,
and therupon prayeng them to spare hym for a little while
departed thence.   And sone, after one hower, betwene
x. and xi., he returned into the chamber among them, al
changed with a wonderful soure angrye countenaunce
knitting the browes, frowning and froting and knawing on
hys lippes, and so sat him downe in hys place ; al the lordes
much dismaied and sore merueiling of this maner of sodain
chaunge, and what thing should him aile.   Then when he
had sitten still a while, thus he began : What were they
worthy to haue, that compasse and ymagine the distruccion
of me, being so nere of blood vnto the king and protectour
of his riall person and his realme ?   At this question, al the
lordes sat sore astonied, musyng much by whome thys
question should be ment, of which euery man wyst himselfe
clere.   Then the lord chamberlen,[1] as he that for the loue
betwene them thoughte he might be boldest with him,
aunswered and sayd, that thei wer worthye to bee punished
as heighnous traitors whatsoeuer they were.   And al the
other affirmed the same.   That is (quod he) yonder sorceres
my brothers wife and other with her, meaning the quene.
At these wordes many of the other Lordes were gretly abashed
that fauoured her.   But the lord Hastinges was in his minde
better content, that it was moued by her, then by any other
whom he loued better.   Albeit hys harte somewhat grudged,
that he was not afore made of counsell in this mater as he
was of the taking of her kynred, and of their putting to
death, which were by his assent before deuised to bee
byhedded at Pountfreit,[2] this selfe same day, in which he
was not ware that it was by other deuised, that himself
should the same day be behedded at London.   Then said
the protectour ; ye shal al se in what wise that sorceres
and that other witch of her counsel Shoris wife [3] with their

[1] Lord Hastings.   [2] Pontefract.
[3] Jane Shore, mistress of Edward IV.

26

affynite, haue by their sorcery and witchcraft wasted my
body. And therwith he plucked vp hys doublet sleue to
his elbow vpon his left arme, where he shewed a werish [1]
withered arme and small, as it was neuer other. And thereupon euery mannes mind sore misgaue them, well perceiuing
that this matter was but a quarel. For wel thei wist, that
the quene was to wise to go aboute any such folye. And
also if she would, yet wold she of all folke leste make Shoris
wife of counsaile, whom of al women she most hated, as that
concubine whom the king her husband had most loued.
And also no man was there present, but wel knew that his
harme was euer such since his birth. Natheles the lorde
Chamberlen aunswered and sayd : certainly my lorde if
they haue so heinously done, thei be worthy heinouse
punishement. What, quod the protectour, thou seruest me,
I wene, with iffes and with andes, I tel the thei haue so done,
and that I will make good on thy body, traitour. And
therwith as in a great anger, he clapped his fist vpon the
borde a great rappe. At which token giuen, one cried
treason without the c(h)ambre. Therewith a dore clapped,
and in come there rushing men in harneys as many as the
chambre might hold. And anon the protectour sayd to the
lorde Hastinges : I arest the, traitour. What me, my
Lorde ? quod he. Yea the, traitour, quod the protectour.
And another let flee at the Lorde Standley which shronke
at the stroke and fel vnderthe table, or els his hed had ben
clefte to the tethe : for as shortely as he shranke, yet ranne
the blood aboute hys eares. Then were they al quickly
bestowed in diuerse chambres, except the lorde Chamberlen,
whom the protectour bade spede and shryue hym [2] apace,
for by saynt Poule (quod he) I wil not to dinner tel I se thy
hed of. It boted him not to aske why, but heuely he toke
a priest at aduenture, and made a short shrift, for a longer
would not be suffered, the protectour made so much hast
to dyner ; which he might not go to til this wer done for
sauing of his othe. So was he brought forth into the grene
beside the chappel within the Tower, and his head laid down
vpon a long log of timbre, and there striken of, and afterward his body with the hed entred at Windsore beside
the body of kinge Edward, whose both soules our Lord
pardon.

[1] illshapen or ugly.   [2] *i.e.* make his confession.

A merueilouse case is it to here, either the warninges of that he shoulde haue voided, or the tokens of that he could not voide. For the self night next before his death, the lord Standley sent a trustie secret messenger vnto him at midnight in al the hast, requiring hym to rise and ryde away with hym, for he was disposed vtterly no lenger to bide ; he had so fereful a dreme, in which him thoughte that a bore with his tuskes so raced them both bi the heddes, that the blood ranne aboute both their shoulders. And forasmuch as the protector gaue the bore for his cognisaunce, this dreme made so fereful an impression in his hart, that he was throughly determined no lenger to tary, but had his horse redy, if the lord Hastinges wold go with him to ride so far yet the same night, that thei shold be out of danger ere dai. Ey, good lord, quod the lord Hastinges to this messenger, leneth mi lord thi master so much to such trifles, and hath such faith in dremes, which either his own fere fantasieth or do rise in the nightes rest by reson of his daye thoughtes ? Tel him it is plaine witchcraft to beleue in such dremes ; which if they wer tokens of thinges to come, why thinketh he not that we might be as likely to make them true by our going if we were caught and brought back (as frendes fayle fleers) for then had the bore a cause likely to race vs with his tuskes, as folke that fled for some falshed, wherfore either is there no peryl ; nor none there is in dede ; or if any be, it is rather in going then biding. And if we should, nedes cost, fall in perill one way or other ; yet had I leuer that men should se it wer by other mens falshed, then thinke it were either our owne faulte or faint hart. And therfore go to thy master, man, and commende me to him, and pray him be mery and haue no fere : for I ensure hym I am as sure of the man that he woteth of, as I am of my own hand. God sende grace, sir, quod the messenger, and went his way.

Certain is it also, that in the riding toward the Tower, the same morning in which he was behedded, his hors twise or thrice stumbled with him almost to the falling ; which thing albeit eche man wote wel daily happeneth to them to whom no such mischaunce is toward, yet hath it ben, of an olde rite and custome, obserued as a token often times notably foregoing some great misfortune. Now this that foloweth was no warning, but an enemiouse scorne. The

šame morning ere he were vp, came a knight [1] unto him, as
it were of curtesy to accompany hym to the counsaile, but
of trouth sent by the protector to hast him thitherward,
wyth whom he was of secret confederacy in that purpose, a
meane man at that time, and now of gret auctorite. This
knight when it happed the lord Chamberlen by the way to
stay his horse, and comen a while with a priest whome he
met in the Tower strete, brake his tale and said merely to
him : What, my lord, I pray you come on, whereto talke
you so long with that priest, you haue no nede of a priest
yet ; and therwith he laughed vpon him, as though he would
say, ye shal haue sone. But litle wist that tother what he
ment, and so little mistrusted that he was neuer merier nor
neuer so full of good hope in his life ; which self thing is
often sene a signe of chaunge.

[1] According to Hall this was " Sir Thomas Haward sonne to Lord
Haward."

INDEX

(The figures refer to pages. The dates enclosed in brackets after persons' names are those of their births and deaths respectively.)